Contents

1 New Features of Red Hat Linux 6.0   **1**

  1.1 Installation-Related Enhancements 1

  1.2 Desktop and Window Managers 3

  1.3 Miscellaneous New Features 4

2 Before You Begin   **5**

  2.1 Getting Documentation 6

  2.2 Getting the Right Red Hat Linux Components 6

  2.3 Things You Should Know 10

  2.4 Installation Methods 14

  2.5 Need a Network Boot Disk? 18

  2.6 Need a PCMCIA Support Diskette? 18

  2.7 Installation Classes 19

  2.8 Disk Partitions 21

  2.9 A Note About Kernel Drivers 32

  2.10 If You Have Problems. 32

  2.11 One Last Note 32

3 Starting the Installation   **33**

  3.1 The Installation Program User Interface 33

  3.2 Starting the Installation Program 36

  3.3 Beginning the Installation 39

3.4   Selecting an Installation Method 41

4   Local Media Installations   **43**

4.1   Selecting an Installation Method 43

4.2   Installing from CD-ROM 43

4.3   Installing from a Hard Drive 45

4.4   Upgrading or Installing 45

4.5   Installation Class 46

4.6   SCSI Support 47

4.7   Creating Partitions for Red Hat Linux 48

4.8   Initializing Swap Space 58

4.9   For Hard Drive Installations Only. 58

4.10   Formatting Partitions 60

4.11   Selecting and Installing Packages 60

5   Network Installations   **65**

5.1   Selecting an Installation Method 65

5.2   Installing via NFS 68

5.3   Installing via FTP 69

5.4   Installing via HTTP 69

5.5   Upgrading or Installing 70

5.6   Installation Class 72

5.7   SCSI Support 74

5.8   Creating Partitions for Red Hat Linux 74

5.9   Initializing Swap Space 85

5.10   Formatting Partitions 85

5.11   Selecting and Installing Packages 86

6   Finishing the Installation   **91**

6.1   Configuring a Mouse 91

6.2   Configuring Networking   92

6.3   Configuring the Time Zone   95

6.4   Selecting Services for Start on Reboot   95

6.5   Configuring a Printer   96

6.6   Setting a Root Password   102

6.7   Authentication Configuration   103

6.8   Creating a Boot Diskette   104

6.9   Installing LILO   105

6.10 Configuring the X Window System   108

6.11 Finishing Up   109

7   Finding Documentation   **111**

7.1   On Line Help   111

7.2   Help from the Internet Community   117

8   System Configuration   **119**

8.1   System Configuration With Linuxconf   120

8.2   System Configuration with the Control Panel   158

9   Package Management with RPM   **173**

9.1   RPM Design Goals   174

9.2   Using RPM   174

9.3   Impressing Your Friends with RPM   180

9.4   Other RPM Resources   182

10 GnoRPM   **183**

10.1 Starting GnoRPM   184

10.2 The Package Display   185

10.3 Installing New Packages   187

10.4 Configuration   188

10.5 Package Manipulation 191

11 System Administration   **195**

11.1 Filesystem Structure 195

11.2 Special Red Hat File Locations 199

11.3 Users, Groups and User-Private Groups 199

11.4 Configuring Console Access 203

11.5 The `floppy` Group 205

11.6 User Authentication with PAM 206

11.7 Shadow Utilities 209

11.8 Building a Custom Kernel 210

11.9 Sendmail 214

11.10 Controlling Access to Services 215

11.11 Anonymous FTP 215

11.12 NFS Configuration 216

11.13 The Boot Process, Init, and Shutdown 217

11.14 Rescue Modes 228

A Getting Technical Support   **229**

A.1 An Overview of Our Support Policy 229

A.2 Getting Support 231

A.3 Support FAQ (Frequently Asked Questions) 234

B Making Installation Diskettes   **237**

B.1 Making a Diskette Under MS-DOS 238

B.2 Making a Diskette Under a Linux-like O/S 238

C An Introduction to Disk Partitions   **239**

C.1 Hard Disk Basic Concepts 239

D Package List   **247**

D.1 Amusements 249

D.2 Applications 252

D.3 Base 287

D.4 Development 288

D.5 Documentation 305

D.6 System Environment 311

D.7 User Interface 337

E General Parameters and Modules   **349**

E.1 CD-ROM parameters 350

E.2 SCSI parameters 351

E.3 Ethernet parameters 353

F Information Specific to Red Hat Linux/SPARC   **359**

F.1 Supported Hardware 359

F.2 Installation Overview 360

F.3 Console Commands 361

F.4 Ramdisk-based Installation Criteria 361

F.5 Choosing a Boot Method 362

F.6 Choosing an Installation Method 366

F.7 Installation Using a Serial Terminal 367

F.8 SILO Configuration 367

F.9 Partitioning 368

G Glossary   **369**

H Kickstart Installations   **379**

H.1 Where to Put A Kickstart File 379

H.2 Starting a Kickstart Installation 381

H.3 The Kickstart File 381

Index   **393**

Index of Packages   **403**

Preface

Welcome! And thanks for your interest in Red Hat Linux. We have what we think is the best Linux distribution on the market today, and we work hard to keep it that way. Red Hat Linux 6.0 is the latest in a long line of software from Red Hat Software. We hope you like it, and that you enjoy using Red Hat Linux as much as we've enjoyed making it for you.

While Linux is popular and well-known by a certain segment of the computer-using population, there are many people out there that are only now hearing about Linux. For this group of people, the following section should provide enough background to help you get acquainted with Linux and Red Hat Software.

What is Linux?

Back in August of 1991, a student from Finland began a post to the `comp.os.minix` newsgroup with the words:

```
Hello everybody out there using minix -
I'm doing a (free) operating system (just a hobby,
won't be big and professional like gnu) for
386(486) AT clones.
```

The student was Linus Torvalds, and the "hobby" he spoke of eventually became what we know today as Linux.

A full-featured POSIX-like operating system, Linux has been developed not just by Linus, but by hundreds of programmers around the world. The interesting thing about this is that this massive, world-wide development effort is largely uncoordinated. Sure, Linus calls the shots where the kernel is concerned, but Linux is more than just the kernel. There's no management infrastructure; a student in Russia gets a new motherboard, and writes a driver to support a neat feature the motherboard has. A system administrator in Maryland needs backup software, writes it, and gives it away to anyone that needs it. The right things just seem to happen at the right time.

Another interesting thing is that Linux can be obtained for absolutely no money. That's right, most of the software is available (at no charge) to anyone with the time and inclination to download it. But not everyone has that much time...

What is Red Hat Linux?

Enter a group of programmers based in North Carolina. Their goal was to make it easier for people to give Linux a try. Like many other such groups, their approach was to bundle all the necessary bits and pieces into a cohesive *distribution*, relieving "newbies" from some of the more esoteric aspects of bootstrapping a new operating system on their PCs.

However, unlike other distributions, this one was fundamentally different. The difference? Instead of being a snapshot of a hard disk that had a working copy of Linux on it, or a set of diskettes from which different parts of the operating system could be dumped, this distribution was based on *packages*.

Software development in the Linux world is fast-paced, so new versions of old software come out continually. With other distributions, upgrading software was painful – a complete upgrade usually meant deleting everything on your hard drive and starting over.

Each package provided a different piece of software, fully tested, configured, and ready to run. Want to try a new editor? Download the package and install it. In seconds, you can give it a try. Don't like it? Issue a single command, and the package is removed.

If that was all there was to it, this distribution would be pretty nifty. But being package-based meant there was one additional advantage:

This Linux distribution could be easily upgraded.

By now you've probably guessed that the group of programmers in North Carolina is Red Hat Software, and the package-based distribution is Red Hat Linux.

Since Red Hat Linux's introduction in the summer of 1994, Linux and Red Hat Software have grown by leaps and bounds. Much has changed; support for more esoteric hardware, huge increases in reliability, and the growing use of Linux by companies around the world.

But much still remains the same. Linux is still developed by people world-wide; Linus is still involved. Red Hat Software is still located in North Carolina; still trying to make Linux easier for people to use.

And Red Hat Linux is still package-based; always has been, always will be.

Since the release of version 4.0, Red Hat Linux runs on three leading computing platforms: Intel compatible PCs, Digital Alpha computers, and Sun SPARC equipment. Our unified source tree and the benefits of RPM (Red Hat Package Management) technology enable us to deploy Red Hat Linux for each platform with a minimum of effort. This in turn enables our users to manage and port software between these platforms as easily as possible.

We make Red Hat Linux available by unrestricted FTP from our site and many mirror sites on the

Internet. Red Hat Linux is also available on CD-ROM. For current information on our product offerings and links to other Linux resources please check Red Hat Software's web site at `http://www.redhat.com`.

On most systems, Red Hat Linux is easy to install; the installation program can walk you through the process in as little as 15 minutes. The system itself is very flexible. With RPM, you can install and uninstall individual software packages with minimal effort. Because of RPM, Red Hat Linux is also easy to maintain – package installations can be verified and corrected, and packages can be installed and uninstalled simply and reliably. Furthermore, Red Hat Linux is easy to administer. Included are a rich set of administrative tools which reduce the hassle of everyday system administration. Complete source code is provided for the freely distributable components of the system.

An Overview of This Manual

This manual is organized to guide you through the process of installing Red Hat Linux quickly and easily. Toward that goal, let's take a quick look at each chapter to help you get acclimated:

Chapter 1, *New Features Of Red Hat Linux 6.0* contains information concerning new functionality that has been added to Red Hat Linux 6.0.

Chapter 2, *Before You Begin* contains information on tasks you should perform prior to starting the Red Hat Linux installation.

Chapter 3, *Starting the Installation* contains detailed instructions for starting the Red Hat Linux installation process.

Chapter 4, *Local Media Installations* contains instructions on installing Red Hat Linux from a CD-ROM or hard drive.

Chapter 5, *Network Installations* contains instructions on installing Red Hat Linux via NFS, FTP, or HTTP.

Chapter 6, *Finishing the Installation* contains instructions on the last steps required to complete the installation process.

Chapters 7 – 11 explain how to find documentation on your system, and how to use the various system management and administration tools which accompany Red Hat Linux. They also include an explanation of what's special about your Red Hat Linux system, including where special files live and more.

Appendixes contain extra information about Red Hat Linux, including an explanation of Red Hat Software's support offerings, packages lists, and more.

Quick Start Information

Those of you that have installed Red Hat Linux/Intel before and are in a hurry to get started need only boot from a boot diskette (or the Red Hat Linux/Intel CD-ROM, if your computer supports booting directly from CD-ROM). There are two separate boot disks, one for CD-ROM and hard drive installations and another for NFS, FTP, and HTTP installations[1]. Next, select the desired installation method. If you will be using a PCMCIA device during the installation, you will need to use the PCMCIA support disk[2].

If you are attempting to install Red Hat Linux for either the Alpha or the SPARC, you really should read Chapter 2 on page 5. It will refer you to information specific to your non-Intel-based system.

Upgrading from a Prior Version of Red Hat Linux

The installation process for Red Hat Linux 6.0 includes the ability to upgrade from prior versions of Red Hat Linux (2.0 through 5.2, inclusive) which are based on RPM technology. Upgrading your system installs the modular 2.2.x kernel as well as updated versions of the packages that are installed on your machine. The upgrade process preserves existing configuration files using a .rpmsave extension (e.g., sendmail.cf.rpmsave) and leaves a log telling what actions it took in /tmp/upgrade.log. As software evolves, configuration file formats can change, so you should carefully compare your original configuration files to the new files before integrating your changes.

A Word From the Developers

We would like to thank all our beta testers for entrusting their systems to early versions of Red Hat Linux and for taking the time to submit bug reports from the front, especially those of you who have been with Red Hat since the "Halloween" release and earlier. We would also like to thank Linus Torvalds and the hundreds of developers around the world for creating, truly, one of the wonders of distributed development.

And, again, we'd like to thank *you* for your interest in Red Hat Linux!

The Red Hat Development Team

---

[1] If you need a boot disk for network type installations, you will have to create one. See section 2.5 on page 18 for that informtaion

[2] If you will be using a PCMCIA device during the install you will need to create a PCMCIA support disk. Section 2.6 on page 18 will describe how that disk is made

Notes from the Editor

Our evolutionary process of expanding the scope of this Installation Guide continues. As before, we've updated the chapters related to the actual installation process. We've also updated the New Features chapter to reflect all the good stuff that's been added to Red Hat Linux 6.0. We consider this to be "business as usual."

We've also made some changes as a direct result of customer feedback. Some people have expressed confusion over all the different terms, abbreviations and acronyms that seem to surround computer technology in general, and Linux in particular. For those people, we've added a glossary. While it's not our goal to include a complete data processing dictionary with every copy of Red Hat Linux, if you think a particular word should be present but is not, feel free to let us know via docs@redhat.com.

As the linuxconf system configuration tool continues to mature, we've created a new system configuration chapter containing task-based linuxconf documentation, as well as those vestiges of the control-panel tools that still remain. Our goal is to continue adding linuxconf documentation; what you see here is just a first step in that process.

The package list has proven to be quite popular; this time we've improved it by adding icons showing whether a given package is part of a pre-defined set of packages.

All of this has resulted in the Installation Guide putting on a little weight. This is a trend that we expect to continue, which leads us right into the next subject. . .

We Need Feedback!

If you spot a typo in the Installation Guide, or if you've thought of a way to make this manual better, we'd love to hear from you! Be sure to mention the manual's identifier:

Inst-6.0-Print-RHS (04/99)

That way we'll know exactly which version of the guide you have.

Please send mail to:

docs@redhat.com

If you have a suggestion, try to be as specific as possible when describing it. If you've found an error, please include the section number and some of the surrounding text so we can find it easily. We may not be able to respond to every message sent to us, but you can be sure that we'll be reading them all!

I Couldn't Have Done it Without. . .

Many thanks go out to the past authors of this manual. A great deal of their work is still here. Thanks also go out to the developers and testers who have patiently listened to my questions and even more patiently given me answers. Without their help, I wouldn't have been able to put this manual together.

A "BIG" thank you also goes out to two of the members of the documentation team. Paul Gallagher, our editor, has done a wonderful job of proof reading and editing this manual. He has also written the GnoRPM chapter of this book and the Official Red Hat Linux Getting Started Guide. Edward Bailey, "fearless leader" and head of the documentation team, has done a fabulous job at keeping me up to speed and helping me go in the right direction. He is also credited with the new partition appendix in this Installation Guide. Without his leadership and guidance, this would have been an impossible task for me. You both have been wonderful to work with and I just can't say thank you enough.

Thanks are also due to all the readers of past Installation Guides. Without their corrections, suggestions and even occassional praises, I wouldn't know if I were on the right track. Your feedback has been incorporated as much as possible (pagecount and deadlines permitting). Please keep the feedback coming.

Many thanks to Cynthia Dale for updating the Frequently Asked Questions chapter and Jeff Goldin for correlating it for publication. Unfortunaly, we could not print it due to lack of space in the manual. However, you can find the most up-to-date FAQ at
`http://www.redhat.com/knowledgebase/index.html`.

Finally, thanks goes out to the support group at Red Hat Software. They have given many insightful suggestions regarding this manual, based on extensive experience with thousands of Red Hat Linux customers. If you find yourself going through this Installation Guide with greater ease, a large part of that is due to all of their effort.

Thank you to everyone at Red Hat Software for your help and support.

Sandra A. Moore

1

New Features of Red Hat Linux 6.0

This chapter describes features that are new to Red Hat Linux 6.0.

1.1   Installation-Related Enhancements

Here is a list of the many changes which have been made in order to make the Red Hat Linux installation process even easier:

- New HTTP Installation Method
- "Out-of-the-Box" Processor Optimized Kernel Support
- New Boot Disks
- Improved Package Selection Screen
- New Authentication Configuration Screen
- Xconfigurator Now Part of Install

Let's take a look at each one in a bit more detail.

New HTTP Installation Method

The Red Hat Linux 6.0 installation program has added HTTP to its available list of network-class installations. Similar to the way you would perform an FTP installation, you are now able to log in to a website and install Linux.

For more information on network-class installations, please refer to Chapter 5 on page 65.

'Out-of-the-Box' Processor Optimized Kernel Support

Optimized kernels for the Pentium Pro, Pentium II, and Pentium III processors and APM enabled kernels are now supported. Additionally, the Red Hat Linux 6.0 installation now has SMP motherboard support. The installation process will probe your system and if more than one processor is detected, an SMP enabled kernel will be automatically installed.

New Boot Disks

There are now two boot disks for Red Hat Linux. One is for installing from local media (CD-ROM installs, hard drive installs) and the other is for network based installs (NFS, FTP, or HTTP).

Additionally, the supplemental disk has been replaced by the PCMCIA support disk. All install methods now require only one disk, unless you need PCMCIA support during the install. If needed, you will be prompted for the PCMCIA support disk.

Improved Package Selection Screen

Individual package selection has been improved, with collapsible and expandable tree menus to allow easy selection of packages during the installation process.

New Authentication Configuration Screen

The Authentication Configuration screen gives you the option of enabling three different types of passwords:

- **Enable NIS** – allows you to run a group of computers in the same Network Information Service domain with a common password and group file. There are two options here to choose from:
    - **NIS Domain** – this option allows you to specify which domain or group of computers your system will belong to.
    - **NIS Server** – this option causes your computer to use a specific NIS server, rather than "broadcasting" a message to the local area network asking for any available server to host your system.

- **Enable Shadow Passwords** – provides a very secure method of retaining passwords for you.

- **Enable MD5 Passwords** – allows passwords up to 256 characters, rather than the standard eight.

Xconfigurator Now Part of the Install

Xconfigurator is now run at the very end of the install, after all filesystem components have been installed. In the past, if Xconfigurator were to hang, you would likely have to start the installation over. Now it is possible to boot Red Hat Linux and configure X after the installation has completed.

Additionally, Xconfigurator tests X during the installation to make sure it is configured correctly for your system. Xconfigurator also offers you the option of booting into the X Window System immediately after the installation.

1.2   Desktop and Window Managers

Red Hat Linux 6.0 provides additional choices in graphical user interfaces.

- GNOME with Enlightenment Included
- KDE Included

GNOME with Enlightenment Included

GNOME is now included in Red Hat Linux 6.0 as the default desktop manager. GNOME features a graphical interface which enables users to easily use and configure their systems. GNOME also supports Drag and Drop protocols which help you use applications that are not GNOME-compliant.

Enlightenment is included as the default window manager. Enlightenment provides a window manager with a great graphical interface, and is designed to allow the user to manipulate it in any way fashionable.

KDE Included

Red Hat Linux 6.0 also includes KDE. A very popular and powerful desktop environment, KDE offers a great graphical interface, window manager, file manager and much more.

1.3   Miscellaneous New Features

Other miscellaneous features of Red Hat Linux 6.0 are:

- Enhanced Font Support
- Enhanced Initscripts
- Switchdesk Feature
- Latest Stable 2.2 Kernel Included

Enhanced Font Support

TrueType fonts are now supported in Red Hat Linux 6.0.

Dynamic font loading is now supported and can be used as a font-server on a local machine.

Please Note: Those of you who upgrade will not have this feature until you edit your fontpaths. To do this you must edit the `/etc/X11/XF86Config` file. Scroll down until you see fontpaths listed. Replace them all with `FontPath ''tcp/localhost:7100''`. You must also verify that `xfs`, the X Font Server, is running. By issuing the command `/sbin/chkconfig --add xfs` you will insure that it starts at system boot time.

Enhanced Initscripts

While booting and shutting down the system, Red Hat Linux 6.0 users are now able to easily see if a service has failed by displaying `OK`, `PASSED` or `FAILED` at the right-hand side of the screen.

Switchdesk Feature

Switchdesk, just as the name implies, allows you to easily switch between different desktop environments such as GNOME, AnotherLevel or KDE. Simply run "switchdesk" and choose your desired interface.

Latest Stable 2.2 Kernel Included

Red Hat Linux 6.0 includes the latest stable version of the 2.2 Linux kernel.

2

Before You Begin

While installing Red Hat Linux is a straightforward process, taking some time prior to starting the installation can make things go much more smoothly. In this chapter, we'll discuss the steps that should be performed before you start the installation.

Please Note: If you are currently running a version 2.0 (or greater) Red Hat Linux system, you can perform an upgrade. Skim this chapter to review the basic issues relating to installation, and read the following chapters in order, following the directions as you go. The upgrade procedure starts out identically to the installation procedure; you will be directed to choose an installation or upgrade after booting the installation program and answering a few questions.

There are five things you should do prior to installing Red Hat Linux:

1. Make sure you have sufficient documentation to effectively use your Red Hat Linux system after the installation.

2. Make sure you have access to the Red Hat Linux components required for installation.

3. Make sure you know your computer's hardware configuration and networking information.

4. Decide, based on the first two tasks, what method you will use to install Red Hat Linux.

5. Determine where on your hard drive(s) Red Hat Linux will reside.

Let's start by making sure you have the documentation you'll need after you install Red Hat Linux.

2.1   Getting Documentation

Red Hat Linux is a powerful, full-featured operating system. Unless you're a Linux wizard, you're going to need additional documentation to make the most of your Red Hat Linux system. We strongly suggest reading over the Official Red Hat Linux Getting Started Guide to see what it can offer you in terms of both use and support. It has been written guide you through using Red Hat Linux once the installation has been completed.

Everyone should review the Official Red Hat Linux Getting Started Guide for more information on available Linux documentation as well as using Red Hat Linux 6.0 to its full potential. While many people will find the resources described in the Getting Started Guide to be very helpful, people who are just starting to use Linux will likely need additional information. The information that will be most helpful to you depends on your level of Linux expertise:

New To Linux – If this is your first time using Linux (or any Linux-like operating system, for that matter), you'll need solid introductory information on basic UNIX concepts. For example, O'Reilly and Associates (`http://www.ora.com/`) produce a wide variety of Linux and UNIX-related books. Give their more general titles a try.

Some Linux Experience – If you've used other Linux distributions (or a Linux-like operating system), you'll probably find what you're looking for in some of the more in-depth reference material available. For example O'Reilly's more specialized titles are valuable when you need a lot of information on a particular subject.

Old Timer – If you're a long-time Red Hat Linux user, you probably don't need us telling you what documentation to read. Thanks for reading this far!

2.2   Getting the Right Red Hat Linux Components

If you've purchased the Red Hat Linux boxed set, you're ready to go! However, mistakes occasionally happen, so now is a good time to double-check the contents of your boxed set. If you haven't purchased a Red Hat Linux boxed set, skip to Section 2.2.3 on page 9.

2.2.1   Contents of the Red Hat Linux Boxed Set

The Red Hat Linux boxed set contains the following items:

- The Official Red Hat Linux Installation Guide
- Official Red Hat Linux Getting Started Guide

> **ALPHA**
>
> - The Alpha Installation Addendum.

- Red Hat Linux CDs 1 and 2.

INTEL
• The Linux Applications CD Pack.

INTEL
Boot diskette.

•

- License and Registration information, located on the insert in the jewel case.

Let's take a quick look at each item:

Installation Guide

The Official Red Hat Linux Installation Guide is what you're currently reading. It contains the information necessary to install Red Hat Linux. In addition, it contains information about aspects of the operating system that are unique to Red Hat Linux.

Official Red Hat Linux Getting Started Guide

The Official Red Hat Linux Getting Started Guide contains information on what to do after the installation has taken place. It will be referred to on many occasions in this text. We believe it is both well written and informative, and will guide you through the necessary steps of actually using your system once the install is in place.

The Official Red Hat Linux Getting Started Guide covers topics ranging from the learning the basics of your system to navigating your system to Gnome.

Alpha Installation Addendum

ALPHA
The Red Hat Linux Alpha Installation Addendum contains additional information of interest to owners of Alpha-based computer systems. It contains information that will make installation of Red Hat Linux more straightforward. (The Alpha Installation Addendum is only included in Red Hat Linux/Alpha boxed sets.)

CDs 1 and 2

These two Compact Discs contain the entire Red Hat Linux distribution, including source code. CD 1 contains all the binary packages built for the type of computer (Intel, Alpha, or SPARC) that you have . CD 2 contains the source packages that were used to build the binary packages on CD 1.

Linux Applications CD Pack

INTEL

This Compact Disc pack contains demonstration versions of a number of commercial Linux software products. For more information, please refer to the README file in this pack.

Please Note: This CD-ROM pack and its contents are *completely unsupported* by Red Hat Software. All questions and issues concerning any software in this pack should be directed to the responsible company, and *not* Red Hat Software.

Boot Diskette

INTEL

This diskette is used to start the installation process for Red Hat Linux/Intel. Depending on your computer's configuration and the type of installation you select, you may or may not need the boot diskette. In addition, you may require a *support* diskette, again depending on your system's hardware configuration, and the installation method you choose. When we discuss the different installation methods later in this chapter, we'll explain which diskettes are needed for each type of installation, and give you instructions for producing any diskettes you require.

ALPHA

Alpha owners should refer to the Red Hat Linux Alpha Installation Addendum for information on which diskettes are required.

SPARC

SPARC owners should turn to Section F.5.1 on page 363 for information on their diskette needs.

License and Registration Information

The CD-ROM jewel case insert includes the license terms for Red Hat Linux, in addition to the license terms for any commercial software that may be included on the Red Hat Linux CD.

In addition, information about registering your copy of Red Hat Linux with Red Hat Software can be found here. Once registered, you can receive installation support. Red Hat Software's installation support program is discussed in Appendix A on page 229.

Please Note: There is an alphanumeric registration string printed on the CD-ROM case. It is used to register you for Red Hat Software's installation support. Please make sure you don't lose your registration string – you won't be able to get installation support without it!

2.2.2   Missing Something?

If you've purchased the Official Red Hat Linux boxed set from Red Hat Software, (or one of its distributors) and you're missing one or more of the items listed above, please let us know!

One thing to keep in mind is that Red Hat Software partners with companies (international and domestic) so that we can make Red Hat Linux available to you in the most convenient form. Because of this, you might find that your Red Hat Linux boxed set may not have been actually produced by Red Hat Software.

Not sure how to identify our official boxed set? Here's how: The bottom of our box has an ISBN number next to one of the bar codes. That ISBN number should be in the form:

$$1\text{-}888172\text{-}xx\text{-}y$$

(Where xx and y may vary.) If your box has an ISBN number in this form, and you're missing something, feel free to call us at 1-888-733-4281 (+1-919-547-0012 outside the USA), or to send mail to `orders@redhat.com`.

If your box has a different ISBN number (or none at all), you'll need to contact the company that produced your boxed set. Normally, third-party producers will include their logo and/or contact information on the outside of the box; an official Red Hat Linux boxed set has only our name and contact info on the outside...

If your Red Hat Linux boxed set is complete, please skip ahead to section 2.2.4 on the next page.

2.2.3   No Boxed Set? No Problem!

Of course, not everyone purchases a Red Hat Linux boxed set. It's entirely possible to install Red Hat Linux using a CD created by another company, or even via FTP. In these cases, you may need to create one or more diskettes to get started.

> **INTEL**
> For people installing Red Hat Linux/Intel, you'll need a boot diskette, and if using a PCMCIA device during the installation, a PCMCIA support diskette. It may also be possible to start the installation directly from the CD, under certain conditions. We'll discuss this in more detail when we outline the various installation methods available.

> **ALPHA**
> People with Alpha-based systems should refer to the Red Hat Linux Alpha Installation Addendum for additional information on the diskettes they may need.

> **SPARC**
> SPARC owners should refer to section F.5.1 on page 363 for information on which diskettes they'll need.

2.2.4   Checking for Updated Diskette Images

From time to time, we find that the installation may fail, and that a revised diskette image is required in order for the installation to work properly. In these cases, we make special images available via the Red Hat Linux Errata.

Since this is a relatively rare occurrence, you will in general save time if you try to use the standard diskette images first, and then review the Errata only if you experience any problems completing the installation.

There are two ways to review the Errata:

1. **World Wide Web** – By pointing your web browser at `http://www.redhat.com/errata`, you can read the Errata on-line, and download diskette images easily.

2. **Electronic Mail** – By sending an empty mail message to `errata@redhat.com`, you will receive a mail message containing the complete Errata. Also included are URLs to each updated package and diskette image in the Errata. By using these URLs, you can then download any necessary diskette images. Remember to use binary mode when transferring a diskette image!

For now, concentrate only on the Errata entries that include new diskette images (the filenames always end in `.img`). If you find an entry that seems to apply to your problem, get a copy of the diskette images, and create them using the instructions in Appendix B on page 237.

2.3   Things You Should Know

In order to prevent any surprises during the installation, you should collect some information before attempting to install Red Hat Linux. You can find most of this information in the documentation that came with your system, or from the system's vendor or manufacturer.

Please Note: The most recent list of hardware supported by Red Hat Linux can be found at Red Hat Software's World Wide Web site at `http://www.redhat.com/hardware`. It's a good idea to check your hardware against this list before proceeding.

2.3.1   Basic Hardware Configuration

You should have a basic understanding of the hardware installed in your computer, including:

- **hard drive(s)** – Specifically, the number, size, and type. If you have more than one, it's helpful to know which one is first, second, and so on. It is also good to know if your drives are IDE or SCSI. If you have IDE drives, you should check your computer's BIOS to see if you are accessing them in *LBA* mode. Please refer to your computer's documentation for the proper key sequence to access the BIOS. Note that your computer's BIOS may refer to LBA mode by other names, such as "large disk mode". Again, your computer's documentation should be consulted for clarification.

- **memory** – The amount of RAM installed in your computer.

- **CD-ROM** – Most importantly, the unit's interface type (IDE, SCSI, or other interface) and, for non-IDE, non-SCSI CD-ROMs, the make and model number. IDE CD-ROMs (also known as ATAPI) are the most common type in recently manufactured, PC-compatible computers.

- **SCSI adapter (if one is present)** – The adapter's make and model number.

- **network card (if one is present)** – The card's make and model number.

- **mouse** – The mouse's type (serial, PS/2, or bus mouse), protocol (Microsoft, Logitech, Mouse-Man, etc.), and number of buttons; also, for serial mice, the serial port it is connected to.

On many newer systems, the installation program is able to automatically identify most hardware. However, it's a good idea to collect this information anyway, just to be sure.

ALPHA
In addition to the latest hardware compatibility list on Red Hat Software's website, owners of Alpha-based systems should refer to the Red Hat Linux Alpha Installation Addendum for more information on supported hardware configurations.

SPARC
In addition to the latest hardware compatibility list on Red Hat Software's website, SPARC owners should refer to Section F.1 on page 359 for a list of supported hardware.

Learning About Your Hardware With Windows®

If your computer is already running Windows 9x, you can use the following procedure to get additional configuration information:

- With Windows running, click on the "My Computer" icon using the secondary (normally the right) mouse button. A pop-up menu should appear.

- Select "Properties." The "System Properties" window should appear (see Figure 2.1 on the next page). Note the information listed under "Computer:" – in particular the amount of RAM listed.

- Click on the "Device Manager" tab. You will then see a graphical representation of your computer's hardware configuration. Make sure the "View devices by type" button is selected.

At this point, you can either double-click on the icons (or single-click on the plus sign ⊕) to look at each entry in more detail (see Figure 2.2 on page 13). Look under the following icons for more information:

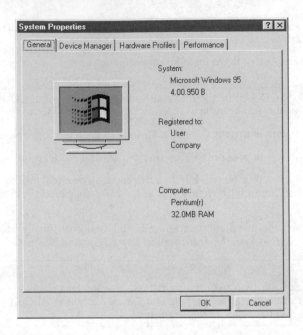

Figure 2.1: Windows System Properties Window

- **Disk drives** – You will find the type (IDE or SCSI) of hard drive here. (IDE drives will normally include the word "IDE," while SCSI drives won't.)

- **Hard disk controllers** – You can get more information about your hard drive controller here.

- **CDROM** – Here is where you'll find out about any CD-ROM drives connected to your computer.

  Please Note: In some cases, there may be no CD-ROM icon, yet your computer has a functioning CD-ROM drive. This is normal, depending on how Windows was originally installed. In this case, you may be able to learn additional information by looking at the CD-ROM driver loaded in your computer's `config.sys` file.

- **Mouse** – The type of mouse present on your computer can be found here.

- **Display adapters** – If you're interested in running the X Window System, you should write down the information you find here.

- **Sound, video and game controllers** – If your computer has sound capabilities, you'll find more information about that here.

- **Network adapters** – Here you'll find additional info on your computer's network card (if you have one).

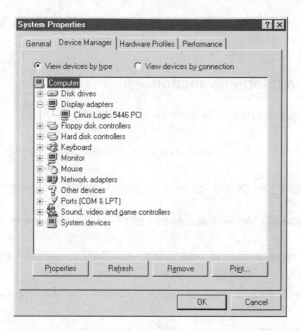

Figure 2.2: Device Manager Under Windows 95

- **SCSI controllers** – If your computer uses SCSI peripherals, you'll find additional info on the SCSI controller here.

While this method is not a complete substitute for opening your computer's case and physically examining each component, in many cases it can provide sufficient information to continue with the installation.

Please Note: This information can also be printed by clicking on the "Print..." button. A second window will appear, allowing you to choose the printer, as well as the type of report (the "All Devices and System Summary" report type is the most complete).

2.3.2   Video Configuration

If you will be installing the X Window System, you should also be familiar with the following:

- **your video card** – The card's make and model number (or the video chipset it uses), and the amount of video RAM it has. (Most PCI-based cards are auto-detected by the installation program.)

- **your monitor** – The unit's make and model number, along with allowable ranges for horizontal and vertical refresh rates.

2.3.3   Network-related Information

If you will be connected to a network, be sure you know your:

- **IP address** – Usually represented as a set of four numbers separated by dots, such as `10.0.2.15`.

- **netmask** – Another set of four numbers separated by dots. An example netmask would be `255.255.248.0`.

- **gateway IP address** – Yet another set of four dot-separated numbers. For instance, `10.0.2.254`.

- **one or more name server IP addresses** – One or more sets of dot-separated numbers. `10.0.2.1` might be the address of a name server.

- **domain name** – The name given to your organization. For instance, Red Hat Software has a domain name of `redhat.com`.

- **hostname** – The name of your computer. A computer might be named `pooh`, for instance.

Please Note: The information given above is an example only! Do *not* use it when you install Red Hat Linux! If you don't know the proper values for your network, ask your network administrator.

2.4   Installation Methods

> **ALPHA**
> Alpha owners should take a moment to review the Red Hat Linux Alpha Installation Addendum, particularly the first chapter. It covers aspects of the installation process that differ from a typical Red Hat Linux/Intel installation.

> **SPARC**
> People with SPARC systems should take a moment to read Appendix F on page 359. This appendix covers aspects of the installation process that differ from a typical Red Hat Linux/Intel installation.

You can install or upgrade Red Hat Linux via any of several different methods. Each method works best in different situations, and has different requirements. But before we discuss each installation method, let's take a look at an issue that may affect some of you.

2.4.1   PCMCIA Support During the Installation

> **INTEL**
> This section is specific to Intel-based computers only

Most Intel-based laptop computers support PCMCIA (also known as PC Card). Computers that support PCMCIA devices contain a controller having one or more slots in which a PCMCIA device can be installed. These devices may be modems, LAN adapters, SCSI adapters, and so on.

When installing Red Hat Linux/Intel on a PCMCIA-capable computer, it is important to note if a PCMCIA device will be used during installation. For example, if you want to install Red Hat Linux/-Intel from a CD-ROM, and your CD-ROM drive is connected to a PCMCIA adapter, the installation program will require PCMCIA support. Likewise, if you are going to use one of the network-based installation methods, you will need PCMCIA support if your network adapter is PCMCIA-based.

Please Note: You don't need install-time PCMCIA support if you're installing Red Hat Linux on a laptop, and using the laptop's built-in CD-ROM drive.

PCMCIA support is dependent on two things:

1. The type of PCMCIA controller in your computer system.

2. The type of PCMCIA device that you wish to use during the installation.

While nearly every PCMCIA controller and most popular PCMCIA devices are supported, there are some exceptions. For more information, please consult the Red Hat Linux Hardware Compatibility List at http://www.redhat.com/hardware.

The main thing to keep in mind is that if you require install-time PCMCIA support, you will need a support diskette. We'll show you how to do this after you've determined which installation method is best for you.

> **ALPHA**
> PCMCIA support is not available for the Alpha.

> **SPARC**
> PCMCIA support is not available for the SPARC.

2.4.2   Installing From a CD-ROM

If you have a Red Hat Linux CD-ROM, and your computer has a supported CD-ROM drive, you should consider this installation method. Installing directly from CD-ROM is the most straightforward approach. When installing from CD-ROM, the packages you select are read from the CD-ROM, and are installed on your hard drive.

How To Do It

As the name implies, you'll need a Red Hat Linux CD-ROM, a supported CD-ROM drive, and a means of starting the installation program.

> **INTEL**
>
> Intel systems will need to use the boot diskette (and the PCMCIA support diskette if a PCMCIA device is used during the install). There is an alternate method of installing from CD-ROM that uses no diskettes, but requires that the system be running DOS. We'll discuss this approach (known as *autoboot*) in Section 3.2.1 on page 38. For now, note that PCMCIA support is not available when using *autoboot*.
>
> **Please Note:** The Red Hat Linux/Intel CD-ROM can also be booted by newer computers that support bootable CD-ROMs. Not all computers support this feature, so if yours can't boot from CD-ROM, you'll have to use a boot diskette (or autoboot from DOS) to get things started. Note that you may need to change BIOS settings in your computer to enable this feature.

If you've determined that this installation method is most applicable to your situation, please skip ahead to Section 2.6 on page 18.

2.4.3   Installing From an FTP Site

If you don't have a Red Hat Linux CD-ROM or a CD-ROM drive, but you do have network access, then an FTP installation may be for you. When installing via FTP, the Red Hat Linux packages you select are downloaded (using FTP) across the network to your computer, and are installed on your hard drive.

How To Do It

When doing an FTP install, you'll need LAN-based access to a network; a dialup connection via modem won't cut it. If your Local Area Network has Internet access, you can use one of the many FTP sites that mirror Red Hat Linux. You can find a list of mirror sites at
`http://www.redhat.com/mirrors.html`.

If your LAN doesn't have Internet access, all is not lost. If there is a computer on your LAN that can accept anonymous FTP requests, simply put a copy of the Red Hat Linux distribution on that system, and you're ready to go.

Please Note: Your FTP server must be able to handle long filenames.

> **INTEL**
>
> For an FTP installation, you must use the network installation boot diskette specific to, and a PCM-CIA support diskette if using a PCMCIA device during the installation. You will need to have a valid nameserver configured or you must specify the IP address of the FTP server you will be using. You will also need the path to the Red Hat Linux directory on the FTP server.

If you've determined that this installation method is most applicable to your situation, please skip ahead to Section 2.6 on the following page.

2.4.4 Installing From an HTTP Site

If you don't have a Red Hat Linux CD-ROM or a CD-ROM drive, but you do have network access, then an HTTP installation may be for you. When installing via HTTP, the Red Hat Linux packages you select are downloaded (using HTTP) across the network to your computer, and are installed on your hard drive.

How To Do It

> INTEL
> For an HTTP installation, you must use the network installation boot disk and if you are using a PCMCIA device during the installation, a PCMCIA support diskette. You will need to have a valid nameserver configured or you must specify the IP address of the HTTP server you will be using. You will also need the path to the Red Hat Linux directory on the HTTP server.

If you've determined that this installation method is most applicable to your situation, please skip ahead to Section 2.6 on the next page.

2.4.5 Installing From an NFS Server

If your system doesn't have a CD-ROM drive, but you do have network access, then an NFS installation may be for you. When installing via NFS, the Red Hat Linux packages you select are NFS-served to your computer from an NFS server system. The packages are then installed on your hard drive.

How To Do It

If you wish to perform an NFS installation, you will need to mount the Red Hat Linux CD-ROM on a machine that supports ISO-9660 file systems with Rock Ridge extensions. The machine must also support NFS. Export the CD-ROM file system via NFS. You will need to have a nameserver configured, or know the NFS server's IP address, as well as the path to the exported CD-ROM.

Please Note: Your NFS server must be able to handle long filenames.

> INTEL
> For an NFS installation, you'll need a boot diskette only.

If you've determined that this installation method is most applicable to your situation, please skip ahead to Section 2.6 on the following page.

2.4.6 Installing From a Hard Drive

If none of the other installation methods will work for you, but you have some means of getting the Red Hat Linux package files written to your system's hard drive, you can install from your hard drive. In this installation method, the Red Hat Linux packages you select are read from one partition on a hard drive, and are installed on another partition (or set of partitions).

How To Do It

The hard drive installation method requires a bit of up-front effort on your part, as you must copy all the necessary files to a partition before starting the Red Hat Linux installation program. You must first create a `RedHat` directory at the top level of your directory tree. Everything you will install should be placed in that directory. First copy the `base` subdirectory and its contents.

Next, copy the packages you want to install to another subdirectory called `RPMS`. You can use available space on an existing DOS partition or a Linux partition that is not required in the install procedure (for example, a partition that would be used for data storage on the installed system).

INTEL

If you are using a DOS filesystem, you will not be able to use the full Linux filenames for the `RPM` packages. The installation process does not care what the filenames look like, but it is a good idea that you keep track of them.
You'll need a boot diskette, and if using a PCMCIA device during the installation, a PCMCIA support diskette, when installing from a hard drive.

2.5 Need a Network Boot Disk?

If you are performing an installation via FTP, HTTP, or NFS you will need to create your own network boot diskette. The network boot diskette image file is `bootnet.img`, and is located in the `images` directory on your Red Hat Linux/Intel CD. Please turn to Appendix B on page 237 and follow the instructions there. Then, return here, and read on.

2.6 Need a PCMCIA Support Diskette?

INTEL

This section is specific to Intel-based computers only. If you are using an Alpha or SPARC computer, please skip ahead to 2.8 on page 21.

Here's a checklist that you can use to see if you'll need to create a PCMCIA support diskette:

- **Installing From a PCMCIA-Connected CD-ROM** – If you'll be installing Red Hat Linux from a CD-ROM, and your CD-ROM drive is attached to your computer through a PCMCIA card, you'll need a support diskette.

- **Installing using a PCMCIA Network Card** – If you will be using a PCMCIA network adapter during the installation, you'll need a support diskette.

If you have determined you will need a support diskette, you will have to make one. The PCMCIA support diskette image file is `pcmcia.img`, and is located in the `images` directory on your Red Hat Linux/Intel CD. Please turn to Appendix B on page 237 and follow the instructions there. Then, return here, and read on.

2.7 Installation Classes

Red Hat Linux includes defines three different classes, or types of installations. They are:

- **Workstation**
- **Server**
- **Custom**

These classes give you the option of simplifying the installation process (with some loss of configuration flexibility), or retaining complete flexibility with a slightly more complex installation process. Let's take a look at each class in more detail, so you can see which one is right for you.

Only the custom-class install allows you complete flexibility. The workstation-class and server-class installs automatically goes through the installation process for you and omits certain steps.

2.7.1 The Workstation-Class Installation

A workstation-class installation is most appropriate for you if you're new to the world of Linux, and would like to give it a try. By answering very few installation questions, you can be up and running Red Hat Linux in no time!

What Does It Do?

A workstation-class installation removes any linux-related partitions on all installed hard drives (and uses all free unpartitioned disk space) to create the following partitions:

- A 64MB swap partition.

  INTEL

- A 16MB partition (mounted as /boot) in which the Linux kernel and related files reside.

  ALPHA

- A 2MB partition (mounted as /dos) in which the MILO boot loader is located.

- A variable-sized (the exact size is dependent on available disk space) partition (mounted as /) in which all other files are stored.

This approach to disk partitioning results in the simplest filesystem configuration possible.

Please Note: You will need approximately 600MB of free disk space in order to perform a workstation-class installation.

If your system already runs Windows, a workstation-class installation will automatically configure your system to dual-boot using LILO.

Please Note: A workstation-class installation will remove any existing Linux partition on any hard drive on your system. It will also attempt to set up a dual boot environment automatically on your system.

2.7.2   The Server-Class Installation

A server-class installation is most appropriate for you if you'd like your system to function as a Linux-based server, and you don't want to heavily customize your system configuration.

What Does It Do?

A server-class installation removes *all* existing partitions on all installed hard drives, so choose this installation class only if you're sure you have nothing you want saved! When the installation is complete, you'll find the following partitions:

- A 64MB swap partition.

  INTEL

- A 16MB partition (mounted as /boot) in which the Linux kernel and related files are kept.

  ALPHA

- A 2MB partition (mounted as /dos) in which the MILO boot loader is kept.

- A 256MB partition (mounted as /).

- A partition of at least 512MB (mounted as /usr).

- A partition of at least 512MB (mounted as /home).

- A 256MB partition (mounted as /var).

This approach to disk partitioning results in a reasonably flexible filesystem configuration for most server-class tasks.

Please Note: You will need approximately 1.6GB of free disk space in order to perform a server-class installation.

Please Note: A server-class installation will remove any existing partitions of any type on all existing hard drives of your system. All drives will be erased of all information and existing operating systems, regardless if they are Linux partitions or not.

2.7.3   The Custom-Class Installation

As you might guess from the name, a custom-class installation puts the emphasis on flexibility. During a custom-class installation, it is up to *you* how disk space should be partitioned. You have complete control over the packages that will be installed on your system. You can also determine whether you'll use LILO to boot your system.

For those of you with prior Red Hat Linux installation experience, you've already done a custom-class installation – it is the same installation procedure we've used in past versions of Red Hat Linux.

2.8   Disk Partitions

Nearly every modern-day operating system uses disk partitions, and Red Hat Linux is no exception. When installing Red Hat Linux, it will be necessary to work with disk partitions. If you have not worked with disk partitions before (or would like a quick review of the basic concepts) please read Appendix C on page 239 before proceeding.

Please Note: If you intend to perform a workstation- or server-class installation, and you already have sufficient *unpartitioned* disk space, you do not need to read this section, and may turn to Section 2.9 on page 32. Otherwise, please read this section in order to determine the best approach to freeing disk space for your Red Hat Linux installation.

In order to install Red Hat Linux, you must make disk space available for it. This disk space needs to be separate from the disk space used by other operating systems you may have installed on your computer, such as Windows, OS/2, or even a different version of Linux. This is done by dedicating one or more *partitions* to Red Hat Linux.

Before you start the installation process, one of the following conditions must be met:

- Your computer must have enough *unpartitioned* disk space available to install Red Hat Linux.

- Your computer must have one or more partitions that may be deleted, thereby freeing up enough disk space to install Red Hat Linux.

Let's look at how this can be done.

2.8.1   Making Room For Red Hat Linux

There are three possible scenarios you may face when attempting to repartition your hard disk:

- Unpartitioned free space is available.

- An unused partition is available.

- Free space in an actively used partition is available.

Let's look at each scenario in order.

Please Note: The figures in this section are based on those used in Appendix C on page 239, and represent the sequence of events necessary to free disk space for Red Hat Linux. If these figures do not make sense to you, you should read Appendix C before proceeding any further. Keep in mind that these illustrations are simplified in the interest of clarity, and do not reflect the exact partition layout that you will encounter when actually installing Red Hat Linux.

Using Unpartitioned Free Space

In this situation, the partitions already defined do not span the entire hard disk, leaving unallocated space that is not part of any defined partition. Figure 2.3 on the next page shows what this might look like.

If you think about it, an unused hard disk also falls into this category; the only difference is that *all* the space is not part of any defined partition.

In any case, you can simply create the necessary partitions from the unused space. Unfortunately, this scenario, although very simple, is not very likely (unless you've just purchased a new disk just for Red Hat Linux).

Let's move on to a slightly more common situation.

Using Space From An Unused Partition

In this case, maybe you have one or more partitions that you just don't use any longer. Perhaps you've dabbled with another operating system in the past, and the partition(s) you've dedicated to it never seem to be used anymore. Figure 2.4 on the facing page illustrates such a situation.

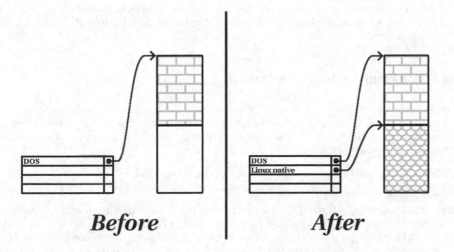

Figure 2.3: Disk Drive with Unpartitioned Free Space

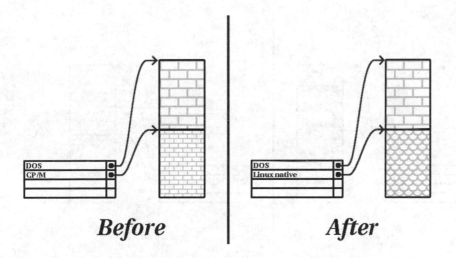

Figure 2.4: Disk Drive With an Unused Partition

If you find yourself in this situation, you can use the space allocated to the unused partition. You'll first need to delete the partition, and then create the appropriate Linux partition(s) in its place. You can either delete the partition using DOS `fdisk`, or you'll be given the opportunity to do so during a custom-class installation.

Using Free Space From An Active Partition

This is the most common situation. It is also, unfortunately, the hardest to work with. The main problem is that, even if you have enough free space, it's presently allocated to a partition that is in use. If you purchased a computer with pre-installed software, the hard disk most likely has one massive partition holding the operating system and data.

Aside from adding a new hard drive to your system, you have two choices:

Destructive Repartitioning – Basically, you delete the single large partition, and create several smaller ones. As you might imagine, any data you had in the original partition is destroyed. This means that making a complete backup is necessary. For your own sake, make two back-ups, use verification (if available in your backup software), and try to read data from your backup *before* you delete the partition. Note also that if there was an operating system of some type installed on that partition, it will need to be reinstalled as well.

After creating a smaller partition for your existing software, you can reinstall any software, restore your data, and continue with your Red Hat Linux installation. Figure 2.5 shows this being done.

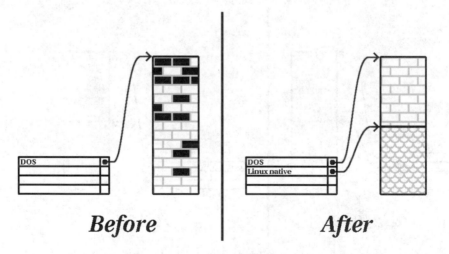

Before   *After*

Figure 2.5: Disk Drive Being Destructively Repartitioned

Please Note: As Figure 2.5 on the facing page shows, any data present in the original partition will be lost without proper backup!

Non-Destructive Repartitioning – Here, you run a program that does the seemingly impossible: it makes a big partition smaller without losing any of the files stored in that partition. Many people have found this method to be reliable and trouble-free. What software should you use to perform this feat? There are several disk management software products on the market; you'll have to do some research to find the one that is best for your situation.

While the process of non-destructive repartitioning is rather straightforward, there are a number of steps involved:

- Compress existing data
- Resize partition
- Create new partition(s)

Let's take a look at each step in a bit more detail.

Compress existing data – As Figure 2.6 shows, the first step is to compress the data in your existing partition. The reason for doing this is to rearrange the data such that it maximizes the available free space at the "end" of the partition.

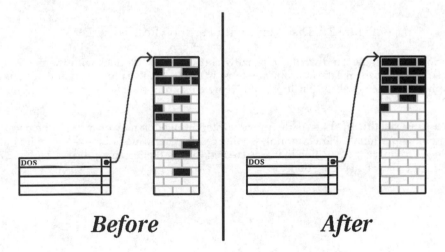

Before | *After*

Figure 2.6: Disk Drive Being Compressed

This step is crucial; without it, it is possible that the location of your data could prevent the partition from being resized to the extent desired. Note also that, for one reason or another, some data cannot be moved. If this is the case (and it restricts the size of your new partition(s)), you may be forced to destructively repartition your disk.

Resize partition – Figure 2.7 shows the actual resizing process. While the actual end-product of the resizing operation varies depending on the software used, in most cases the newly freed space is used to create an unformatted partition of the same type as the original partition.

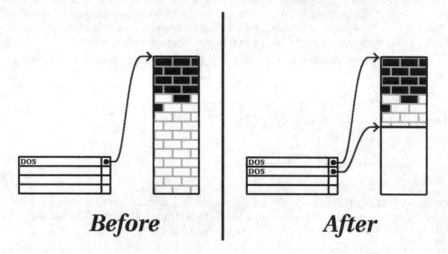

Figure 2.7: Disk Drive with Partition Resized

It's important to understand what the resizing software you use does with the newly freed space, so that you can take the appropriate steps. In the case we've illustrated, it would be best to simply delete the new DOS partition, and create the appropriate Linux partition(s).

Create new partition(s) – As the previous step implied, it may or may not be necessary to create new partitions. However, unless your resizing software is Linux-aware, it is likely you'll need to delete the partition that was created during the resizing process. Figure 2.8 on the next page shows this being done.

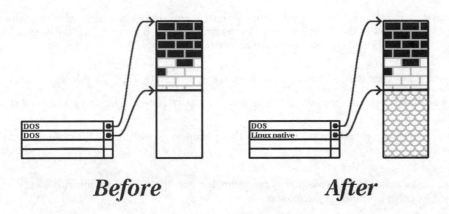

Before   *After*

Figure 2.8: Disk Drive with Final Partition Configuration

INTEL

As a convenience to our customers, we provide the `fips` utility. This is a freely available program that can resize FAT (File Allocation Table) partitions. It's included on the Red Hat Linux/Intel CD-ROM in the `dosutils` directory.

Please Note: Many people have successfully used `fips` to repartition their hard drives. However, because of the nature of the operations carried out by `fips`, and the wide variety of hardware and software configurations under which it must run, Red Hat Software cannot guarantee that `fips` will work properly on your system. Therefore, no installation support whatsoever is available for `fips`; use it at your own risk.

That said, if you decide to repartition your hard drive with `fips`, it is *vital* that you do two things:

- **Perform a Backup** – Make two copies of all the important data on your computer. These copies should be to removable media (such as tape or diskettes), and you should make sure they are readable before proceeding.

- **Read the Documentation** – Completely read the `fips` documentation, located in the `/dosutils/fipsdocs` subdirectory on Red Hat Linux/Intel CD 1.

Should you decide to use `fips`, be aware that after `fips` runs you will be left with *two* partitions: the one you resized, and the one `fips` created out of the newly freed space. If your goal is to use that space to install Red Hat Linux, you should delete the newly created partition, either by using `fdisk` under your current operating system, or while setting up partitions during a custom-class installation.

2.8.2   Partition Naming Scheme

Linux refers to disk partitions using a combination of letters and numbers which may be confusing, particularly if you're used to the "C drive" way of referring to hard disks and their partitions. In the DOS/Windows world, here is how partitions are named:

- Each partition's type is checked to determine if it can be read by DOS/Windows.

- If the partition's type is compatible, it is assigned a "drive letter." The drive letters start with "C".

- The drive letter can then be used to refer to that partition as well as the filesystem contained on that partition.

Red Hat Linux uses a naming scheme that is more flexible and conveys more information than the approach used by other operating systems.

The naming scheme is file-based, with filenames in the form:

$$/dev/xxyN$$

Here's how to decipher the partition naming scheme:

/dev/ – This string is the name of the directory in which all device files reside. Since partitions reside on hard disks, and hard disks are devices, the files representing all possible partitions reside in /dev/.

xx – The first two letters of the partition name indicate the type of device on which the partition resides. You'll normally see either hd (for IDE disks), or sd (for SCSI disks).

y – This letter indicates which device the partition is on. For example, /dev/hda (the first IDE hard disk) or /dev/sdb (the second SCSI disk).

N – The final number denotes the partition. The first four (primary or extended) partitions are numbered 1 through 4. Logical partitions start at 5. E.g., /dev/hda3 is the third primary or extended partition on the first IDE hard disk; /dev/sdb6 is the second logical partition on the second SCSI hard disk.

Please Note: There is no part of this naming convention that is based on partition type; unlike DOS/Windows, *all* partitions can be identified under Red Hat Linux. Of course, this doesn't mean that Red Hat Linux can access data on every type of partition, but in many cases it is possible to access data on a partition dedicated to another operating system.

Keep this information in mind; it will make things easier to understand when you're setting up the partitions Red Hat Linux requires.

2.8.3   Disk Partitions and Other Operating Systems

If your Red Hat Linux partitions will be sharing a hard disk with partitions used by other operating systems, most of the time you'll have no problems. However, there are certain combinations of Linux and other operating systems that require extra care. Information on creating disk partitions compatible with other operating systems is available in several HOWTOs and Mini-HOWTOs, available on the Red Hat Linux CD in the `doc/HOWTO` and `doc/HOWTO/mini` directories. In particular, the Mini-HOWTOs whose names start with `Linux+` are quite helpful.

> **INTEL**
>
> If Red Hat Linux/Intel will coexist on your machine with OS/2, you must create your disk partitions with the OS/2 partitioning software—otherwise, OS/2 may not recognize the disk partitions. During the installation, do not create any new partitions, but do set the proper partition types for your Linux partitions using the Linux `fdisk`.

2.8.4   Disk Partitions and Mount Points

One area that many people new to Linux find confusing is the matter of how partitions are used and accessed by the Linux operating system. In DOS/Windows, it is relatively simple: If you have more than one partition, each partition gets a "drive letter." You then use the drive letter to refer to files and directories on a given partition.

This is entirely different from how Red Hat Linux deals with partitions and, for that matter, with disk storage in general. The main difference is that each partition is used to form part of the storage necessary to support a single set of files and directories. This is done by associating a partition with a directory through a process known as *mounting*. Mounting a partition makes its storage available starting at the specified directory (known as a *mount point*).

For example, if partition `/dev/hda5` were mounted on `/usr`, that would mean that all files and directories under `/usr` would physically reside on `/dev/hda5`. So the file `/usr/doc/FAQ/txt/Linux-FAQ` would be stored on `/dev/hda5`, while the file `/etc/X11/gdm/Sessions/Gnome` would not.

Continuing our example, it is also possible that one or more directories below `/usr` would be mount points for other partitions. For instance, a partition (say, `/dev/hda7`) could be mounted on `/usr/local`, meaning that, for example, `/usr/local/man/whatis` would then reside on `/dev/hda7` rather than `/dev/hda5`.

2.8.5   How Many Partitions?

At this point in the process of preparing to install Red Hat Linux, you will need to give some consideration to the number and size of the partitions to be used by your new operating system. The question of "how many partitions" continues to spark debate within the Linux community and, without any end to the debate in sight, it's safe to say that there are probably as many partition layouts as there are people debating the issue.

Keeping this in mind, we recommend that, unless you have a reason for doing otherwise, you should create the following partitions:

- **A swap partition** – Swap partitions are used to support virtual memory. If your computer has 16 MB of RAM or less, you *must* create a swap partition. Even if you have more memory, a swap partition is still recommended. The minimum size of your swap partition should be equal to your computer's RAM, or 16 MB (whichever is larger). The largest useable swap partition is roughly 127 MB, so making a swap partition larger than that will result in wasted space. Note, however, that you can create and use more than one swap partition if your system requires more than 127MB of swap.

  > **INTEL**
  > The following partition is specific to Red Hat Linux/Intel installations.

- **A** /boot **partition** – The partition mounted on /boot contains the operating system kernel, along with a few other files used during the bootstrap process. Due to the limitations of most PC BIOSes, creating a small partition to hold these files is a good idea. This partition should be no larger than 16MB.

  Please Note: Make sure you read Section 2.8.6 – the information there applies to the /boot partition!

  > **ALPHA**
  > The following partition is specific to Red Hat Linux/Alpha installations.

- **A MILO partition** – Alpha owners that will be using MILO to boot their systems should create a 2MB DOS partition where MILO can be copied after the installation is complete. We recommend using /dos as the mount point.

- **A root partition** – The root partition is where / (the root directory) resides. In this partitioning layout, all files (except those stored in /boot) reside on the root partition. Because of this, it's in your best interest to maximize the size of your root partition. A 500MB root partition will permit the equivalent of a workstation-class installation (with *very* little free space), while a 1GB root partition will let you install every package.

2.8.6   One Last Wrinkle: Using LILO

> **INTEL**
> LILO (the LInux LOader) is the most commonly used method to boot Red Hat Linux on Intel-based systems. An operating system loader, LILO operates "outside" of any operating system, using only the Basic I/O System (or BIOS) built into the computer hardware itself. This section describes LILO's interactions with PC BIOSes, and is specific to Intel-compatible computers.

> **ALPHA**
> Alpha owners may skip ahead to Section 2.9 on page 32.

SPARC

SPARC owners may skip ahead to Section 2.9 on the following page.

BIOS-Related Limitations Impacting LILO

LILO is subject to some limitations imposed by the BIOS in most Intel-based computers. Specifically, most BIOSes can't access more than two hard drives and they can't access any data stored beyond cylinder 1023 of any drive. Note that some recent BIOSes do not have these limitations, but this is by no means universal.

All the data LILO needs to access at boot time (including the Linux kernel) are located in the `/boot` directory. If you follow the partition layout recommended above, or you are performing a workstation- or server-class install, the `/boot` directory will be in a small, separate partition. Otherwise, it will reside in the root partition. In either case, the partition in which `/boot` resides must conform to the following guidelines if you are going to use LILO to boot your Red Hat Linux system:

On First Two IDE Drives – If you have 2 IDE (or EIDE) drives, `/boot` must be located on one of them. Note that this two-drive limit also includes any IDE CD-ROM drives on your primary IDE controller. So, if you have one IDE hard drive, and one IDE CD-ROM on your primary controller, `/boot` must be located on the first hard drive *only*, even if you have other hard drives on your secondary IDE controller.

On First IDE or First SCSI Drive – If you have one IDE (or EIDE) drive and one or more SCSI drives, `/boot` must be located either on the IDE drive or the SCSI drive at ID 0. No other SCSI IDs will work.

On First Two SCSI Drives – If you have only SCSI hard drives, `/boot` must be located on a drive at ID 0 or ID 1. No other SCSI IDs will work.

Partition *Completely* Below Cylinder 1023 – No matter which of the above configurations apply, the partition that holds `/boot` must be located entirely below cylinder 1023. If the partition holding `/boot` straddles cylinder 1023, you may face a situation where LILO will work initially (because all the necessary information is below cylinder 1023), but will fail if a new kernel is to be loaded, and that kernel resides above cylinder 1023.

As mentioned earlier, it is possible that some of the newer BIOSes may permit LILO to work with configurations that don't meet our guidelines. Likewise, some of LILO's more esoteric features may be used to get a Linux system started, even if the configuration doesn't meet our guidelines. However, due to the number of variables involved, Red Hat Software cannot support such extraordinary efforts.

Please Note: Disk Druid as well as the workstation- and server-class installs take these BIOS-related limitations into account. However, if you decide to use `fdisk` instead, it is your responsibility to ensure that you keep these limitations in mind.

2.9   A Note About Kernel Drivers

During installation of Red Hat Linux, there are some limits placed on the filesystems and other drivers supported by the kernel. However, after installation there is support for all filesystems available under Linux. At install time the modularized kernel has support for (E)IDE devices, (including ATAPI CD-ROM drives), SCSI adapters, and network cards. Additionally, all mice, SLIP, CSLIP, PPP, PLIP, FPU emulation, console selection, ELF, SysV IPC, IP forwarding, firewalling and accounting, reverse ARP, QIC tape and parallel printers, are supported.

Please Note: Because Red Hat Linux supports installation on many different types of hardware, many drivers (including those for SCSI adapters, network cards, and many CD-ROMs) are not built into the Linux kernel used during installation; rather, they are available as *modules* and loaded as you need them during the installation process. If necessary, you will have the chance to specify options for these modules at the time they are loaded, and in fact these drivers will ignore any options you specify for them at the `boot:` prompt.

After the installation is complete you may want to rebuild a kernel that includes support for your specific hardware configuration. See Section 11.8 on page 210 for information on building a customized kernel. Note that, in most cases, a custom-built kernel is not necessary.

2.10   If You Have Problems...

If you have problems before, during, or after the installation, check the list of Red Hat Linux Frequently Asked Questions. You can find the FAQ at:

```
http://www.redhat.com/knowledgebase/index.html
```

In many cases, a quick check of the FAQ can quickly get you back in action.

2.11   One Last Note

Please read all of the installation instructions *before* starting; this will prepare you for any decisions you need to make and should eliminate potential surprises.

3

Starting the Installation

This chapter explains how to start the Red Hat Linux 6.0 installation process. We'll cover the following areas in this chapter:

- Getting familiar with the installation program's user interface;
- Starting the installation program;
- Selecting an installation method.

By the end of this chapter, the installation program will be running on your system, and the appropriate installation method will have been selected.

3.1   The Installation Program User Interface

The Red Hat Linux installation program uses a screen-based interface that includes most of the on-screen "widgets" commonly found on graphical user interfaces. They may look a little different than their more graphical counterparts; Figures 3.1 on page 35 and 3.2 on page 36 are included here to make them easier to identify. Here's a list of the most important widgets:

- **Window** – Windows (also referred to as *dialog boxes* in this manual) will appear on your screen throughout the installation process. At times, one window may overlay another; in these cases, you may only interact with the window on top. When finished with that window, it will disappear, allowing you to continue with the window that was underneath.

- **Text Input** – Text input lines are regions where you can enter information required by the installation program. When the cursor rests on a text input line, you may enter and/or edit information on that line.

- **Check Box** – Check boxes allow you to select or deselect a particular feature offered to you by the installation program. When the cursor rests within a check box, pressing (Space) causes the check box to toggle between a selected and unselected state.

- **Text Widget** – Text widgets are regions of the screen that are devoted to the display of text. At times, text widgets may also contain other widgets, such as check boxes. It is possible that a text widget may contain more information than could be displayed at one time. In these cases, the text widget will have a scroll bar next to it; if you position the cursor within the text widget, you can then use the (↑) and (↓) keys to scroll through all the information available.

- **Scroll Bar** – Scroll bars provide a visual indication of your relative position in the information being displayed in a text widget. Your current position is shown by a # character, which will move up and down the scroll bar as you scroll back and forth.

- **Button Widget** – Button widgets are the primary method of interacting with the installation program. By "pressing" these buttons, you will progress through the series of windows that make up the installation process. Buttons may be pressed when they are highlighted by the cursor.

- **Cursor** – Although not a widget, the cursor is used to select (and interact) with a particular widget. As the cursor is moved from widget to widget, it may cause the widget to change color, or you may only see the cursor itself positioned in or next to the widget. In Figure 3.1 on the facing page, the cursor is positioned on the **Ok** button. Figure 3.2 on page 36 shows the cursor on the first line of the text widget at the top of the window.

As you might have guessed by our description of these widgets, the installation program is character-based, and does not use a mouse. This is due to the fact that the installation program must run on a wide variety of computers, some of which may not even have a mouse. The following section describes the keystrokes necessary to interact with the installation program.

3.1.1   Using the Keyboard to Navigate

You can navigate around the installation dialogs using a simple set of keystrokes. You will need to move the cursor around by using various keys such as (←), (→), (↑), and (↓). You can also use (Tab), and (Alt)-(Tab) to cycle forward or backward through each widget on the screen. In most cases, there is a summary of available function keys presented at the bottom of each screen.

To "press" a button, position the cursor over the button (using (Tab), for instance) and press (Space) (or (Enter)). To select an item from a list of items, move the cursor to the item you wish to select and

Window   Text Input

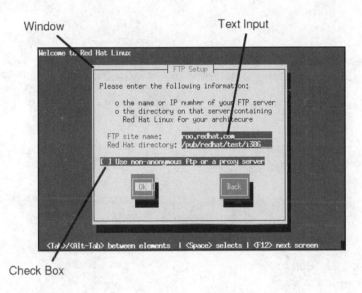

Check Box

Figure 3.1: Installation Program Widgets

press Enter. To select an item with a *check box*, move the cursor to the check box and press Space to select an item. To deselect, press Space a second time.

Pressing F12 accepts the current values and proceeds to the next dialog; it is usually equivalent to pressing the **Ok** button.

Please Note: Unless a dialog box is waiting for your input, do not press any keys during the installation process – it may result in unpredictable behavior.

3.1.2 A Note about Virtual Consoles

There is more to the Red Hat Linux installation program than the dialog boxes it presents as it guides you through the installation process.

In fact, the installation program makes several different kinds of diagnostic messages available to you, in addition to giving you a way to enter commands from a shell prompt. It presents this information on five *virtual consoles* which you can switch between using a single keystroke.

These virtual consoles can be very helpful if you encounter a problem while installing Red Hat Linux.

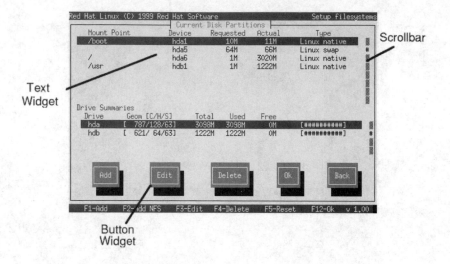

Figure 3.2: More Installation Program Widgets

Messages displayed on the install or system consoles can help pinpoint the problem. Please see Figure 3.3 on the facing page for a listing of the virtual consoles, the keystrokes to switch to them, and their contents.

In general, there should be no reason to leave virtual console #1 unless you are attempting to diagnose installation problems. But if you are the curious type, feel free to look around.

3.2 Starting the Installation Program

Now it's time to start installing Red Hat Linux. To start the installation, it is first necessary to boot the installation program. Before we start, please make sure you have all the resources you'll need for the installation. If you've already read through Chapter 2, and followed the instructions, you should be ready.

Console	Keystroke	Contents
1	Alt-F1	installation dialog
2	Alt-F2	shell prompt
3	Alt-F3	install log (messages from install program)
4	Alt-F4	system log (messages from kernel, etc.)
5	Alt-F5	other messages

Figure 3.3: Virtual Console Information

ALPHA

If you haven't created your diskettes yet, please refer to the first chapter of the Red Hat Linux Alpha Installation Addendum, and create them now. After you've created the necessary diskettes, please finish reading the first chapter of the Red Hat Linux Alpha Installation Addendum for information on starting the installation.

SPARC

If you haven't prepared for the installation yet, please read Sections F.2 on page 360 through F.5. Determine how you will boot the installation program, and issue the boot command that will start the installation.

3.2.1 Booting the Installation Program

To start installing Red Hat Linux, insert the boot diskette into your computer's first diskette drive and reboot (or boot from the Red Hat Linux CD-ROM, if your computer supports it). Your BIOS settings may need to be changed to allow you to boot from the diskette or CD-ROM.

After a short delay, a screen containing the boot: prompt should appear. The screen contains information on a variety of boot options. Each boot option also has one or more help screens associated with it. To access a given help screen, press the appropriate function key as listed in the line at the bottom of the screen.

You should keep two things in mind:

- The initial screen will automatically start the installation program if you take no action within the first minute. To disable this feature, press one of the help screen function keys.

- If you press a help screen function key, there will be a slight delay as the help screen is read from diskette.

Normally, you'll only need to press Enter to boot. Watch the boot messages to see whether the Linux kernel detects your hardware. If it does not properly detect your hardware, you may need to restart the installation in "expert" mode.

Expert mode disables most hardware probing, and gives you the option of entering options for the drivers loaded during the installation. Expert mode can be entered using the following boot command:

```
boot: expert
```

Please Note: The initial boot messages will not contain any references to SCSI or network cards. These devices are supported by modules that are loaded during the installation process.

Options can also be passed to the kernel. For example, to instruct the kernel to use all the RAM in a 128 MB system, enter:

```
boot: linux mem=128M
```

However, with most computers, there is no need to pass this argument to the kernel. The kernel will detect the amount of memory your system has in most cases. To be sure that all of your memory has been detected, at a shell prompt type:

```
cat /proc/meminfo
```

This will display the amount of memory detected by the kernel in the form of total, used, free, etc.

If MemTotal is not correct for your system, you will need to modify your lilo.conf to pass that amount of memory to the kernel at boot time. Such as, if your computer has 96 megabytes of RAM, you will add:

```
append="mem=96M"
```

After entering any options, press (Enter) to boot using those options. If you do need to specify boot options to identify your hardware, please make note of them – they will be needed later.

INTEL

Installing Without Using a Boot Diskette   The Red Hat Linux/Intel CD-ROM can also be booted by newer computers that support bootable CD-ROMs. Not all computers support this feature, so if yours can't boot from the CD-ROM, there is one other way to start the installation without using a boot diskette. The following method is specific to Intel-based computers only.

If you have MS-DOS installed on your computer, you can boot the installation system directly from the CD without using any diskettes.

To do this (assuming your CD is drive d:),, use the following commands:

```
C:\> d:
D:\> cd \dosutils
D:\dosutils> autoboot.bat
```

Note that this method will not work if run in a DOS window – the `autoboot.bat` file must be executed with DOS as the only operating system. In other words, Windows cannot be running.

If your computer can't boot directly from CD-ROM (and you can't use a DOS-based autoboot), you'll have to use a boot diskette to get things started.

3.3 Beginning the Installation

After booting, the installation program begins by displaying a welcome message. Press (Enter) to begin the installation. If you wish to abort the installation process at this time, simply eject the boot diskette now and reboot your machine.

3.3.1 Choosing a Language

After the welcome dialog, the installation program asks you to select the language to be used during the installation process (see Figure 3.4). Using the ↑ and ↓ keys, select the appropriate language. A scroll bar may appear to the right of the languages – if present, it indicates that there are more entries than can be displayed at one time. You'll be seeing scroll bars like this throughout the installation program.

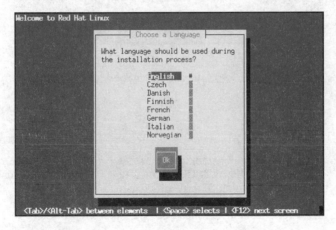

Figure 3.4: Selecting a Language

3.3.2   Selecting a Keyboard Type

Next, the installation program gives you an opportunity to select a keyboard type (see Figure 3.5). You may navigate this dialog box the same way you did with the language selection dialog.

After selecting the appropriate keyboard type, press (Enter); the keyboard type you select will be loaded automatically both for the remainder of the installation process and each time you boot your Red Hat Linux system.

If you wish to change your keyboard type after you have installed your Red Hat Linux system, you may use the /usr/sbin/kbdconfig command or you may type setup at the root prompt.

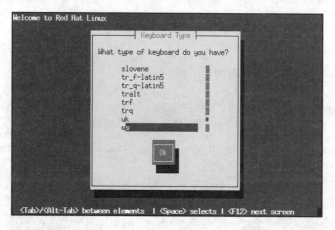

Figure 3.5: Selecting a Keyboard Type

3.3.3   PCMCIA Support

Next, the installation program will probe your system to determine if your system requires PCMCIA (also known as PC Card) support. If a PCMCIA controller is found, you'll be asked if you require PCMCIA support during the installation. If you will be using a PCMCIA device during the installation (for example, you have a PCMCIA ethernet card and you'll be installing via NFS, or you have a PCMCIA SCSI card and will be installing from a SCSI CD), you should select **Yes**.

Please Note: This question applies *only* to PCMCIA support during the actual installation. Your installed Red Hat Linux system will still support PCMCIA, even if you say **No** here (assuming that you do not deselect the kernel-pcmcia-cs package during the subsequent installation).

If you require PCMCIA support, you will then be asked to insert the PCMCIA support diskette. Select **Ok** when you've done so.

The installation program will then display a progress bar as the support diskette is loaded.

3.4 Selecting an Installation Method

Next, you will be asked what type of installation method you wish to use. You can install Red Hat Linux via any of five basic methods (see Section 2.4 on page 14), which require the use of a support diskette if you are using a PCMCIA device during the install. To summarize, you can install Red Hat Linux from:

CD-ROM – If you have a CD-ROM drive and the Red Hat Linux CD-ROM. Requires a PCMCIA support disk only if you will be using a PCMCIA device during the install. Please refer to Section 4.2 on page 43 to select the CD-ROM installation method.

Hard Drive – If you copied the Red Hat Linux files to a local hard drive. Requires a PCMCIA support disk only if you will be using a PCMCIA device during the install. Please refer to Section 4.3 on page 45 to select the hard drive installation method.

NFS Image If you are installing from an NFS Image server which is exporting the Red Hat Linux CD-ROM or a mirror image of Red Hat Linux. Requires a PCMCIA support disk only if you will be using a PCMCIA device during the install. Requires a network boot disk. Please refer to Section 5.2 on page 68 to select the NFS installation method.

FTP – If you are installing directly from an FTP server. Requires a PCMCIA support disk only if you will be using a PCMCIA device during the install. Requires a network boot disk. Please refer to Section 5.3 on page 69 to select the FTP installation method.

HTTP – If you are installing directly from an HTTP Web server. Requires a PCMCIA support disk only if you will be using a PCMCIA device during the install. Requires a network boot disk. Please refer to Section 5.4 on page 69 to select the HTTP installation method.

If you choose to perform a CD-ROM or a hard drive install, please refer to Chapter 4 on page 43 for those installation instructions.

If you choose to perform a network-based install (NFS, FTP, or HTTP), please refer to Chapter 5 on page 65 for those installation instructions.

4

Local Media Installations

4.1 Selecting an Installation Method

Now you must decide what type of installation method you wish to use (see Figure 4.1 on the following page). Highlight the appropriate choice and select **Ok**, or press ⌊Enter⌋.

If you are *not* performing a local media type installation (CD-ROM or hard drive), then please skip ahead to Chapter 5 on page 65 for network type installations.

If you *are* planning to do a local media type installation, please read on.

4.2 Installing from CD-ROM

If you are going to install Red Hat Linux from CD-ROM, choose "CD-ROM," and select **Ok**. The installation program will then prompt you to insert your Red Hat Linux CD-ROM into your CD-ROM drive. When you've done so, select **Ok**, and press ⌊Enter⌋. The installation program will then probe your system and attempt to identify your CD-ROM drive. It will start by looking for an IDE (also known as ATAPI) CD-ROM drive. If one is found, the installation will continue. If the installation program cannot automatically detect your CD-ROM drive, you will be asked what type of CD-ROM you have. You can choose from the following types:

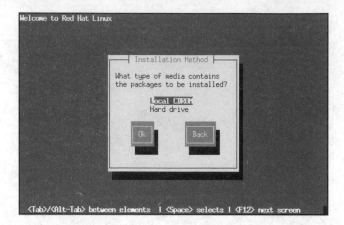

Figure 4.1: Selecting an Installation Method

SCSI Select this if your CD-ROM is attached to a supported SCSI adapter; the installation program
will then ask you to choose a SCSI driver. Choose the driver that most closely resembles your
adapter. You may specify options for the driver if necessary; however, most drivers will detect
your SCSI adapter automatically.

Other If your CD-ROM is neither an IDE nor a SCSI CD-ROM, it's an "other." Sound cards with
proprietary CD-ROM interfaces are good examples of this CD-ROM type. The installation
program presents a list of drivers for supported CD-ROMs – choose a driver and, if necessary,
specify any driver options.

Please Note: A partial list of optional parameters for CD-ROMs can be found in Appendix E on
page 349. If you have an ATAPI CD-ROM and the installation program fails to find it (in other
words, it asks you what type of CD-ROM you have), you must restart the installation, and enter
`linux hdX=cdrom`. Replace the X with one of the following letters, depending on the interface the
unit is connected to, and whether it is configured as master or slave:

- **a** – First IDE controller, master
- **b** – First IDE controller, slave
- **c** – Second IDE controller, master
- **d** – Second IDE controller, slave

(If you have a third and/or fourth controller, simply continue assigning letters in alphabetical order,
going from controller to controller, and master to slave.)

Once your CD-ROM drive has been identified, you will be asked to insert the Red Hat Linux CD-ROM into your CD-ROM drive. Select **Ok** when you have done so. After a short delay, the next dialog box will appear. Continue to section 4.4 for upgrade or full-installation instructions.

4.3 Installing from a Hard Drive

If you are going to install Red Hat Linux from a locally-attached hard drive, highlight "hard drive" and select **Ok**.

Before you started the installation program, you must first have copied all the necessary files to a partition on a locally-attached hard drive. If you haven't done this yet, please refer to Section 2.4.6 on page 18. Continue to section 4.4 for upgrade or full-installation instructions.

4.4 Upgrading or Installing

After you choose an installation method, the installation program prompts you to either *install* or *upgrade* (see Figure 4.2).

Figure 4.2: Upgrading or Installing

4.4.1 Installing

You usually install Red Hat Linux on a clean disk partition or set of partitions, or over another installation of Linux.

Please Note: Installing Red Hat Linux over another installation of Linux (including Red Hat Linux) does *not* preserve any information (files or data) from the prior installation. Make sure you save any important files! If you are worried about saving the current data on your existing system (without making a backup on your own), you should consider performing an upgrade instead.

If you wish to perform a full install, choose **Install**, and skip to section 4.5.

4.4.2   Upgrading

The installation process for Red Hat Linux 6.0 includes the ability to upgrade from prior versions of Red Hat Linux (version 2.0 and later) which are based on RPM technology.

Upgrading your system installs the modular 2.2.*x* kernel as well as updated versions of the packages which are currently installed on your machine. The upgrade process preserves existing configuration files by renaming them using a `.rpmsave` extension (e.g., `sendmail.cf.rpmsave`) and leaves a log telling what actions it took in `/tmp/upgrade.log`. As software evolves, configuration file formats can change, so you should carefully compare your original configuration files to the new files before integrating your changes.

If you wish to upgrade your Red Hat Linux system, choose **Upgrade**.

Please Note: Some upgraded packages may require that other packages are also installed for proper operation. The upgrade procedure takes care of these *dependencies*, but it may need to install additional packages which are not on your existing system.

Please Note: If you already have the X Window System (and possibly an older version of GNOME) on your machine you may see a screen that prompts you to install the latest version of GNOME included in this release.

4.5   Installation Class

If you chose to perform a full install, the installation program will ask you to choose an installation class (see Figure 4.3 on the facing page). You will not see this screen if you chose to perform an upgrade. You may choose from the following installation classes:

- **Workstation** – A workstation-class installation will automatically erase *all Linux partitions* from your computer's hard drive(s). This installation type will also attempt to set up a dual boot environment automatically.

- **Server** – A server-class installation will automatically erase *all partitions* (Linux or others) from your computer's hard drive(s).

- **Custom** – A custom-class installation gives you complete control over partitioning-related issues. If you have installed Red Hat Linux in the past, the custom-class installation is most similar to past installations.

Figure 4.3: Installation Class

Please Note: If you choose either **Workstation** or **Server**, part (or all) of your computer's stored data on all drives *will* be erased! You will be asked to confirm your decision; however, please keep in mind that once the installation program receives your confirmation, the erasure is irrevocable.

Please Note: **WARNING** – If you choose to perform a workstation-class or server-class installation, data erasure will be irrevocable. The severity of erased data varies according to type of installation:

- **Workstation-class** – Data on any existing Linux partition on any hard drive on your system will be erased.

- **Server-class** – Data on all partitions of all drives will be completely erased, regardless if it is on an existing Linux partition or not.

If you choose a workstation- or server-class installation, you will be able to skip over some of the steps that the custom-class install requires.

For a hard drive installation, please keep reading. For the CD-ROM workstation- or server-class installation, you should turn to Chapter 6 on page 91 to continue with the install..

4.6   SCSI Support

Next the installation program will probe your system for SCSI adapters. In some cases, the installation program will ask you whether you have any SCSI adapters.

If you choose **Yes**, the next dialog presents a list of SCSI drivers. Choose the driver that most closely resembles your SCSI adapter. The installation program then gives you an opportunity to specify options for the SCSI driver you selected; most SCSI drivers should detect your hardware automatically, however.

4.7   Creating Partitions for Red Hat Linux

At this point, it's necessary to let the installation program know where it should install Red Hat Linux. This is done by defining *mount points* for one or more disk partitions in which Red Hat Linux will be installed. You may also need to create and/or delete partitions at this time.

Please Note: If you have not yet planned how you will set up your partitions, please turn to Section 2.8 on page 21, and review everything up to Section 2.9 on page 32. As a bare minimum, you'll need an appropriately-sized root partition, and a swap partition of at least 16 MB.

If you're still unsure on how to set up your partitions, please refer to Appendix C on page 239.

The installation program then presents a dialog box that allows you to choose from two disk partitioning tools (see Figure 4.4). The choices you have are:

- **Disk Druid** – This is Red Hat Linux's install-time disk management utility. It can create and delete disk partitions according to user-supplied requirements, in addition to managing mount points for each partition.

- **fdisk** – This is the traditional Linux disk partitioning tool. While it is somewhat more flexible than Disk Druid, the downside is that `fdisk` assumes you have some experience with disk partitioning, and are comfortable with its somewhat terse user interface.

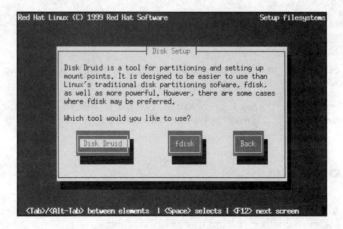

Figure 4.4: Selecting Disk Setup Method

With the exception of certain esoteric situations, Disk Druid can handle the partitioning requirements for a typical Red Hat Linux installation.

SPARC

Note that there are some points you should be aware of if you decide to use Disk Druid under Red Hat Linux/SPARC. Please refer to Appendix F on page 359 for more information.

ALPHA

Note that there are some points you should be aware of if you decide to use Disk Druid under Red Hat Linux/Alpha. Please refer to the Alpha Installation Addendum for more information.

Select the disk partitioning tool you'd like to use, and press Enter. If you choose Disk Druid, continue reading. If you'd rather use fdisk, please turn to Section 4.7.3 on page 54.

4.7.1 Using Disk Druid

If you selected Disk Druid, you will be presented with a screen that looks like figure 4.5. While it may look overwhelming at first, it really isn't. Let's go over each of Disk Druid's three sections.

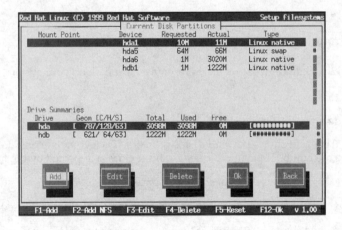

Figure 4.5: Disk Druid Main Screen

The "Current Disk Partitions" Section

Each line in the "Current Disk Partitions" section represents a disk partition. You'll note that this section has a scroll bar to the right, which means that there might be more partitions than can be displayed at one time. If you use the ⬆ and ⬇ keys, you can see if there are any additional partitions. Each line in this section has five different fields:

Mount Point – This field indicates where the partition will be mounted when Red Hat Linux is installed and running.

Device – This field displays the partition's device name.

Requested – The "Requested" field shows the minimum size requested when the partition was defined.

Actual – The "Actual" field shows the space currently allocated to the partition.

Type – This field shows the partition's type.

Another Type of Partition   As you scroll through the "Current Disk Partitions" section, you might see an "Unallocated Requested Partitions" title bar, followed by one or more partitions. As the title implies, these are partitions that have been requested but, for one reason or another, have not been allocated. A common reason for having an unallocated partition is a lack of sufficient free space for the partition. In any case, the reason the partition remains unallocated will be displayed after the partition's mount point.

The "Drive Summaries" Section

Each line in the "Drive Summaries" section represents a hard disk on your system. Each line has the following fields:

Drive – This field shows the hard disk's device name.

Geom [C/H/S] – This field shows the hard disk's *geometry*. The geometry consists of three numbers representing the number of cylinders, heads and sectors as reported by the hard disk.

Total – The "Total" field shows the total available space on the hard disk.

Used – This field shows how much of the hard disk's space is currently allocated to partitions.

Free – The "Free" field shows how much of the hard disk's space is still unallocated.

Bar Graph – This field presents a visual representation of the space currently used on the hard disk. The more pound signs there are between the square braces, the less free space there is. In Figure 4.5 on the page before, the bar graph shows no free space.

Please Note: The "Drive Summaries" section is displayed only to indicate your computer's disk configuration. It is not meant to be used as a means of specifying the target hard drive for a given partition. This is described more completely in the **Adding a Partition**, Section 4.7.1 on page 52.

Disk Druid's Buttons

These buttons control Disk Druid's actions. They are used to add and delete partitions, and to change partition attributes. In addition, there are buttons that are used to accept the changes you've made, or to exit Disk Druid entirely. Let's take a look at each button in order.

Add — The "Add" button is used to request a new partition. When selected, a dialog box will appear containing fields that must be filled in.

Edit – The "Edit" button is used to modify attributes of the partition currently highlighted in the "Current Disk Partitions" section. Selecting this button will cause a dialog box to appear. Some or all of the fields in the "Edit Partition" dialog box may be changed, depending on whether the partition information has already been written to disk or not.

Delete – The "Delete" button is used to delete the partition currently highlighted in the "Current Disk Partitions" section. Selecting this button will cause a dialog box to appear asking you to confirm the deletion.

Ok – The "Ok" button causes any changes made to your system's partitions to be written to disk. You will be asked to confirm your changes before Disk Druid rewrites your hard disk partition table(s). In addition, any mount points you've defined are passed to the installation program, and will eventually be used by your Red Hat Linux system to define the filesystem layout.

Back – This button causes Disk Druid to abort without saving any changes you've made. When this button is selected, the installation program will take you back to the previous screen, so you can start over.

Handy Function Keys

While there is some overlap between Disk Druid's buttons and the available functions keys, there are two function keys that have no corresponding buttons:

- **F2** **(Add NFS)** – This function key is used to add a read-only NFS-served filesystem to the set of mount points on your Red Hat Linux system. When selected, a dialog box will appear containing fields that must be filled in.

- **F5** **(Reset)** – This function key is used to discard all changes you may have made while in Disk Druid, and return the list of partitions to those read from the partition table(s) on your hard disk(s). When selected, you'll be asked to confirm whether you want to discard the changes. Note that any mount points you've specified will be lost, and will need to be reentered.

Please Note: You will need to dedicate at least one partition to Red Hat Linux, and optionally more. This is discussed more completely in Section 2.8.5 on page 29.

Now let's see how Disk Druid is used to set up partitions for your Red Hat Linux system.

Adding a Partition

To Add a new partition, select the **Add** button, and press [Space] or [Enter]. A dialog box entitled "Edit New Partition" will appear (see Figure 4.6). It contains the following fields:

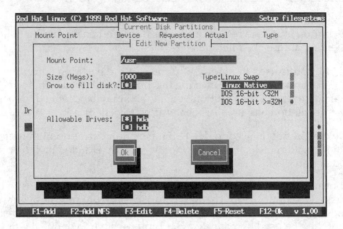

Figure 4.6: Creating a New Partition

- **Mount Point** – Highlight this field and enter the partition's mount point. For example, if this partition should be the root partition, enter /; enter /usr for the usr partition, and so on.

- **Size (Megs)** – In this field, enter the size (in megabytes) of the partition. Note that this field starts with a "1" in it, meaning that unless you change it, you'll end up with a 1 MB partition. Delete it using the [Backspace] key, and enter the desired partition size.

- **Growable?** – This check box indicates whether the size you entered in the previous field is to be considered the partition's exact size, or its minimum size. Press [Space] to check and uncheck the box. When checked, the partition will grow to fill all available space on the hard disk. In this case, the partition's size will expand and contract as other partitions are modified. Note that you can make more than one partition growable; if you do so, the additional free space will be shared between all growable partitions.

- **Type** – This field contains a list of different partition types. Select the appropriate partition type by using the [↑] and [↓] keys.

- **Allowable Drives** – This field contains a list of the hard disks installed on your system, with a check box for each. If a hard disk's box is checked, then this partition may be created on that hard disk. If the box is *not* checked, then the partition will *never* be created on that hard disk. By using different check box settings, you can direct Disk Druid to place partitions as you see fit, or let Disk Druid decide where partitions should go.

- **Ok** – Select this button and press [Space] when you are satisfied with the partition's settings, and wish to create it.

- **Cancel** – Select this button and press [Space] when you don't want to create the partition.

4.7.2   Problems When Adding a Partition

Please Note: If you are having problems adding a partition, you may want to reference Appendix C on page 239 to get more information.

If you attempt to add a partition and Disk Druid can't carry out your request, you'll see a dialog box like the one in Figure 4.7. In the box are listed any partitions that are currently unallocated, along with the reason they could not be allocated. Select the **Ok** button, and press [Space] to continue. Note that the unallocated partition(s) are also displayed on Disk Druid's main screen (though you may have to scroll the "Current Disk Partitions" section to see them).

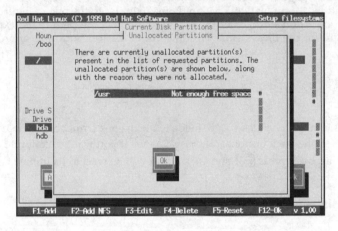

Figure 4.7: Unallocated Partition Warning

Deleting a Partition

To delete a partition, highlight the partition in the "Current Disk Partitions" section, select the **Delete** button, and press [Space]. You will be asked to confirm the deletion.

Editing a Partition

To change a partition's settings, highlight the partition in the "Current Disk Partitions" section, select the **Edit** button, and press [Space]. You will be presented with a dialog box very similar to the one shown in Figure 4.6 on page 52. Make the appropriate changes, select **Ok**, and press [Space].

Please Note: If the partition already existed on your hard disk, you will only be able to change the partition's mount point. If you want to make any other changes, you will need to delete the partition and recreate it.

Adding an NFS Mount

To add a read-only NFS-served filesystem, press [F2]. If you have not selected a network-related installation method, you will be presented with several dialog boxes concerning network configuration (turn to Section 5.1.1 on page 65 for more information). Fill in the boxes appropriately. You will then see a dialog box entitled, "Edit Network Mount Point" (similar to the one in Figure 4.12 on page 58). In this dialog box you will need to enter the NFS server name, the path to the exported filesystem, and the mount point for the filesystem. Select the **Ok** or **Cancel** button as appropriate, and press [Space].

Starting Over

If you'd like to abandon any changes you've made while in Disk Druid, and would rather use `fdisk` instead, you can select the **Back** button, and press [Space]. If you want to continue using Disk Druid, but would like to start over, press [F5], and Disk Druid will be reset to its initial state.

When You're Finished...

Once you've finished configuring partitions and entering mount points, your screen should look something like the one in Figure 4.8 on the facing page. Select **Ok**, and press [Space]. Then turn to Section 4.8 on page 58.

4.7.3 Using `fdisk`

If you'd rather use `fdisk` to manage partitions, this is the section for you. Once you've selected `fdisk`, you'll be presented with a dialog box entitled "Partition Disks" (see Figure 4.9 on the facing page). In this box is a list of every disk on your computer. Move the highlight to the disk you'd like to partition, select **Edit**, and press [Space]. You will then enter `fdisk` and can partition the disk you selected. Repeat this process for each disk you want to partition. When you're done, select "Done."

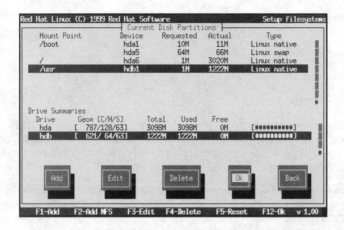

Figure 4.8: Partitions and Mount Points Defined

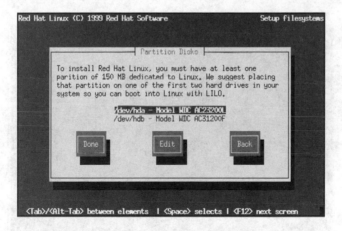

Figure 4.9: Selecting a Disk for Partitioning

An Overview of fdisk

fdisk includes online help which is terse but useful. Here are a few tips:

- The command for help is m.

- To list the current partition table, use the p command (see Figure 4.10).

- To add a new partition, use n.

- Linux fdisk creates partitions of type Linux native by default. When you create a swap partition, don't forget to change it to type Linux swap using the t command. The value for the Linux swap type is 82. For other partition types, use the l command to see a list of partition types and values.

- Linux allows up to four (4) partitions on one disk. If you wish to create more than that, one (and only one) of the four may be an *extended* partition, which acts as a container for one or more *logical* partitions. Since it acts as a container, the extended partition must be at least as large as the total size of all the logical partitions it is to contain.

- It's a good idea to write down which partitions (e.g., /dev/hda2) are meant for which filesystems (e.g., /usr) as you create each one.

- **Please Note:** None of the changes you make take effect until you save them and exit fdisk using the w command. You may quit fdisk at any time without saving changes by using the q command.

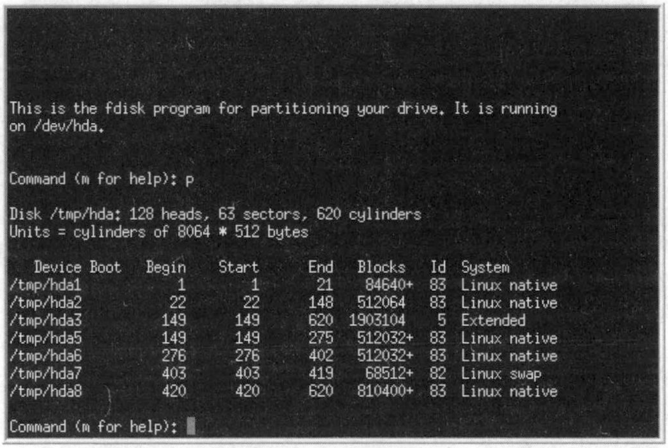

```
This is the fdisk program for partitioning your drive. It is running
on /dev/hda.

Command (m for help): p

Disk /tmp/hda: 128 heads, 63 sectors, 620 cylinders
Units = cylinders of 8064 * 512 bytes

   Device Boot    Begin    Start     End    Blocks   Id  System
/tmp/hda1             1        1      21    84640+   83  Linux native
/tmp/hda2            22       22     148   512064    83  Linux native
/tmp/hda3           149      149     620  1903104     5  Extended
/tmp/hda5           149      149     275   512032+   83  Linux native
/tmp/hda6           276      276     402   512032+   83  Linux native
/tmp/hda7           403      403     419    68512+   82  Linux swap
/tmp/hda8           420      420     620   810400+   83  Linux native

Command (m for help):
```

Figure 4.10: Sample Output From fdisk

Changing the Partition Table

When you are finished partitioning your disks, press **Done**; you may see a message indicating that the installation program needs to reboot. This is a normal occurrence after changing a disk's partition data; it usually happens if you created, changed or deleted any extended partitions. After you press **Ok**, your machine will reboot. Follow the same installation steps you did up until **Partitioning Disks**; then simply choose **Done**.

4.7.4   Filesystem Configuration

The next dialog box contains a list of all disk partitions with filesystems readable by Red Hat Linux, including partitions for MS-DOS or Windows. This gives you the opportunity to assign these partitions to different parts of your Red Hat Linux filesystem. The partitions you assign will be automatically mounted when your Red Hat Linux system boots. Select the partition you wish to assign and press Enter (or choose **Edit**); then enter the *mount point* for that partition, e.g., /usr (see Figure 4.11).

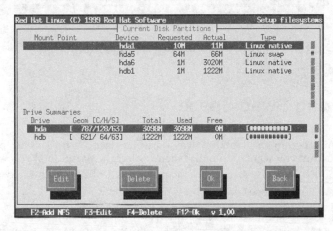

Figure 4.11: Filesystem Configuration

If you are performing an upgrade, the installation program tries to find your root partition automatically; if it does, it obtains all this information automatically, and goes on to the next step.

Adding an NFS Mount

Red Hat Linux also allows you to mount read-only NFS volumes when your system boots; this allows directory trees to be shared across a network. To do so, press F2. If you have not selected a network-related installation method, you will be presented with several dialog boxes concerning network configuration (turn to Section 5.1.2 on page 66 for more information). Fill them in appropriately. You will then see a dialog box entitled "Edit Network Mount Point." Enter the NFS server's hostname, the path to the NFS volume, and the local mount point for that volume (see Figure 4.12).

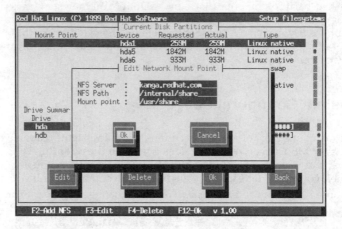

Figure 4.12: Adding an NFS Mount

4.8   Initializing Swap Space

Now the installation program will look for swap partitions (see Figure 4.13 on the next page). If it finds any, it asks whether you want to initialize them. Select the partition(s) you wish to initialize as swap space using ⌈Space⌋; if you wish to check the partitions for bad blocks, select the **Check for bad blocks during format** box. Choose **Ok**, and press ⌈Space⌋.

If the installation program can't find a swap partition and you're sure one exists, make sure you have set the partition type to Linux swap; see Section 4.7 on page 48 for information on how this is done with Disk Druid or fdisk.

4.9   For Hard Drive Installations Only...

If you are *not* performing a hard drive installation, please skip ahead to Section 4.10 on page 60. Otherwise, read on.

At this point, a dialog box entitled "Select Partition" is displayed (see Figure 4.14 on the facing page). Enter the device name of the partition holding the RedHat directory tree. There is also a field labelled "Directory." If the RedHat directory is not in the root directory of that partition (for example, /test/new/RedHat), enter the path to the RedHat directory (in our example, /test/new).

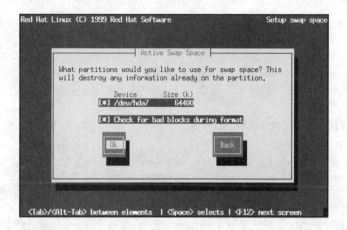

Figure 4.13: Initializing Swap Space

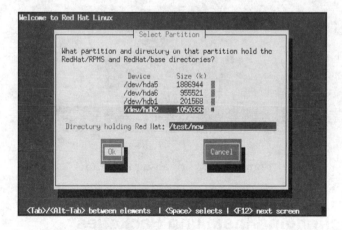

Figure 4.14: Selecting Partition for Hard Drive Install

If the installation program was unable to find the necessary files on the partition and directory you've specified, you'll be returned to the "Select Partition" dialog box to make the necessary corrections.

If everything has been specified properly, you should see a message box indicating that the packages are being scanned.

If you are doing a workstation- or server-class installation, please turn to Chapter 6 on page 91. Move on to the next section to continue the custom installation of Red Hat Linux.

4.10   Formatting Partitions

The next dialog box presents a list of partitions to format (see Figure 4.15). All newly-created partitions should be formatted. In addition, any existing partitions that contain old data you no longer need should be formatted. However, partitions such as /home or /usr/local must not be formatted if they contain data you wish to keep. Select each partition to format and press Space. If you wish to check for bad blocks while formatting each filesystem, select **Check for bad blocks during format**. Select **Ok**, and press Space.

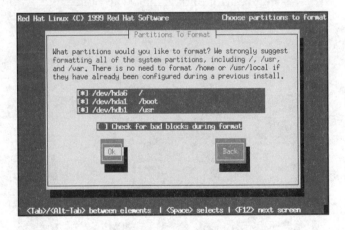

Figure 4.15: Formatting Partitions

4.11   Selecting and Installing Packages

After your partitions have been configured and selected for formatting, you are ready to select packages for installation. You can select *components*, which group packages together according to function, individual packages, or a combination of the two.

4.11.1 Selecting Components

Components group packages together according to the functionality they provide. For example, **C Development**, **Networked Workstation**, or **Web Server**. Select each component you wish to install and press Space. Selecting **Everything** (which can be found at the end of the component list) installs all packages included with Red Hat Linux (see Figure 4.16). Selecting every package will require close to 1 GIG of free disk space.

Figure 4.16: Selecting System Components

If you wish to select or deselect individual packages, check the **Select individual packages** check box.

4.11.2 Selecting Individual Packages

After selecting the components you wish to install, you may select or deselect individual packages. The installation program presents a list of the package groups available; using the arrow keys, select a group to examine and press Enter or Space. The installation program presents a list of the packages in that group, which you may select or deselect by using the arrow keys to highlight a package, and pressing Space (see Figure 4.17 on the following page).

Please Note: Some packages (such as the kernel and certain libraries) are required for every Red Hat Linux system and are not available to select or deselect.

Quick Keys

- o – shows that at least one of the packages in that component group has been selected.

- *∗* – shows that all the packages of a component group has been selected.

- *−* – removes all packages in a component group.

- *∗* – selects all packages in a component group.

Please Note: In the upper right-hand corner of the screen you will see the approximate system size of the components you have selected to install.

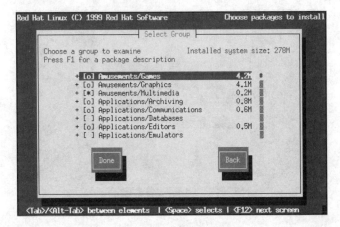

Figure 4.17: Selecting Packages

When you are finished selecting individual packages, press **Ok** in the **Select Group** dialog box.

Getting Information about a Package

You may view a detailed description of the currently-highlighted package by pressing F1 . A dialog box will appear containing a description of the package. You can use the arrow keys to scroll through the description if it cannot fit on the screen. When you're done reading the description, press **Ok**, and the box will disappear. You can then continue selecting packages.

Please Note: If you'd rather read the package descriptions on paper, please turn to Appendix D on page 247.

4.11.3   Package Dependencies

Many software packages, in order to work correctly, depend on other software packages or libraries that must be installed on your system. For example, many of the graphical Red Hat system administration tools require the `python` and `pythonlib` packages. To make sure your system has all the

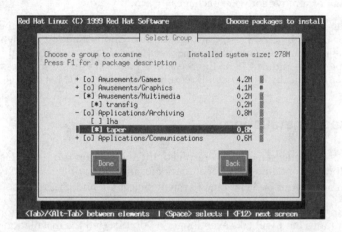

Figure 4.18: Selecting Packages – Expanded View

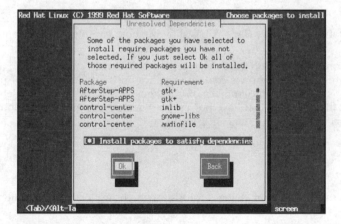

Figure 4.19: Unresolved Dependencies

packages it needs in order to be fully functional, Red Hat Linux checks these package *dependencies* each time you install or remove software packages.

After you have finished selecting packages to install, the installation program checks the list of selected packages for dependencies. If any package requires another package which you have not selected to install, the program presents a list of these *unresolved dependencies* and gives you the opportunity to resolve them (see Figure 4.19 on the preceding page). If you simply press **Ok**, the program will resolve them automatically by adding all required packages to the list of selected packages.

4.11.4   Package Installation

After all package dependencies have been resolved, the installation program presents a dialog box telling you that a log file containing a list of all packages installed will be written to /tmp/install.log on your Red Hat Linux system. Select **Ok** and press Space to continue.

At this point, the installation program will format every partition you selected for formatting. This can take several minutes (and will take even longer if you directed the installation program to check for bad blocks).

Once all partitions have been formatted, the installation program starts to install packages. A window entitled "Install Status" is displayed with the following information:

Package – The name of the package currently being installed.

Size – The size of the package (in kilobytes).

Summary – A short description of the package.

Package Installation Progress Bar – A bar showing how complete the current package installation is.

Statistics Section – This section has three rows labeled "Total," "Completed," and "Remaining." As you might guess, these rows contain statistics on the total number of packages that will be installed, statistics on the number of packages that have been completely installed, and statistics on the packages that have not yet been installed. The information tracked on these three rows includes:

    Packages – The number of packages.
    Bytes – The size.
    Time – The amount of time.

Overall Progress Bar – This bar changes color showing how close to completion the entire installation is.

At this point there's nothing left for you to do until all the packages have been installed. How quickly this happens depends on the number of packages you've selected, and your computer's speed.

Once all the packages have been installed, please turn to Chapter 6 on page 91 to finish your installation of Red Hat Linux.

5

Network Installations

5.1 Selecting an Installation Method

Now you must decide what type of installation method you wish to use (see Figure 5.1 on the following page). Highlight the appropriate choice and select **Ok**, or press (Enter).

If you are *not* performing a network type installation (NFS, FTP, or HTTP) then please skip ahead to Chapter 6 on page 91 to finish the installation process, or back to Chapter 4 on page 43 if you need to perform a CD-ROM or hard drive installation.

If you *are* planning to do a network type installation, please read on.

5.1.1 Network Driver Configuration

Next, the installation program will probe your system and attempt to identify your network card. Most of the time, the driver can locate the card automatically. If it is not able to identify your network card, you'll be asked to choose the driver that supports your network card and to specify any options necessary for the driver to locate and recognize it.

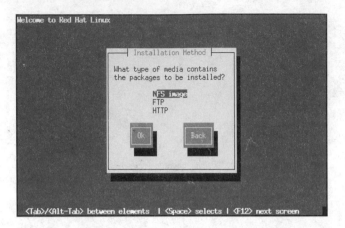

Figure 5.1: Selecting an Installation Method

5.1.2   Configuring TCP/IP Networking

After the installation program has configured your network card, it presents several dialogs for configuring your system's TCP/IP networking. The first screen (shown in Figure 5.2 on the next page) allows you to select from one of three approaches to network configuration:

- **Static IP address** – You must supply all the necessary network-related information manually.

- **BOOTP** – The necessary network-related information is automatically provided using a `bootp` request.

- **DHCP** – The necessary network-related information is automatically provided using a `dhcp` request.

Please Note: The **BOOTP** and **DHCP** selections require an active, properly configured bootp (or dhcp) server running on your local area network.

If you choose **BOOTP** or **DHCP**, your network configuration will be set automatically, and you can skip the rest of this section.

If you've selected **Static IP address**, you'll need to specify all the networking information yourself. Figure 5.3 on the facing page contains an example of networking information similar to what you'll be needing.

Please Note: The information in figure 5.3 on the next page is a sample only! You should obtain the proper information for your network from your network administrator.

The first dialog asks you for IP and other network addresses (see Figure 5.4 on page 68). Enter the **IP address** you are using during installation and press ⏎Enter. The installation program attempts to

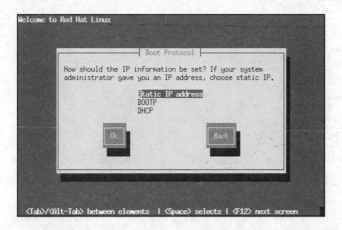

Figure 5.2: Selecting Method of Network Configuration

Field	Example Value
IP Address	10.0.2.15
Netmask	255.255.255.0
Default Gateway	10.0.2.254
Primary Nameserver	10.0.2.1
Domain Name	redhat.com
Hostname	pooh.redhat.com

Figure 5.3: Sample Networking Information

guess your **Netmask** based on your IP address; you may change the netmask if it is incorrect. Press
(Enter). The installation program guesses the **Default gateway** and **Primary nameserver** addresses
from your IP address and netmask; you may change them if they are incorrect.

Choose **Ok** to continue.

After the first dialog box, you may see a second one. It will prompt you for a domain name, a
hostname, and other networking information (see Figure 5.5 on page 69). Enter the **Domain name**
for your system and press (Enter); the installation program carries the domain name down to the **Host
name** field. Enter the hostname you are using in front of the domain name to form a fully-qualified
domain name (FQDN). If your network has more than one nameserver, you may enter IP addresses
for additional nameservers in the **Secondary nameserver** and **Tertiary nameserver** fields. Choose
Ok to continue.

Please Note: If you're performing an FTP installation, go to Section 5.3 on page 69 and continue
from there. If you're doing an NFS installation, read on.

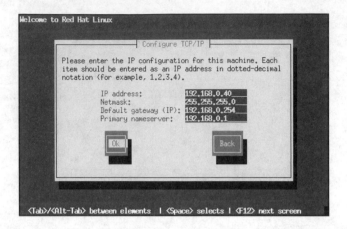

Figure 5.4: Configuring TCP/IP

5.2   Installing via NFS

If you are installing Red Hat Linux 6.0 via NFS, you will now need to configure your NFS server information.

5.2.1   NFS Server Information

The next dialog requests information about the NFS server (see Figure 5.6 on page 70). Enter the name (which must be a fully-qualified domain name) or IP address of your NFS server, and the name of the exported directory that contains the Red Hat Linux CD. For example, if the NFS server has the Red Hat Linux CD mounted on /mnt/cdrom, enter /mnt/cdrom in the **Red Hat directory** field. If the NFS server is exporting a mirror of the Red Hat Linux installation tree instead of a CD, enter the directory which contains the RedHat directory. For example, if your NFS server contains the directory /mirrors/redhat/i386/RedHat,
enter /mirrors/redhat/i386.

After a short delay, the next dialog box will appear.

Please Note: An NFS install does not require a support diskette in the installation process, unless you are using a PCMCIA device to complete the installation. If so, you will need to use the PCMCIA support disk when prompted.

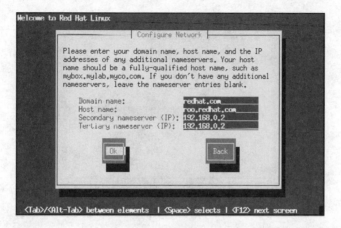

Figure 5.5: Configuring Networking

5.3 Installing via FTP

You should now be looking at the "FTP Setup" dialog box. Here's where you point the installation program at the FTP site of your choice (see Figure 5.7 on page 71). Enter the name or IP address of the FTP site you are installing from, and the name of the directory there which contains the `RedHat` directory for your architecture. For example, if the FTP site contains the directory `/pub/mirrors/redhat/i386/RedHat`, enter `/pub/mirrors/redhat/i386`. If you are not using anonymous FTP, or if you need to use a proxy FTP server (if you're behind a firewall, for example), check the check box, and another dialog box will request the FTP account and proxy information.

If everything has been specified properly, you should see a message box indicating that `base/hdlist` is being retrieved.

Continue to section 5.5 on the next page for upgrade or full-installation instructions.

5.4 Installing via HTTP

You should now be looking at the "HTTP Setup" dialog box. Here's where you point the installation program at the HTTP site of your choice. Enter the name or IP address of the HTTP site you are installing from, and the name of the directory there which contains the `RedHat` directory for your architecture. For example, if the HTTP site contains the directory `/pub/mirrors/redhat/i386/RedHat`, enter `/pub/mirrors/redhat/i386`. If you are not using anonymous HTTP, or if you need to use a proxy HTTP server (if you're behind a firewall, for example), check the check box, and another dialog box will request the HTTP account and proxy

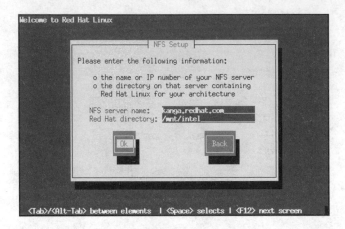

Figure 5.6: Installing via NFS

information.

If everything has been specified properly, you should see a message box indicating that `base/hdlist` is being retrieved.

Continue to section 5.5 for upgrade or full-installation instructions.

5.5 Upgrading or Installing

After you choose an installation method, the installation program prompts you to either *install* or *upgrade* (see Figure 5.9 on page 72).

5.5.1 Installing

You usually install Red Hat Linux on a clean disk partition or set of partitions, or over another installation of Linux.

Please Note: Installing Red Hat Linux over another installation of Linux (including Red Hat Linux) does *not* preserve any information (files or data) from the prior installation. Make sure you save any important files! If you are worried about saving the current data on your existing system (without making a backup on your own), you should consider performing an upgrade instead.

If you wish to perform a full install, choose **Install**, and skip to section 5.6 on page 72.

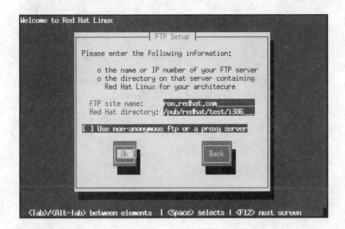

Figure 5.7: Installing via FTP

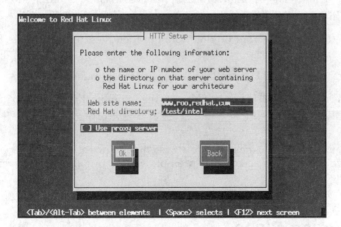

Figure 5.8: Installing via HTTP

Figure 5.9: Upgrading or Installing

5.5.2   Upgrading

The installation process for Red Hat Linux 6.0 includes the ability to upgrade from prior versions of Red Hat Linux (version 2.0 and later) which are based on RPM technology. Upgrading your system installs the modular 2.2.*x* kernel as well as updated versions of the packages which are currently installed on your machine. The upgrade process preserves existing configuration files by renaming them using an .rpmsave extension (e.g., sendmail.cf.rpmsave) and leaves a log telling what actions it took in /tmp/upgrade.log. As software evolves, configuration file formats can change, so you should carefully compare your original configuration files to the new files before integrating your changes.

If you wish to upgrade your Red Hat Linux system, choose **Upgrade**.

Please Note: Some upgraded packages may require that other packages are also installed for proper operation. The upgrade procedure takes care of these *dependencies*, but it may need to install additional packages.

Please Note: If you already have the X Window System (and possibly an older version of GNOME) on you machine you may see a screen that prompts you to install the latest version of GNOME included in this release.

5.6   Installation Class

If you chose to perform a full install, the installation program will ask you to choose an installation class (see Figure 5.10 on the next page). You will not see this screen if you chose to perform an upgrade. You may choose from the following installation classes:

Figure 5.10: Installation Class

- **Workstation** – A workstation-class installation will automatically erase all Linux partitions from your computer's hard drive(s). This type of installation will attempt to set up a dual boot environment automatically.

- **Server** – A server-class installation will automatically erase *all partitions* from your computer's hard drive(s).

- **Custom** – A custom-class installation gives you complete control over partitioning-related issues. If you have installed Red Hat Linux in the past, the custom-class installation is most similar to past installations.

Please Note: If you choose either **Workstation** or **Server**, part (or all) of your computer's stored data on all drives *will* be erased! You will be asked to confirm your decision; however, please keep in mind that once the installation program receives your confirmation, the erasure is irrevocable.

Please Note: WARNING – If you choose to perform a workstation-class or server-class installation, data erasure will be irrevocable. The severity of erased data varies according to type of installation:

- **Workstation-class** – Data on any existing Linux partition on any hard drive on your system will be erased.

- **Server-class** – Data on all partitions of all drives will be completely erased, regardless if it is on an existing Linux partition or not.

If you choose a workstation- or server-class installation, you will be able to skip over some of the steps that the custom-class install requires.

5.7   SCSI Support

After you choose the appropriate installation class, the installation program will probe your system for SCSI adapters. In some cases, the installation program will ask you whether you have any SCSI adapters. If you choose **Yes**, the following dialog presents a list of SCSI drivers. Choose the driver that most closely resembles your SCSI adapter. The installation program then gives you an opportunity to specify options for the SCSI driver you selected; most SCSI drivers should detect your hardware automatically, however.

For either the workstation- or server-class installation, you should turn Chapter 6 on page 91 to finish the installation process.

5.8   Creating Partitions for Red Hat Linux

At this point, it's necessary to let the installation program know where it should install Red Hat Linux. This is done by defining *mount points* for one or more disk partitions in which Red Hat Linux will be installed. You may also need to create and/or delete partitions at this time.

Please Note: If you have not yet planned how you will set up your partitions, please turn to Section 2.8 on page 21, and review everything up to Section 2.9 on page 32. As a bare minimum, you'll need an appropriately-sized root partition, and a swap partition of at least 16 MB.

If you are still unsure about how to set up your partitions, please refer to Appendix C on page 239 for more information.

The installation program then presents a dialog box that allows you to choose from two disk partitioning tools (see Figure 5.11 on the facing page). The two choices you have are:

- **Disk Druid** – This is Red Hat Linux's install-time disk management utility. It can create and delete disk partitions according to user-supplied requirements, in addition to managing mount points for each partition.

- **fdisk** – This is the traditional Linux disk partitioning tool. While it is somewhat more flexible than Disk Druid, the downside is that `fdisk` assumes you have some experience with disk partitioning, and are comfortable with its somewhat terse user interface.

With the exception of certain esoteric situations, Disk Druid can handle the partitioning requirements for a typical Red Hat Linux installation.

SPARC

Note that there are some points you should be aware of if you decide to use Disk Druid under Red Hat Linux/SPARC. Please refer to Appendix F on page 359 for more information.

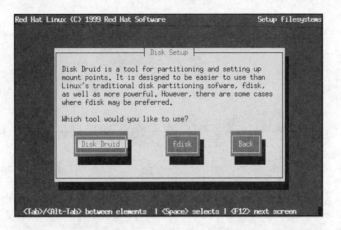

Figure 5.11: Selecting Disk Setup Method

ALPHA

Note that there are some points you should be aware of if you decide to use Disk Druid under Red Hat Linux/Alpha. Please refer to the Alpha Installation Addendum for more information.

Select the disk partitioning tool you'd like to use, and press Enter. If you choose Disk Druid, continue reading. If you'd rather use fdisk, please turn to Section 5.8.3 on page 81.

5.8.1 Using Disk Druid

If you selected Disk Druid, you will be presented with a screen that looks like figure 5.12 on the next page. While it may look overwhelming at first, it really isn't. Let's go over each of Disk Druid's three sections.

The "Current Disk Partitions" Section

Each line in the "Current Disk Partitions" section represents a disk partition. You'll note that this section has a scroll bar to the right, which means that there might be more partitions than can be displayed at one time. If you use the ↑ and ↓ keys, you can see if there are any additional partitions there. Each line in this section has five different fields:

Mount Point – This field indicates where the partition will be mounted when Red Hat Linux is installed and running.

Device – This field displays the partition's device name.

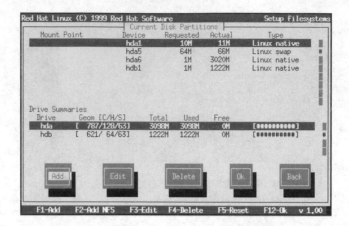

Figure 5.12: Disk Druid Main Screen

Requested – The "Requested" field shows the minimum size requested when the partition was defined.

Actual – The "Actual" field shows the space currently allocated to the partition.

Type – This field shows the partition's type.

Another Type of Partition – As you scroll through the "Current Disk Partitions" section, you might see an "Unallocated Requested Partitions" title bar, followed by one or more partitions. As the title implies, these are partitions that have been requested but, for one reason or another, have not been allocated. A common reason for having an unallocated partition is a lack of sufficient free space for the partition. In any case, the reason the partition remains unallocated will be displayed after the partition's mount point.

The "Drive Summaries" Section

Each line in the "Drive Summaries" section represents a hard disk on your system. Each line has the following fields:

Drive – This field shows the hard disk's device name.

Geom [C/H/S] – This field shows the hard disk's *geometry*. The geometry consists of three numbers representing the number of cylinders, heads, and sectors as reported by the hard disk.

Total – The "Total" field shows the total available space on the hard disk.

Used – This field shows how much of the hard disk's space is currently allocated to partitions.

Free – The "Free" field shows how much of the hard disk's space is still unallocated.

Bar Graph – This field presents a visual representation of the space currently used on the hard disk. The more pound signs there are between the square braces, the less free space there is. In Figure 5.12 on the facing page, the bar graph shows no free space.

Please Note: The "Drive Summaries" section is displayed only to indicate your computer's disk configuration. It is not meant to be used as a means of specifying the target hard drive for a given partition. This is described more completely in **Adding a Partition** later in this section.

Disk Druid's Buttons

These buttons control Disk Druid's actions. They are used to add and delete partitions, and to change partition attributes. In addition, there are buttons that are used to accept the changes you've made, or to exit Disk Druid entirely. Let's take a look at each button in order.

Add – The "Add" button is used to request a new partition. When selected, a dialog box will appear containing fields that must be filled in.

Edit – The "Edit" button is used to modify attributes of the partition currently highlighted in the "Current Disk Partitions" section. Selecting this button will cause a dialog box to appear. Some or all of the fields in the "Edit Partition" dialog box may be changed, depending on whether the partition information has already been written to the disk.

Delete – The "Delete" button is used to delete the partition currently highlighted in the "Current Disk Partitions" section. Selecting this button will cause a dialog box to appear asking you to confirm the deletion.

Ok – The "Ok" button causes any changes made to your system's partitions to be written to disk. You will be asked to confirm your changes before Disk Druid rewrites your hard disk partition table(s). In addition, any mount points you've defined are passed to the installation program, and will eventually be used by your Red Hat Linux system to define the filesystem layout.

Back – This button causes Disk Druid to abort without saving any changes you've made. When this button is selected, the installation program will take you back to the previous screen, so you can start over.

Handy Function Keys

While there is some overlap between Disk Druid's buttons and the available functions keys, there are two function keys that have no corresponding buttons:

- **F2 (Add NFS)** – This function key is used to add a read-only NFS-served filesystem to the set of mount points on your Red Hat Linux system. When selected, a dialog box will appear containing fields that must be filled in.

- **F5 (Reset)** – This function key is used to discard all changes you may have made while in Disk Druid, and return the list of partitions to those read from the partition table(s) on your hard disk(s). When selected, you'll be asked to confirm whether you want the changes discarded or not. Note that any mount points you've specified will be lost, and will need to be reentered.

Please Note: You will need to dedicate at least one partition to Red Hat Linux, and optionally more. This is discussed more completely in Section 2.8.5 on page 29.

Now let's see how Disk Druid is used to set up partitions for your Red Hat Linux system.

Adding a Partition

To Add a new partition, select the **Add** button, and press Space or Enter. A dialog box entitled "Edit New Partition" will appear (see Figure 5.13). It contains the following fields:

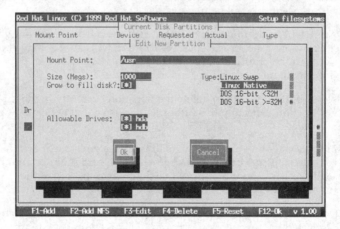

Figure 5.13: Creating a New Partition

- **Mount Point** – Highlight this field, and enter the partition's mount point. For example, if this partition should be the root partition, enter /; enter /usr for the usr partition, and so on.

- **Size (Megs)** – In this field, enter the size (in megabytes) of the partition. Note that this field starts with a "1" in it, meaning that unless you change it, you'll end up with a 1 MB partition. Delete it using the Backspace key, and enter the desired partition size.

- **Growable?** – This check box indicates whether the size you entered in the previous field is to be considered the partition's exact size, or its minimum size. Press $\boxed{\text{Space}}$ to check and uncheck the box. When checked, the partition will grow to fill all available space on the hard disk. In this case, the partition's size will expand and contract as other partitions are modified. Note that you can make more than one partition growable; if you do so, the additional free space will be shared between all growable partitions.

- **Type** – This field contains a list of different partition types. Select the appropriate partition type by using the $\boxed{\uparrow}$ and $\boxed{\downarrow}$ keys.

- **Allowable Drives** – This field contains a list of the hard disks installed on your system, with a check box for each. If a hard disk's box is checked, then this partition may be created on that hard disk. If the box is *not* checked, then the partition will *never* be created on that hard disk. By using different check box settings, you can direct Disk Druid to place partitions as you see fit, or let Disk Druid decide where partitions should go.

- **Ok** – Select this button and press $\boxed{\text{Space}}$ when you are satisfied with the partition's settings, and wish to create it.

- **Cancel** – Select this button and press $\boxed{\text{Space}}$ when you don't want to create the partition.

5.8.2 Problems When Adding a Partition

Please Note: If you are having problems setting up your partitions, please refer to Appendix C on page 239 for more information.

If you attempt to add a partition and Disk Druid can't carry out your request, you'll see a dialog box like the one in Figure 5.14 on the following page. In the box are listed any partitions that are currently unallocated, along with the reason they could not be allocated. Select the **Ok** button, and press $\boxed{\text{Space}}$ to continue. Note that the unallocated partition(s) are also displayed on Disk Druid's main screen (though you may have to scroll the "Current Disk Partitions" section to see them).

Deleting a Partition

To delete a partition, highlight the partition in the "Current Disk Partitions" section, select the **Delete** button, and press $\boxed{\text{Space}}$. You will be asked to confirm the deletion.

Editing a Partition

To change a partition's settings, highlight the partition in the "Current Disk Partitions" section, select the **Edit** button, and press $\boxed{\text{Space}}$. You will be presented with a dialog box very similar to the one shown in Figure 5.13 on the preceding page. Make the appropriate changes, select **Ok**, and press $\boxed{\text{Space}}$.

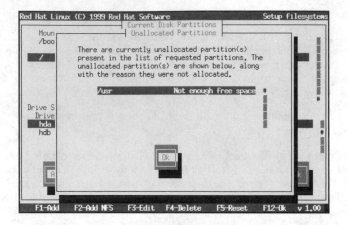

Figure 5.14: Unallocated Partition Warning

Please Note: If the partition already existed on your hard disk, you will only be able to change the partition's mount point. If you want to make any other changes, you will need to delete the partition and recreate it.

Adding an NFS Mount

To add a read-only NFS-served filesystem, press [F2]. If you have not selected a network-related installation method, you will be presented with several dialog boxes concerning network configuration (turn to Section 5.1.1 on page 65 for more information). Fill in the boxes appropriately. You will then see a dialog box entitled, "Edit Network Mount Point" (similar to the one in Figure 5.19 on page 84). In this dialog box you will need to enter the NFS server name, the path to the exported filesystem, and the mount point for the filesystem. Select the **Ok** or **Cancel** button as appropriate, and press [Space].

Starting Over

If you'd like to abandon any changes you've made while in Disk Druid, and would rather use `fdisk` instead, you can select the **Back** button, and press [Space]. If you want to continue using Disk Druid, but would like to start over, press [F5], and Disk Druid will be reset to its initial state.

When You're Finished...

Once you've finished configuring partitions and entering mount points, your screen should look something like the one in Figure 5.15. Select **Ok**, and press Space. Then turn to Section 4.8 on page 58.

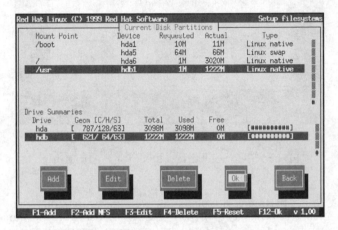

Figure 5.15: Partitions and Mount Points Defined

5.8.3 Using fdisk

If you'd rather use fdisk to manage partitions, this is the section for you. Once you've selected fdisk, you'll be presented with a dialog box entitled "Partition Disks" (see Figure 5.16 on the following page). In this box is a list of every disk on your computer. Move the highlight to the disk you'd like to partition, select **Edit**, and press Space. You will then enter fdisk and can partition the disk you selected. Repeat this process for each disk you want to partition. When you're done, select "Done."

An Overview of fdisk

fdisk includes online help which is terse but useful. Here are a few tips:

- The command for help is m.

- To list the current partition table, use the p command (see Figure 5.17 on page 83).

- To add a new partition, use n.

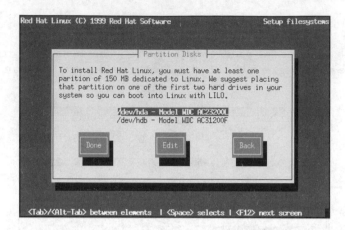

Figure 5.16: Selecting a Disk for Partitioning

- Linux `fdisk` creates partitions of type `Linux native` by default. When you create a swap partition, don't forget to change it to type `Linux swap` using the `t` command. The value for the `Linux swap` type is `82`. For other partition types, use the `l` command to see a list of partition types and values.

- Linux allows up to four (4) partitions on one disk. If you wish to create more than that, one (and only one) of the four may be an *extended* partition, which acts as a container for one or more *logical* partitions. Since it acts as a container, the extended partition must be at least as large as the total size of all the logical partitions it is to contain.

- It's a good idea to write down which partitions (e.g., `/dev/hda2`) are meant for which filesystems (e.g., `/usr`) as you create each one.

- **Please Note:** None of the changes you make take effect until you save them and exit `fdisk` using the `w` command. You may quit `fdisk` at any time without saving changes by using the `q` command.

Changing the Partition Table

When you are finished partitioning your disks, press **Done**; you may see a message indicating that the installation program needs to reboot. This is a normal occurrence after changing a disk's partition data; it usually happens if you created, changed, or deleted any extended partitions. After you press **Ok**, your machine will reboot. Follow the same installation steps you did up until **Partitioning Disks**; then simply choose **Done**.

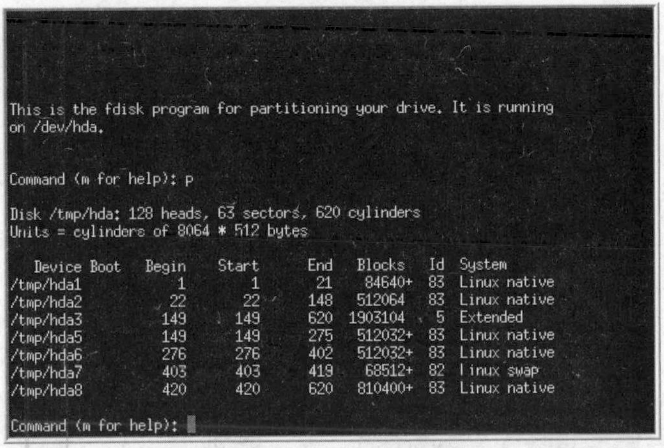

```
This is the fdisk program for partitioning your drive. It is running
on /dev/hda.

Command (m for help): p

Disk /tmp/hda: 128 heads, 63 sectors, 620 cylinders
Units = cylinders of 8064 * 512 bytes

   Device Boot   Begin   Start    End   Blocks   Id  System
/tmp/hda1            1       1     21   84640+   83  Linux native
/tmp/hda2           22      22    148   512064   83  Linux native
/tmp/hda3          149     149    620  1903104    5  Extended
/tmp/hda5          149     149    275   512032+  83  Linux native
/tmp/hda6          276     276    402   512032+  83  Linux native
/tmp/hda7          403     403    419   68512+   82  linux swap
/tmp/hda8          420     420    620   810400+  83  Linux native

Command (m for help):
```

Figure 5.17: Sample Output from `fdisk`

5.8.4   Filesystem Configuration

The next dialog box contains a list of all disk partitions with filesystems readable by Red Hat Linux, including partitions for MS-DOS or Windows. This gives you the opportunity to assign these partitions to different parts of your Red Hat Linux filesystem. The partitions you assign will be automatically mounted when your Red Hat Linux system boots. Select the partition you wish to assign and press Enter (or choose **Edit**); then enter the *mount point* for that partition, e.g., /usr (see Figure 5.18 on the following page).

If you are performing an upgrade, the installation program tries to find your root partition automatically; if it does, it obtains all this information automatically, and goes on to the next step.

Adding an NFS Mount

Red Hat Linux also allows you to mount read-only NFS volumes when your system boots; this allows directory trees to be shared across a network. To do so, press F2. If you have not selected a network-related installation method, you will be presented with several dialog boxes concerning network configuration (turn to Section 5.1.2 on page 66 for more information). Fill them in appropriately. You will then see a dialog box entitled "Edit Network Mount Point." Enter the NFS server's hostname, the path to the NFS volume, and the local mount point for that volume (see Figure 5.19 on the following page).

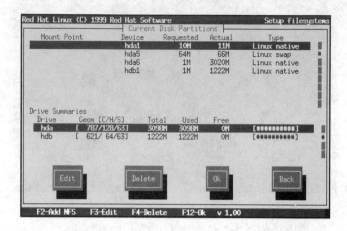

Figure 5.18: Filesystem Configuration

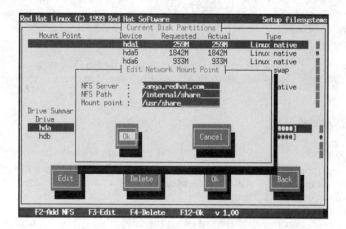

Figure 5.19: Adding an NFS Mount

5.9   Initializing Swap Space

After you've created partitions for Red Hat Linux, the installation program looks for swap partitions (see Figure 5.20). If it finds any, it asks whether you want to initialize them. Select the partition(s) you wish to initialize as swap space using [Space]; if you wish to check the partitions for bad blocks, make sure the **Check for bad blocks during format** box is checked. Choose **Ok**, and press [Space].

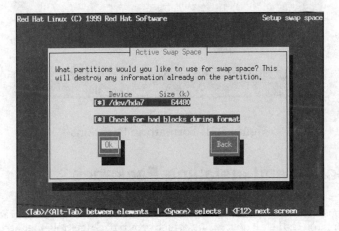

Figure 5.20: Initializing Swap Space

If the installation program can't find a swap partition and you're sure one exists, make sure you have set the partition type to Linux swap; see Section 5.8 on page 74 for information on how this is done with Disk Druid or fdisk.

5.10   Formatting Partitions

The next dialog box presents a list of partitions to format (see Figure 5.21 on the next page). All newly created partitions should be formatted. In addition, any existing partitions that contain old data you no longer need should be formatted. However, partitions such as /home or /usr/local must not be formatted if they contain data you wish to keep. Select each partition to format and press [Space]. If you wish to check for bad blocks while formatting each filesystem, select **Check for bad blocks during format**. Select **Ok**, and press [Space].

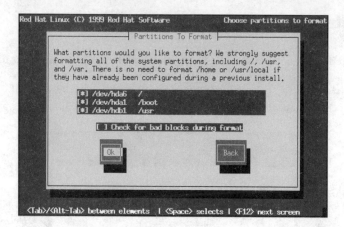

Figure 5.21: Formatting Partitions

5.11   Selecting and Installing Packages

After your partitions have been configured and selected for formatting, you are ready to select packages for installation. You can select *components*, which group packages together according to function, individual packages, or a combination of the two.

5.11.1   Selecting Components

Components group packages together according to the functionality they provide. For example, **C Development**, **Networked Workstation**, or **Web Server**. Select each component you wish to install and press Space. Selecting **Everything** (which can be found at the end of the component list) installs all packages included with Red Hat Linux (see Figure 5.22 on the facing page). Selecting every package will require close to 1 GIG of free disk space.

If you wish to select or deselect individual packages, check the **Select individual packages** check box.

5.11.2   Selecting Individual Packages

After selecting the components you wish to install, you may select or deselect individual packages. The installation program presents a list of the package groups available; using the arrow keys, select a group to examine and press Enter or Space. The installation program presents a list of the packages in that group, which you may select or deselect by using the arrow keys to highlight a package, and

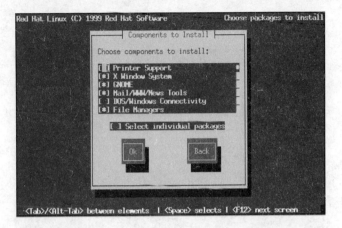

Figure 5.22: Selecting System Components

pressing [Space] (see Figure 5.23 on the next page).

Please Note: Some packages (such as the kernel and certain libraries) are required for every Red Hat Linux system and are not available to select or deselect.

Quick Keys

- o – shows that at least one of the packages in that component group has been selected.

- * – shows that all the packages of a component group have been selected.

- – – removes all packages in a component group.

- * – selects all packages in a component group.

Please Note: In the upper right-hand corner of the screen you will see the approximate system size of the components you have selected to install.

When you are finished selecting individual packages, press **Ok** in the **Select Group** dialog box.

Getting Information about a Package

You may view a detailed description of the currently highlighted package by pressing [F1]. A dialog box will appear containing a description of the package. You can use the arrow keys to scroll through the description if there is more than can fit on the screen. When you're done reading the description,

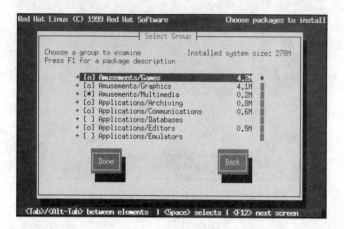

Figure 5.23: Selecting Packages

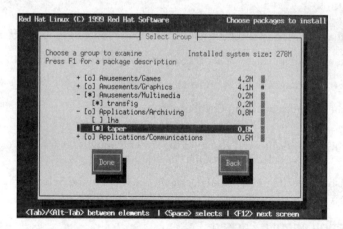

Figure 5.24: Selecting Packages – Expanded View

press **Ok**, and the box will disappear. You can then continue selecting packages (and viewing their descriptions).

Please Note: If you'd rather read the package descriptions on paper, please turn to Appendix D on page 247.

5.11.3 Package Dependencies

Many software packages, in order to work correctly, depend on other software packages or libraries that must be installed on your system. For example, many of the graphical Red Hat system administration tools require the `python` and `pythonlib` packages. To make sure your system has all the packages it needs in order to be fully functional, Red Hat Linux checks these package *dependencies* each time you install or remove software packages.

After you have finished selecting packages to install, the installation program checks the list of selected packages for dependencies. If any package requires another package which you have not selected to install, the program presents a list of these *unresolved dependencies* and gives you the opportunity to resolve them (see Figure 5.25). If you simply press **Ok**, the program will resolve them automatically by adding all required packages to the list of selected packages.

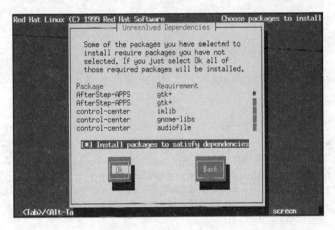

Figure 5.25: Unresolved Dependencies

5.11.4 Package Installation

After all package dependencies have been resolved, the installation program presents a dialog box telling you that a log file containing a list of all packages installed will be written to `/tmp/install.log` on your Red Hat Linux system. Select **Ok** and press ⎵Space⎵ to continue.

At this point, the installation program will format every partition you selected for formatting. This can take several minutes (and will take even longer if you directed the installation program to check for bad blocks).

Once all partitions have been formatted, the installation program starts to install packages. A window entitled "Install Status" is displayed with the following information:

Package – The name of the package currently being installed.

Size – The size of the package (in kilobytes).

Summary – A short description of the package.

Package Installation Progress Bar – A bar showing how complete the current package installation is.

Statistics Section – This section has three rows labeled "Total," "Completed," and "Remaining." As you might guess, these rows contain statistics on the total number of packages that will be installed, statistics on the number of packages that have been completely installed, and statistics on the packages that have not yet been installed. The information tracked on these three rows includes:

Packages – The number of packages.

Bytes – The size.

Time – The amount of time.

Overall Progress Bar – This bar changes color showing how close to completion the entire installation is.

Please Note: If you're doing an FTP or HTTP installation, a message box will pop up as each package is retrieved from the site.

At this point there's nothing left for you to do until all the packages have been installed. How quickly this happens depends on the number of packages you've selected, and your computer's speed. Once all the packages have been installed, please turn to Chapter 6 on the facing page to finish your installation of Red Hat Linux.

6

Finishing the Installation

6.1 Configuring a Mouse

Next, your system will be probed to find a mouse. Some mice may be detected automatically; in this case, a dialog box is displayed showing the port on which the mouse was found. You may then be asked to give additional information, such as whether you have a two-button mouse, and would like it to emulate a three-button mouse. Make the appropriate selections, and continue to the next section.

More commonly, you will see a screen similar to the one in Figure 6.1 on the next page.

The installation program's "best guess" as to your system's mouse type will be highlighted. If the mouse type is not accurate, use the $\uparrow$ and $\downarrow$ keys to scroll through the different mouse types. In general, you should use the following approach to selecting your system's mouse type:

- If you find an *exact* match for your mouse in the list, highlight that entry.

- If you find a mouse that you are *certain*[1] is compatible with your mouse, highlight that entry.

- Otherwise, select one of the **Generic** entries, based on your mouse's number of buttons, and its interface. To determine your mouse's interface, follow the mouse cable back to where it plugs into your system. If the connector at the end of the mouse cable plugs into a rectangular

---

[1]No guessing allowed!

Figure 6.1: Mouse Configuration

connector, you have a serial mouse. On the other hand, if the connector is round, you have a PS/2 mouse. If you are installing Red Hat Linux on a laptop computer, in most cases the pointing device will be PS/2 compatible.

The **Emulate 3 Buttons** check box allows you to use a two-button mouse as if it had three buttons. In general, it's easiest to use the X Window System if you have a three-button mouse. If you select this check box, you can emulate a third, "middle" button by pressing both mouse buttons simultaneously.

If you've selected a mouse with a serial interface, you will then see a screen similar to the one shown in Figure 6.2 on the facing page. Simply highlight the appropriate serial port for your mouse, select **Ok**, and press Space.

If you wish to change your mouse configuration after you have booted your Red Hat Linux system, you may use the /usr/sbin/mouseconfig command.

If wish to configure your mouse as a left-handed mouse, you can reset the order of the mouse buttons. This may be done after you have booted your Red Hat Linux system, by typing gpm -B 321.

6.2   Configuring Networking

Next, the installation program gives you an opportunity to configure (or reconfigure) networking. If you are installing from CD-ROM or from a local hard disk, the installation program asks if you want to configure networking. If you choose **No**, your Red Hat Linux system will be a standalone workstation. If you choose **Yes**, you may configure networking as described below.

If you are installing via network media you have already entered temporary networking information

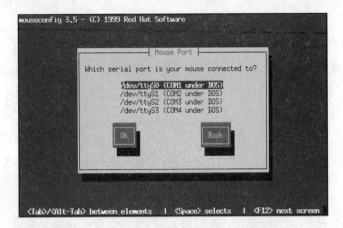

Figure 6.2: Serial Mouse Port Selection

that was used during the installation. The install program offers you three choices (see Figure6.3 and 6.4):

- **Keep this setup** – Keeps the network configuration you used during the installation. All the networking information you entered previously becomes part of your system's permanent configuration.

- **Reconfigure network now** – The installation program presents the network configuration dialogs in Section 5.1.1 on page 65. The values you used during installation will be filled in as defaults. Choose this if your system will be installed on a network other than the one you used to install Red Hat Linux.

- **Don't setup networking** – Don't set up networking at all. Your system will not have networking configured. Choose this if you installed your system over a network, but it will be used as a standalone workstation.

6.2.1   Network Configuration Dialogs

If you elected to configure networking at this time, you will be presented with a series of dialog boxes. Please turn to Section 5.1.2 on page 66 for more information.

Figure 6.3: Network Configuration Options – Local Media Install

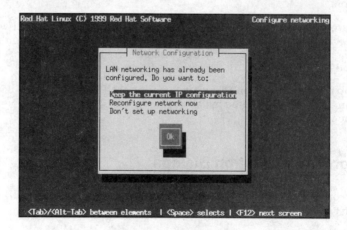

Figure 6.4: Network Configuration Options – Network Install

6.3   Configuring the Time Zone

Next, the installation program presents a dialog to help you configure your system's time zone (see Figure 6.5).

If you wish to set the hardware (CMOS) clock to GMT (Greenwich Mean Time, also known as UTC, or Coordinated Universal Time), select **Hardware clock set to GMT**. Setting it to GMT means your system will properly handle daylight-saving time, if your time zone uses it. Most networks use GMT.

Please Note: If your computer runs another operating system from time to time, setting the clock to GMT may cause the other operating system to display the incorrect time. Also keep in mind that if more than one operating system is allowed to automatically change the time to compensate for daylight-saving time, it is likely that the time will be improperly set.

Figure 6.5: Configuring Time Zones

Select the time zone your system will be operating in froom the list, and press ⟨Enter⟩.

If you wish to change your time zone configuration after you have booted your Red Hat Linux system, you may use the /usr/sbin/timeconfig command.

6.4   Selecting Services for Start on Reboot

Please Note: If you're performing a workstation- or server-class installation, this part of the installation is automatically done for you. Please skip ahead to Section 6.5 on the following page.

Next you'll see a dialog box entitled "Services" (see Figure 6.6 on the next page). Displayed in this box is a list of services with a check box by each. Scroll through this list, and check every service that you would like automatically started every time your Red Hat Linux system boots. If you're not sure what a particular service is, move the highlight to it and press [F1]. You'll then get a brief description of the service.

Figure 6.6: Selecting Services

Note that you can run /usr/sbin/ntsysv or /sbin/chkconfig after the installation to change which services automatically start on reboot.

6.5   Configuring a Printer

Next you will be asked if you want to configure a printer. If you choose **Yes**, a dialog box will ask you to indicate how the printer is connected to your computer (see Figure 6.7 on the facing page).

Here is a brief description of the three types of printer connections available:

Local – The printer is directly connected to your computer.

Remote lpd – The printer is connected to your local area network (either through another computer, or directly), and is capable of communicating via lpr/lpd.

SMB/Windows 95/NT – The printer is connected to another computer which shares the printer via SMB networking, such as a printer shared by a Windows 95 or Windows NT computer.

Netware – The printer is connected to another computer which shares the printer via Novell NetWare.

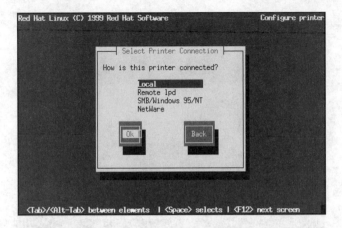

Figure 6.7: Selecting Printer Type

After selecting a printer type, you'll be presented with a dialog box entitled "Standard Printer Options" (see Figure 6.8 on the next page). Enter the name of the queue and the spool directory you'd like to use, or accept the default information.

The dialog box you'll see next depends on the printer connection type you selected.

6.5.1 Locally Attached Printers

If you selected "Local" as your printer's connection type, you'll see a dialog box similar to the one in Figure 6.9 on the following page.

Enter the printer device name in the field provided. As a convenience, the installation program attempts to determine which printer ports are available on your computer. Select **Next**, and press Space. Now turn to Section 6.5.5 on page 99 to continue.

6.5.2 Remote lpd Printers

If you selected "Remote lpd" as your printer's connection type, you'll see a dialog box similar to the one in Figure 6.10 on page 99.

Enter the name of the computer to which the printer is directly connected in the "Remote hostname" field. The name of the queue *on the remote computer* that is associated with the remote printer goes in the "remote queue" field. Select **Next**, and press Space. Now turn to Section 6.5.5 on page 99 to continue.

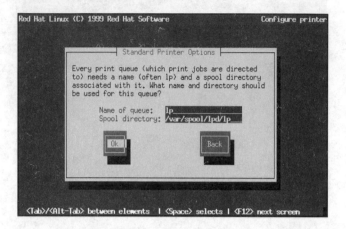

Figure 6.8: Standard Printer Options

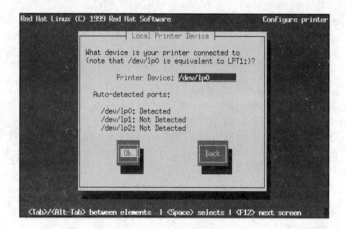

Figure 6.9: Local Printer Device

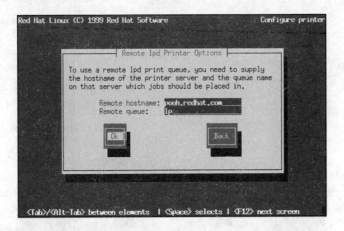

Figure 6.10: Remote lpd Printer Options

6.5.3 SMB, Windows 95/NT Printers

If you selected "SMB, Windows 95/NT" as your printer's connection type, you'll see a dialog box similar to the one in Figure 6.11 on the following page. Enter the necessary information in the fields provided. Select **Next**, and press [Space].

6.5.4 NetWare Printers

If you selected "NetWare" as your printer's connection type, you'll see a dialog box similar to the one in Figure 6.12 on the next page. Enter the necessary information in the fields provided. Select **Next**, and press [Space].

6.5.5 Finalizing Printer Setup

Next, you'll see a dialog box entitled "Configure Printer" (see Figure 6.13 on page 101). Select the printer type that most closely matches your printer. Select **Next**, and press [Space] to continue.

After selecting the printer type, you will see a dialog box similar to the one in Figure 6.14 on page 101. Set the paper size and resolution appropriately. The **Fix stair-stepping of text** check box should be checked if your printer does not automatically perform a carriage return after each line.

If your printer supports it, you will see a dialog box in which you can configure the color options of your printer, or a similar one, in which you can configure the color and resolutions options of the uniprint driver your printer uses. Set these options appropriately.

Figure 6.11: SMB and Windows95/NT Printer Options

Figure 6.12: Netware Printer Options

Figure 6.13: Configure Printer

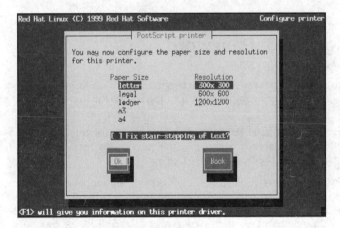

Figure 6.14: Printer Settings

Finally, you'll see a dialog box that contains all the information pertaining to your printer (see Figure 6.15). Verify that the information is correct. If everything looks OK, select **Done**. If you need to make changes, select **Edit**. You can also select **Cancel** if you'd rather not configure a printer at this time.

Figure 6.15: Verifying Printer Information

If you select **Done**, you will be given the option to configure another printer, or you may continue with the installation.

6.6   Setting a Root Password

The installation program will next prompt you to set a *root password* for your system (see Figure 6.16 on the next page). You'll use the root password to log into your Red Hat Linux system for the first time.

The root password must be at least six characters long; the password you type is not echoed to the screen. You must enter the password twice; if the two passwords do not match, the installation program will ask you to enter them again.

You ought to make the root password something you can remember, but not something that is easy for someone else to guess. Your name, your phone number, `qwerty`, `password`, `root`, `123456`, and `anteater` are all examples of poor passwords. Good passwords mix numerals with upper and lower case letters and do not contain dictionary words: `Aard387vark` or `420BMttNT`, for example. Remember that the password is case-sensitive. Write down this password and keep it in a secure place.

Please Note: The *root* user (also known as the *superuser*) has complete access to the entire system; for this reason, logging in as the root user is best done *only* to perform system maintenance or admin-

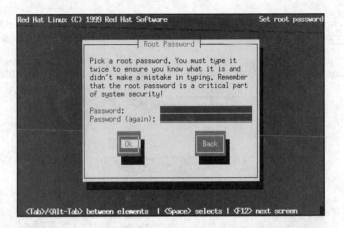

Figure 6.16: Root Password

istration. Please see Chapter 8 on page 119 for instructions on how to add a user account for yourself after you reboot your system. A more basic method of creating a new user account can also be found in the Official Red Hat Linux Getting Started Guide in the `Welcome to Linux` chapter.

6.7 Authentication Configuration

After you have set up your root password, you will have the option of setting up different network password authentications:

- **Enable NIS** allows you to run a group of computers in the same Network Information Service domain with a common password and group file. There are two options here to choose from:

  - **NIS Domain** – this option allows you to specify which domain or group of computers your system will belong to.

  - **NIS Server** – this option causes your computer to use a specific NIS server, rather than "broadcasting" a message to the local area network asking for any available server to host your system.

- **Enable Shadow Passwords** – provides a very secure method of retaining passwords for you. The `/etc/psswd` file is replaced by `/etc/shadow` which is only readable by root.

- **MD5 Password** allows a long password to be used up to 256 characters, instead of the standard eight letters or less.

Please Note: To configure the NIS option, you must be connected to an NIS network. If you are unsure whether or not you are connected to an NIS network, please ask you system administrator.

Unless you are setting up a NIS password, you will notice that both Shadow password and MD5 are selected. We recommend you use both to make your machine as secure as possible (see Figure 6.17).

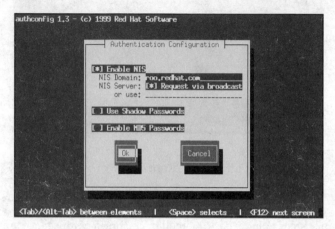

Figure 6.17: Authentication Configuration

6.8   Creating a Boot Diskette

Next, you'll be given the opportunity to create a customized boot diskette for your Red Hat Linux system (see Figure 6.18 on the facing page).

A boot diskette can be handy for a number of reasons:

- **Use It Instead of LILO** – You can use a boot diskette instead of LILO. This is handy if you're trying Red Hat Linux for the first time, and you'd feel more comfortable if the boot process for your other operating system is left unchanged. With a boot diskette, going back to your other operating system is as easy as removing the boot diskette and rebooting.

- **Use It In Emergencies** – The boot diskette can also be used in conjunction with a rescue disk, which will give you the tools necessary to get an ailing system back on its feet again[2].

- **Use It When Another Operating System Overwrites LILO** – Other operating systems may not be as flexible as Red Hat Linux when it comes to supported boot methods. Quite often,

---

[2]To do this, you'll need to create a rescue diskette from the rescue.img image contained in the images directory of your Red Hat Linux CD-ROM. Appendix B on page 237 explains how to do this.

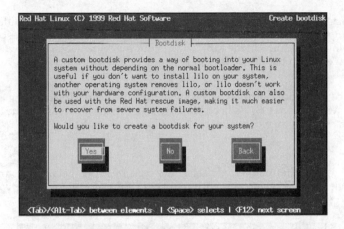

Figure 6.18: Creating a Boot Diskette

installing or updating another operating system can cause the master boot record (originally containing LILO) to be overwritten, making it impossible to boot your Red Hat Linux installation. The boot diskette can then be used to boot Red Hat Linux so you can reinstall LILO.

Given these reasons to create a boot diskette, you should seriously consider doing so. Select **Yes** and press Space to create a boot diskette. Next, you'll see a dialog box directing you to insert a blank diskette in your computer's diskette drive. Select **Ok**, and press Space when you've done so.

After a short delay, your boot diskette will be done. After removing it from your diskette drive, label it clearly. Note that if you would like to create a boot diskette after the installation, you'll be able to do so. If you boot your system with the boot diskette (instead of LILO), make sure you create a new boot diskette if you make any changes to your kernel. For more information, please see the mkbootdisk man page, by typing man mkbootdisk at the shell prompt.

6.9 Installing LILO

Please Note: If you are performing a custom-class installation, please keep reading. If you are performing a workstation-class or server-class installation, this part of the installation process is automatically done for you. Please skip ahead to Section 6.10 on page 108.

In order to be able to boot your Red Hat Linux system, you usually need to install LILO (the LInux LOader). You may install LILO in one of two places:

The Master Boot Record (MBR) is the recommended place to install LILO, unless the MBR already starts another operating system loader, such System Commander or OS/2's Boot Manager. The master boot record is a special area on your hard drive that is automatically loaded by your computer's BIOS, and is the earliest point at which LILO can take control of the boot process. If you install LILO in the MBR, when your machine boots, LILO will present a `boot:` prompt; you can then boot Red Hat Linux or any other operating system you configure LILO to boot (see below).

The first sector of your root partition is recommended if you are already using another boot loader on your system (such as OS/2's Boot Manager). In this case, your other boot loader will take control first. You can then configure that boot loader to start LILO (which will then boot Red Hat Linux).

A dialog box will appear that will let you select the type of LILO installation you desire (see Figure 6.19). Select the location where you wish to install LILO and press **Ok**. If you do not wish to install LILO, press **Skip**.

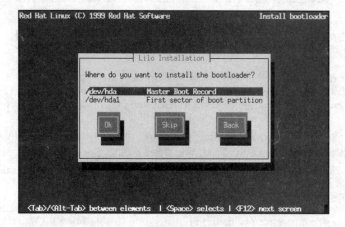

Figure 6.19: Installing LILO

Please Note: If you choose **Skip**, you will not be able to boot your Red Hat Linux system directly, and will need to use another boot method (such as a boot diskette). Use this option only if you know you have another way of booting your Red Hat Linux system!

6.9.1   SMP Motherboards and LILO

This section is specific to SMP motherboards only. If the installer detects a SMP motherboard on your system, it will automatically create two `lilo.conf` entries as opposed to the usual single entry.

One entry will be called `smp` and the other will be called `linux`. The `smp` will boot by default. However, if you have trouble with the smp kernel, you can elect to boot the `linux` entry instead. You will retain all the functionality as before, but you will only be operating with a single processor.

6.9.2 Adding Options to the LILO Boot Command Line

Next, the installation program will ask if you wish to add default options to the LILO boot command (see Figure 6.20). Any options you enter will be passed to the Linux kernel every time it boots. When you reviewed your computer's BIOS settings in Section 2.3.1 on page 10, if you found your computer accesses a hard drive in LBA mode, check **Use linear mode**. Select **Ok** and press (Space) when finished.

Figure 6.20: LILO options

Finally, the installation program will display a screen similar to the one in Figure 6.21 on the following page. Every partition that may be bootable is listed, including partitions used by other operating systems. The "Boot label" column will be filled in with the word linux on the partition holding your Red Hat Linux system's root filesystem. Other partitions may also have boot labels. If you would like to add boot labels for other partitions (or change an existing boot label), use the arrow keys to highlight the desired partition. Then use the (Tab) key to select the **Edit** button, and press (Space). You'll then see a small dialog box permitting you to enter/modify the partition's boot label. Press **Ok** when done.

Please Note: The contents of the "Boot label" column will be what you will need to enter at LILO's Boot: prompt in order to boot the desired operating system. However, if you forget the boot labels defined on your system, you can always press (?) at LILO's Boot: prompt to display a list of defined boot labels.

There is also a column labeled "Default." Only one partition will contain an asterisk under that column. The partition marked as the default will be the partition LILO will boot if there is no user input during the boot process. Initially the root partition for your Red Hat Linux installation will be selected as the default. If you'd like to change this, use the arrow keys to highlight the partition you'd like to make the default, and press (F2). The asterisk should move to the selected partition. When you've finished, select **Ok**, and press (Space).

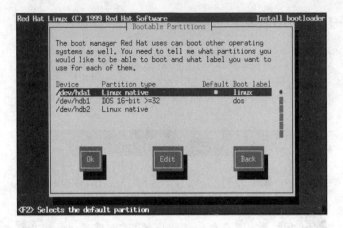

Figure 6.21: Selecting Bootable Partitions

6.9.3 Alternatives to LILO

If you do not wish to use LILO to boot your Red Hat Linux system, there are a few alternatives:

Boot Diskette You can use the boot diskette created by the installation program (if you elected to create one).

LOADLIN can load Linux from MS-DOS; unfortunately, it requires a copy of the Linux kernel (and an initial RAM disk, if you have a SCSI adapter) to be available on an MS-DOS partition. The only way to accomplish this is to boot your Red Hat Linux system using some other method (e.g., from LILO on a diskette) and then copy the kernel to an MS-DOS partition. LOADLIN is available from
`ftp://metalab.unc.edu/pub/Linux/system/boot/dualboot/` and associated mirror sites.

SYSLINUX is an MS-DOS program very similar to LOADLIN; it is also available from
`ftp://metalab.unc.edu/pub/Linux/system/boot/loaders/` and associated mirror sites.

Some commercial bootloaders, such as System Commander, are able to boot Linux (but still require LILO to be installed in your Linux root partition).

6.10 Configuring the X Window System

If you decided to install the X Window System packages, you now will have the opportunity to configure X server for your system. If you did not choose to install the X Window System packages, you may skip ahead to Section 6.11 on the next page.

6.10.1   Configuring an XFree86 Server

If you wish to use XFree86, the installation program launches the Xconfigurator utility.

Xconfigurator first probes your system in an attempt to determine what type of video card you have. Failing that, Xconfigurator will present a list of video cards. Select your video card from the list and press (Enter). If your video card does not appear on the list, XFree86 may not support it. However, if you have technical knowledge about your card, you may choose **Unlisted Card** and attempt to configure it by matching your card's video chipset with one of the available X servers.

Once you have selected your video card, the installation program installs the appropriate XFree86 server, and Xconfigurator presents a list of monitors. If your monitor appears on the list, select it and press (Enter). Otherwise, select **Custom**. If you do select **Custom**, Xconfigurator prompts you to select the horizontal sync range and vertical sync range of your monitor (these values are generally available in the documentation which accompanies your monitor, or from your monitor's vendor or manufacturer).

Caution: It is not recommended to select a monitor "similar" to your monitor unless you are certain that the monitor you are selecting does not exceed the capabilities of your monitor. If you do so, it is possible you may overclock your monitor and damage or destroy it.

Next, Xconfigurator prompts you for the amount of video memory installed on your video card. If you are not sure, please consult the documentation accompanying your video card. It will not damage your video card by choosing more memory than is available, but the XFree86 server may not start correctly if you do.

If the video card you selected might have a video clockchip, Xconfigurator presents a list of clockchips. The recommended choice is **No Clockchip Setting**, since XFree86 can automatically detect the proper clockchip in most cases.

Next, Xconfigurator prompts you to select the video modes you wish to use; select one or more modes by pressing (Space). Xconfigurator then writes a configuration file containing all of your choices to /etc/X11/XF86Config.

Finally, you will see a screen which gives you the option of running the X Windows System when you reboot. If you choose to have X run, GNOME will be the default desktop manager you see.

6.11   Finishing Up...

After you have configured the X Windows System, the installation program will prompt you to prepare your system for reboot (see Figure 6.22 on the following page). Don't forget to remove any diskette that might be in the diskette drive, or CD that might be in the CD-ROM drive if your system is able to boot from the CD-ROM (unless you decided to skip the standard LILO installation, in which case you'll need to use the boot diskette created during the installation).

After your computer's normal power-up sequence has completed, you should see LILO's standard prompt, which is boot:. At the boot: prompt, you can do any of the following things:

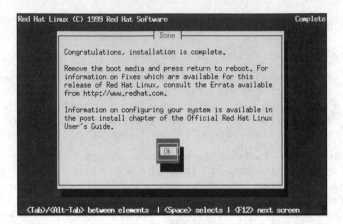

Figure 6.22: Ready for Reboot

- **Pressing** (Enter) – Causes LILO's default boot entry (as defined by the dialog box shown in Figure 6.21 on page 108) to be booted.

- **Entering a Boot Label, followed by** (Enter) – Causes LILO to boot the operating system corresponding to the entered boot label.

- **Doing Nothing** – After LILO's timeout period, (which, by default, is five seconds) LILO will automatically boot the default boot entry.

Do whatever is appropriate to boot Red Hat Linux. You should see one or more screens worth of messages scroll by. Eventually, you should see a `login:` prompt.

Congratulations! Your Red Hat Linux installation is complete!

If you're not sure what to do next, we suggest you begin with the Official Red Hat Linux Getting Started Guide as an introduction to using Linux. The Official Red Hat Linux Getting Started Guide covers topics such as "learning the basics of your system" to "navigating your system" and much more.

7

Finding Documentation

Red Hat Linux includes thousands of pages of online documentation to help you learn how to use the system. The man pages, info documents, and plain text files included provide information on almost every aspect of Linux. If you've installed it, Red Hat Linux also includes documentation produced by the Linux Documentation Project.

7.1 On Line Help

When you are looking for general help on commands and error messages, the best place to start is right on your system. There are several different sources of information at your fingertips:

- **Man Pages** – Authoritative reference material for commands, file formats, and system calls.

- **Package Documentation** – Many packages include additional documentation; RPM can help you find it.

- **HOWTOs and FAQs** – Helpful information from the Linux Documentation Project.

- **The** `locate` **Command** – A command that can help bridge the gap between a command and its documentation.

- `info` **Pages** – Hypertext documentation without the Web.

Let's take a look at each information source.

7.1.1 Man Pages

Almost every command on your system has an associated "man" page. This is documentation that you can get to instantly should you have questions or problems. For example, if you were having trouble with the `ls` command, you could use man to get more information by entering `man ls`. This will bring up the man page for `ls`.

The man page is viewed through the `less` program (which makes it easy to page forward and backward screen by screen), so all of the options to `less` will work while in a man page. The more important keystrokes for `less` are:

- $\boxed{q}$ to quit

- $\boxed{Enter}$ to page down line by line

- $\boxed{Space}$ to page down page by page

- $\boxed{b}$ to page back up by one page

- $\boxed{/}$ followed by a string and $\boxed{Enter}$ to search for a string

- $\boxed{n}$ to find the next occurrence of the previous search

There are times when it's just a lot more convenient to read something from a sheet of paper. Providing you have a working printer, you can print man pages as well. If you don't have Postscript printing capability and just want to print ASCII, you can print man pages with:

```
man COMMAND | lpr
```

If you do have a postscript printer, you will probably want to print with:

```
man -t COMMAND | lpr
```

In both of those commands substitute "COMMAND" for the command you are trying to get help for.

Sometimes you'll find that certain system components have more than one man page. Here is a table showing the sections that are used to divide man pages:

Section	Contents
1	user commands
8	system commands
2	system calls
3	library calls
4	devices
5	file formats
6	games
7	miscellaneous
9	kernel internals
n	Tcl/Tk commands

This is also the order in which the sections are searched. This can be important; here's an example:

Let's say that you want to see the man page for the swapon system call. So, you type man swapon. You will actually get the man page for swapon(8), which is the command used to control swapping. Using the chart above, you can see that what you want is a "system call" and is located in section 2. You can then type man 2 swapon. All of this is because man searches the man directories in the order shown above, which means that the swapon(8) man page would be found before the swapon(2) man page.

You can also search the man pages for strings. You do this using man -k string_to_search_for. This won't work, however, unless the makewhatis database has been created. Under Red Hat Linux, this is done by a cron job overnight. If you don't leave your system running overnight the database won't get created. If that is the case, run the following command as the root user:

```
/etc/cron.weekly/makewhatis.cron
```

Once you've done that (note that it might take a while), you could enter man -k swapon. That command would return:

```
# man -k swapon
swapon, swapoff (2) - start/stop swapping to file/device
swapon, swapoff (8) - enable/disable devices and files for
                      paging and swapping
```

So you can see that there are pages in section 2 and 8 both referring to swapon (and swapoff in this case).

How to Read a Man Page

Man pages provide a great deal of information in very little space. Because of this, they can be difficult to read. Here's a quick overview of the major sections in most man pages:

- **Name** – The name of the program or programs documented in the man page. There may be more than one name, if the programs are closely related.

- **Synopsis** – An overview of the program's command syntax, showing all options and arguments.

- **Description** – A short description of the program's function.

- **Options** – A list of all options, with a short description of each (often combined with the previous section).

- **See Also** – If present, lists the names of other programs that are related in some way to this program.

- **Files** – If present, contains a list of files that are used and/or modified by the program.

- **History** – If present, indicates important milestones in the program's development.

- **Authors** – The people that wrote the program.

If you are new to Linux, don't expect to be able to use man pages as tutorials; they are meant as concise reference material. Trying to learn about Linux using the man pages is similar to trying to learn how to speak English from reading a dictionary. But there are other sources of information that may be more useful to those people just starting out with Linux; let's continue our search for documentation...

7.1.2   Package Documentation

Many packages have README files and other documentation as part of the source package. Packages built for Red Hat Linux define a standard place to install those documents so that you don't have to search through the sources to find the documents. Every package containing documentation (other than man pages, and files that need to be in specific locations) places their documentation in a subdirectory of /usr/doc.

The name of the subdirectory depends on the package name and version number. For example, the tin package might be at version 1.22. Therefore, the path to its documentation would be /usr/doc/tin-1.22.

For the most part, the documents in /usr/doc are in ASCII. You can view them with more *filename* or less *filename*.

Having this special documentation area can be handy, but what if you're looking for documentation on a specific command (or file), and you don't know what package that command came from? No problem! Take, for example, the file /usr/bin/rtin. You're not sure what package it's part of, but you'd like to learn a bit more about it. Simply enter:

```
rpm -qdf /usr/bin/rtin
```

This command will return a listing of all the documentation (including man pages) from the package containing the file /usr/bin/rtin. RPM is capable of a lot more than this simple example. For more information on RPM, turn to Chapter 9 on page 173.

Of course, maybe this kind of information is not exactly what you're looking for. Maybe you're more interested in task-oriented documentation. If so, read on...

7.1.3 HOWTOs and FAQs

If you elected to install it, most of the contents of the Linux Documentation Project (LDP) are available in /usr/doc on your system.

The directory /usr/doc/HOWTO contains the ASCII versions of all the available HOWTOs at the time your Red Hat Linux CD-ROM was mastered. These files are viewable by using the less command.

```
less Installation-HOWTO
```

You may also encounter files that end with .gz. They are compressed with gzip to save space, so you'll need to decompress them before reading. One way of reading compressed HOWTOs without cluttering your disk with uncompressed versions is to use zless:

```
zless 3Dfx-HOWTO.gz
```

The zless command uses the same keystrokes as less, so you can easily move back and forth through a HOWTO.

/usr/doc/HOWTO/mini contains the ASCII versions of all the available mini-HOWTOs. They are not compressed and can be viewed with more or less.
/usr/doc/HOWTO/other-formats/html contains the HTML versions of all the HOWTOs and the *Linux Installation and Getting Started* guide. To view things here, just use the web browser of your choice.

/usr/doc/FAQ contains ASCII versions (and some HTML versions) of some popular FAQs, including the RedHat-FAQ. They can be viewed using more or less, or (in the case of HTML files) with the web browser of your choice.

7.1.4 The "locate" Command

When you don't know the full name of a command or file, but need to find it, you can usually find it with locate. locate uses a database to find all files on your system. Normally, this database gets built from a cron job every night. This won't happen, however, if your machine isn't booted into Linux all the time. So, if that is the case, you may occasionally want to run the following command:

```
/etc/cron.daily/updatedb.cron
```

You will need to be root on your system when doing that. That will allow locate to work properly.

So, if you know you need to find all the "finger" files, you could run:

```
locate finger
```

It should return something like:

```
/usr/bin/finger
/usr/lib/irc/script/finger
/usr/man/man1/finger.1
/usr/man/man8/in.fingerd.8
/usr/sbin/in.fingerd
```

One thing to note, however, is that locate not only returns hits based on file name, but also on path name. So if you have a /home/djb/finger/ directory on your system, it would get returned along with all files in the directory.

7.1.5   "info" Pages

While man is the most ubiquitous documentation format, info is much more powerful. It provides hypertext links to make reading large documents much easier and many features for the documentation writer. There are some very complete info documents on various aspects of Red Hat (especially the portions from the GNU project).

To read info documentation, use the info program without any arguments. It will present you with a list of available documentation. If it can't find something, it's probably because you don't have the package installed that includes that documentation. Install it with RPM and try again.

If you're comfortable using emacs, it has a built in browser for info documentation. Use the Ctrl-h i key sequence to see it.

The info system is a hypertext based system. Any highlighted text that appears is a link leading to more information. Use Tab to move the cursor to the link, and press Enter to follow the link. Pressing p returns you to the previous page, n moves you to the next page, and U goes up one level of documentation. To exit info, press Ctrl-x Ctrl-c (control-x followed by control-c).

The best way to learn how to use info is to read the info documentation on it. If you read the first screen that info presents you'll be able to get started.

7.2 Help from the Internet Community

7.2.1 Red Hat Mailing Lists

If you can't find help for your problem on line and you have WWW access, you should see `http://www.redhat.com/support/mailing-lists/`. Here you can search the archives of the redhat-list. Many questions have already been answered there.

The subscription addresses for our lists follow this format:

```
<list-name>-request@redhat.com
```

Simply replace `<list-name>` with one of the following:

```
apollo-list
applixware-list
axp-list
blinux-list
cde-list
gnome-announce
gtk-list
hurricane-list
linux-alert
linux-security
m68k-list
pam-list
redhat-announce-list
redhat-devel-list
redhat-install-list
redhat-list
redhat-ppp-list
rpm-list
sound-list
sparc-list
```

To subscribe, send mail to the address of the list you want to subscribe to with `subscribe` in the `Subject:` line.

To unsubscribe, send mail to the address of the list you want to unsubscribe from with `unsubscribe` in the `Subject:` line.

Then to send mail to the list, you just send it to the address above without the `-request` in the name.

7.2.2 USENET Newsgroups

Another good source of help is the `comp.os.linux` hierarchy on USENET. If you are familiar with news, you should check it out.

Red Hat-Specific Newsgroups

Red Hat Software currently hosts a number of newgroups specifically for users of our software. You can either read these groups directly from news.redhat.com, or ask your news admin to add the redhat.* hierarchy to their news server.

8

System Configuration

After installing your Red Hat Linux system, it's easy to think that the decisions you made during the installation are engraved in granite, never to be changed again. Nothing could be further from the truth!

One of the main strengths of Linux is that the operating system can be configured to do just about anything. Here at Red Hat Software, we try to make system configuration as easy and accessible as possible. To that end, we've worked hard on two fronts:

- By developing system configuration tools in-house;

- By working with outside developers of world-class system configuration tools.

Anyone familiar with Red Hat Linux over the years has probably seen what we call our "control panel" system configuration tools. These tools have been developed by Red Hat Software to make system configuration easier. And while these tools *do* make life easier for the Red Hat Linux user, we began a search for a system configuration tool with even more flexibility and power.

Our search ended with the inclusion of Linuxconf into Red Hat Linux 5.1 in June 1998. Now, with this version of Red Hat Linux, we've been able to more fully document the popular aspects of system configuration using Linuxconf.

Note that we said "popular aspects." One of Linuxconf's greatest strengths – the incredible range of configuration options under its control – is actually a liability when it comes time to document them all. Rest assured, however, that we will continue to expand Linuxconf documentation as new versions of Red Hat Linux are released.

But what about the control panel tools? They're still there. While Linuxconf at present can do nearly everything the control panel tools can, there are two areas in which the control panel still holds the upper hand:

- Printer configuration

- Kernel daemon control

To that end, we've left the control panel documentation in this manual as the second half of this chapter.

But now, let's take a look at Linuxconf...

8.1   System Configuration With Linuxconf

Linuxconf is a utility that allows you to configure and control various aspects of your system, and is capable of handling a wide range of programs and tasks. Fully documenting Linuxconf could be a separate book in its own right and certainly more than we can cover in this chapter. So we'll focus on those areas that address common tasks such as adding new users and getting connected to a network.

More information on Linuxconf, including its status, most recent release, and more can be found at the Linuxconf Project homepage:

`http://www.solucorp.qc.ca/linuxconf/`

This website includes fairly extensive information on Linuxconf including description, rationale, history, list of contacts and a lot of other information in addition to the software itself. It is maintained by Linuxconf's creator, Jacques Gelinas, so it's the best source of Linuxconf information on the Internet.

Notation

Accurately describing the location of specific screens within Linuxconf is easy, but lengthy given Linuxconf's hierarchical nature. If the structure was a family tree, most of the data entry screens are in the fourth generation. To describe the path to the screen where you would add new users to your system, we could write this out as:

> "Select the Config option from the main screen, then the users accounts option off of that; on the users accounts screen that appears, select the normal option and then select the user accounts option."

Rather lengthy and not immediately accessible. Given the structural similarity to a family tree, we could write it as:

"main window beget Users accounts tab, beget Normal tab..."

But that's an awful lot of begets. Instead, we'll use the following format:

(Config) ⇒ (Users accounts) ⇒ (Normal) ⇒ (User accounts)

It's much more concise and clear. It assumes as its base the Linuxconf entry screen. The other advantage to this approach is that it's not interface specific, so regardless of which interface you're using, you know exactly where the information is. You're happy, we're happy, and the trees which lobbied against lengthy descriptions are happy. What could be better?

8.1.1 Running Linuxconf

To run Linuxconf you must have root access. If you are logged in as something other than root, there is an easy way to handle this situation. Use the su command to become root.

In case you aren't familiar with it yet, type su at the shell prompt and hit (Enter). The password it asks you for is the root account's. Once you've entered that correctly you'll have phenomenal cosmic power! Well, complete control of your system at any rate[1]. Anyway, type linuxconf at the shell prompt to begin the program. Linuxconf has the following user interfaces:

- **Command line** – Linuxconf's command-line mode is handy for manipulating your system's configuration in scripts.

- **Character-Cell** – Using the same user interface style as the Red Hat Linux installation program, the character-cell interface makes it easy to navigate your way through Linuxconf, even if you aren't running X.

- **X Window-Based** – Linuxconf can take advantage of X, and give you an easy-to-use "point and click" tree menu interface. This form of navigation is new in Linuxconf! Please see the **Tree Menu Interface** subsection of section 8.1.1 on the next page for more information. This is the interface we'll use for illustrations throughout this chapter.

- **Web-Based** – A Web-based interface makes remote system administration a breeze. The Web interface will even play nice with the Lynx character-cell Web browser!

Linuxconf will normally start in either character-cell or X mode, depending on the DISPLAY environment variable. The first time you run Linuxconf, an introductory message will be shown; although it is only displayed once, accessing help from the main screen will give you the same basic information.

Linuxconf has context-specific help available. For information on any specific aspect of Linuxconf, please select **Help** from the screen you'd like help with. Note that not all help screens are complete at this time; as help screens are updated, they will be included in subsequent versions of Linuxconf.

---

[1]One could argue that it's pretty much the same thing.

Tree Menu Interface

The new version of Linuxconf comes complete with a tree menu interface.

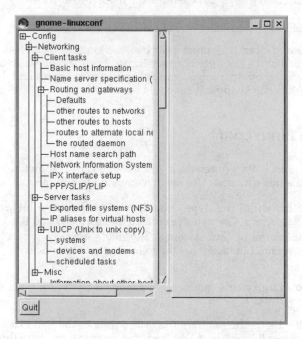

Figure 8.1: Linuxconf Entry Screen

Finding the appropriate panel should be simple and fast. You can collapse and expand sections by clicking on the menu item icons. Click the icon once to activate it for that particular sub-menu. A single click will then collapse it; another single click will expand it again.

Selected entries will appear as tabs in the right-hand panel and will remain there until closed. This will greatly reduce the clutter of windows on your desktop that Linuxconf has typically caused. If you end up with more tabs open than you like, just hit **Cancel** on the bottom of each tab to close it without making any changes, or **Accept** to implement them.

Please Note: If you've grown fond of your previous X Window System interface, it's still available. To return to it:

1. Start Linuxconf by typing `linuxconf` at the shell prompt

2. Open (Control) ⇒ (Control files and systems) ⇒ (Linuxconf modules)

3. De-select the **This module is active** check box for the **treemenu** module.

4. Click **Accept**

5. Click **Quit**

6. Restart Linuxconf

Enabling Web-Based Linuxconf Access

For security reasons, Web-based access to Linuxconf is disabled by default. Before attempting to access Linuxconf with a Web browser, you'll need to enable access. Here's how to do it from the text-mode interface:

1. Start Linuxconf by typing `linuxconf` at the shell prompt

2. Open [Config] ⇒ [Networking] ⇒ [Misc] ⇒ [Linuxconf network access]

3. In the **Linuxconf html access control** dialog box, enter the hostname of any computers that should be allowed access to Linuxconf. This would also include your own system, if you wish to use the Web-based interface locally. Web accesses related to Linuxconf may be logged to your system's `htmlaccess.log` file by selecting the check box shown.

4. Select the **Accept** button and press [Space]. Then select the **Quit** buttons on each dialog box to back out of the menu hierarchy. When you come to a dialog box labeled **Status of the system**, press [Enter] to take the default action, which is to apply the changes you've made.

At this point, Web-based access has been enabled. To test it out, go to one of the systems that you added to the access control list. Launch your Web browser, and enter the following URL:

```
http://<host>:98/
```

(Replacing `<host>` with your system's hostname, of course.) You should see the main Linuxconf page. Note that you will need to enter your system's root password to gain access beyond the first page.

Adding a User Account – Quick Reference

1. Start Linuxconf by typing `linuxconf` at the shell prompt

2. Open [Config] ⇒ [Users accounts] ⇒ [Normal] ⇒ [User accounts]

3. Select **Add**

4. Enter the account's login and full names

5. Enter information in other fields only as necessary

6. Select **Accept**

7. Enter the initial password for the account

8. Reenter the initial password for the account in the **Confirmation** field

9. Select **Accept**

Adding a User Account – General Overview

Adding a user is one of the most basic tasks you will encounter in administering your system. To add a user:

- Start Linuxconf by typing `linuxconf` at the shell prompt.

- Open [Config] ⇒ [Users accounts] ⇒ [Normal] ⇒ [User accounts] This will open the **Users accounts** tab (see figure 8.3 on page 126).

- If you have more than 15 accounts on the system, Linuxconf will provide you with a filter screen (see figure 8.2 on the next page). You can use this to select a smaller range of accounts than the full list. To get the full list, select **Accept** without changing any of the parameters. For detailed information on the various filters, select the **Help** button on the **Filter control** screen.

- Select **Add**. This will open the **User account creation** tab (see figure 8.4 on page 127).

The **User account creation** tab is where you enter all the information on the new account. There are a number of fields you should be aware of, some required, some optional.

Required Fields:

- **Login name** – the name of the account. Usually all lowercase letters. First or last names, initials or some combination thereof are fairly common login names. For a user named John T. Smith, "smith," "john," "jts," or "jsmith" would be common user names. Of course "spike" or something else works just fine, too. You can also use numbers, so "jts2" would be fine if you had a second person with the same initials. There is no default for this field.

Optional Fields:

- **Full name** – this is the name of the user or the account. For an individual, it would be their name, "John T. Smith" for example. If the account represents a position rather than a person, the full name might be the title. So an account called "webmaster" might have a full name of "Red Hat Webmaster" or just "Webmaster." There is no default for this field.

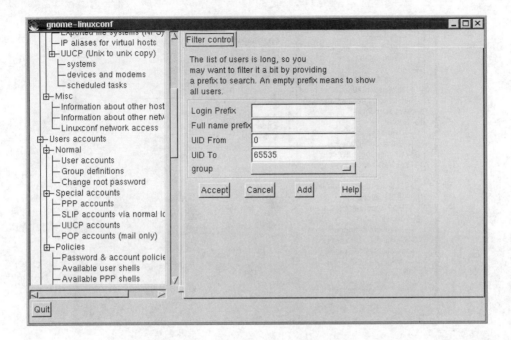

Figure 8.2: Filter Control Screen

- **group** – here you can specify the group associated with the account. The default is a group that's the same as the login name. So "jsmith" would have the group "jsmith."

- **Supplementary groups** – here is where you can specify any additional groups. We suggest that if you want to add a user to a group or groups, you do so here, rather than changing the **group** field. Group names should be separated by spaces. The default for this field is blank, meaning no supplementary groups.

- **Home directory** – specifies the home or login directory for the account. The default is /home/*login*, where *login* is replaced by the login name. A home directory is your starting point in the directory structure when you log in, or if in X, for each xterm window opened. This is also where account specific preference files are stored.

- **Command interpreter** – specifies the location of the command interpreter. Command interpreters are usually referred to as shells. The default is displayed in the drop down box.

- **User ID** – the number associated with each user account. This is automatically generated by the system when the account is created.

The **User account creation** screen has a number of fields; only the login name is required, though filling in the **Full name** field is strongly recommended. Once you have entered the login name and

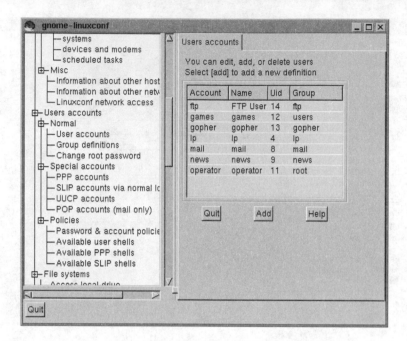

Figure 8.3: Users Accounts Screen

any other desired information select the **Accept** button at the bottom of the screen. If you decide against creating a new user, hit **Cancel** instead.

Upon hitting **Accept** Linuxconf will prompt you to enter the password. There is also a field called **Confirmation** where you will need to type the password again. This is to prevent you from mistyping the password. Passwords must be at least 6 characters in length. They may contain numbers as well as a mix of lowercase and uppercase letters. Hit **Accept** when finished.

Modifying a User Account – Quick Reference

Please Note: Although you can change the settings in any user account, it is usually a bad idea to change the settings in a pre-created account. It is best to change settings and explore options in an account that you have created yourself.

1. Start Linuxconf by typing linuxconf at the shell prompt.

2. Open Config ⇒ Users accounts ⇒ Normal ⇒ User accounts.

3. Select the user account.

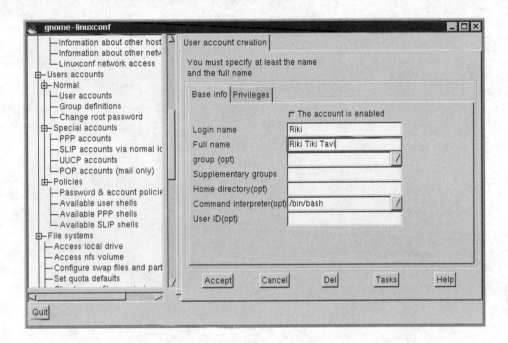

Figure 8.4: User Account Creation

4. Modify entries as desired.

5. Select **Accept**.

Modifying a User Account – General Overview

- Start Linuxconf by typing `linuxconf` at the shell prompt.

- Open [Config] ⇒ [Users accounts] ⇒ [Normal] ⇒ [User accounts]. This will open the **Users accounts** tab (see figure 8.3 on the preceding page).

- If you have more than 15 accounts on the system, Linuxconf will provide you with a filter screen (see figure 8.2 on page 125). You can use this to select a smaller range of accounts than the full list. To get the full list, select **Accept** without changing any of the parameters. For detailed information on the various filters, select the **Help** button on the **Filter control** screen.

- Select the account you wish to modify. This will open the **User information** tab.

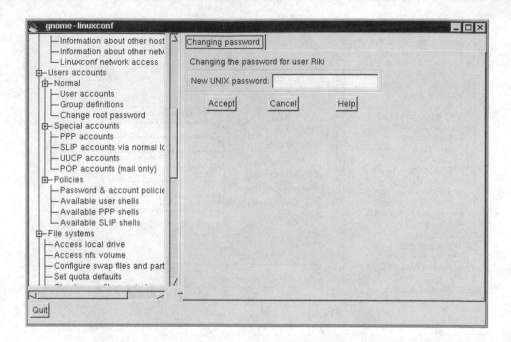

Figure 8.5: Change Password Screen

On the **User information** screen, the information can be changed as desired. To implement the changes select **Accept**. If you decide against making any changes select **Cancel**. This guarantees that no changes are made.

Changing a User's Password – Quick Reference

1. Start Linuxconf by typing `linuxconf` at the shell prompt.

2. Open (Config) ⇒ (Users accounts) ⇒ (Normal) ⇒ (User accounts).

3. Select the user account.

4. Select **Passwd**.

5. Enter the user's new password.

6. Reenter the user's new password in the **Confirmation** field.

7. Select **Accept**.

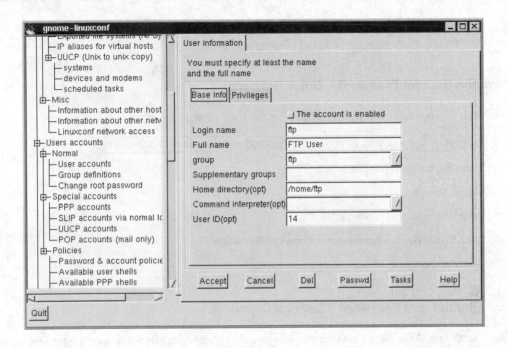

Figure 8.6: User Information Screen

Changing a User's Password – General Overview

- Start Linuxconf by typing `linuxconf` at the shell prompt.

- Open [Config] ⇒ [Users accounts] ⇒ [Normal] ⇒ [User accounts]. This will open the **Users accounts** tab (see figure 8.3 on page 126).

- If you have more than 15 accounts on the system, Linuxconf will provide you with a filter screen (see figure 8.2 on page 125). You can use this to select a smaller range of accounts than the full list. To get the full list, select **Accept** without changing any of the parameters. For detailed information on the various filters, select the **Help** button on the **Filter control** screen.

- Select the account whose password you wish to change. This will open the **User information** tab (see figure 8.6).

- Select **Passwd** from the options at the bottom of the screen.

Linuxconf will then prompt you to enter the new password. There is also a field called **Confirmation** where you will need to type the password again. This is to prevent you from mistyping the password. Passwords must be at least 6 characters in length. They may contain numbers as well as a mix of lowercase and uppercase letters. If you decide against changing the password, just hit **Cancel**. Once you have entered the new password select **Accept**.

Changing the root Password – Quick Reference

1. Start Linuxconf by typing `linuxconf` at the shell prompt.

2. Open [Config] ⇒ [Users accounts] ⇒ [Normal] ⇒ [Change root password].

3. Enter the current root password.

4. Select **Accept**.

5. Enter the new root password.

6. Reenter the new root password in the **Confirmation** field.

7. Select **Accept**.

Changing the root Password – General Overview

Changing the roots password isn't handled in the same manner as changing a user's password. Because of both the importance and security considerations surrounding root access, Linuxconf requires you to verify that you currently have access to the root account.

- Start Linuxconf by typing `linuxconf` at the shell prompt.

- Open [Config] ⇒ [Users accounts] ⇒ [Normal] ⇒ [Change root password].

The screen is a little confusing because neither the title, nor the description really explains the screen's purpose. Linuxconf seems to be asking for the new password, which isn't actually the case. Instead, Linuxconf wants the current root password to verify access to the root account. Linuxconf does require root access to run, but once running there's nothing to keep anyone from sitting down at the computer if the person using Linuxconf steps out for a minute. The potential pitfalls are extensive! If the person who was originally using Linuxconf logs out of root, they won't be able to get back into it. A lack of validation would also give free reign over the computer to whoever had changed root's password.

Once you have entered root's current password, it will prompt you for a new password. There is also a field called **Confirmation** where you will need to type the password again (see figure 8.5 on page 128). This is to prevent you from mistyping the password. Passwords must be at least 6 characters in length. They may contain numbers as well as a mix of lowercase and uppercase letters. If you decide against changing the root password, just hit **Cancel**. Once you have entered the new password select **Accept**. The change takes place immediately and is effective not only for logging in as root, but also for becoming root using the `su` command.

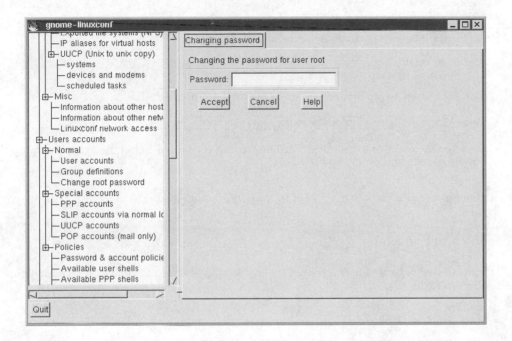

Figure 8.7: Root Password Verification Screen

Disabling a User Account – Quick Reference

1. Start Linuxconf by typing `linuxconf` at the shell prompt.

2. Open [Config] ⇒ [Users accounts] ⇒ [Normal] ⇒ [User accounts].

3. Select the account.

4. De-select **the account is enabled** check box.

5. Select **Accept**.

Disabling a User Account – General Overview

Why disable an account? Good question! There's no single answer, but we can provide some reasons why this option is available. The biggest reason is security. For example, you may have created a special account to be used by clients, co-workers, or friends to access specific files on your system. This account gets used from time to time, but should only be used when you know there's a need. Leaving an unused account around is a target for people who'd want to break into your system.

Deleting it requires you to recreate it every time you want to use it. Disabling an account solves both problems by allowing you to simply select or de-select a check-box.

To disable an account:

- Start Linuxconf by typing `linuxconf` at the shell prompt.
- Open (Config) ⇒ (Users accounts) ⇒ (Normal) ⇒ (User accounts).
- De-select the check-box that states that **The account is enabled**. Select the **Accept** button at the bottom of the window and you're all set.

The account is disabled and can be enabled later using a similar method.

Enabling a User Account

By default, all newly created user accounts are enabled. If you need to enable an account, you can use Linuxconf to do it.

- Start Linuxconf by typing `linuxconf` at the shell prompt.
- Open (Config) ⇒ (Users accounts) ⇒ (Normal) ⇒ (User accounts).
- Select the account you want to enable.
- Select the **The account is enabled** check-box and then select **Accept** at the bottom of the screen.

Deleting a User Account – Quick Reference

1. Start Linuxconf by typing `linuxconf` at the shell prompt.
2. Open (Config) ⇒ (Users accounts) ⇒ (User accounts).
3. Select the account you wish to delete.
4. On the **User information** screen select **Del**.
5. On the **Deleting account...** screen, choose the appropriate option for the account's data.
6. Select **Accept**.

Deleting a User Account – General Overview

Please Note: While there are a couple options that let you retain files associated with an account, any information or files deleted are gone and effectively unrecoverable. Take care when using this option!

To delete an account:

- Start Linuxconf by typing `linuxconf` at the shell prompt.

- Open (Config) ⇒ (Users accounts) ⇒ (User accounts).

- On the **User accounts** screen (see figure 8.3 on page 126) select the account you wish to delete.

- At the bottom of the **User information** screen (see figure 8.6 on page 129) select **Del** to delete the account.

Linuxconf will then prompt you with a list of options.

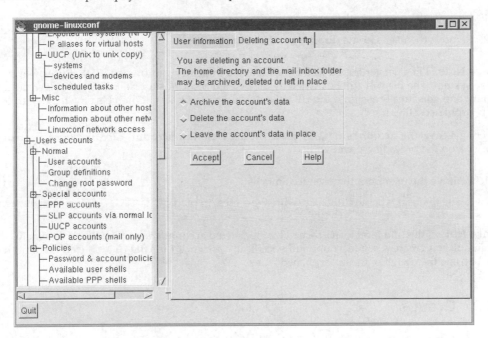

Figure 8.8: Deleting Account Screen

The default option is to archive the account's data. The archive option has the following effects:

1. Removes the user from the user accounts list;

2. Takes everything contained in the user's home directory and archives it (using tar and gzip compression), storing the resulting file in a directory called `oldaccounts`. For an account named `useraccount` the file name would be similar to:

   `useraccount-1999-10-10-497.tar.gz`

   The date indicates when the account was deleted, and the number following it is the ID of the process that actually performed the deletion. The `oldaccounts` directory is created in the same place as all of your user directories, and is created automatically the first time you remove a user account using this option.

3. Files not contained in the user's home directory, but owned by that user remain. The file is owned by the deleted account's user ID (UID). If you create a new account and specifically assign it the UID of a deleted account, it will then become the owner of any remaining files.

Selecting **Delete the account's data** on the **Deleting account** *<accountname>* screen (see figure 8.8 on the page before) will:

1. Remove the user from the user accounts list;

2. Remove the user's home directory and all its contents.

Please Note: Files not contained in the user's home directory, but owned by that user will remain on the system. The file will still be owned by the deleted account's user ID (UID). If you create a new account and specifically assign it the UID of a deleted account, it will then become the owner of any such "orphaned" files.

Selecting **Leave the account's data in place** on the **Deleting account** *<accountname>* screen (see figure 8.8 on the preceding page) will:

1. Remove the user from the user accounts list;

2. Leave the user's home directory (with all its files) in place.

Please Note: Files and directories owned by the deleted account's user ID (UID) will remain on the system. If you create a new account and specifically assign it the UID of a deleted account, it will then become the owner of these "orphaned" files.

8.1.2   Groups

All users belong to one or more groups. Just as each file has a specific owner, each file belongs to a particular group as well. The group might be specific to the owner of the file, or may be a group shared by all users. The ability to read, write or execute a file can be assigned to a group; this is separate from the owner's rights. For example, the owner of a file will be able to write to a document, while other group members may only be able to read it.

Creating a Group – Quick Reference

1. Start Linuxconf by typing `linuxconf` at the shell prompt.

2. Open [Config] $\Rightarrow$ [Users accounts] $\Rightarrow$ [Normal] $\Rightarrow$ [Group definition].

3. Select **Add**.

4. Enter the Group name, and optionally alternate members.

5. Select **Accept**.

Creating a Group – General Overview

To create a new group:

- Start Linuxconf by typing `linuxconf` at the shell prompt.

- Open [Config] $\Rightarrow$ [Users accounts] $\Rightarrow$ [Normal] $\Rightarrow$ [Group definition].

If you have more than 15 groups, you will be given the option to select the groups by providing a prefix.

You may add a group directly from this screen, or move on to the **User groups** screen. To move on select choiceAccept with or without a prefix, to add a new group, hit choiceAdd.

Select **Add** at the bottom of the **User groups** screen.

Enter a group name. You may also wish to specify members of the group and can do so in the **Alternate members** field. The list of users should be space delimited, meaning that each username must have a space between it and the next one. When you're finished, select **Accept** and the group will be created.

Deleting a Group – Quick Reference

1. Start Linuxconf by typing `linuxconf` at the shell prompt.

2. Open [Config] $\Rightarrow$ [Users accounts] $\Rightarrow$ [Normal] $\Rightarrow$ [Group definitions].

3. Select the group you wish to delete.

4. Select **Del**.

5. Confirm deletion.

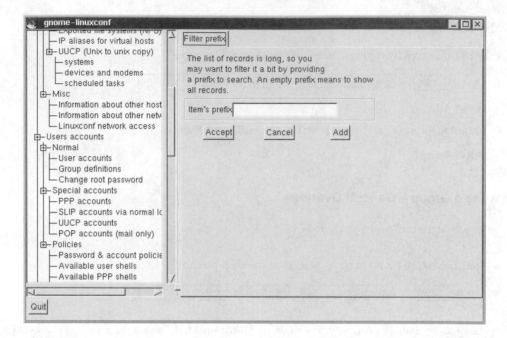

Figure 8.9: Group Filter Screen

Deleting a Group – General Overview

To delete a group:

- Start Linuxconf by typing `linuxconf` at the shell prompt.

- Open $\boxed{\text{Config}} \Rightarrow \boxed{\text{Users accounts}} \Rightarrow \boxed{\text{Normal}} \Rightarrow \boxed{\text{Group definitions}}$.

If you have more than 15 groups, you will be given a filter screen (see figure 8.9) to narrow your choice of groups by specifying a prefix.

- With or without a prefix select **Accept** at the bottom of the screen.

- On the **User groups** screen (see figure 8.10 on the facing page) select the group you wish to delete.

- You'll be presented with the **Group specification** screen (see figure 8.11 on page 138).

- Select **Del** to delete the group. Linuxconf will then prompt you to confirm the deletion. Choose **yes** to delete the group.

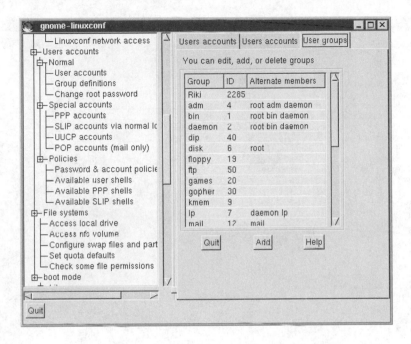

Figure 8.10: User Groups Screen

The group's files will still remain and their respective owners will still have sole control over them. The group name will be replaced with the deleted group's ID. The files may be assigned to a new group by using the chgrp command. More information on chgrp can be found by typing the command info chgrp or man chgrp at the shell prompt. If a new group is created and the deleted group's ID is specified then the new group will have access to the deleted group's files. Don't worry, Linuxconf doesn't recycle old group numbers any more than it does old user IDs, so it won't happen by accident.

Modifying Group Membership

There are two ways to modify the list of users that belong to a group. You can either update each user account itself, or you can update the group definitions. In general, the fastest way is to update each of the group definitions. If you're planning on changing more information for each user than just the group information, then updating each user account may prove easier.

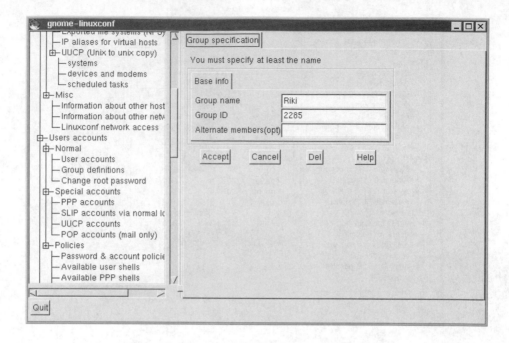

Figure 8.11: Group Specification Screen

Modifying Group Membership – Quick Reference

- Under Groups

1. Start Linuxconf by typing linuxconf at the shell prompt.

2. Open Config ⇒ Users accounts ⇒ Normal ⇒ Group definitions.

3. Select the group to which you wish to add or remove users.

4. Add or remove new users to the **Alternate members(opt)** field; make sure all user names are separated with a space " " character.

5. Select **Accept**.

Modifying Group Membership – Quick Reference

- Under Users

1. Start Linuxconf by typing `linuxconf` at the shell prompt.

2. Open [Config] ⇒ [Users accounts] ⇒ [Normal] ⇒ [User accounts].

3. Select a user to which you wish to add or remove groups.

   Adjust the **Supplementary groups** field accordingly; make sure all the group names are separated with a space " " character.

4. Select **Accept**.

5. Repeat steps 3 through 5 for each additional user to be added.

Modifying Group Membership – General Overview

We'll start by detailing the group definitions method.

- Start Linuxconf by typing `linuxconf` at the shell prompt.

- Open [Config] ⇒ [Users accounts] ⇒ [Normal] ⇒ [Group definitions].

If you have more than 15 groups, you will be given a filter screen (see figure 8.9 on page 136) to narrow your choice of groups by specifying a prefix.

- With or without a prefix, select **Accept** at the bottom of the screen.

- Select the group you wish to modify. This will open the **Group specification** screen (see figure 8.11 on the preceding page).

- Add or remove each user from the **Alternate members** field. Make sure that all of the user names are separated by a space " " character.

- Once you've done this select **Accept** which can be found at the bottom of the screen.

This will automatically update each user account with the group showing up in the **Supplementary groups** field if added or absent if removed.

Adding and removing groups can also be done by modifying each individual user account.

- Start Linuxconf by typing `linuxconf` at the shell prompt.

- Open Config ⇒ Users accounts ⇒ Normal ⇒ User accounts.

If you have more than 15 accounts on the system, Linuxconf will provide you with a filter screen (see figure 8.2 on page 125).

- On the **User accounts** screen (see figure 8.3 on page 126), select a user that you wish to update. You will be presented with the **User information** screen (see figure 8.6 on page 129).

- Add or remove the desired groups from the, **Supplementary groups** field. Each group should be separated by a space " " character.

- Once you've made all the changes you'd like, select **Accept** at the bottom of the screen.

This will automatically update the group definitions. Repeat the process for each user.

8.1.3   CD-ROMs, Diskettes, Hard Drives and Filesystems – the Inside Track

A filesystem is composed of files and directories, all starting from a single root directory. The root directory may contain any number of files and other directories, with each directory in turn following suit. The average filesystem often looks like an inverted tree with the directories as branches and the files as leaves. Filesystems reside on mass storage devices such as diskette drives, hard drives, and CD-ROMs.

For example, a diskette drive on DOS and Windows machines is typically referenced by `A:\`. This describes both the device (`A:`), and the root directory on that device (`\`). The primary hard drive on the same systems is typically referred to as the "C" drive because the device specification for the first hard drive is `C:`. To specify the root directory on the C drive, you would use `C:\`.

Under this arrangement, there are two filesystems – the one on `A:`, and the one on `C:`. In order to specify *any* file on a DOS/Windows filesystem, you must either explicitly specify the device on which the file resides, or it must be on the system's default drive (which is where DOS' infamous C prompt comes from – that's the default drive in a system with a single hard drive).

Under Linux, it is possible to link the filesystems on several mass storage devices together into a single, larger, filesystem. This is done by placing one device's filesystem "under" a directory on another device's filesystem. So while the root directory of a diskette drive on a DOS machine may be referred to as `A:\`, the same drive on a Linux system may be accessible as `/mnt/floppy`.

The process of merging filesystems in this way is known as *mounting*. When a device is mounted, it is then accessible to the system's users. The directory "under" which a mounted device's filesystem becomes accessible is known as the *mount point*. In the previous paragraph's example, `/mnt/floppy` was the diskette drive's mount point. Note that there are no restrictions (other than common conventions) as to the naming of mount points. We could have just as easily mounted the floppy to `/long/path/to/the/floppy/drive`.

One thing to keep in mind is that all of a device's files and directories are relative to its mount point. Consider the following example:

- **A Linux System**

    - / — system root directory
    - /foo — mount point for the CD-ROM

- **A CD-ROM**

    - / — CD-ROM's root directory
    - /images — a directory of images on the CD-ROM
    - /images/old — a directory of old images

So, if the above describes the individual filesystems, and you mount the CD-ROM at /foo, the new operating system directory structure would be:

- **A Linux System (with the CD-ROM mounted)**

    - / — system root directory
    - /foo — CD-ROM root directory
    - /foo/images — a directory of images on the CD-ROM
    - /foo/images/old — a directory of old images

To mount a filesystem make sure to be logged in as root, or become root using the su command. For the latter, type su at the shell prompt and then enter the root password. Once you are root, type mount followed by the device and then the mount point. For example, to mount the first diskette drive on /mnt/floppy, you would type the command mount /dev/fd0 /mnt/floppy.

At installation, Red Hat Linux will create /etc/fstab. This file contains information on devices and associated mount points. The advantage to this file is that it allows you to shorten your mount commands[2]. Using the information in /etc/fstab, you can type mount and then either the mount point or the device. The mount command will look for the rest of the information in /etc/fstab. It's possible to modify this file by hand, or by using Linuxconf. To use Linuxconf, please see Section **Reviewing Your Current Filesystem** immediately following.

Reviewing Your Current Filesystem – Quick Reference

1. Start Linuxconf by typing linuxconf at the shell prompt.

2. Open (Config) ⇒ (File systems) ⇒ (Access local drive) or to look at your network environment: Open (Config) ⇒ (File systems) ⇒ (Access nfs volume).

---

[2]It also controls which filesystems are automatically mounted when the system is booted.

Reviewing Your Current Filesystem – General Overview

We'll start by looking at your current directory structure.

- Start Linuxconf by typing `linuxconf` at the shell prompt.

- Open (Config) ⇒ (File systems) ⇒ (Access local drive).

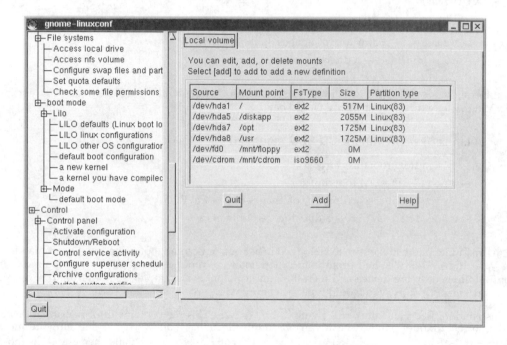

Figure 8.12: Local Volume Screen

The fields are:

- **Source** – The physical hardware; `hd` indicates an IDE hard drive, `fd` indicates a diskette drive, and `cdrom` typically indicates a CD-ROM drive. If your system has a SCSI drive, you will see an `sd` instead. More than one drive of a type are listed by letters, so `hda` represents the first IDE drive, while `hdb` would be the second. In some cases, you'll see numbers following these letters; on hard drives, the numbers represent the partitions on that drive, while for diskette drives, this number refers to the actual unit.

- **Mount point** – This is where in the system the drive is to be mapped when mounted.

- **FsType** – This is where the type of filesystem is indicated. A standard Linux partition uses the ext2 filesystem type. A filesystem type of vfat indicates a DOS filesystem with long filename support, while a fat filesystem type is for DOS filesystems supporting traditional 8.3 filenames. The iso9660 filesystem type indicates a CD-ROM drive, as seen in figure 8.12 on the preceding page.

  Please Note: Red Hat Linux 6.0 can access FAT32 filesystems using the **vfat** filesystem type.

- **Size** – Size indicates the size of the filesystem in megabytes (M). For removable media devices such as diskette and CD-ROM drives the stated size is listed as zero.

- **Partition type** – A description of the filesystem used on that partition.

Filesystems from other machines on a network may also be available. These can range from single small directories to entire volumes. No information on Size or Partition type is available for these partitions, either. Additional information on these filesystems (should you have any available) will be contained under:

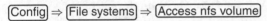

$\boxed{\text{Config}} \Rightarrow \boxed{\text{File systems}} \Rightarrow \boxed{\text{Access nfs volume}}$

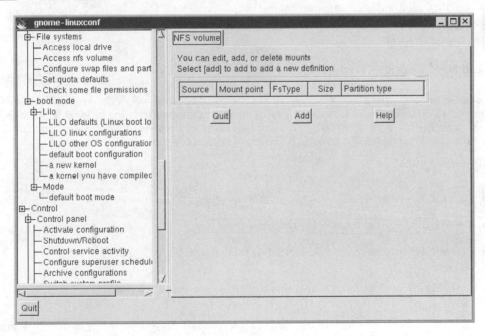

Figure 8.13: NFS Volume Screen

The screen is similar to the **Local volume** screen (see figure 8.12 on the facing page), with some notable differences in the information provided for each entry:

- **Source** – This will be the name of the machine serving the filesystem, followed by the remote directory. For example: `foo:/var/spool/mail` where `foo` is the machine serving the directory, and `/var/spool/mail` is the directory being served.

- **FsType** – This will always be "nfs."

Adding NFS Mounts – Quick Reference

1. Start Linuxconf by typing `linuxconf` at the shell prompt.

2. Open (Config) ⇒ (File systems) ⇒ (Access nfs volume).

3. Select **Add**.

4. Enter the host name where the filesystem resides.

5. Enter the path to the remote filesystem in the **Volume** field. For example, `/var/spool/mail`.

6. Specify the mount point on your system. For example, `/mnt/foo`.
   Select **Accept**.

Adding NFS Mounts – General Overview

NFS stands for Network FileSystem. It is a way for computers to share sections of their local filesystem across a network. These sections may be as small as a single directory, or include thousands of files in a vast hierarchy of directories. For example, many companies will have a single mail server with individuals' mail files served as an NFS mount to each users' local systems.

To add an NFS mount:

- Start Linuxconf by typing `linuxconf` at the shell prompt.

- Open (Config) ⇒ (File systems) ⇒ (Access nfs volume).

- On the **NFS volume** screen (see figure 8.13 on the page before), select **Add**.

The three fields on the **Base** tab are what you'll need to concern yourself with.

- **Server** – The host name of the machine the desired filesystem resides on. For example, `foo.bar.com`.

- **Volume** – The filesystem you wish to add. For example, `/var/spool/mail`.

- **Mount point** – Where in your system you want the remote file system accessible from. For example, `/mnt/mail`.

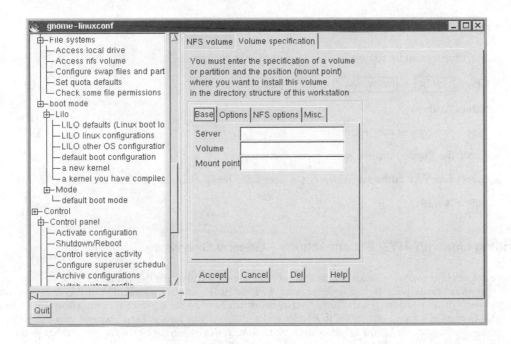

Figure 8.14: Volume Specification Screen

This is all you need to get the mount created. Linuxconf will update your `/etc/fstab` file accordingly. If you are aware of additional requirements, please read the help file on the **Volume specification** screen and see the `mount` man page for more information.

Once you have entered the information, select **Accept**.

8.1.4 Getting Connected (Network Configuration)

The first thing to determine when getting hooked up is whether you're connecting to a local area network, such as a group of computers in an office, or a wide area network, such as the Internet. Before continuing, it's important to know what hardware you have and how you intend to connect. If you're going to dial into another computer, then make sure your modem is installed and that the cables are arranged properly. If you're using a network card, make sure it is installed properly and that the cables are correctly connected. Regardless of what network configuration you specify, if every phone line or cable is not in place, you'll never get connected. We'll start with modem connections and then move on to using network cards.

Adding Modem/PPP/SLIP connections – Quick Reference

1. Start Linuxconf by typing `linuxconf` at the shell prompt.

2. Open [Config] ⇒ [Networking] ⇒ [PPP/SLIP/PLIP].

3. Select **Add**.

4. Select the type of connection.

5. Enter the Phone number, login name and password.

6. Select **Use PAP authentication** only if necessary (only available for PPP accounts).

7. Select **Accept**.

Adding Modem/PPP/SLIP connections – General Overview

There are several pieces of information you will need to get from your ISP (Internet Service Provider) or systems administrator before getting your PPP or SLIP account working. In the case of some providers, you may have to sort through directions on how to set up a PPP connection on a Linux system. Some ISPs are ill-equipped to handle individuals using Linux. Don't worry, you can still get connected; you just need some additional information from your ISP. The following is what you need for a connection with Red Hat Linux. The ISP representatives may respond that you don't need this information, or may suggest that you need more than this. Red Hat has streamlined the information needed using intelligent defaults and tools such as Linuxconf to simplify this process for you. Unless they have a document specifically for Red Hat Linux, just request the information below and go from there. Specifically, you'll need:

- the IP address for a domain nameserver (DNS);

- the telephone number to dial;

- your login and password;

- an IP address for your machine if the network you are connecting to isn't going to provide you with a dynamic one;

- whether or not your ISP uses an authentication method such as PAP, CHAP or MS-CHAP. If so, you will need a "secret" to enable authentication. The secret will be a word or sequence of characters. CHAP and MS-CHAP are not currently supported using Linuxconf, and are rarely used.

Additional information which may be helpful, but isn't necessary includes a secondary nameserver address, and a search domain. Once you have all this information, you're ready to get connected.

- Start Linuxconf by typing `linuxconf` at the shell prompt.

- Open [Config] ⇒ [Networking] ⇒ [PPP/SLIP/PLIP].

- Select **Add**.

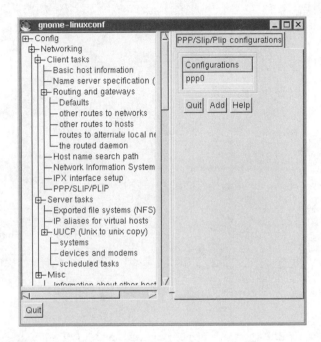

Figure 8.15: PPP/SLIP/PLIP Configurations Screen

Initially there won't be any configurations specified. When you select **Add** you will be given a choice between PPP, SLIP and PLIP.

PPP is the most commonly used interface and is the default. To set up a PPP connection select **PPP** and hit **Accept**.

You'll see the following fields:

- Phone number - number used to access to remote system;

- Modem port - indicates where your modem is. Should already be set.

- Use PAP authentication (check box) - check if you know that the system you are dialing into requires this;

- Login name - your login name for the PPP account;

- Password - your password for the PPP account.

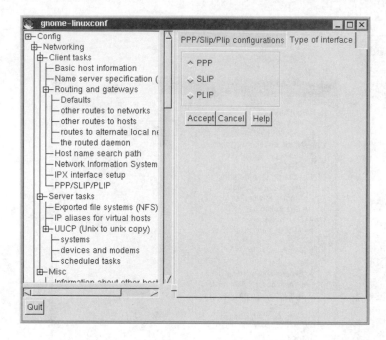

Figure 8.16: Type of Interface Screen

Notice that the title bar is **PPP interface ppp0**. ppp0 is the first PPP interface, ppp1 would be the second and so on. It's important to keep track of which interface you're using if you have more than one. SLIP connections use sl instead of ppp for their interface prefix. With the exception of a PAP authentication option, the entry screens for adding a PPP or a SLIP account are identical.

Enter the complete phone number for the remote machine, and make sure to include any numbers required to access outside lines. For example, if you need to dial "9" and then the number, and the computer you're connecting to has a telephone number of "555-0111", then you'd enter "95550111". The next thing it asks you for is the modem port. This is a drop down box of available ports. If you're using a dual-boot Linux/Windows system and you know the COM port your modem is on, the following map may be of use:

Map to Windows COM ports are as follows:

- cua0 – COM1: under MS-DOS;

- cua1 – COM2: under MS-DOS;

- cua2 – COM3: under MS-DOS;

- cua3 – COM4: under MS-DOS.

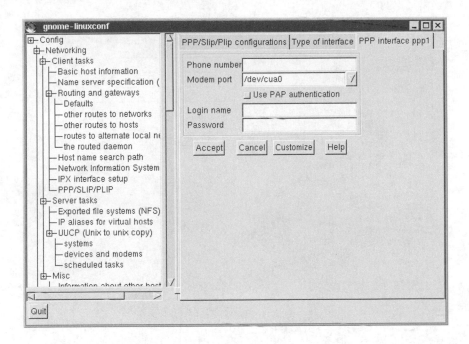

Figure 8.17: PPP Interface Screen

The login name is the one for the PPP account. The password you enter will be shown in plain text, so be careful who you have around when you enter it! If you will be using PAP authentication, check the box; when you've entered the other required information, select the **Customize** button at the bottom of the screen. All the other information is provided on the various tabs and can be set within the **Customize** screen, but it's easier to find the information all in one place on the primary screen.

Select the **PAP** tab and enter your username and then the secret the ISP has provided you in the **Secret** field. The other defaults should be sufficient, but if you need to, you can edit the initial settings using the **Customize** option.

Modifying a PPP or SLIP Configuration – Quick Reference

1. Start Linuxconf by typing `linuxconf` at the shell prompt.

2. Open [Config] ⇒ [Networking] ⇒ [PPP/SLIP/PLIP].

3. Select the configuration to modify.

4. Change the desired settings; most are on the **Communications** tab.

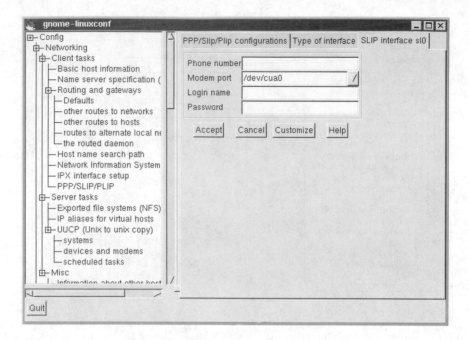

Figure 8.18: SLIP Interface Screen

5. Select **Accept**.

Modifying a PPP or SLIP Configuration – General Overview

You can edit an existing configuration as well as delete it by selecting it from the list on the **PPP/SLIP/PLIP configurations** screen.

- Start Linuxconf by typing `linuxconf` at the shell prompt.

- Open Config ⇒ Networking ⇒ PPP/SLIP/PLIP.

- You will then be presented with the **PPP/SLIP/PLIP configurations** screen (see figure 8.15 on page 147). Select the configuration you would like to modify or delete.

This will open the appropriate interface screen for your configuration. If you wish to delete the configuration, the handy **Del** button is there at the bottom of the screen. The Modem port is on the **Hardware** tab and is a drop down menu. If you want to change the other settings you entered when you originally created the configuration, select the **Communication** tab. The first **Send** field contains

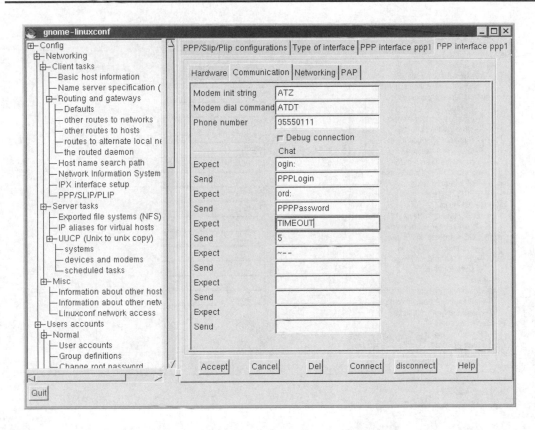

Figure 8.19: PPP Interface Customization Screen

your login, and the next **Send** field contains your password. The **Expect** fields correspond to the `login:` and `password:` prompts, which explains the `ogin:` and `ord:` entries.

Please Note: The `ogin:` and `ord:` entries may not be the same for your system. Different **ISP/PPP** servers may use different text and should be changed to fit the needs of whatever server type you are logging in to. Instead, you may see such prompts as `User ID` and `authentification`.

Once you have made your changes, you can test to see if your configuration is working. Select **Connect** from the bottom of the screen. This will attempt to connect you to the remote system using the information you've entered. Once you've finished configuring and testing your setup, we recommend using the `usernet` utility to control your dial-up networking connection on a daily basis. See the `usernet` man page for more information.

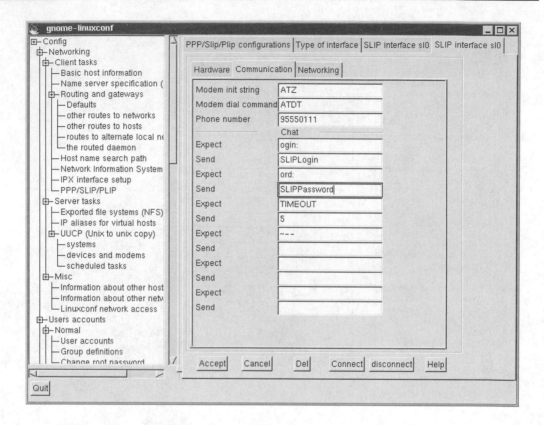

Figure 8.20: SLIP Interface Customization Screen

Other Network Connections – Quick Reference

Due to the number of possible choices and sub-choices, no quick reference is available for this section.

Other Network Connections – General Overview

Setting up a network connection over ethernet requires an entirely different type of setup. Network connections to token ring or arcnet networks follow a similar procedure, but will not be discussed here.

- First you will need to have an Ethernet card installed.
- Start Linuxconf by typing `linuxconf` at the shell prompt.

- Open ⌈Config⌉ ⇒ ⌈Networking⌉ ⇒ ⌈Client tasks⌉ ⇒ ⌈Basic host information⌉. The **Host name** tab will request a host name, which should be specified by default unless you did not setup your networking during the installation process. If it is not already specified, please take the time now to configure it. Skip this tab. Select the tab for **Adaptor 1**.

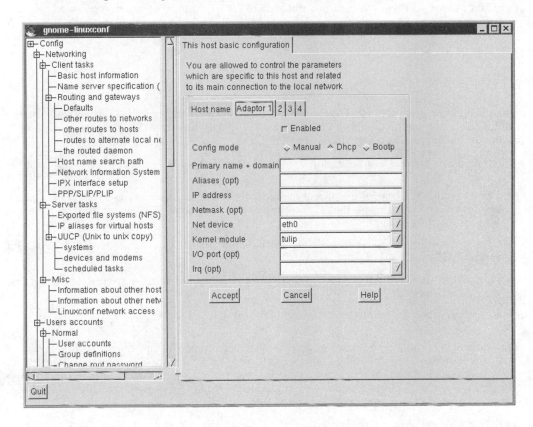

Figure 8.21: Adaptor 1

The first item on this screen is a check box to indicate whether this adaptor is enabled or not. It should be checked if this is the one you intend to use. Below that is a choice of Config modes. **Manual** means that you will be providing all the information and entering it yourself. **DHCP** and **bootp** retrieve their information from a remote server of the corresponding kind. If you're not sure what option to choose, talk to your systems administrator.

DHCP and bootp Required fields:

- Net device - The type of network card you are using; for example, `eth0` would be the appropriate entry to use the first Ethernet card.

- Kernel module - The correct module based on your network card; for further information see the list below.

For DHCP and bootp configurations you only need to specify the **Net device** and the **Kernel module**. For the **Net device**, you will choose from a list where the `eth` prefix represents ethernet cards, the `arc` specifies an arcnet card and the `tr` specifies token ring cards. A complete list of network cards and their respective modules can be found in Section E.3 on page 353. For the most recent up-to-date list, please see our website at:

```
http://www.redhat.com
```

The netmask information will be set by default, although depending on what kind of network you are setting up, or becoming a part of, you may need to specify this. If you are connecting to an ISP, ask them for the information. Most likely it will be `255.255.255.0` (the default).

Required fields for **Manual Configuration**:

- Primary name + domain – the primary name is the name of your computer, while the domain is how your network is specified. For example, `foo.bar.com`; `foo` is the primary name and `bar.com` is the domain.

- IP address – this is the address of the machine and will follow the pattern of *x.x.x.x*. For example, `192.168.0.13`.

- Net device – type of network card you are using; eth0 would be the appropriate entry to use the first ethernet card.

- Kernel module – the correct module based on your network card.

Information on net devices and kernel modules is described above. The appropriate primary name + domain and IP address will depend on whether you are adding the computer to an existing network or creating a new network. For connecting to an existing network, contact your systems administrator for the information. Getting a network connected to the Internet is beyond the scope of this book, and we recommend the following starting point:

TCP/IP Network Administration, 2nd Edition, by Craig Hunt (O'Reilly and Associates).

If you're setting up a private network that won't *ever* be connected to the Internet, then you can choose any primary name + domain name you would like and have several choices for IP addresses (See Figure 8.22 on the facing page).

The three sets of numbers above correspond to class a, b, and c networks respectively. The classes are used to describe the number of IP addresses available as well as the range of numbers used to described each. The numbers above have been set aside for private networks.

Please Note: You should not use these IP addresses if you connect to the Internet since 192.168.0.* and 192.168.255.* are not reliably considered private. If you want your network to be connected to the Internet, or think you might want to at some point in the future, do yourself a favor and get yourself non-private addresses now.

Addresses available	Examples
10.0.0.0 - 10.255.255.255	10.5.12.14
172.16.0.0 - 172.31.255.255	172.16.9.1, 172.28.2.5
192.168.0.0 - 192.168.255.255	192.168.0.13

Figure 8.22: Private Address Ranges

Nameserver Specification

A nameserver and default domain are also needed to establish a network connection. The nameserver is used to translate host names such as `private.network.com` to their corresponding IP address such as `192.168.7.3`. The default domain tells the computer where to look if a fully qualified hostname isn't specified. Fully qualified means that the full address is given, so `foo.redhat.com` is the fully qualified hostname, while the hostname is simply `foo`. If you specified your default domain as `redhat.com`, then you could use just the hostname to connect successfully. For example `ftp foo` would be sufficient if your search domain is `redhat.com`, while `ftp foo.redhat.com` would be required if it wasn't.

To specify the nameserver, open [Config] ⇒ [Networking] ⇒ [Name server specification (DNS)].

Nameservers are ranked according to the order in which they are accessed, so it's not unusual to see nameservers referred to as primary, secondary, tertiary and so on down the list if more than one is specified. Each of these must be an IP address and not a name. The computer has no way to resolve the name until it connects to a nameserver. Screamingly obvious when stated, but occasionally overlooked when people are simply asked to supply an address for a computer.

In addition to a default domain, you can also specify search domains. Search domains work differently; they progress from one to six in a similar manner to the nameserver. However, they all take precedence over the default domain! Keep this in mind when specifying search domains. Search domains are not commonly used.

The one item not yet covered is the check box for DNS usage. If you are running a small private network with no Internet connection, then using `/etc/hosts` files and keeping them all synchronized will work. As you add more and more machines, the complexity increases until it is easier to have a single machine run a DNS than to continue to sync `/etc/hosts` files.

There is another reason for not using DNS, and that is if your network is going to use NIS instead. Note that NIS can be used in conjunction with DNS. So to sum it all up, unless you know why using `/etc/hosts` or NIS would be best for your situation, DNS is probably going to be your best choice.

You can add, modify, or delete entries from the `/etc/hosts` file using Linuxconf. Open [Config] ⇒ [Networking] ⇒ [Misc] ⇒ [Information about other hosts].

To modify or delete an entry select it. To delete the entry, select **Del** at the bottom of the **host/network definition** screen.

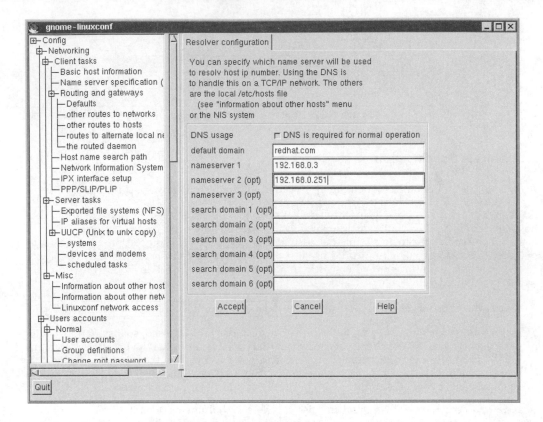

Figure 8.23: Resolver Configuration Screen

To modify it, change the information as necessary. To add a new entry, select **Add** at the bottom of the /etc/hosts screen. This will also open the **host/network definition** screen.

Required Fields:

- **Primary name + domain** – the primary name is the name of the computer, while the domain is how the network it is attached to is specified. For example, given foo.bar.com, foo is the primary name and bar.com is the domain.

- **IP number** – also referred to as IP address; this is the address of the machine and will follow the pattern of *x.x.x.x*. For example, 192.168.0.13

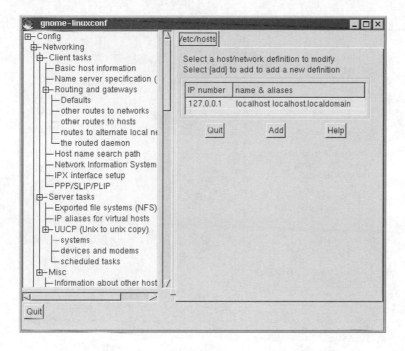

Figure 8.24: /etc/hosts Screen

Optional Fields:

- **Alias** – A shorthand for the fully qualified domain name. This is often the same as the primary name. So, for example, if the fully qualified domain name is foo.bar.com, you could select foo as the alias.

- **Comment** – a comment on the machine. For example, "The remote nameserver."

You will need to specify both the primary name + domain and the IP number. The other fields are optional. Once finished, select **Accept**.

Date and Time

To get to the **date & time** control panel:

- Start Linuxconf by typing linuxconf at the shell prompt.

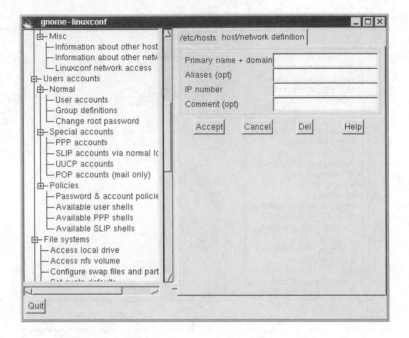

Figure 8.25: Host/Network Definition Screen

- Enter root's password when prompted (if not already root).

- Open (Control) $\Rightarrow$ (Date & Time).

The **zone** field is a pull-down list that is long and extensive. It is often designated by a large region and then a city or zone within it. Examples include `Europe/Vienna` and `US/Eastern`. There is a check box to **Store date in CMOS in GMT format**. Hours are specified from 0 (midnight) to 23 (11 PM). Months are specified by number as well. For the year, please specify all four digits. All other fields should be self-explanatory.

8.2 System Configuration with the Control Panel

Please Note: Most of what can be done with the control panel applications can also be done using Linuxconf. In addition, Linuxconf supports both character-cell *and* graphical user interfaces. Please refer to Section 8.1 on page 120 for an introduction to Linuxconf.

The control panel is a launching pad for a number of different system administration tools (see Figure 8.27 on page 160). These tools make your life easier by letting you configure things without

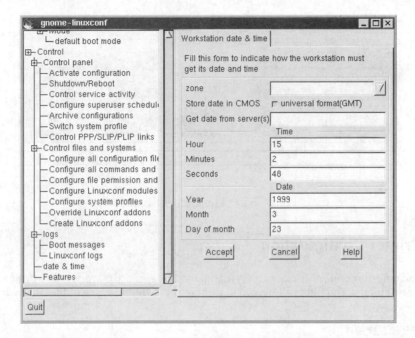

Figure 8.26: Workstation Date & Time

remembering configuration file formats and awkward command line options.

To start the control-panel, start the X Window System as root with `startx` and type `control-panel` in an xterm. You will need to be root to run the control-panel tools successfully. You can do this as well if you already have X running as a normal user. Just type `su -c control-panel` and then type the root password when prompted. If you plan to do other tasks as root, you could type `su` followed by the root password when prompted.

Please Note: If you are not running X as root, you may need to give root access to your system's X server. To do this, enter the following command on a *non-root* terminal window:

```
xhost +localhost
```

After starting the control panel, simply clicking on an icon starts up a tool. Please note that you are not prevented from starting two instances of any tool, but doing so is a very bad idea because you may try to edit the same files in two places and end up overwriting your own changes. If you do accidentally start a second copy of a tool, you should quit it immediately. Also, do not manually edit any files managed by the control-panel tools while the tools are running. Similarly, do not run any other programs (such as Linuxconf) that may change those files while the tools are running.

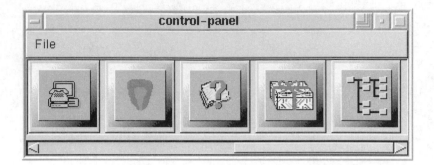

Figure 8.27: The Control Panel

8.2.1   Printer Configuration

The printer configuration tool (`printtool`) maintains the `/etc/printcap` file, print spool directories, and print filters. The filters allow you to print many different types of files, including:

- plain text (ASCII) files

- PostScript files

- TEX `.dvi` files

- GIF, JPEG, TIFF, and other graphics formats

- RPMs

In other words, simply printing a GIF or RPM file using the `lpr` command will result in the printer doing "the right thing."

In order to create a new *print queue*, choose **Add**. Then, select what type of printer is being added. There are four types of print queues which can be configured with printtool:

- **Local** print queues are for printers attached to a printer or serial port on your Red Hat Linux system.

- **Remote** print queues are attached to a different system which you can access over a TCP/IP network.

- **SMB** print queues are attached to a different system which uses LAN-Manager-type (SMB) networking.

- **NCP** print queues are attached to a different system which uses Novell's NetWare network technology.

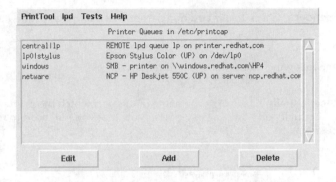

Figure 8.28: Print Tool

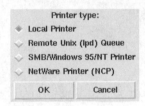

Figure 8.29: Selecting a Printer Type

After choosing the printer type, a dialog box requests further information about the print queue (see Figure 8.30 on the next page). All types of print queues require the following information:

- **Queue Name**: What the queue will be called. Multiple names can be specifed with the | (pipe) character separating entries.

- **Spool Directory**: This is the directory on the local machine where files are stored before printing occurs. Be careful to not have more than one printer queue use a given spool directory.

- **File Limit**: Maximum size print job accepted, in kilobytes (1 kb = 1024 bytes). A size of 0 indicates no limit should be imposed.

- **Input Filter**: Filters convert printed files into a format the printer can handle. Press **Select** to choose the filter which best matches your printer (see Figure 8.31 on the following page).

  In addition to configuring print queues able to print graphical and PostScript output, you can configure a *text-only* printer, which will only print plain ASCII text. Most printer drivers are also able to print ASCII text without converting it to PostScript first; simply choose **Fast text printing** when you configure the filter. **Please Note:** This only works for non-PostScript printers.

- **Suppress Headers**: Check this if you don't want a header page printed at the beginning of each print job.

For *local* printers, the following information is also required:

- **Printer Device**: Usually `/dev/lp1`; the name of the port which the printer is attached to. Serial printers are usually on `/dev/ttyS?` ports. Note that you will need to manually configure serial parameters.

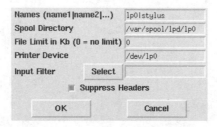

Figure 8.30: Adding a Local Printer

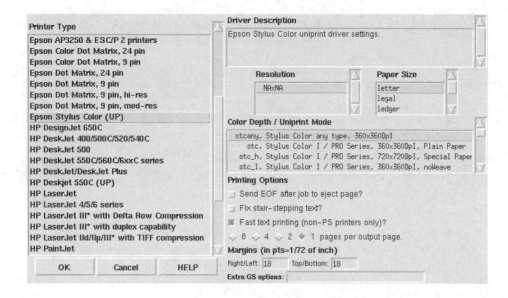

Figure 8.31: Configuring a Print Filter

For *remote* printers, the dialog box contains additional fields; fill in the following information:

- **Remote Host**: Hostname of the remote machine hosting the printer.

- **Remote Queue**: Name of the queue to print to on the remote machine.

The remote machine must be configured to allow the local machine to print on the desired queue. Typically /etc/hosts.lpd controls this.

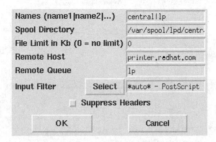

Figure 8.32: Adding a Remote Printer

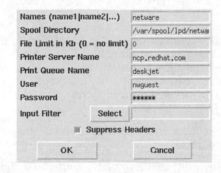

Figure 8.33: Adding an NCP Printer

For SMB and NCP printers, fill in the following information:

- **Hostname of Printer Server**: Name of the machine to which the printer you want to use is attached.

- **IP number of Server**: The IP address of the machine to which the printer you want to use is attached; this is optional and only relevant for SMB printers.

- **Printer Name**: Name of the printer on which you want to print.

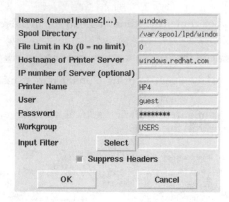

Figure 8.34: Adding an SMB Printer

- **User**: Name of user you must login as to access the printer (typically guest for Windows servers, or nobody for samba servers).

- **Password**: Password (if required) to use the printer (typically blank). Someone should be able to tell you this if you do not already know it.

Please Note: If you need to use a username and password for an SMB (LAN Manager) or NCP (NetWare) print queue, they are stored unencrypted in a local script. Thus, it is possible for another person to learn the username and password. It is therefore recommended that the username and password for use of the printer to be different than that for a user account on the local Red Hat Linux system, so that the only possible security compromise would be unauthorized use of the printer. If there are file shares from the SMB server, it is recommended that they also use a different password than the one for the print queue.

After you have added your print queue, you may need to restart the printer daemon (lpd). To do so, choose **Restart lpd** from the **lpd** menu.

You may print a *test page* for any print queue you have configured. Select the type of test page you would like to print from the **Tests** menu.

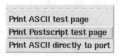

Figure 8.35: Printing a Test Page

8.2.2 Kernel Daemon Configuration

Red Hat Linux includes `kerneld`, the Kernel Daemon, which automatically loads some software and hardware support into memory as it is needed, and unloads it when it is no longer being used.

The tool shown in Figure 8.36 manages the configuration file for kerneld. While kerneld can load some things, such as filesystems, without explicit configuration, it needs to be told what hardware support to load when it is presented with a generic hardware request.

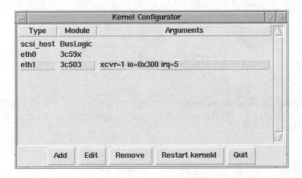

Figure 8.36: Kernel Module Management

For instance, when the kernel wants to load support for ethernet, kerneld needs to know which ethernet card you have, and if your ethernet card requires special configuration, it needs to know about that, too.

Changing Module Options

To change the options being given to a module when it is loaded, click on the line to select it, then click the **Edit** button. kernelcfg will bring up a window which looks like Figure 8.37 on the following page. The options kernelcfg knows about (normally all available options) will each have their own field. Normally, you will want to ignore the **Other arguments** field. Some modules normally take no arguments; just in case, they have an **Arguments** field which allows you to enter configuration information.

Changing Modules

To change which module gets invoked to provide a generic service, such as an ethernet card or SCSI host adapter module, you need to delete the old one and add a new one. To delete a module, select it by clicking on it, then click on **Remove**. Then click on **Add** to add the new module, as explained in the following section.

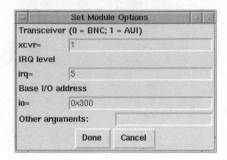

Figure 8.37: Editing Module Options

If you have changed your SCSI controller (`scsi_hostadapter`), remember to make a new initial ramdisk with the `/sbin/mkinitrd` command as documented in section 11.8.2 on page 213.

Adding Modules

To add a module of any type, click on the **Add** button. You will be presented with a dialog box (Figure 8.38) asking you to choose a module type. Ethernet is `eth`, Token Ring is `tr`, SCSI controllers are `scsi_hostadapter`, and so on. Click **Ok** to continue to the next dialog box.

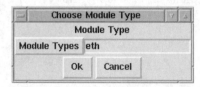

Figure 8.38: Adding a module

If there is more than one module which can be used for the module type you have chosen, you will be presented with a dialog box (Figure 8.39 on the next page) which asks which module you want to use, and may also ask for specifics about the type of module; for ethernet, for example, you need to choose from `eth0`, `eth1`, etc. When you are done, click **Ok** again to continue to specify any module options in the next dialog box (Figure 8.39 on the facing page), which is the same as the dialog for editing a module.

Restarting Kerneld

The changes that you make with the Kernel Daemon Configuration tool will be made in the `/etc/conf.modules` file, which kerneld reads whenever it is started. Once you have made changes,

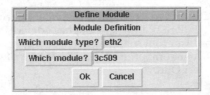

Figure 8.39: Selecting From Available Modules

you can restart kerneld by clicking on the **Restart kerneld** button. This will **not** cause any modules which are currently in use to be reloaded, it will only notify kerneld to use the configuration when it loads more modules in the future.

8.2.3 Network Configuration

Please Note: Documentation on network configuration using Linuxconf can be found in Section 8.1.4 on page 145.

The network configuration tool (`netcfg`) shown in Figure 8.40 is designed to allow easy manipulation of parameters such as IP address, gateway address, and network address, as well as name servers and `/etc/hosts`.

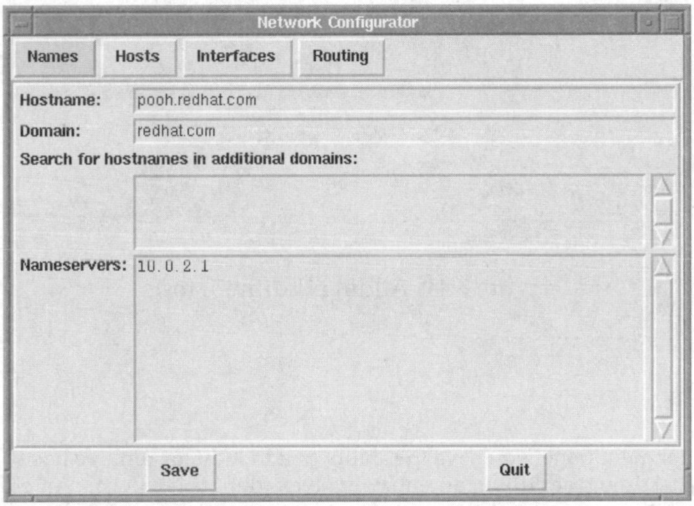

Figure 8.40: Network Configuration Panel

Network devices can be added, removed, configured, activated, deactivated and aliased. Ethernet, arcnet, token ring, pocket (ATP), PPP, SLIP, PLIP and loopback devices are supported. PPP/SLIP/PLIP support works well on most hardware, but some hardware setups may exhibit unpredictable behavior. When using the Network Configuration Tool click **Save** to write your changes to disk, to quit without making any changes select **Quit**.

Managing Names

The **Names** panel of the Network Configuration tool serves two primary purposes: setting the hostname and domain of the computer, and determining which name server will be used to look up other hosts on the network. The Network tool is not capable of configuring a machine as a nameserver. To edit a field or add information to a field simply click on the field with the left mouse button and type the new information.

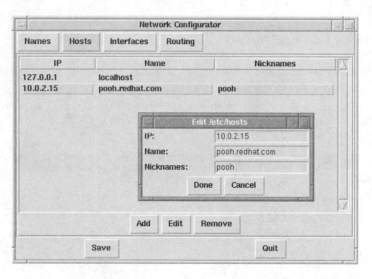

Figure 8.41: Adding/Editing Hosts

Managing Hosts

In the **Hosts** management panel you have the ability to add, edit, or remove hosts from the /etc/hosts file. Adding or editing an entry involves identical actions. An edit dialog box will appear, simply type the new information and click **Done** when you are finished. See Figure 8.41 for an example.

Adding a Networking Interface

If you have added a networking interface to your machine since installing Red Hat Linux, or you didn't configure your ethernet card at install time, you can configure it with a few clicks of a mouse.

Please Note: You may need to configure `kerneld` to load a driver for the network interface you are adding (e.g., `eth0`); see Section 8.2.2 on page 165 for more information.

Begin adding an interface by clicking on **Interfaces** in the main panel. This will bring up a window of configured devices with a row of available options, see Figure 8.42.

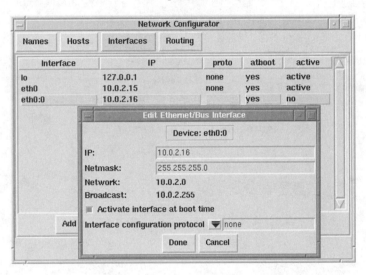

Figure 8.42: Configured Interfaces

To add a device, first click the **Add** button then select the type of interface you want to configure from the box that appears (See Figure 8.43 on the following page).

Please Note: There is now a **clone** button available in `netcfg`. This button can be used to create a "clone" of an already-existing interface. By using clone interfaces, it is possible for a laptop to have one Ethernet interface defined for a work LAN, and a clone Ethernet device defined for a home LAN.

PPP Interface – Adding a PPP interface can be as simple as supplying the phone number, login name and password in the **Create PPP Interface** dialog shown in Figure 8.44 on the next page. If you need to use PAP authentication for your PPP connection, choose **Use PAP authentication**. In many cases some degree of customization will be needed to establish a PPP connection. Choosing the **Customize** button will allow you to make changes to the hardware, communication, and networking settings for the PPP interface.

Figure 8.43: Choose Interface Type

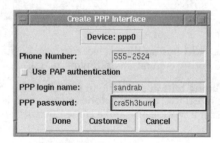

Figure 8.44: Create PPP Interface

SLIP Interface In order to configure a SLIP interface you must first supply a phone number, login name, and password. This will supply the initial parameters for the chat script needed to establish a SLIP connection. When you choose **Done**, a dialog titled **Edit SLIP Interface** appears that enables you to further customize the hardware, communication and networking parameters for your SLIP interface.

PLIP Interface To add a PLIP interface to your system you only have to supply the IP address, the remote IP address, and the Netmask. You can also select if you want to activate the interface at boot time.

Ethernet, Arcnet, Token Ring and Pocket Adaptor Interfaces If you are adding an ethernet, arcnet, token ring or pocket adapter to your computer you will need to supply the following information:

- **Device**: This is determined by netconfig based on the devices already configured.

- **IP Address**: Enter an IP address for your network device.

- **Netmask**: Enter the network mask for your network device.

  The network and broadcast addresses are calculated automatically based on the IP address and netmask you enter.

- **Activate interface at boot time**: If you want the device to be configured automatically when your machine boots select this by clicking on the box.

- **Allow any user to (de)activate interface**: Check this if you want any user to be able to activate or deactivate the interface.

- **Interface configuration protocol**: If you have a BOOTP or DHCP server on your network and would like to use it to configure the interface, choose the appropriate option; otherwise, choose **none**.

After providing the configuration information for your new device, click **Done**. The device should appear in your **Interfaces** list as an inactive device. (The active column should have a label of **no**.) To activate the new device, first select it with a mouse click and then choose on the **Activate** button. If it does not come up properly, you may need to reconfigure it by choosing on **Edit**.

Managing Routes

In the Routes management screen you have the ability to add, edit, or remove static networking routes. Adding or editing an entry involves identical actions, just like the Hosts panel. An edit dialog box will appear; simply type the new information and click **Done** when you are finished. See Figure 8.45 on the following page for an example.

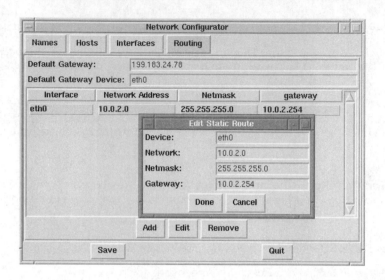

Figure 8.45: Adding/Editing Routes

8.2.4   Time and Date

Please Note: Documentation on setting your system's time and date using Linuxconf can be found in Section 8.1.4 on page 157.

The time machine allows you to change the time and date by clicking on the appropriate part of the time and date display and clicking on the arrows to change the value.

The system clock is not changed until you click on the **Set System Clock** button.

Click on **Reset Time** to set the time machine time back to that of the system.

Please Note: Changing the time can seriously confuse programs that depend on the normal progression of time, and could possibly cause problems. Try to quit as many applications and processes as possible before changing the time or date.

9

Package Management with RPM

The **R**ed Hat **P**ackage **M**anager (RPM), is an open packaging system available for anyone to use, and works on Red Hat Linux as well as other Linux and UNIX systems. Red Hat Software encourages other vendors to take the time to look at RPM and use it for their own products. RPM is distributable under the terms of the GPL.

For the end user, RPM provides many features that make maintaining a system far easier than it has ever been. Installing, uninstalling, and upgrading RPM packages are all one line commands, and all the messy details have been taken care of for you. RPM maintains a database of installed packages and their files, which allows you to perform powerful queries and verification of your system. During upgrades RPM handles configuration files specially, so that you never lose your customizations – a feature that is impossible with straight `.tar.gz` files.

For the developer, RPM allows you to take source code for software and package it into source and binary packages for end users. This process is quite simple and is driven from a single file and optional patches that you create. This clear delineation of "pristine" sources and your patches and build instructions eases the maintenance of the package as new versions of the software are released.

Please Note: Although it does not hurt to understand the concepts behind RPM, there is an alternative for installing, uninstalling and upgrading packages. For those of you that prefer a graphical interface to the command line, we suggest you use GnoRPM. Please see Chapter 10 on page 183 for more information.

9.1   RPM Design Goals

Before trying to understand how to use RPM, it helps to have an idea of what the design goals are.

Upgradability With RPM you can upgrade individual components of your system without completely reinstalling. When you get a new release of an operating system based on RPM (such as Red Hat Linux), you don't need to reinstall on your machine (as you do with operating systems based on other packaging systems). RPM allows intelligent, fully-automated, in-place upgrades of your system. Configuration files in packages are preserved across upgrades, so you won't lose your customizations.

Powerful Querying RPM is also designed to have powerful querying options. You can do searches through your entire database for packages or just certain files. You can also easily find out what package a file belongs to and where it came from. The files an RPM package contains are in a compressed archive, with a custom binary header containing useful information about the package and its contents, allowing you to query individual packages quickly and easily.

System Verification Another powerful feature is the ability to verify packages. If you are worried that you deleted an important file for some package, simply verify the package. You will be notified of any anomalies. At that point, you can reinstall the package if necessary. Any configuration files that you modified are preserved during reinstallation.

Pristine Sources A crucial design goal was to allow the use of "pristine" software sources, as distributed by the original authors of the software. With RPM, you have the pristine sources along with any patches that were used, plus complete build instructions. This is a big advantage for several reasons. For instance, if a new version of a program comes out, you don't necessarily have to start from scratch to get it to compile. You can look at the patch to see what you *might* need to do. All the compiled-in defaults, and all of the changes that were made to get the software to build properly are easily visible this way.

This goal may only seem important for developers, but it results in higher quality software for end users too. We would like to thank the folks from the BOGUS distribution for originating the pristine source concept.

9.2   Using RPM

RPM has five basic modes of operation (not counting package building): installing, uninstalling, upgrading, querying, and verifying. This section contains an overview of each mode. For complete details and options try `rpm --help`, or turn to Section 9.4 on page 182 for more information on RPM.

9.2.1 Installing

RPM packages typically have file names like foo-1.0-1.i386.rpm, which includes the package name (foo), version (1.0), release (1), and architecture (i386). Installing a package is as simple as:

```
# rpm -ivh foo-1.0-1.i386.rpm
foo                           ###################################
#
```

As you can see, RPM prints out the name of the package (which is not necessarily the same as the file name, which could have been 1.rpm), and then prints a succession of hash marks as the package is installed, as a sort of progress meter.

Installing packages is designed to be simple, but you can get a few errors:

Package Already Installed

If the package is already installed, you will see:

```
# rpm -ivh foo-1.0-1.i386.rpm
foo                   package foo-1.0-1 is already installed
error: foo-1.0-1.i386.rpm cannot be installed
#
```

If you really want to install the package anyway, you can use --replacepkgs on the command line, which tells RPM to ignore the error:

```
# rpm -ivh --replacepkgs foo-1.0-1.i386.rpm
foo                           ###################################
#
```

Conflicting Files

If you attempt to install a package that contains a file that has already been installed by another package, you'll see:

```
# rpm -ivh foo-1.0-1.i386.rpm
foo             /usr/bin/foo conflicts with file from bar-1.0-1
error: foo-1.0-1.i386.rpm cannot be installed
#
```

To cause RPM to ignore that error, use `--replacefiles` on the command line:

```
# rpm -ivh --replacefiles foo-1.0-1.i386.rpm
foo                         ##################################
#
```

Unresolved Dependency

RPM packages can "depend" on other packages, which means that they require other packages to be installed in order to run properly. If you try to install a package for which there is such an unresolved dependency, you'll see:

```
# rpm -ivh bar-1.0-1.i386.rpm
failed dependencies:
        foo is needed by bar-1.0-1
#
```

To handle this error you should install the requested packages. If you want to force the installation anyway (a bad idea since the package probably will not run correctly), use `--nodeps` on the command line.

9.2.2   Uninstalling

Uninstalling a package is just as simple as installing:

```
# rpm -e foo
#
```

Notice that we used the package *name* "foo," not the name of the original package *file* "foo-1.0-1.i386.rpm".

You can encounter a dependency error when uninstalling a package if some other installed package depends on the one you are trying to remove. For example:

```
# rpm -e foo
removing these packages would break dependencies:
        foo is needed by bar-1.0-1
#
```

To cause RPM to ignore that error and uninstall the package anyway (which is also a bad idea since the package that depends on it will probably fail to work properly), use `--nodeps` on the command line.

9.2.3 Upgrading

Upgrading a package is almost just like installing.

```
# rpm -Uvh foo-2.0-1.i386.rpm
foo                                ####################################
#
```

What you don't see above is that RPM automatically uninstalled any old versions of the foo package. In fact you may want to always use -U to install packages, since it works fine even when there are no previous versions of the package installed.

Since RPM performs intelligent upgrading of packages with configuration files, you may see a message like:

```
saving /etc/foo.conf as /etc/foo.conf.rpmsave
```

This means that your changes to the configuration file may not be "forward compatible" with the new configuration file in the package, so RPM saved your original file, and installed a new one. You should investigate and resolve the differences between the two files as soon as possible to ensure that your system continues to function properly.

Since upgrading is really a combination of uninstalling and installing, you can encounter any errors from those modes, plus one more: If RPM thinks you are trying to upgrade to a package with an *older* version number, you will see:

```
# rpm -Uvh foo-1.0-1.i386.rpm
foo     package foo-2.0-1 (which is newer) is already installed
error: foo-1.0-1.i386.rpm cannot be installed
#
```

To cause RPM to "upgrade" anyway, use --oldpackage on the command line:

```
# rpm -Uvh --oldpackage foo-1.0-1.i386.rpm
foo                                ####################################
#
```

9.2.4 Freshening

Freshening a package is similar to upgrading:

```
# rpm -Fvh foo-1.2-1.i386.rpm
foo                             ###################################
#
```

RPM's freshen option checks the versions of the packages specified on the command line against the versions of packages that have already been installed on your system. When a newer version of an already-installed package is processed by RPM's freshen option, it will be upgraded to the newer version. However, RPM's freshen option will not install a package if no previously-installed package of the same name exists. This differs from RPM's upgrade option, as an upgrade *will* install packages, whether or not an older version of the package was already installed.

RPM's freshen option works well with single packages or with a group of packages. It's especially handy if you've just downloaded a large number of different packages, and you only want to upgrade those packages that are already installed on your system. Using the freshen option means that you won't have to pick through the downloaded packages, deleting any unwanted ones before using RPM.

In this case, you can simply issue the following command:

```
# rpm -Fvh *.rpm
```

RPM will automatically upgrade only those packages that have already been installed.

9.2.5   Querying

Querying the database of installed packages is accomplished with rpm -q. A simple use is rpm -q foo which will print the package name, version, and release number of the installed package foo:

```
# rpm -q foo
foo-2.0-1
#
```

Instead of specifying the package name, you can use the following options with -q to specify what package(s) you want to query. These are called *Package Specification Options*.

- -a queries all currently installed packages.
- -f <file> will query the package owning <file>.
- -p <packagefile> queries the package <packagefile>.

There are a number of ways to specify what information to display about queried packages. The following options are used to select the information you are interested in. These are called *Information Selection Options*.

- -i displays package information such as name, description, release, size, build date, install date, vendor, and other miscellaneous information.

- -l displays the list of files that the package "owns".

- -s displays the state of all the files in the package.

- -d displays a list of files marked as documentation (man pages, info pages, README's, etc).

- -c displays a list of files marked as configuration files. These are the files you change after installation to adapt the package to your system (sendmail.cf, passwd, inittab, etc).

For those options that display file lists, you can add -v to your command line to get the lists in a familiar ls -l format.

9.2.6 Verifying

Verifying a package compares information about files installed from a package with the same information from the original package. Among other things, verifying compares the size, MD5 sum, permissions, type, owner and group of each file.

rpm -V verifies a package. You can use any of the *Package Selection Options* listed for querying to specify the packages you wish to verify. A simple use is rpm -V foo which verifies that all the files in the foo package are as they were when they were originally installed. For example:

- To verify a package containing particular file:

      rpm -Vf /bin/vi

- To verify ALL installed packages:

      rpm -Va

- To verify an installed package against an RPM package file:

      rpm -Vp foo-1.0-1.i386.rpm

  This can be useful if you suspect that your RPM databases are corrupt.

If everything verified properly there will be no output. If there are any discrepancies they will be displayed. The format of the output is a string of 8 characters, a possible "c" denoting a configuration file, and then the file name. Each of the 8 characters denotes the result of a comparison of one attribute of the file to the value of that attribute recorded in the RPM database. A single "." (period) means the test passed. The following characters denote failure of certain tests:

5 MD5 checksum

S File size

L Symbolic link

T File modification time

D Device

U User

G Group

M Mode (includes permissions and file type)

If you see any output, use your best judgment to determine if you should remove or reinstall the package, or somehow fix the problem.

9.3   Impressing Your Friends with RPM

RPM is a very useful tool for both managing your system and diagnosing and fixing problems. The best way to make sense of all the options is to look at some examples.

- Let's say you delete some files by accident, but you aren't sure what you deleted. If you want to verify your entire system and see what might be missing, you would enter:

  ```
  rpm -Va
  ```

  If some files are missing, or appear to have been corrupted, you should probably either re-install the package or uninstall, then re-install the package.

- Let's say you run across a file that you don't recognize. To find out which package owns it, you would enter:

  ```
  rpm -qf /usr/X11R6/bin/xjewel
  ```

  The output would look like:

  ```
  xjewel-1.6-1
  ```

- We can combine the above two examples in the following scenario. Say you are having problems with /usr/bin/paste. You would like to verify the package that owns that program but you don't know which package that is. Simply enter:

  ```
  rpm -Vf /usr/bin/paste
  ```

  and the appropriate package will be verified.

- If you are using a program and want to find out more information about it, you can enter the following to find out what documentation came with the package that "owns" that program (in this case `ispell`):

  ```
  rpm -qdf /usr/bin/ispell
  ```

The output would be:

```
/usr/man/man4/ispell.4
/usr/man/man4/english.4
/usr/man/man1/unsq.1
/usr/man/man1/tryaffix.1
/usr/man/man1/sq.1
/usr/man/man1/munchlist.1
/usr/man/man1/ispell.1
/usr/man/man1/findaffix.1
/usr/man/man1/buildhash.1
/usr/info/ispell.info.gz
/usr/doc/ispell-3.1.18-1/README
```

- You find a new koules RPM, but you don't know what it is. To find out some information on it, enter:

  ```
  rpm -qip koules-1.2-2.i386.rpm
  ```

The output would be:

```
Name         : koules Distribution: Red Hat Linux Colgate
Version      : 1.2          Vendor: Red Hat Software
Release      : 2        Build Date: Mon Sep 02 11:59:12 1996
Install date: (none)   Build Host: porky.redhat.com
Group        : Games    Source RPM: koules-1.2-2.src.rpm
Size         : 614939
Summary      : SVGAlib action game; multiplayer, network
Description :
This arcade-style game is novel in conception and
excellent in execution.  No shooting, no blood, no guts,
no gore.  The play is simple, but you still must develop
skill to play.  This version uses SVGAlib to run on a
graphics console.
```

- Now you want to see what files the koules RPM installs. You would enter:

  ```
  rpm -qlp koules-1.2-2.i386.rpm
  ```

The output is:

```
/usr/man/man6/koules.6
/usr/lib/games/kouleslib/start.raw
/usr/lib/games/kouleslib/end.raw
/usr/lib/games/kouleslib/destroy2.raw
/usr/lib/games/kouleslib/destroy1.raw
/usr/lib/games/kouleslib/creator2.raw
/usr/lib/games/kouleslib/creator1.raw
/usr/lib/games/kouleslib/colize.raw
/usr/lib/games/kouleslib
/usr/games/koules
```

These are just several examples. As you use the system you will find many more uses for RPM.

9.4   Other RPM Resources

For more information on RPM, check out the man page, the help screen (`rpm --help`), and the RPM documents available at

> `http://www.rpm.org/`

There is also an RPM book available. It's called Maximum RPM , and it is available from Red Hat Software and your local bookstore. It contains a wealth of information about RPM for both the end-user and the package builder. An on-line version of the book is available at `http://www.rpm.org/`.

There is also a mailing list for discussion of RPM related issues, called `rpm-list@redhat.com`. The list is archived on `http://www.redhat.com/support/mailing-lists/`. To subscribe, send mail to `rpm-list-request@redhat.com` with the word `subscribe` in the subject line.

10

GnoRPM

New to Red Hat Linux 6.0 is GnoRPM, a graphical tool which runs under the X Window System. Written by James Henstridge (james@daa.com.au), GnoRPM replaces GLINT. Although GnoRPM shares some similarities with GLINT, it is faster, more powerful and holds a more user-friendly interface.

GnoRPM is "GNOME-compliant," meaning that it seamlessly integrates into GNOME, the X Window System desktop environment.

With GnoRPM, you can easily

- install RPM packages
- uninstall RPM packages
- upgrade RPM packages
- find new RPM packages
- query RPM packages
- verify RPM packages

The interface features a menu, a toolbar, a tree and a display window of currently installed packages.

Operations are performed in GnoRPM by finding and selecting packages, then choosing the type of operation to perform via push-button on the toolbar or through the menu.

- Installing a package places all of the components of that package on your system in the correct locations.

- Uninstalling one removes all traces of the package except for configuration files you have modified.

- Upgrading a package installs the newly available version and uninstalls all other versions that were previously installed. This allows quick upgrading to the latest releases of packages. Refer to Section 10.4 on page 188 for information about how to alter the default settings for installing and uninstalling packages.

You can also use the **Web find** option to search the Internet for newly released packages. You can direct GnoRPM to search for particular distributions when you want to look for new packages. (If you have a slow connection, this option can take some time to fully execute.) See Section 10.4 on page 188 for more information about this feature.

Please Note: Exercise caution if you choose to use the **Web find** option, since there is no way to verify the integrity of the many packages which are available at numerous repositories. Before installing packages, you should perform a query on that package to help you determine whether it can be trusted. Packages not produced by Red Hat Software are not supported in any way by Red Hat Software.

Using GnoRPM to perform all of these and many other operations is the same as using rpm from the shell prompt. However, the graphical nature of GnoRPM often makes these operations easier to perform.

The normal way to handle GnoRPM is to display the available packages, select the package(s) you want to operate on, and then select an option from the toolbar or menu which performs the operation.

For instance, you can install, upgrade or uninstall several packages with a few button clicks. Similarly, you can query and verify more than one package at a time.

10.1   Starting GnoRPM

You can start GnoRPM from either an X terminal window or from the GNOME desktop panel, under **System**.

To start GnoRPM from an X terminal window, at the shell prompt, simply type

```
gnorpm &
```

That will bring up the main GnoRPM window (as shown in Figure 10.1).

Please Note: If you would like to install, upgrade or uninstall packages, you must be in root. The easiest way to do this is to type su root and then the root password at a shell prompt. However, you do not need to be in root to query and verify packages.

There are several parts to the GnoRPM interface.

- **Package Panel -** On the left; allows you to browse and select packages on your system.

- **Display window -** To the right of the package panel; shows you contents from folders in the panel.

- **Toolbar -** Above the display and panel; a graphical display of package tools.

- **Menu -** Above the toolbar; contains text-based commands, as well as help info, preferences and other settings.

- **Status bar -** Beneath the panel and display windows; shows the total number of selected packages.

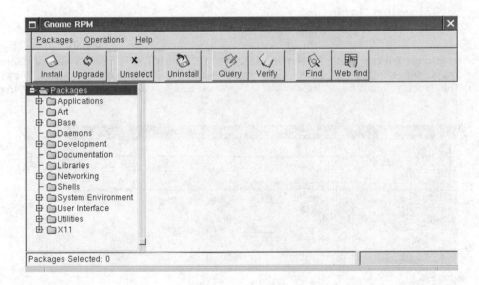

Figure 10.1: Main GnoRPM Window

10.2   The Package Display

Each folder icon in the tree view at left represents a group of packages. Each group can contain subgroups. Groups are used to place packages that perform similar functions in similar locations. For example, the folder Editors contains text editors such as ed, vim and GXedit. From the tree view on the left, you might find another folder beneath Editors called Emacs, which would contain both emacs and emacs-X11.

The tree view is also arranged in an expandable and collapsible manner, which helps you to easily navigate through the packages. A folder which appears with a + next to it indicates that there are subfolders within that category.

To view the packages and subgroups within a group, click once on a folder or a + with your left mouse button. The display window will then show you the contents of that folder. By default, you will be presented with icons to represent the packages. You can change that view to a list view by selecting **View as list** from the **Interface** tab you'll find under **Operations** ⇒ **Preferences**.

In this manner, you can move about the tree view, opening and expanding folders containing applications, games, tools and more. The contents of each folder will be displayed at the right.

10.2.1   Selecting Packages

To select a single package, click on it with the left mouse button. You'll notice that highlighting will appear around the package's title (as shown in Figure 10.2) which shows that it's currently selected. To unselect it, either click on an empty space in the display panel with the left mouse button, or click on the Unselect button on the toolbar. When you unselect a package, the highlighting will disappear.

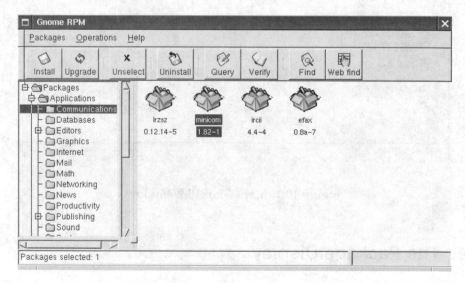

Figure 10.2: Selecting Packages in GnoRPM

You can select and unselect more than one package at a time, in more than one folder in the tree panel. To select more than one package incrementally, left-click with your mouse button, while holding down the Control key; you'll see highlighting around each additional selection.

To select more than one package "globally," that is, make larger selections within a folder, left-click one package, then, while holding down the Shift key, left-click on the final package you wish to select. By doing so, you'll notice that individual packages between your starting and ending selections will also be highlighted for selection. Using this option makes selecting groups of packages much quicker than selecting each package individually.

The status bar at the bottom of GnoRPM will display the total number of packages you have selected.

10.3   Installing New Packages

To install new packages, choose **Install** from the toolbar. A new window will open, revealing a space for new packages to be installed. Remember, however, that you must be logged in as **root** to install, upgrade and uninstall.

Choose the **Add** button. By default, GnoRPM will search in /mnt/cdrom/RedHat/RPMS for new packages. (You can find this option in the **Interface** tab of the **Preferences** dialog. See the Configuration section for more information on this feature.) If no packages are available in the default path, you'll be presented with an **Add Packages** window from which you can select the appropriate location of your new package.

To choose an item, double-click on it with your left mouse button, or click on the **Add** button. The selected package(s) will be added to the **Install** window. You can also install more than one package in the same manner; each selection will be added to the **Install** window.

In addition to choosing to install the packages from within the **Install** window, you can install after performing a query on the selected package. Click on **Query**, which will open the **Package Info** window. Here, you can find a variety of details about the file(s) you've selected to install. Information will include the origination of the package, the date it was built, its size and more.

Within this **Package Info** window, you have the option of installing or upgrading packages: If the package has not been installed on your system, you'll find an **Install** button at the bottom of the window.

If the package already exists on your system and you're querying a newer release, the **Package Info** window provides an **Upgrade** button, which will perform an upgrade to newer releases.

You can also "drag and drop" packages from GNOME Midnight Commander File Manager and place them into the **Install** window. To accomplish this, open the file manager (for example, by going to the GNOME Panel, clicking on the GNOME footprint and opening the **File Manager** menu). Locate the directory in which your packages can be found, click on the directory in the tree menu on the left. In the display window to the right, left-click on the package name and, when it's highlighted, "drag" the file by keeping your finger pressed on the mouse button, releasing the pressure (and the package) once you're over the **Install** window.

You'll see a progress indicator when your package is being installed.

10.4 Configuration

GnoRPM offers a wide selection of choices for installing and uninstalling packages, documentation and other features. You can customize GnoRPM through the **Preferences** dialog, which you can access from **Operations** ⇒ **Preferences** on the menu. To make selections in the **Preferences** dialog, select the check boxes next to the options.

Under the **Behavior** tab, you'll find a number of options for configuring the way GnoRPM installs, uninstalls and upgrades packages. The Behavior tab is split into five sections: Install, Upgrade, Other, Database and Architecture. Note that by default these boxes not checked.

Under **Install Options**, you have the following choices:

- **No dependency checks -** When selected, this will install or upgrade a package without checking for other types of files on which the program may be dependent in order to work. However, unless you know what you're doing we strongly suggest you not use this option as some packages may depend on other packages for files, libraries or programs to function correctly.

- **No reordering -** This option is useful if RPM is unable to change the installation order of some packages to satisfy dependencies.

- **Don't run scripts -** Pre- and post-install scripts are sequences of commands that are sometimes included in packages to assist with installation. This check box is similar to the `--noscripts` option when installing from the shell prompt.

Under **Upgrade Options**, you can select the following:

- **Allow replacement of packages -** Replaces a package with a new copy of itself. Similar to the `--replacepkgs` option from the shell prompt. This option can be useful if an already-installed package has become damaged or may require other repair to function correctly.

- **Allow replacement of files -** Allows the replacement of files which are owned by another package. The shell prompt equivalent for this RPM option is `--replacefiles`. This option can sometimes be useful when there are two packages with the same file name but different contents.

- **Allow upgrade to old version -** Like the shell prompt RPM option equivalent `--oldpackage`, this option allows you to "upgrade" to an earlier package. It can sometimes be useful if the latest version of a package doesn't function correctly for your system.

- **Keep packages made obsolete -** Prevents packages listed in an Obsoletes header from being removed.

In **Other Options**, you can select:

- **Don't install documentation -** Like `--excludedocs`, this option can save on disk space by excluding documentation such as man pages or other information related to the package.

- **Install all files -** Installs all files in the package.

The choices available in **Database Options** and **Architecture Options** allow you to decide, among other things, whether you want to perform a "test" installation (which will check for file conflicts without actually performing an install), or whether you want to exclude packages for other operating systems or system architectures.

In the **Interface** tab, you'll find a choice of displays for your packages: either as icons, which will be graphically-based, or as a list, which is not graphical but can provide more information about the packages.

Beneath these choices, you can specify the path through which GnoRPM can find new RPMs on your system. When you're using your Red Hat Linux CD-ROM, this will probably be

```
/mnt/cdrom/RedHat/RPMS
```

which is set as the default path for GnoRPM. If you download new RPMs from the Internet or want to install RPMs via a NFS mounted CD-ROM this path will be different for you.

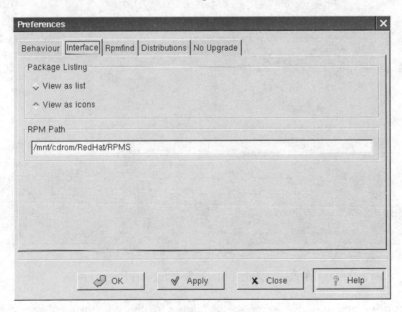

Figure 10.3: Interface Window

To change this path, type the full path to the RPMs you'd like to work with. Choosing the **Apply** or **OK** buttons will save this path, making it the default for future sessions.

After changing this path and closing the dialog box, you can use the **Install** button to view the packages available in the new location.

Optionally, if the path for your RPMs doesn't match the default path in your preferences, you'll be presented with a browser window, which will allow you to select the correct path for your new RPMs.

In addition to using the file dialog to add files to your install list, you can "drag" files from the GNOME Midnight Commander File Manager to add them to the list.

In the **Rpmfind** tab, you'll find settings and options which correspond to the **Web find** feature. The **Metadata server** sets the server to be used for searches. The **Download dir:** entry allows you to specify where you want the files to be stored. The **Local Hostname:** entry allows you to set your hostname (so that **Rpmfind** can guess the closest mirror).

Additionally, you can specify the vendor, distribution name and whether to find sources and/or the latest files.

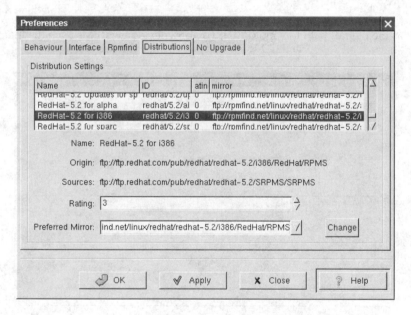

Figure 10.4: Distribution Settings in Preferences

In the **Distribution Settings** tab, you can set the options for choosing the most appropriate package out of the selections **Rpmfind** returns, as well as which mirror you would like to use. The higher the rating you indicate for your selection (as shown in Figure 10.4) the higher the priority it will receive; the lower rating, such as -1, will specify that packages not be recommended.

10.5 Package Manipulation

10.5.1 Querying Packages

The easiest way to query packages is to use the **Query** option from the menu at the top. If you want to query more than one package, make all your selections then press the **Query** button on the menu.

You'll be presented with a window like the one shown in Figure 10.5. The more packages you've queried, the more "tabs" you'll find within the **Query** box, each tab representing a **Query** window for a package.

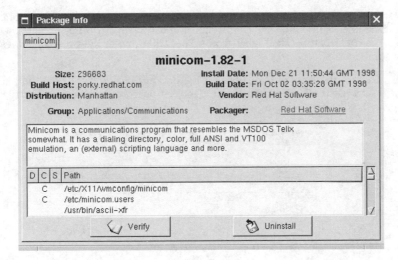

Figure 10.5: Query Window

The name of the package is centered at the top of the box. Below, the box is divided into two columns of listed information; below this information, you'll see a display area showing package files.

In the left column in the information list, you'll find the size of the file, the machine on which the file is found, the name of the package distribution and the group to which its function belongs.

In the right column, you'll find the date of the package's installation on your machine, the date the package was built, the name of the vendor and the name of the group who packaged the software. If the package has not been installed on your machine, that space will simply read, "not installed."

Below the description is a list of the files contained in the package. If a D appears in its related column to the left of the path, that file is a documentation file and would be a good thing to read for help on using the application. If a C appears in its respective column, the file is a configuration file. Under the S column, you can view the "state" of the package; here, you'll receive information if any files are reported as "missing" from the package (and therefore probably mean there's a problem with the package).

If you're querying a package that's already installed, you'll also find two additional buttons beneath at the bottom of this window: **Verify** and **Uninstall**. If you're performing a query on a package that hasn't been installed yet, the buttons on the bottom will be labeled **Install**, **Upgrade** and **Check Sig**.

To close the query window without performing any action, left-click on the **X** at the top right of the window bar.

10.5.2   Verifying Packages

Verifying a package checks all of the files in the package to ensure they match the ones present on your system. The checksum, file size, permissions, and owner attributes are all checked against the database. This check can be used when you suspect that one of the program's files has become corrupted for some reason.

Choosing the packages to verify is like choosing the packages to query. Select the packages in the display window and use the **Verify** button on the toolbar or from **Packages** ⇒ **Verify** on the menu. A window opens like the one in Figure 10.6.

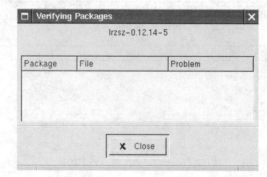

Figure 10.6: Verify Window

As the package is being checked, you'll see the progress in the **Verify** window. If there are any problems discovered during the verify process, they'll be described in the main display area.

10.5.3   Uninstalling Packages

Uninstalling a package removes the application and associated files from your machine. When a package is uninstalled, any files it uses that are not needed by other packages on your system are also removed. Changed configuration files are copied to `<filename>.rpmsave` so you can reuse them later.

Please Note: Remember that you must be root to uninstall packages.

If uninstalling a package would break "dependencies" (which could hobble other applications that require one or more of the removed files in the package), a dialog will pop up, asking you to confirm the deletion. This will occur if you haven't selected the "No dependency checks" box from the **Preferences** menu (as shown in Figure 10.7).

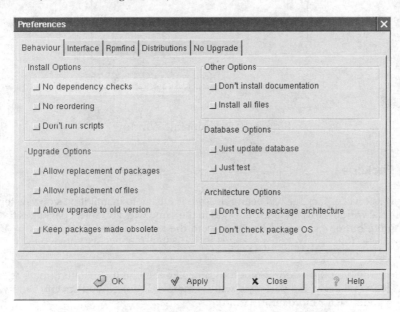

Figure 10.7: The Behavior Tab in Preferences

There are a variety of methods through which you can remove a selected package: from the menu, under **Packages**; from the toolbar and from the **Query** function. If you decide to remove more than one package at a time, you can choose either an incremental or global selection in the same way as you would when installing, querying or verifying. The total of your selections will be reflected in the status bar on the bottom of the main window. Because you can remove more than one package at a time, use caution to select only those which you wish to remove.

Once you've begun the uninstall, GnoRPM asks for confirmation, showing a window like the one in Figure 10.8. All of the packages that are about to be uninstalled are listed. You should look at them all to ensure you're not about to remove something you want to keep. Clicking the **Yes** button will start the uninstallation process. After it completes, the packages and groups that have been removed will disappear from any windows they were in.

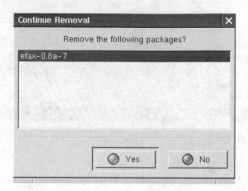

Figure 10.8: Uninstall Window

Upgrading Packages

When a new version of a package has been released, it is easy to install it on your system. Select the packages from the window of available packages in the same way you select packages for installation. Both the **Upgrade** button on the toolbar and, from the menu, under **Operations** ⇒ **Upgrade** will begin the process. You simply Add packages in the same manner as you would a new package installation.

During the upgrade, you'll see a progress indicator like the one for installing packages. When it's finished, any old versions of the packages will be removed, unless you specify otherwise (refer to Section 10.4 on page 188 for more information).

It is much better to use the upgrade option than to uninstall the old versions of a package and then install the new one. Using upgrade ensures that any changes you made to package configuration files are preserved properly, while uninstalling and then reinstalling a new package could cause those changes to be lost.

If you run out of disk space during an installation, the install will fail. However, the package which was being installed when the error occurred may leave some files around. To clean this up, reinstall the package after you've made more disk space available.

11

System Administration

This chapter is an overview of the Red Hat Linux system. It will illustrate things that you may not know about the system and things that are somewhat different from other UNIX systems.

11.1 Filesystem Structure

Red Hat Software is committed to the Linux File System Standard, a collaborative document that defines the names and locations of many files and directories. We will continue to track the standard to keep Red Hat compliant.

While compliance with the standard means many things, the two most important are compatibility with other compliant systems, and the ability to mount the /usr partition read-only. The /usr partition contains common executables and is not meant to be changed by users. Because of this, the /usr partition can be mounted from the CD-ROM or from another machine via read-only NFS. The current Linux Filesystem Standard (FSSTND) document is the authoritative reference to any FSSTND compliant filesystem, but the standard leaves many areas undefined or extensible. In this section we provide an overview of the standard and a description of the parts of the filesystem not covered by the standard.

The complete standard can be viewed at:

```
http://www.pathname.com/fhs/
```

11.1.1   Overview of the FSSTND

The directories and files noted here are a small subset of those specified by the FSSTND document. Check the latest FSSTND document for the most up-to-date and complete information.

The /dev **Directory**   The /dev directory contains file system entries that represent devices that are attached to the system. These files are essential for the system to function properly.

The /etc **Directory**   The /etc directory is reserved for configuration files that are local to your machine. No binaries are to be put in /etc. Binaries that were in the past put in /etc should now go into /sbin or possibly /bin.

The X11 and skel directories should be subdirectories of /etc:

```
/etc
  |- X11
  +- skel
```

The X11 directory is for X11 configuration files such as XF86Config. The skel directory is for "skeleton" user files, which are files used to populate a home directory when a user is first created.

The /lib **Directory**   The /lib directory should contain only those libraries that are needed to execute the binaries in /bin and /sbin.

The /proc **Directory**   The /proc directory contains special files that either extract information or send information to the kernel. It is an easy method of accessing information about the operating system using the cat command.

The /sbin **Directory**   The /sbin directory is for executables used only by the root user, and only those executables needed to boot and mount /usr and perform system recovery operations. The FSSTND says:

> "/sbin typically contains files essential for booting the system in addition to the binaries in /bin. Anything executed after /usr is known to be mounted (when there are no problems) should be placed in /usr/sbin. Local-only system administration binaries should be placed into /usr/local/sbin."

At a minimum, the following programs should be in /sbin:

```
clock, getty, init, update, mkswap, swapon, swapoff, halt,
reboot, shutdown, fdisk, fsck.*, mkfs.*, lilo, arp, ifconfig,
route
```

The /usr **Directory**   The /usr directory is for files that are shareable across a whole site. The /usr directory usually has its own partition, and it should be mountable read only. The following directories should be subdirectories of /usr:

```
/usr
    |- X11R6
    |- bin
    |- dict
    |- doc
    |- etc
    |- games
    |- include
    |- info
    |- lib
    |- local
    |- man
    |- sbin
    |- share
    +- src
```

The X11R6 directory is for the X Window System (XFree86 on Red Hat Linux), bin is for executables, doc is for random non-man-page documentation, etc is for site-wide configuration files, include is for C header files, info is for GNU info files, lib is for libraries, man is for man pages, sbin is for system administration binaries (those that do not belong in /sbin), and src is for source code.

The /usr/local **Directory**   The FSSTND says:

> "The /usr/local hierarchy is for use by the system administrator when installing software locally. It needs to be safe from being overwritten when the system software is updated. It may be used for programs and data that are shareable amongst a group of machines, but not found in /usr."

The /usr/local directory is similar in structure to the /usr directory. It has the following subdirectories, which are similar in purpose to those in the /usr directory:

```
/usr/local
        |- bin
        |- doc
        |- etc
        |- games
        |- include
        |- info
```

```
|- lib
|- man
|- sbin
+- src
```

The /var **Directory**   Since the FSSTND requires that you be able to mount /usr read-only, any programs that write log files or need spool or lock directories probably should write them to the /var directory. The FSSTND states /var is for

> "... variable data files. This includes spool directories and files, administrative and logging data, and transient and temporary files."

The following directories should be subdirectories of /var:

```
/var
   |- log
   |- catman
   |- lib
   |- local
   |- named
   |- nis
   |- preserve
   |- run
   |- lock
   |- tmp
   +- spool
       |- at
       |- cron
       |- lpd
       |- mail
       |- mqueue
       |- rwho
       |- smail
       |- uucp
       +- news
```

System log files such as wtmp and lastlog go in /var/log. The /var/lib directory also contains the RPM system databases. Formatted man pages go in /var/catman, and lock files go in /var/lock. The /var/spool directory has subdirectories for various systems that need to store data files.

11.1.2 `/usr/local` **in Red Hat Linux**

In Red Hat Linux, the intended use for `/usr/local` is slightly different from that specified by the FSSTND. The FSSTND says that `/usr/local` should be where you store software that is to remain safe from system software upgrades. Since system upgrades from Red Hat Software are done safely with the RPM system and GnoRPM, you don't need to protect files by putting them in `/usr/local`. Instead, we recommend you use `/usr/local` for software that is local to your machine.

For instance, let's say you have mounted `/usr` via read-only NFS from *beavis*. If there is a package or program you would like to install, but you are not allowed to write to *beavis*, you should install it under `/usr/local`. Later perhaps, if you've managed to convince the system administrator of *beavis* to install the program on `/usr`, you can uninstall it from `/usr/local`.

11.2   Special Red Hat File Locations

In addition to the files pertaining to the RPM system that reside in `/var/lib/rpm` (see Chapter 9), there are two other special locations that are reserved for Red Hat Linux configuration and operation.

The control-panel and related tools put lots of stuff in `/usr/lib/rhs`. There is probably nothing here that you would want to edit. It is mostly small scripts, bitmaps and text files.

The other location, `/etc/sysconfig`, stores configuration information. The major users of the files in this directory are the scripts that run at boot time. It is possible to edit these by hand, but it would be better to use the proper control-panel tool.

11.3   Users, Groups and User-Private Groups

Managing users and groups has traditionally been tedious. Red Hat Linux has a few tools and conventions that make user and groups easier to manage, and more useful.

The easiest way to manage users and groups is through Linuxconf (see Chapter 8). However, you can also use `adduser` to create a new user from the command line.

11.3.1 Standard Users

Table 11.3.1 lists the standard users set up by the installation process (this is essentially the `/etc/passwd` file). The group id (GID) in this table is the *primary group* for the user. See Section 11.3.3 for details on how groups are used.

User	UID	GID	Home Directory	Shell
root	0	0	/root	/bin/bash
bin	1	1	/bin	
daemon	2	2	/sbin	
adm	3	4	/var/adm	
lp	4	7	/var/spool/lpd	
sync	5	0	/sbin	/bin/sync
shutdown	6	0	/sbin	/sbin/shutdown
halt	7	0	/sbin	/sbin/halt
mail	8	12	/var/spool/mail	
news	9	13	/var/spool/news	
uucp	10	14	/var/spool/uucp	
operator	11	0	/root	
games	12	100	/usr/games	
gopher	13	30	/usr/lib/gopher-data	
ftp	14	50	/home/ftp	
nobody	99	99	/	

Figure 11.1: Standard Users

11.3.2   Standard Groups

Table 11.3.2 lists the standard groups as set up by the installation process (this is essentially the /etc/group file).

11.3.3   User Private Groups

Red Hat Linux uses a user private group (UPG) scheme, which makes UNIX groups much easier to use. The UPG scheme does not add or change anything in the standard UNIX way of handling groups. It simply offers a new convention for handling groups. Whenever you create a new user, by default, he or she has a unique group. The scheme works as follows:

User Private Group Each user has its own primary group, of which only it is a member.

umask = 002 The traditional UNIX umask is 022, which prevents other users *and other members of a user's primary group* from modifying a user's files. Since every user has their own private group in the UPG scheme, this "group protection" is not needed. A umask of 002 will prevent users from modifying other users' private files. The umask is set in /etc/profile.

setgid bit on Directories If you set the setgid bit on a directory (with chmod g+s *directory*), files created in that directory will have their group set to the directory's group.

Group	GID	Members
root	0	root
bin	1	root,bin,daemon
daemon	2	root,bin,daemon
sys	3	root,bin,adm
adm	4	root,adm,daemon
tty	5	
disk	6	root
lp	7	daemon,lp
mem	8	
kmem	9	
wheel	10	root
mail	12	mail
news	13	news
uucp	14	uucp
man	15	
games	20	
gopher	30	
dip	40	
ftp	50	
nobody	99	
users	100	
floppy	19	

Figure 11.2: Standard Groups

Most computing sites like to create a group for each major project and assign people to the groups they need to be in. Managing files traditionally has been difficult, though, because when someone creates a file it is owned by the primary group he or she belongs to. When a single person works on multiple projects, it becomes hard to make the files owned by the group that is associated with that project. In the UPG scheme, groups are automatically assigned to files on a project-by-project basis, which makes managing group projects very simple.

Let's say you have a big project called *devel*, with many people editing the devel files in a `devel` directory. Make a group called `devel`, `chgrp` the `devel` directory to `devel`, and add the all the devel users to the `devel` group. Now, all devel users will be able to edit the devel files and create new files in the `devel` directory, and these files will always retain their `devel` group. Thus, they will always be edit-able by other devel users.

If you have multiple projects like *devel*, and users who are working on multiple projects, these users will never have to change their umask or group when they move from project to project. The setgid bit on each project's main directory "selects" the proper group.

Since each user's HOME directory is owned by the user and their private group, it is safe to set the setgid bit on the HOME directory. However, by default, files are created with the primary group of the user, so the setgid bit would be redundant.

User Private Group Rationale

Although UPG is not new to Red Hat Linux 6.0, many people still have questions about it, such as why UPG is necessary. The following is the rationale for the scheme.

- You'd like to have a group of people work on a set of files in say, the `/usr/lib/emacs/site-lisp` directory. You trust a few people to mess around in there, but certainly not everyone.

- So you enter:

```
chown -R root.emacs /usr/lib/emacs/site-lisp
```

and you add the proper users to the group.

- To allow the users to actually create files in the directory you enter:

```
chmod 775 /usr/lib/emacs/site-lisp
```

- But when a user creates a new file it is assigned the group of the user's default group (usually `users`). To prevent this you enter

```
chmod 2775 /usr/lib/emacs/site-lisp
```

which causes everything in the directory to be created with the "emacs" group.

- But the new file needs to be mode 664 for another user in the emacs group to be able to edit it. To do this you make the default umask 002.

- Well, this all works fine, except that if your default group is "users," every file you create in your home directory will be writable by everybody in "users" (usually everyone).

- To fix this, you make each user have a "private group" as their default group.

At this point, by making the default umask 002 and giving everyone a private default group, you can easily set up groups that users can take advantage of without doing any magic. Just create the group, add the users, and do the above chown and chmod on the group's directories.

11.4   Configuring Console Access

When normal (non-root) users log in to a computer locally, they are given two types of special permission; they can run certain programs that they would not otherwise be able to run, and they can access certain files (normally special device files used to access diskettes, CD-ROMS, etc.) that they would not otherwise be able to access.

Since there are multiple consoles on a single computer, and multiple users can be logged into the computer locally at the same time, one of the users has to "win" the fight to access the files. The first user to log in at the console owns those files. Once the first user logs out, the next user who logs in will own the files.

In contrast, *every* user who logs in on the console will be allowed to run programs normally restricted to the root user. By default, those programs will ask for the user's password. This will be done graphically if X is running which makes it possible to make these actions menu items from within a graphical user interface. As shipped, the console-accessible programs are shutdown, halt, and reboot.

Disabling Console Program Access   In environments where the console is otherwise secured (BIOS and LILO passwords are set, control-alt-delete is disabled, the power and reset switches are disabled, etc.), it may not be desirable to allow arbitrary users at the console to run shutdown, halt, and reboot.

In order to disable all access by console users to console programs, you should run the command:

```
rm -f /etc/security/console.apps/*
```

Disabling All Console Access   In order to disable all console access, including program and file access, in the /etc/pam.d/ directory, comment out all lines that refer to pam_console.so. The following script will do the trick:

```
cd /etc/pam.d
for i in * ; do
  sed '/[^#].*pam_console.so/s/^/#/' < $i > foo && mv foo $i
done
```

Defining the Console   The `/etc/security/console.perms` file defines the console group. The syntax of that file is very flexible, so it's possible to edit that file so that these instructions no longer apply. However, the default file has a line that looks like this:

```
<console>=tty[0-9][0-9]* :[0-9]
.[0-9] :[0-9]
```

When users log in, they are attached to some sort of named terminal, either an X server with a name like :0 or mymachine.example.com:1.0; or a device like /dev/tty0 or /dev/pts/2. The default is to define that local virtual consoles and local X servers are considered local, but if you want to consider the serial terminal next to you on port /dev/ttyS1 to also be local, you can change that line to read:

```
<console>=tty[0-9][0-9]* :[0-9]
.[0-9] :[0-9] /dev/ttyS1
```

Making Files Console-Accessible   In /etc/security/console.perms, there is a section with lines like:

```
<cdrom>=/dev/cdrom
```

You can also add your own lines:

```
<scanner>=/dev/sga
```

(of course, make sure that /dev/sga is really your scanner and not, say, your hard drive).

That's the first part. The second part is to define what is done with those files. Look in the last section of /etc/security/console.perms for lines similar to

```
<console> 0600 <cdrom>  0600 root
```

and add a line like

```
<console> 0600 <scanner> 0600 root
```

Then when you log in at the console, you will be given ownership of the /dev/sga device and the permissions will be 0600 (readable and writable by you only). When you log out, the device will be owned by root and still have 0600 (now: readable and writable by root only) permissions.

Enabling Console Access for Other Applications   If you wish to make other applications besides `shutdown`, `reboot`, and `halt` accessible to console users, you will have to do just a little bit more work.

First of all, console access *only* works for applications which reside in `/sbin` or `/usr/sbin`, so the application that you wish to run must be there.

Create a link from the name of your application to the `/usr/bin/consolehelper` application:

```
cd /usr/bin
ln -s consolehelper foo
```

Create the file `/etc/security/console.apps/foo`

```
touch /etc/security/console.apps/foo
```

Create a PAM configuration file for the foo service in `/etc/pam.d/`. We suggest that you start with a copy of the shutdown service, then change it if you want to change the behavior:

```
cp /etc/pam.d/shutdown /etc/pam.d/foo
```

Now, when you run `/usr/bin/foo`, it will call consolehelper, which with the help of `/usr/sbin/userhelper` will authenticate the user (asking for the users password if `/etc/pam.d/foo` is a copy of `/etc/pam.d/shutdown`; otherwise, it will do precisely what is specified in `/etc/pam.d/foo`) and then run `/usr/sbin/foo` with root permissions.

11.5   The `floppy` Group

If, for whatever reason, console access is not appropriate for you, and you need to give non-root users access to your system's diskette drive, this can be done using the `floppy` group. Simply add the user(s) to the `floppy` group using the tool of your choice. Here's an example showing how `gpasswd` can be used to add user `fred` to the `floppy` group:

```
[root@bigdog root]# gpasswd -a fred floppy
Adding user fred to group floppy
[root@bigdog root]#
```

User `fred` will now be able to access the system's diskette drive (using the `mtools` utility programs, for instance).

11.6   User Authentication with PAM

Programs which give users access to privileges of any sort need to be able to authenticate the users. When you log into a system, you provide your name and password, and the login process uses those to authenticate the login – to verify that you are who you say you are. Other forms of authentication than passwords are possible, and it is possible for the passwords to be stored in different ways.

PAM, which stands for "Pluggable Authentication Modules," is a way of allowing the system administrator to set authentication policy without having to recompile programs which do authentication. With PAM, you control how the modules are plugged into the programs by editing a configuration file.

Most Red Hat Linux users will never need to touch this configuration file. When you use RPM to install programs that need to do authentication, they automatically make the changes that are needed to do normal password authentication. However, you may want to customize your configuration, in which case you need to understand the configuration file.

11.6.1   PAM Modules

There are four types of modules defined by the PAM standard. `auth` modules provide the actual authentication, perhaps asking for and checking a password, and set "credentials" such as group membership or kerberos "tickets." `account` modules check to make sure that the authentication is allowed (the account has not expired, the user is allowed to log in at this time of day, etc.). `password` modules are used to set passwords. `session` modules are used once a user has been authenticated to make it possible for them to use their account, perhaps mounting the user's home directory or making their mailbox available.

These modules may be *stacked*, so that multiple modules are used. For instance, rlogin normally makes use of at least two authentication methods: if "rhosts" authentication succeeds, it is sufficient to allow the connection; if it fails, then standard password authentication is done.

New modules can be added at any time, and PAM-aware applications can then be made to use them. For instance, if you have a one-time-password calculator system, and you can write a module to support it (documentation on writing modules is included with the system), PAM-aware programs can use the new module and work with the new one-time-password calculators without being recompiled or otherwise modified in any way.

11.6.2   Services

Each program using PAM defines its own "service" name. The login program defines the service type `login`, ftpd defines the service type `ftp`, etc. In general, the service type is the name of the program used to **access** the service, not (if there is a difference) the program used to **provide** the service.

11.6.3   The Configuration Files

The directory /etc/pam.d is used to configure all PAM applications. (This used to be /etc/pam.conf in earlier PAM versions; while the pam.conf file is still read if no /etc/pam.d/ entry is found, its use is deprecated.) Each application (really, each **service**) has its own file. A file looks like this:

```
#%PAM-1.0
auth       required    /lib/security/pam_securetty.so
auth       required    /lib/security/pam_pwdb.so shadow nullok
auth       required    /lib/security/pam_nologin.so
account    required    /lib/security/pam_pwdb.so
password   required    /lib/security/pam_cracklib.so
password   required    /lib/security/pam_pwdb.so shadow ↵
                                          nullok use_authtok
session    required    /lib/security/pam_pwdb.so
```

The first line is a comment. Any line that starts with a # character is a comment. Lines two through four stack up three modules to use for login authorization. Line two makes sure that *if* the user is trying to log in as root, the tty on which they are logging in is listed in the /etc/securetty file *if* that file exists. Line three causes the user to be asked for a password and the password checked. Line four checks to see if the file /etc/nologin exists, and if it does, displays the contents of the file, and if the user is not root, does not let him or her log in.

Note that all three modules are checked, *even if the first module fails*. This is a security decision—it is designed to not let the user know why their authentication was disallowed, because knowing why it was disallowed might allow them to break the authentication more easily. You can change this behavior by changing required to requisite; if any requisite module returns failure, PAM fails immediately without calling any other modules.

The fifth line causes any necessary accounting to be done. For example, if shadow passwords have been enabled, the pam_pwdb.so module will check to see if the account has expired, or if the user has not changed his or her password and the grace period for changing the password has expired.

The sixth line subjects a newly changed password to a series of tests to ensure that it cannot, for example, be easily determined by a dictionary-based password cracking program.

The seventh line (which we've had to wrap) specifies that if the login program changes the user's password, it should use the pam_pwdb.so module to do so. (It will do so only if an auth module has determined that the password needs to be changed—ie, if a shadow password has expired.)

The eighth and final line specifies that the pam_pwdb.so module should be used to manage the session. Currently, that module doesn't do anything; it could be replaced (or supplemented by stacking) by any necessary module.

Note that the order of the lines within each file matters. While it doesn't really matter much in which order required modules are called, there are other *control flags* available. While optional is rarely used, and never used by default on a Red Hat Linux system, `sufficient` and `requisite` cause order to become important.

Let's look at the `auth` configuration for `rlogin`:

```
auth    required    /lib/security/pam_securetty.so
auth    sufficient  /lib/security/pam_rhosts_auth.so
auth    required    /lib/security/pam_pwdb.so shadow nullok
auth    required    /lib/security/pam_nologin.so
```

That looks *almost* like the `login` entry, but there's an extra line specifying an extra module, and the modules are specified in a different order.

First, `pam_securetty.so` keeps root logins from happening on insecure terminals. This effectively disallows all root rlogin attempts. If you wish to allow them (in which case we recommend that you either not be internet-connected or be behind a good firewall), you can simply remove that line.

Second, `pam_nologin.so` checks `/etc/nologin`, as specified above.

Third, if `pam_rhosts_auth.so` authenticates the user, PAM immediately returns success to rlogin without any password checking being done. If `pam_rhosts_auth.so` fails to authenticate the user, that failed authentication is ignored.

Finally (if `pam_rhosts_auth.so` has failed to authenticate the user), the `pam_pwdb.so` module performs normal password authentication.

Note that if you do not want to prompt for a password if the securetty check fails, you can change the `pam_securetty.so` module from `required` to `requisite`

11.6.4 Shadow Passwords

The `pam_pwdb.so` module will automatically detect that you are using shadow passwords and make all necessary adjustments. Please refer to Section 11.7 on the next page for more information.

11.6.5 Rexec and PAM

For security reasons, rexec is not enabled in Red Hat Linux 6.0. Should you wish to enable it, you will need to comment out one line in the file `/etc/pam.d/rexec`. Here is a sample of the file (note that your file may differ slightly):

```
#%PAM-1.0
auth       required    /lib/security/pam_pwdb.so shadow nullok
auth       required    /lib/security/pam_nologin.so
account    required    /lib/security/pam_pwdb.so
```

To enable rexec, the line referring to the `pam_nologin.so` module must be commented out:

```
#%PAM-1.0
auth        required    /lib/security/pam_pwdb.so shadow nullok
#auth       required     /lib/security/pam_nologin.so
account     required    /lib/security/pam_pwdb.so
```

After this file is modified, rexec will be enabled.

Please Note: If your `/etc/pam.d/rexec` file contains a line referring to the `pam_securetty.so` module, you will not be able to rexec as root. To do so, you must also comment out the line referring to the `pam_securetty.so` module.

More Information This is just an introduction to PAM. More information is included in the `/usr/doc/pam*` directory, including a *System Administrators' Guide*, a *Module Writers' Manual*, an *Application Developers' Manual*, and the PAM standard, DCE-RFC 86.0. In addition, documentation is available from the Red Hat website, at `http://www.redhat.com/linux-info/pam/`.

11.7 Shadow Utilities

Support for shadow passwords has been enhanced significantly for Red Hat Linux 6.0. Shadow passwords are a method of improving system security by moving the encrypted passwords (normally found in `/etc/passwd`) to another file with more restrictive file access permissions. During the installation, you were given the option of setting up shadow password protection on your system.

The `shadow-utils` package contains a number of utilities that support:

- Conversion from normal to shadowed passwords and back (`pwconv`, `pwunconv`).

- Verification of the password, group, and associated shadow files (`pwck`, `grpck`).

- Industry-standard methods of adding, deleting and modifying user accounts (`useradd`, `usermod`, and `userdel`).

- Industry-standard methods of adding, deleting, and modifying user groups (`groupadd`, `groupmod`, and `groupdel`).

- Industry-standard method of administering the `/etc/group` file (`gpasswd`).

Please Note: There are a few additional points of interest concerning these utilities:

- The utilities will work properly whether shadowing is enabled or not.

- The utilities have been slightly modified to support Red Hat Software's user private group scheme. For a description of the modifications, please see the `useradd` man page. For more information on user private groups, please turn to Section 11.3.3 on page 200.

- The `adduser` script has been replaced with a symlink to `/usr/sbin/useradd`.

11.8   Building a Custom Kernel

With the introduction of modularization in the Linux 2.2.*x* kernel there have been some significant changes in building customized kernels. In the past you were required to compile support into your kernel if you wanted to access a particular hardware or filesystem component. For some hardware configurations the size of the kernel could quickly reach a critical level. To require ready support for items that were only occasionally used was an inefficient use of system resources. With the capabilities of the 2.2.*x* kernel, if there are certain hardware components or filesystems that are used infrequently, driver modules for them can be loaded on demand. For information on handling kernel modules see Chapter 8.2, Section 8.2.2.

Many people new to Linux often ask, "why should I build my own kernel?" Given the advances that have been made in the use of kernel modules, the most accurate response to that question is, "unless you know why you need to build your own kernel, you probably don't." So unless you have a specific reason to build a customized kernel (or you're just the curious sort), you may skip ahead to Section 11.9 on page 214.

11.8.1   Building a modularized kernel

These instructions provide you with the knowledge needed to take advantage of the power and flexibility available through kernel modularization. If you do not wish to take advantage of modularization, please see Section 11.8.3 for an explanation of the different aspects of building and installing a monolithic kernel. It's assumed that you've already installed the `kernel-headers` and `kernel-source` packages and that you issue all commands from the `/usr/src/linux` directory.

It is important to begin a kernel build with the source tree in a known condition. Therefore, it is recommended that you begin with the command `make mrproper`. This will remove any configuration files along with the remains of any previous builds that may be scattered around the source tree. Now you must create a configuration file that will determine which components to include in your new kernel. Depending upon your hardware and personal preferences there are three methods available to configure the kernel.

- `make config` – An interactive text program. Components are presented and you answer with Y (yes), N (no), or M (module).

- `make menuconfig` – A graphic, menu driven program. Components are presented in a menu of categories, you select the desired components in the same manner used in the Red Hat Linux installation program. Toggle the tag corresponding to the item you want included; **Y** (yes), **N** (no), or **M** (module).

- `make xconfig` – An X Windows program. Components are listed in different levels of menus, components are selected using a mouse. Again, select **Y** (yes), **N** (no), or **M** (module).

Please Note: In order to use `kerneld` (see Section 8.2.2 for details) and kernel modules you must answer **Yes** to **kerneld support** and **module version (CONFIG_MODVERSIONS) support** in the configuration.

Please Note: If you are building a Linux/Intel kernel on (or for) a machine that uses a "clone" processor (for example, one made by Cyrix or AMD), it is recommended to choose a **Processor type** of **386**.

If you wish to build a kernel with a configuration file (`/usr/src/linux/.config`) that you have already created with one of the above methods, you can omit the `make mrproper` and `make config` commands and use the command `make dep` followed by `make clean` to prepare the source tree for the build.

The next step consists of the actual compilation of the source code components into a working program that your machine can use to boot. The method described here is the easiest to recover from in the event of a mishap. If you are interested in other possibilities, details can be found in the Kernel-HOWTO or in the `Makefile` in `/usr/src/linux` on your Linux system.

- Build the kernel with `make boot`.

- Build any modules you configured with `make modules`.

- Move the old set of modules out of the way with:

```
rm -rf /lib/modules/2.0.36-old
mv /lib/modules/2.0.36 /lib/modules/2.0.36-old
```

Of course, if you have upgraded your kernel, replace `2.0.36` with the version you are using.

- Install the new modules (even if you didn't build any) with `make modules_install`.

If you have a SCSI adapter and made your SCSI driver modular, build a new `initrd` image (see Section 11.8.2; note that there are few practical reasons to make the SCSI driver modular in a custom kernel).

In order to provide a redundant boot source to protect from a possible error in a new kernel you should keep the original kernel available. Adding a kernel to the LILO menu is as simple as renaming the original kernel in `/boot`, copying the new kernel to `/boot`, adding a few lines in `/etc/lilo.conf` and running `/sbin/lilo`. Here is an example of the default `/etc/lilo.conf` file shipped with Red Hat Linux:

```
boot=/dev/hda
map=/boot/map
install=/boot/boot.b
prompt
timeout=100
image=/boot/vmlinuz
        label=linux
        root=/dev/hda1
        read-only
```

Now you must update /etc/lilo.conf. If you built a new initrd image you must tell LILO to use it. In this example of /etc/lilo.conf we have added four lines in the middle of the file to indicate another kernel to boot from. We have renamed /boot/vmlinuz to /boot/vmlinuz.old and changed its label to old. We have also added an initrd line for the new kernel:

```
boot=/dev/hda
map=/boot/map
install=/boot/boot.b
prompt
timeout=100
image=/boot/vmlinuz
        label=linux
        initrd=/boot/initrd
        root=/dev/hda1
        read-only
image=/boot/vmlinuz.old
        label=old
        root=/dev/hda1
        read-only
```

Now when the system boots and you press (Tab) at the LILO boot: prompt two choices will be shown;

```
LILO boot:
linux    old
```

To boot the new kernel (linux) simply press (Enter), or wait for LILO to time out. If you want to boot the old kernel (old), type old and press (Enter).

Here is a summary of the steps:

- mv /boot/vmlinuz /boot/vmlinuz.old
- cp /usr/src/linux/arch/i386/boot/zImage /boot/vmlinuz

- edit `/etc/lilo.conf`

- run `/sbin/lilo`

You can begin testing your new kernel by rebooting your computer and watching the messages to ensure your hardware is detected properly.

11.8.2 Making an initrd image

An `initrd` image is needed for loading your SCSI module at boot time. The shell script `/sbin/mkinitrd` can build a proper `initrd` image for your machine if the following conditions are met:

- The loopback block device is available.

- The `/etc/conf.modules` file has a line for your SCSI adapter; for example:

      alias scsi_hostadapter BusLogic

To build the new `initrd` image, run `/sbin/mkinitrd` with parameters such as this:

      /sbin/mkinitrd /boot/newinitrd-image 2.0.36

where `/boot/newinitrd-image` is the file to use for your new image, and `2.0.36` is the kernel whose modules (from `/lib/modules`) should be used in the `initrd` image (not necessarily the same as the version number of the currently running kernel).

11.8.3 Building a monolithic kernel

To build a monolithic kernel you follow the same steps as building a modularized kernel with a few exceptions.

- When configuring the kernel only answer **Yes** and **No** to the questions (don't make anything modular).

- Omit the steps:

      make modules
      make modules_install

- Edit the file `/etc/rc.d/rc.sysinit` and comment out the line `depmod -a` by inserting a "#" at the beginning of the line.

11.9   Sendmail

A default `sendmail.cf` file will be installed in `/etc`. The default configuration should work for most SMTP-only sites. It will *not* work for UUCP sites; you will need to generate a new `send-mail.cf` if you must use UUCP mail transfers. To generate a new `sendmail.cf`, you will need to install `m4` and the `sendmail` source package. Read the `README` file in the sendmail sources for more details on creating `sendmail` configuration files. Also, O'Reilly & Associates publishes a good sendmail reference entitled *sendmail*, by Bryan Costales.

One common sendmail configuration is to have a single machine act as a mail gateway for all the machines on your network. For instance, at Red Hat Software we have a machine `mail.redhat.com` that does all our mail. On that machine we simply need to add the names of machines for which `mail.redhat.com` will handle mail to `/etc/sendmail.cw`. Here is an example:

```
# sendmail.cw - include all aliases for your machine
# here.
torgo.redhat.com
poodle.redhat.com
devel.redhat.com
```

Then on the other machines, `torgo`, `poodle`, and `devel`, we need to edit `/etc/sendmail.cf` to "masquerade" as `mail.redhat.com` when sending mail, and to forward any local mail processing to `redhat.com`. Find the `DH` and `DM` lines in `/etc/sendmail.cf` and edit them thusly:

```
# who I send unqualified names to
# (null means deliver locally)
DRmail.redhat.com

# who gets all local email traffic
DHmail.redhat.com

# who I masquerade as (null for no masquerading)
DMredhat.com
```

With this type of configuration, all mail sent will appear as if it were sent from `redhat.com`, and any mail sent to `torgo.redhat.com` or the other hosts will be delivered to `mail.redhat.com`.

Please be aware that if you configure your system to masquerade as another any e-mail sent from your system to your system will be sent to the machine you are masquerading as. For example, in the above illustration, log files that are periodically sent to `root@poodle.redhat.com` by the `cron` daemon would be sent to `root@mail.redhat.com`.

11.10 Controlling Access to Services

As a security measure, most network services are managed by a protective program called a *TCP wrapper*. The protected services are those listed in
`/etc/inetd.conf` that specify `/usr/sbin/tcpd`. `tcpd` can allow or deny access to a service based on the origin of the request, and the configuration in
`/etc/hosts.allow` and `/etc/hosts.deny`.   By default Red Hat Linux allows all service requests. To disable or limit services you can edit `/etc/hosts.allow`. Here is an example `/etc/hosts.allow` file:

```
ALL: redhat.com .redhat.com
in.talkd: ALL
in.ntalkd: ALL
in.fingerd: ALL
in.ftpd: ALL
```

This configuration allows all connections from `redhat.com` and `*.redhat.com` machines. It also allows talk, finger, and ftp requests from all machines.

`tcpd` allows much more sophisticated access control, using a combination of
`/etc/hosts.allow` and `/etc/hosts.deny`. Read the tcpd(8) and hosts_access(5) man pages for complete details.

11.11 Anonymous FTP

Setting up anonymous FTP is simple. All you need to do is install the `anon-ftp` rpm package (which you may have already done at install time). Once it is installed, anonymous FTP will be up and running.

There are a few files you might wish to edit to configure your FTP server.

`/etc/ftpaccess` – This file defines most of the access control for your ftp server. Some of the things that you can do are: set up logical "groups" to control access from different sites, limit the number of simultaneous FTP connections, configure transfer logging, and much more. Read the ftpaccess man page for complete details.

`/etc/ftphosts` – The ftphosts file is used to allow or deny access to certain accounts from various hosts. Read the ftphosts man page for details.

`/etc/ftpusers` – This file lists all the users that are *not* allowed to ftp into your machine. For example, `root` is listed in `/etc/ftpusers` by default. That means that you can not ftp to your machine and log in as root. This is a good security measure, but some administrators prefer to remove `root` from this file.

11.12   NFS Configuration

NFS stands for Network File System, and is a way to share files between machines as if they were on
your local hard drive. Linux can be both an NFS server and an NFS client, which means that it can
export filesystems to other systems, and *mount* filesystems exported from other machines.

Mounting NFS Filesystems   Use the `mount` command to mount an NFS filesystem from another machine:

```
mkdir /mnt/local # Only required if /mnt/local doesn't exist
mount bigdog:/mnt/export /mnt/local
```

In this command, `bigdog` is the hostname of the NFS fileserver, `/mnt/export` is the filesystem
that bigdog is exporting, and `/mnt/local` is a directory on my local machine where we want to
mount the filesystem. After the `mount` command runs (and if we have the proper permissions from
`bigdog`) we can enter `ls /mnt/local` and get a listing of the files in `/mnt/export` on `bigdog`.

Exporting NFS Filesystems   The file that controls what filesystems you wish to export is
`/etc/exports`. Its format is:

```
directory         hostname(options)
```

the `(options)` are optional. For example:

```
/mnt/export       speedy.redhat.com
```

would allow `speedy.redhat.com` to mount `/mnt/export`, but:

```
/mnt/export       speedy.redhat.com(ro)
```

would just allow `speedy` to mount `/mnt/export` read-only.

Each time you change `/etc/exports`, you must tell the NFS daemons to examine it for new information. One simple way to accomplish this is to just stop and start the daemons:

```
/etc/rc.d/init.d/nfs stop
/etc/rc.d/init.d/nfs start
```

The following will also work:

```
killall -HUP rpc.nfsd rpc.mountd
```

See the following man pages for more details: nfsd(8), mountd(8), and exports(5). Another good reference is *Managing NFS and NIS Services*, by Hal Stern, published by O'Reilly & Associates.

11.13   The Boot Process, Init, and Shutdown

This section contains information on what happens when a Red Hat Linux system is booted and shut down. Let's start with information on the files in /etc/sysconfig.

11.13.1   Sysconfig Information

The following information outlines the various files in /etc/sysconfig, their function, and their contents.

Files in /etc/sysconfig

The following files are normally found in /etc/sysconfig:

- /etc/sysconfig/clock
- /etc/sysconfig/keyboard
- /etc/sysconfig/mouse
- /etc/sysconfig/network
- /etc/sysconfig/pcmcia
- /etc/sysconfig/amd
- /etc/sysconfig/tape

Let's take a look at each one.

/etc/sysconfig/clock   – The /etc/sysconfig/clock file controls the interpretation of values read from the system clock. Earlier releases of Red Hat Linux used the following values (which is deprecated):

- **CLOCKMODE=*mode***, where ***mode*** is one of the following:

- **GMT** – indicates that the clock is set to UTC.
- **ARC** – on Alpha only indicates the ARC console's 42-year time offset is in effect.

Currently, the correct values are:

- **UTC=*boolean*,** where **boolean** is one of the following:

  - **true** – indicates that the clock is set to UTC. Any other value indicates that it is set to local time.

- **ARC=*boolean*,** where **boolean** is one of the following:

  - **true** – (for Alpha-based systems only) Indicates the ARC console's 42-year time offset is in effect. Any other value indicates that the normal UNIX epoch is assumed.

/etc/sysconfig/keyboard – The `/etc/sysconfig/keyboard` files controls the behavior of the keyboard. The following values may be used:

- **KEYTABLE=*file*,** where **file** is the name of a keytable file. For example:
  `KEYTABLE="/usr/lib/kbd/keytables/us.map"`

/etc/sysconfig/mouse – The `/etc/sysconfig/mouse` file is used to specify information about the available mouse. The following values may be used:

- **MOUSETYPE=*type*,** where `type` is one of the following:

  - **microsoft** – A Microsoft mouse.
  - **mouseman** – A MouseMan mouse.
  - **mousesystems** – A Mouse Systems mouse.
  - **ps/2** – A PS/2 mouse.
  - **msbm** – A Microsoft bus mouse.
  - **logibm** – A Logitech bus mouse.
  - **atibm** – An ATI bus mouse.
  - **logitech** – A Logitech mouse.
  - **mmseries** – An older MouseMan mouse.
  - **mmhittab** – An mmhittab mouse.

- **XEMU3=*emulation*,** where **emulation** is one of the following:

  - **yes** – Three mouse buttons should be emulated.
  - **no** – The mouse already has three buttons.

In addition, `/dev/mouse` is a symlink that points to the actual mouse device.

/etc/sysconfig/network – The `/etc/sysconfig/network` file is used to specify information about the desired network configuration. The following values may be used:

- **NETWORKING=*answer***, where ***answer*** is one of the following:

  - **yes** – Networking should be configured.
  - **no** – Networking should not be configured.

- **HOSTNAME=*hostname***, where ***hostname*** should be the FQDN (Fully Qualified Domain Name), but can be whatever hostname you want.

  Please Note: For compatibility with older software that people might install (such as `trn`), the `/etc/HOSTNAME` file should contain the same value as here.

- **FORWARD_IPV4=*answer***, where ***answer*** is one of the following:

  - **yes** – Perform IP forwarding.
  - **no** – Do not perform IP forwarding.

  (The current Red Hat Linux installation sets this to "no" by default (for RFC compliance), but if FORWARD_IPV4 is not set at all, forwarding is *enabled* for compatibility with the configuration files used on Red Hat Linux versions 4.2 and earlier.)

- **GATEWAY=*gw-ip***, where ***gw-ip*** is the IP address of the network's gateway.

- **GATEWAYDEV=*gw-dev***, where ***gw-dev*** is the gateway device (e.g. eth0).

- **NISDOMAIN=*dom-name***, where ***dom-name*** is the NIS domain name.

/etc/sysconfig/pcmcia – The `/etc/sysconfig/pcmcia` file is used to specify PCMCIA configuration information. The following values may be used:

- **PCMCIA=*answer***, where ***answer*** is one of the following:

  - **yes** – PCMCIA support should be enabled.
  - **no** – PCMCIA support should not be enabled.

- **PCIC=*pcic-type***, where ***pcic-type*** is one of the following:

  - **i82365** – The computer has an i82365-style PCMCIA socket chipset.
  - **tcic** – The computer has a tcic-style PCMCIA socket chipset.

- **PCIC_OPTS=*option***, where ***option*** is the socket driver (i82365 or tcic) timing parameters.

- **CORE_OPTS=*option***, where ***option*** is the list of pcmcia_core options.

- **CARDMGR_OPTS=*option***, where ***option*** is the list of options for the PCMCIA cardmgr.

/etc/sysconfig/amd – The `/etc/sysconfig/amd` file is used to specify operational parameters for amd. The following values may be used:

- **ADIR=*path***, where ***path*** is the amd directory. It should be "`/.automount.`" and is normally never changed.

- **MOUNTPTS=*mountpts***, where ***mountpts*** is, for example, "`/net /etc/amd.conf`"

- **AMDOPTS=*options***, where ***options*** are any extra options for AMD.

/etc/sysconfig/tape – The `/etc/sysconfig/tape` file is used to specify tape-related configuration information. The following values may be used:

- **DEV=*devnam***, where ***devnam*** is the tape device (for example, "`/dev/nst0`)." Use the non-rewinding device for these scripts.

  For SCSI tapes this is "`/dev/nst#`," where "#" is the number of the tape drive you want to use. If you only have one, then use "`/dev/nst0`."

  For IDE tapes you use "`/dev/ht#`," where "#" is the number of the tape drive you want to use. If you only have one, then use "`/dev/ht0`."

  For floppy tape drives use "`/dev/ftape`."

- **ADMIN=*account***, where ***account*** is the user account to send mail to if the backup fails for any reason. Normally set to "`root`."

- **SLEEP=*time***, where ***time*** is the time to sleep between tape operations. Some drives need a bit more than others, but "5" seems to work for 8mm, 4mm, and DLT.

- **BLOCKSIZE=*size***, where ***size*** is the tape drive's optimal block size. A value of "32768" worked fine for 8mm, then 4mm, and now DLT. An optimal setting is probably however much data your drive writes at one time.

- **SHORTDATE=*date***, where ***date*** is a string that evaluates to a short date string, to be used in backup log filenames. The default setting is: "`$(date +%y:%m:%d:%H:%M)`."

- **DAY=*date***, where ***date*** is a string that evaluates to a date string, to be used for the log file directory. The default setting is: "`$(date +log-%y:%m:%d)`."

- **DATE=*date***, where ***date*** is a string that evaluates to a regular date string, to be used in log files. The default setting is: "`$(date)`."

- **LOGROOT=*path***, where ***path*** is the root of the logging directory.

- **LIST=*file***, where ***file*** is the file name the incremental backup will use to store the incremental list. It will be followed by a sequence number.

- **DOTCOUNT=*count***, where ***count*** is the name of a file used for counting as you go, to know which incremental list to use.

- **COUNTER=*count-file***, where **count-file** is used for rewinding when done.

- **BACKUPTAB=*file***, where **file** is the name of the file in which we keep our list of backup(s) we want to make.

Files in /etc/sysconfig/network-scripts/

The following files are normally found in /etc/sysconfig/network-scripts:

- /etc/sysconfig/network-scripts/ifup
- /etc/sysconfig/network-scripts/ifdown
- /etc/sysconfig/network-scripts/network-functions
- /etc/sysconfig/network-scripts/ifcfg-*<interface-name>*
- /etc/sysconfig/network-scripts/ifcfg-*<interface-name>*-*<clone-name>*
- /etc/sysconfig/network-scripts/chat-*<interface-name>*
- /etc/sysconfig/network-scripts/dip-*<interface-name>*
- /etc/sysconfig/network-scripts/ifup-post
- /etc/sysconfig/network-scripts/ifdhcpc-done

Let's take a look at each one.

/etc/sysconfig/network-scripts/ifup, /etc/sysconfig/network-scripts/ifdown – Symlinks to /sbin/ifup and /sbin/ifdown, respectively. These are the only two scripts in this directory that should be called directly; these two scripts call all the other scripts as needed. These symlinks are here for legacy purposes only – they will probably be removed in future versions, so only /sbin/ifup and /sbin/ifdown should currently be used.

These scripts take one argument normally: the name of the device (e.g. "eth0"). They are called with a second argument of "boot" during the boot sequence so that devices that are not meant to be brought up on boot (ONBOOT=no, [see below]) can be ignored at that time.

/etc/sysconfig/network-scripts/network-functions – Not really a public file. Contains functions which the scripts use for bringing interfaces up and down. In particular, it contains most of the code for handling alternative interface configurations and interface change notification through netreport.

/etc/sysconfig/network-scripts/ifcfg-<***interface-name***>,
/etc/sysconfig/network-scripts/ifcfg-<***interface-name***>-<***clone-name***> – The first
file defines an interface, while the second file contains only the parts of the definition that are different
in a "clone" (or alternative) interface. For example, the network numbers might be different, but
everything else might be the same, so only the network numbers would be in the clone file, while all
the device information would be in the base ifcfg file.

The items that can be defined in an ifcfg file depend on the interface type.

The following values are common to all base files:

- **DEVICE=*name***, where ***name*** is the name of the physical device (except dynamically-allocated
  PPP devices where it is the "logical name").

- **IPADDR=*addr***, where ***addr*** is the IP address.

- **NETMASK=*mask***, where ***mask*** is the netmask value.

- **NETWORK=*addr***, where ***addr*** is the network address.

- **BROADCAST=*addr***, where ***addr*** is the broadcast address.

- **GATEWAY=*addr***, where ***addr*** is the gateway address.

- **ONBOOT=*answer***, where ***answer*** is one of the following:

  - **yes** – This device should be activated at boot-time.
  - **no** – This device should not be activated at boot-time.

- **USERCTL=*answer***, where ***answer*** is one of the following:

  - **yes** – Non-root users are allowed to control this device.
  - **no** – Non-root users are not allowed to control this device.

- **BOOTPROTO=*proto***, where ***proto*** is one of the following:

  - **none** – No boot-time protocol should be used.
  - **bootp** – The bootp protocol should be used.
  - **dhcp** – The dhcp protocol should be used.

The following values are common to all PPP and SLIP files:

- **PERSIST=*answer***, where ***answer*** is one of the following:

  - **yes** – This device should be kept active at all times, even if deactivated after a modem
    hangup.
  - **no** – This device should not be kept active at all times.

- **MODEMPORT=*port***, where *port* is the modem port's device name (for exmaple, "/dev/modem").

- **LINESPEED=*baud***, where *baud* is the modem's linespeed (for example, "115200").

- **DEFABORT=*answer***, where *answer* is one of the following:

  - **yes** – Insert default abort strings when creating/editing the script for this interface.
  - **no** – Do not insert default abort strings when creating/editing the script for this interface.

The following values are common to all PPP files:

- **DEFROUTE=*answer***, where *answer* is one of the following:

  - **yes** – Set this interface as the default route.
  - **no** – Do not set this interface as the default route.

- **ESCAPECHARS=*answer***, where *answer* is one of the following:

  - **yes** – Use the pre-defined asyncmap.
  - **no** – Do not use the pre-defined asyncmap.

  (This represents a simplified interface; it doesn't let people specify which characters to escape. However, almost everyone can use an asyncmap of 00000000 anyway, and it's possible to set PPPOPTIONS to use an arbitrary asyncmap if so desired.)

- **HARDFLOWCTL=*answer***, where *answer* is one of the following:

  - **yes** – Use hardware flow control.
  - **no** – Do not use hardware flow control.

- **PPPOPTIONS=*options***, where *options* is an arbitrary option string. It is placed last on the command line so it can override other options (such as asyncmap) that were specified previously.

- **PAPNAME=*name***, where *name* is used as part of "name $PAPNAME" on the pppd command line.

  Note that the "remotename" option is always specified as the logical PPP device name, like "ppp0" (which might perhaps be the physical device ppp1 if some other PPP device was brought up earlier...), which makes it easy to manage pap/chap files – name/password pairs are associated with the logical PPP device name so that they can be managed together.

  In principle, there shouldn't anything that would keep the logical PPP device names from being "worldnet" or "myISP" instead of "ppp0" – "pppN."

- **REMIP=*addr***, where *addr* is the remote ip address (which is normally unspecified).

- **MTU=*value*,** where ***value*** is the value to be used as MTU.

- **MRU=*value*,** where ***value*** is the value to be used as MRU.

- **DISCONNECTTIMEOUT=*value*,** where ***value*** represents the number of seconds to wait before re-establishing the connection after a successfully-connected session terminated.

- **RETRYTIMEOUT=*value*,** where ***value*** represents the number of seconds to wait before re-attempting to establish a connection after a previous attempt has failed.

/etc/sysconfig/network-scripts/chat-<*interface-name*> – This file is a chat script for PPP or SLIP connections, and is intended to establish the connection. For SLIP devices, a DIP script is written from the chat script; for PPP devices, the chat script is used directly.

/etc/sysconfig/network-scripts/dip-<*interface-name*> – This write-only script is created from the chat script by netcfg. Do not modify this file. In the future, this file may disappear and instead will be created on-the-fly from the chat script.

/etc/sysconfig/network-scripts/ifup-post – This file is called when any network device (except a SLIP device) comes up. Calls `/etc/sysconfig/network-scripts/ifup-routes` to bring up static routes that depend on that device. Brings up aliases for that device. Sets the hostname if it is not already set and a hostname can be found for the IP for that device. Sends SIGIO to any programs that have requested notification of network events.

Could be extended to fix up nameservice configuration, call arbitrary scripts, and more, as needed.

/etc/sysconfig/network-scripts/ifdhcpc-done – This file is called by dhcpcd once dhcp configuration is complete; sets up `/etc/resolv.conf` from the version dhcpcd dropped in `/etc/dhcpc/resolv.conf`.

11.13.2 System V Init

This section is a brief description of the internals of the boot process. It basically covers in detail how the machine boots using SysV init, as well as the differences between the init used in older Linux releases, and SysV init.

Init is the program that gets run by the kernel at boot time. It is in charge of starting all the normal processes that need to run at boot time. These include the getty processes that allow you to log in, NFS daemons, FTP daemons, and anything else you want to run when your machine boots.

SysV init is fast becoming the standard in the Linux world to control the startup of software at boot time. This is because it is easier to use and more powerful and flexible than the traditional BSD init.

SysV init also differs from BSD init in that the config files are in a subdirectory of `/etc` instead of residing directly in `/etc`. This directory is called `rc.d`. In there you will find `rc.sysinit` and the following directories:

```
init.d
rc0.d
rc1.d
rc2.d
rc3.d
rc4.d
rc5.d
rc6.d
```

`init.d` contains a bunch of scripts. Basically, you reqiire one script for each service you may need to start at boot time or when entering another runlevel. Services include things like networking, nfs, sendmail, httpd, etc. Services do not include things like setserial that must only be run once and then exited. Things like that should go in `rc.local` or `rc.serial`.

If you want `rc.local`, it should be in `/etc/rc.d`. Most systems include one even though it doesn't do much. You can also include an rc.serial in `/etc/rc.d` if you need to do serial port specific things at boot time.

The chain of events is as follows:

- The kernel looks in several places for `init` and runs the first one it finds

- `init` runs `/etc/rc.d/rc.sysinit`

- `rc.sysinit` does a bunch of necessary things and then runs `rc.serial` (if it exists)

- `init` runs all the scripts for the default runlevel.

- `init` runs `rc.local`

The default runlevel is decided in `/etc/inittab`. You should have a line close to the top like:

```
id:3:initdefault:
```

From this, you'd look in the second column and see that the default runlevel is 3, as should be the case for most systems. If you want to change it, you can edit `/etc/inittab` by hand and change the 3. Be very careful when you are messing with the inittab. If you do mess up, you can fix it by rebooting and doing:

```
LILO boot:  linux single
```

This *should* allow you to boot into single user mode so you can fix inittab.

Now, how does it run all the right scripts? If you enter `ls -l` on `rc3.d`, you might see something like:

```
lrwxrwxrwx 1 root root 17 3:11 S10network -> ../init.d/network
lrwxrwxrwx 1 root root 16 3:11 S30syslog -> ../init.d/syslog
lrwxrwxrwx 1 root root 14 3:32 S40cron -> ../init.d/cron
lrwxrwxrwx 1 root root 14 3:11 S50inet -> ../init.d/inet
lrwxrwxrwx 1 root root 13 3:11 S60nfs -> ../init.d/nfs
lrwxrwxrwx 1 root root 15 3:11 S70nfsfs -> ../init.d/nfsfs
lrwxrwxrwx 1 root root 18 3:11 S90lpd -> ../init.d/lpd.init
lrwxrwxrwx 1 root root 11 3:11 S99local -> ../rc.local
```

What you'll notice is that there are no real "files" in the directory. Everything there is a link to one of the scripts in the init.d directory. The links also have an "S" and a number at the beginning. The "S" means to start this particular script and a "K" would mean to stop it. The number is there just for ordering purposes. Init will start all the services based on the order in which they appear. You can duplicate numbers, but it will only confuse you somewhat. You only need to use a two digit number, along with an upper case "S" or "K" to start or stop the services you require to.

How does init start and stop services? Simple. Each of the scripts is written to accept an argument which can be "start" and "stop." You can execute those scripts by hand, in fact, with a command like:

```
/etc/rc.d/init.d/httpd.init stop
```

to stop the httpd server. Init just reads the name and if it has a "K," it calls the script with the "stop" argument. If it has an "S" it calls the script with a "start" argument.

Why all these runlevels? Some people want an easy way to set up machines to be multi-purpose. You could have a "server" runlevel that just runs httpd, sendmail, networking, etc. Then you could have a "user" runlevel that runs xdm, networking, etc.

11.13.3 Init Runlevels

Generally, Red Hat Linux operates in run level 3—full multiuser mode. The following runlevels are defined in Red Hat Linux:

0 Halt
1 Single user mode
2 Multiuser mode, without NFS
3 Full multiuser mode
4 Not used

5 Full multiuser mode (with an X-based login screen)

6 Reboot

If your machine gets into a state where it will not boot due to a bad /etc/inittab, or will not let you log in because you have a corrupted /etc/passwd or have simply forgotten your password, boot into single user mode by typing linux 1 at the LILO boot prompt. A very bare system will come up and you will be given a shell from which you can fix things.

11.13.4 Initscript Utilities

The chkconfig utility provides a simple command-line tool for maintaining the /etc/rc.d directory hierarchy. It relieves system administrators from having to directly manipulate the numerous symlinks in /etc/rc.d.

In addition, there is the ntsysv utility, that provides a screen-oriented interface, versus chkconfig's command-line interface.

Please see the chkconfig and ntsysv man pages for more information.

11.13.5 Running Programs at Boot Time

The file /etc/rc.d/rc.local is executed at boot time, after all other initialization is complete, and whenever you change runlevels. You can add additional initialization commands here. For instance, you may want to start up additional daemons, or initialize a printer. In addition, if you require serial port setup, you can edit /etc/rc.d/rc.serial, and it will be executed automatically at boot time.

The default /etc/rc.d/rc.local simply creates a nice login banner with your kernel version and machine type.

11.13.6 Shutting Down

To shut down Red Hat Linux, issue the shutdown command. You can read the shutdown man page for complete details, but the two most common usages are:

```
shutdown -h now
shutdown -r now
```

Each will cleanly shutdown the system. After shutting everything down, the first will halt the machine, and the second will reboot.

Although the reboot and halt commands are now "smart" enough to invoke shutdown if run while the system is in runlevels 1-5, it is a bad habit to get into, as not all Linux-like operating systems have this feature.

11.14   Rescue Modes

When things go wrong, there are several ways to work on fixing them. However, they require that you understand the system well. This manual can't teach you what to do, but we will present the ways that you can use our products to get into rescue modes where you can use your own knowledge to rescue the system.

Through LILO   If your system boots, but does not allow you to log in when it has completed booting, you can use the `single` or `emergency` boot option. At the `LILO boot:` prompt, type `linux single` in order to boot in single-user mode. In single-user mode, your local filesystems will be mounted, but your network will not be activated. In emergency mode, almost nothing will be set up. Only the root filesystem will be mounted, and it will be mounted read-only.

Emergency Boot Diskettes   The boot diskette created during installation of Red Hat Linux 6.0 may be used as part of a rescue diskette set. For more information, please read the file `rescue.txt` in the `/doc` on your Red Hat Linux 6.0 CD-ROM or refer to the Official Red Hat Linux Getting Started Guide.

A Handy Trick

Have you ever rebuilt a kernel and, eager to try out your new handiwork, rebooted before running LILO? And you didn't have an entry for an older kernel in `lilo.conf`? Read on...

Here's a handy trick. In many cases, it's possible to boot your Red Hat Linux/Intel from the Red Hat Linux boot diskette with your root filesystem mounted and ready to go. Here's how:

Enter the following command at the boot diskette's `boot:` prompt:

```
linux single root=/dev/hdXX initrd=
```

(Replace the `XX` in `/dev/hdXX` with the appropriate letter and number for your root partition.)

What does this do? First, it starts the boot in single-user mode, with the root partition set to your root partition. The empty `initrd` specification bypasses the installation-related image on the boot diskette, which will cause you to enter single-user mode immediately.

Is there a downside to this trick? Unfortunately, yes. Because the kernel on the Red Hat Linux boot diskette only has support for IDE built-in, those of you with SCSI-based systems won't be able to use this trick. In that case, you'll have to use the boot/rescue diskette combination mentioned above.

A

Getting Technical Support

This chapter discusses Red Hat Software's support:

- What it is
- How to get it
- Frequently asked questions

A.1 An Overview of Our Support Policy

Red Hat Software provides 90-day installation support for people that have purchased the Official Red Hat Linux product.

Red Hat will provide support to registered purchasers of the Red Hat Linux Boxed Set. This support will be provided by means of electronic mail. In the case that the user doesn't have access to e-mail, fax support will be provided for those requests submitted with complete registration numbers.

In order to receive support it is necessary to register the product via the World Wide Web at http://www.redhat.com/support/register or by sending mail including the registration number to register@redhat.com.

After registering successfully, support may be obtained by sending a specially formatted message to support@redhat.com. The message format is described in the support HOW-TO, located at:

http://www.redhat.com/support/register/support-how2.html

This e-mail will then be delivered to Red Hat Software support where it will be distributed to a Red Hat Support Engineer.

As the name implies, installation support centers on helping you successfully install Red Hat Linux on your computer. This includes support in three distinct areas:

- Answering questions you may have prior to installation, such as:

  - Hardware compatibility issues.
  - Basic approaches to partitioning your hard drive.

- Helping you get through the installation process:

  - Getting any supported hardware necessary for installation recognized by the installation program.
    (See http://www.redhat.com/hardware/)
  - Assisting with the creation of a root and swap partition using the free space available on your hard drive.
  - Using the installation program to configure LILO to boot Red Hat Linux, and one other operating system (such as DOS, Windows 95, or Windows NT) already residing on your hard drive.

- Assisting with final configuration tasks, such as:

  - The successful configuration of the X window system on supported hardware, using either the Metro-X or XFree86 software. (Additional configuration, such as automatically starting X on reboot, or changing/customizing window managers is your responsibility.)
  - Configuring a printer connected directly to the Red Hat Linux system, enabling it to print text.
  - Setting up a mouse to be used with the text-based console, or with the X window system.
  - Getting access to the CD-ROM, so that information can be read from it.

Naturally, although our installation support service will get your system running Red Hat Linux, there are many other optional tasks that you might want to undertake, such as compiling a customized kernel, adding support for devices not included in the installation process, and so on.

For assistance with these tasks, please consider the many books on Linux at your local bookstore, or various on-line resources. A starting point in your on-line search for Linux information should always be:

http://www.redhat.com/support/

for information specific to Red Hat Linux, or:

`http://www.redhat.com/linux-info/`

for more general Linux information. Another good resource is `http://www.linux.org/`.

Red Hat Software can only support customers that have purchased the official Red Hat Linux Box set. If you have obtained Red Hat from any other publisher, you must contact them for support. Examples of other publishers would be:

- Macmillan/Sams
- Cheapbytes
- Pacific Hi-Tech (PHT)
- Infomagic
- Linux Systems Labs (LSL)
- ADRAS Computing

Also, RHL-Intel obtained via any of the following methods does not qualify for support from Red Hat Software:

- Red Hat Linux PowerTools Archive
- Downloaded via FTP on the Internet.
- Included in a package such as Applixware or Motif.
- Copied or installed from another user's CD.

A.2 Getting Support

As of August 1997, Red Hat Software put a new Technical Support system online. The support system automatically routes questions to support technicians. This document describes how to use the Red Hat Software technical support system.

A.2.1 Registration

In order to receive technical support for your Red Hat Software product, you have to register it. Every official Red Hat product comes with registration material located on the insert in the CD-ROM jewel case. The product registration number uniquely identifies a product which you have purchased (such as Red Hat Linux) that includes 90 days of free installation technical support by fax or email.

Registering via the Web

Registering via the Web

You can register your Red Hat Software product online at Red Hat's World Wide Web site at `http://www.redhat.com/support/register/`. Choose **Register a Product**. Please enter all applicable information, and please be accurate with the system information. This information will aid in solving problems and answering questions more quickly and easily, and incorrect information benefits neither us nor our customers. Also, make sure the electronic mail address you give is correct. All support correspondence will be sent to that address. If this should change, please login to the registration pages and edit this information.

Registration has changed. There will be no more annoying support ID numbers to remember. If you don't have a current login to the support database, you will need to create one. Simply enter a name at the **Support Login** and click on the **Create Login** button to begin registration of your product. If you were already registered for support before August 14, 1997 you can login by using your email address as your Support Login and your former support/customer ID as the password. The password can be changed once logged in. If you don't remember it, follow the steps as if you never had a login, and re-enter the registration numbers and information.

Registering via Email

If you don't have access to the World Wide Web, but you do have access to Internet mail, you can send registration details to `register@redhat.com`. Please include the following information:

- Contact Information: name, address, city, state/province, country, zip/postal code, and telephone and fax numbers; also, your support ID if you have one;

- Product Information: name of product you are registering, product registration number (very important!), architecture you're using the product on (Intel, Alpha/AXP, or Sparc), and what you're using the product for (File Server, Internet Server, Workstation, Home Computer, or Other);

- System Information: CPU (i386, i486, i586, i686/PentiumPro, AXP21164, AXP21064, Sparc4C, Sparc4M), CPU speed (MHz), amount of RAM (MB), hard drives (number, size, type, partitions), video card, CD-ROM drive, any network card, and other hardware components (SCSI or ISDN adaptors, etc.).

Registering via Fax or Snail Mail

We do not recommend registering via fax or snail mail, if you have access to either the World Wide Web or Internet mail. If you do so, your registration is likely to be delayed considerably. If you do wish to register via fax, fax a copy of your registration card to Red Hat Software at +1-919-547-0024.

A.2.2   Support Questions

Technical support is a black art: in most cases, support technicians rely solely on communication with the customer to solve installation problems on hardware the technicians have never physically seen. It is extremely important, therefore, to state your question clearly and concisely, including detailed information such as:

- symptoms of the problem ("Red Hat Linux 6.0 doesn't recognize my CD-ROM drive");

- when the problem began ("It stopped working yesterday ...");

- what changes you have made to your system around the time of the problem ("... after I disconnected it from the IDE controller.");

- any diagnostic output specifically related to the problem ("In the bootup messages, it says 'Cannot find /dev/hdb; device disconnected'."). However, this can be taken overboard; don't send us your system logs unless we ask you for them;

- other relevant information ("I'm using the floppy installation method, from the CD.").

How to Send Them

Red Hat's support system is email-based and is partially automated; for this reason, it is important to make sure you send support questions in the correct format, so that your message will be recognized and routed to an appropriate support technician. In order to receive technical support for your Red Hat Software product, you must first register it.

Submitting trouble tickets can be performed in the traditional email way, or can be initiated via the World Wide Web. After providing the information for the registration, you will have a new menu allowing you to edit your registration information or open a trouble ticket. Hurry and login now to open a ticket on the Web! http://www.redhat.com/support/register/

To open a support ticket via email, all you need to do is send the support system a message with a Subject: of [registration #nnnn nnnn nnnn nnnn], where nnnn nnnn nnnn nnnn is the registration number of the product for which you are requesting support. For example, if your registration number is fffe 0fff ff00 ff00, the subject line should read:

```
Subject: [registration #fffe 0fff ff00 ff00]
```

The square brackets, the number sign, and the word 'registration' must be present. If you wish, you may add explanatory text to the subject line:

```
Subject: [registration #fffe 0fff ff00 ff00] CD-ROM problem
```

Once you've opened a ticket, support responses come to you with the support ticket number in the subject line:

```
Subject: [ticket #12015] CD-ROM problem
```

To correspond about the same problem, simply send a reply with the same subject:

```
Subject: Re: [ticket #12015] CD-ROM problem
```

If you feel that the problem has been solved the ticket can also be closed by you. Simply add `close` to the same subject:

```
Subject: Re: [close ticket #12015] CD-ROM problem
```

Once your problem is solved or your question answered, the technician handling your support ticket can close the ticket. This can also be done by you via the website. Either method will result in a message from the support system stating the ticket is closed and will contain a summary of the problem and the solution. You can open a new ticket for your next support question. All past correspondence will be saved in the database under the old ticket number and can be accessed with your account at any time.

Where to Send Them

The address for Red Hat's Technical Support System is `support@redhat.com`; all support questions should go there. There are also several related addresses:

- For a copy of the Red Hat FAQ (Frequently Asked Questions, with answers), send mail to `faq@redhat.com`.
- For a copy of the Red Hat PPP Tips (tips on setting up a PPP connection), send mail to `ppp-tips@redhat.com`.

A.3   Support FAQ (Frequently Asked Questions)

Here are a few questions that the Red Hat Support Staff see frequently, along with the answers:

Question – I've sent several messages to the Red Hat Support System, and I've gotten absolutely no response. Is anybody there?

Answer – Check your registration information to make sure your email address is correct. You can check it by logging in at
`http://www.redhat.com/support/register/`.

Question – I know I have already registered, but I keep getting a message from the support system telling me I'm not registered. Is the system broken?

Answer – Make sure to register via the World Wide Web at
`http://www.redhat.com/support/register/`. If you did not, please do so, by first accessing the registration page. Next, input a login name and click on **Create Login**. After this you will be prompted to input some personal information. When finished click on the **Submit** button and then enter your registration number which should look something like `fffe 0fff ff00 ff00`. Then be sure to enter all the information about your system. This information can be maintained by logging in and accessing your registration information from `http://www.redhat.com/support/register/`.

Question – But I registered via email. Why isn't the support system working?

Answer – When you register via email, your message goes to an actual human who registers you manually. Depending on the backlog of people sending in registrations via this method, this can delay your registration anywhere from several hours to several days.

Question – I've done everything perfectly for my registration, but I'm still getting messages telling me I have an invalid registration number.

Answer – Please make sure you're using a valid product registration number. If you have not purchased the official box set from Red Hat Software or a vendor that sells the official version (it will say "Official" on the box) you will not be able to register, as Red Hat Software cannot support products packaged and sold by other software publishers.

Question – I see this thing on the registration page that asks me what my login is? What is my login anyway?

Answer – If you are a first-time user of the the support system or accessed the support system after August 15, 1997 then the Login can be whatever you want it to be. It must be all one word and if there is already a duplicate you will be warned of an error. If you accessed the system before this time and have a valid registration, your login will be the email address you had when registering and the password will be the old Support ID number. You can change the password if you like; however the login cannot be changed.

Question – I've tried entering a login and password but the system won't accept it. Why won't the system accept the password I'm trying to enter?

Answer – The password must be a minimum of 5 alphanumeric characters long and no more than 8. Make sure you typed in the exact same password both times for both password fields on the registration page.

Question – I hear that it's possible to change my registration information and view all my old tickets and the past correspondence. How do I do that?

Answer – Simply login to the registration page at
`http://www.redhat.com/support/register` and all these options will be available to you. If you need to reference an old trouble ticket, change your system information, or just check up on the status of a trouble ticket, visit this page. You can also open a trouble ticket with valid registration numbers directly from the web from these pages.

Making Installation Diskettes

It is sometimes necessary to create a diskette from an *image file* (for example, you might need to use updated diskette images obtained from the Red Hat Linux Errata).

As the name implies, an image file is a file that contains an exact copy (or image) of a diskette's contents. Since a diskette contains filesystem information in addition to the data contained in files, the image file is not usable until it has been written to a diskette.

To start, you'll need a blank, formatted, high-density (1.44 MB), 3.5-inch diskette. You'll need access to a computer with a 3.5-inch diskette drive, and capable of running a DOS program, or the dd utility program found on most Linux-like operating systems.

The image files are found in the following directories on your Red Hat Linux CD:

- images – Contains the boot and PCMCIA support images for Red Hat Linux/Intel, and the various kernel and ramdisk images for Red Hat Linux/Alpha.

  On the Red Hat Linux/SPARC CD, this directory contains the boot image, and an image for network booting.

- milo – Contains the various images for the Red Hat Linux/Alpha miniloader, MILO. This directory exists only on Red Hat Linux/Alpha CDs.

Once you've selected the proper image, it's time to transfer the image file onto a diskette. As mentioned previously, this can be done on a DOS-capable system, or on a system running a Linux-like operating system.

B.1   Making a Diskette Under MS-DOS

To make a diskette under MS-DOS, use the `rawrite` utility included on the Red Hat Linux CD in the `dosutils` directory. First, label a blank, formatted 3.5-inch diskette appropriately (eg. "Boot Diskette," "Supplemental Diskette," etc). Insert it into the diskette drive. Then, use the following commands (assuming your CD is drive `d:`):

```
C:\> d:
D:\> cd \dosutils
D:\dosutils> rawrite
Enter disk image source file name: ..\images\boot.img
Enter target diskette drive: a:
Please insert a formatted diskette into drive A: and
press --ENTER-- : [Enter]
D:\dosutils>
```

`rawrite` first asks you for the filename of a diskette image; enter the directory and name of the image you wish to write (for example, `..\images\boot.img`). Then `rawrite` asks for a diskette drive to write the image to; enter `a:`. Finally, `rawrite` asks for confirmation that a formatted diskette is in the drive you've selected. After pressing [Enter] to confirm, `rawrite` copies the image file onto the diskette. If you need to make another diskette, label another diskette, and run `rawrite` again, specifying the appropriate image file.

B.2   Making a Diskette Under a Linux-like O/S

To make a diskette under Linux (or any other Linux-like operating system), you must have permission to write to the device representing a 3.5-inch diskette drive (known as `/dev/fd0` under Linux). First, label a blank, formatted diskette appropriately (eg. "Boot Diskette," "Supplemental Diskette," etc.). Insert it into the diskette drive (but don't issue a `mount` command). After mounting the Red Hat Linux CD, change directory to the directory containing the desired image file, and use the following command (changing the name of the image file and diskette device as appropriate):

```
# dd if=boot.img of=/dev/fd0 bs=1440k
```

If you need to make another diskette, label another diskette, and run `dd` again, specifying the appropriate image file.

C

An Introduction to Disk Partitions

Disk partitions are a standard part of the personal computer landscape, and have been for quite some time. However, with so many people purchasing computers featuring preinstalled operating systems, relatively few people understand how partitions work. This chapter attempts to explain how disk partitions work so you'll find your Red Hat Linux installation is as simple as possible.

C.1 Hard Disk Basic Concepts

Hard disks perform a very simple function – they store data and reliably retrieve it on command.

When discussing issues such as disk partitioning, it's important to know a bit about the underlying hardware; unfortunately, it's easy to become bogged down in details. Therefore, let's use a simplified diagram of a disk drive to help us explain what goes on "under the hood." Figure C.1 on the following page shows a brand-new, unused disk drive.

Not much to look at, is it? But if we're talking about disk drives on a basic level, it will do. Let's say that we'd like to store some data on this drive. As things stand now, it won't work. There's something we need to do first...

Figure C.1: An Unused Disk Drive

C.1.1   It's Not What You Write, it's How You Write It

The old-timers in the audience probably got this one of the first try. We need to *format* the drive. Formatting (usually known as "making a *filesystem*" in Linux parlance) writes information to the drive, creating order out of the empty space in an unformatted drive.

As Figure C.2 on the next page implies, the order imposed by a filesystem involves some tradeoffs:

- A small percentage of the drive's available space is used to store filesystem-related data, and can be considered as overhead.

- A filesystem splits the remaining space into small, consistently-sized segments. In the Linux world, these segments are known as *inodes*[1].

Given that filesystems make things like directories and files possible, these tradeoffs are usually seen as a small price to pay.

It's also worth noting that there is no single, universal filesystem; as Figure C.3 on the facing page shows, a disk drive may have one of many different filesystems written on it. As you might guess, different filesystems tend to be incompatible; that is, an operating system that supports one filesystem (or a handful of related filesystem types) may not support another. This last statement is not a hard-and-fast rule, however. For example, Red Hat Linux supports a wide variety of filesystems (including many commonly used by other operating systems), making data interchange easy.

---

[1]Inodes really *are* consistently-sized, unlike our illustrations. Also, keep in mind that an average disk drive contains thousands of inodes. But for the purposes of this discussion, please ignore these minor discrepancies.

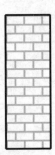

Figure C.2: Disk Drive with a Filesystem

Figure C.3: Disk Drive with a Different Filesystem

Of course, writing a filesystem to disk is only the beginning. The goal of this process is to actually *store* and *retrieve* data. Let's take a look at our drive after some files have been written to it.

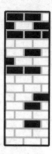

Figure C.4: Disk Drive with Data Written to It

As Figure C.4 shows, 14 of the previously-empty inodes are now holding data. We cannot determine how many files reside on this drive; it may be as few as one or as many as 14, as all files use as least one inode. Another important point to note is that the used inodes do not have to form a contiguous region; used and unused inodes may be interspersed. This is known as *fragmentation*. Fragmentation can play a part when attempting to resize an existing partition.

As with most computer-related technologies, disk drives continued to change over time. In particular, they changed in one specific way – they got bigger. Not bigger in size, but bigger in capacity. And it was this additional capacity that drove a change in the way disk drives were used.

C.1.2   Partitions – Turning One Drive Into Many

As disk drive capacities soared, some people started wondering if having all that space in one big chunk wasn't such a great idea. This line of thinking was driven by several issues, some philosophical, some technical. On the philosophical side, above a certain size, it just seemed that the additional space provided by a larger drive made for more clutter. On the technical side, some filesystems were never designed to support larger drives. Or the filesystems *could* support larger drives, but the overhead imposed by the filesystem became excessive.

The solution to this problem was to divide disks into *partitions*. Each partition can be accessed as if it was a separate disk. This is done through the addition of a *partition table*.

Please Note: While the diagrams in this chapter show the partition table as being separate from the actual disk drive, this is not entirely accurate. In reality, the partition table is stored at the very start of the disk, before any filesystem or user data. But for clarity, we'll keep it separate in our diagrams.

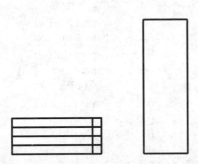

Figure C.5: Disk Drive with Partition Table

As Figure C.5 shows, the partition table is divided into four sections. Each section can hold the information necessary to define a single partition, meaning that the partition table can define no more than four partitions.

Each partition table entry contains several important characteristics of the partition:

- The points on the disk where the partition starts and ends;
- Whether the partition is "active";
- The partition's type.

Let's take a closer look at each of these characteristics. The starting and ending points actually define the partition's size and location on the disk. The "active" flag is used by some operating systems' boot loaders. In other words, the operating system in the partition that is marked "active" will be booted.

The partition's type can be a bit confusing. The type is a number that identifies the partition's anticipated usage. If that statement sounds a bit vague, that's because the meaning of the partition type is a bit vague. Some operating systems use the partition type to denote a specific filesystem type, to flag the partition as being associated with a particular operating system, to indicate that the partition contains a bootable operating system, or some combination of the three.

Figure C.6 on the next page contains a listing of some popular (and obscure) partition types, along with their numeric values.

Partition Type	Value	Partition Type	Value
Empty	00	Novell Netware 386	65
DOS 12-bit FAT	01	PC/IX	75
XENIX root	02	Old MINIX	80
XENIX usr	03	Linux/MINIX	81
DOS 16-bit <=32M	04	Linux swap	82
Extended	05	Linux native	83
DOS 16-bit >=32M	06	Linux extended	85
OS/2 HPFS	07	Amoeba	93
AIX	08	Amoeba BBT	94
AIX bootable	09	BSD/386	a5
OS/2 Boot Manager	0a	OpenBSD	a6
Win95 FAT32	0b	NEXTSTEP	a7
Win95 FAT32 (LBA)	0c	BSDI fs	b7
Win95 FAT16 (LBA)	0e	BSDI swap	b8
Win95 Extended (LBA)	0f	Syrinx	c7
Venix 80286	40	CP/M	db
Novell?	51	DOS access	e1
Microport	52	DOS R/O	e3
GNU HURD	63	DOS secondary	f2
Novell Netware 286	64	BBT	ff

Figure C.6: Partition Types

Now you might be wondering how all this additional complexity is normally used. See Figure C.7 on the facing page for an example.

That's right – in many cases there is but a single partition spanning the entire disk, essentially duplicating the pre-partitioned days of yore. The partition table has only one entry used, and it points to the start of the partition. We've labeled this partition as being of type "DOS," although as you can see from Figure C.6, that's a bit simplistic, but adequate for the purposes of this discussion. This is a typical partition layout for most newly purchased computers with some version of Windows pre-installed.

C.1.3   Partitions within Partitions – An Overview of Extended Partitions

Of course, in time it became obvious that four partitions would not be enough. As disk drives continued to grow, it became more and more likely that a person could configure four reasonably-sized

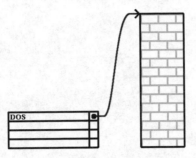

Figure C.7: Disk Drive With Single Partition

partitions and still have disk space left over. There needed to be some way of creating more partitions.

Enter the extended partition. As you may have noticed in Figure C.6 on the facing page, there is an "Extended" partition type; it is this partition type that is at the heart of extended partitions. Here's how it works.

When a partition is created and its type is set to "Extended," an extended partition table is created. In essence, the extended partition is like a disk drive in its own right – it has a partition table that points to one or more partitions (now called *logical partitions*, as opposed to the four *primary partitions*) contained entirely within the extended partition itself. Figure C.8 on the next page shows a disk drive with one primary partition, and one extended partition containing two logical partitions (along with some unpartitioned free space).

As this figure implies, there is a difference between primary and logical partitions – there can only be four primary partitions, but there is no fixed limit to the number of logical partitions that can exist. (However, in reality it is probably not a good idea to try to define and use more than 12 logical partitions on a single disk drive.)

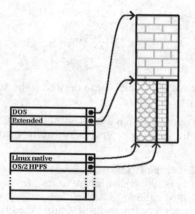

Figure C.8: Disk Drive With Extended Partition

D

Package List

This appendix lists the packages that make up Red Hat Linux. In each entry, you'll find the following information:

- The name of the package
- The packaged software's version number
- The size of the packaged software, in kilobytes
- A short description of the software

In addition, some packages will have one or more of the following icons alongside the package name:

B   This package is part of the Red Hat Linux *base*, meaning that it is always installed.

W   Workstation-class installations include this package.

S   Server-class installations include this package.

Please Note: This package list was automatically generated right before Red Hat Linux 6.0 went into production. Because of the short timeframes involved, you might find minor typesetting problems in the package lists. However, we felt that an up-to-date package list was more important than a picture-perfect package list. We hope you'll agree...

You may also notice that some packages have different versions, and that packages listed here are not mentioned in the installation program (and vice versa). Any differences in package versions are normally due to the normal bug fixing process. It's possible that "missing" or "extra" packages are the result of last-minute changes prior to pressing CDROMs. Also note that all the packages in the "Base" group (and subgroups) are always installed, therefore you will not see them mentioned explicitly during the installation process.

Using the Package List After Installation   This list can come in handy even after you've installed Red Hat Linux. You can use it search for documentation. Here's how:

1. Find the package in this list.

2. Note the package name (The very first thing listed in bold at the start of each package description).

3. Enter the following command, taking care to enter the package name *exactly* as it is shown in the list (the package name is case-sensitive):

   ```
   rpm -qd package-name
   ```

(Replacing `package-name` with the actual name of the package, of course.)

If you installed the package, you should get a list of filenames. Each file contains documentation relating to the package you specified. Here are some of the types of filenames you'll see:

- **/usr/man... something.n** – This is a man page. You can view it by using the `man` command (for example, `man something`. You might also need to include the file's ending number in the `man` command (as in `man n something`.

- **/usr/X11R6/man... something.nx** – This is a man page for part of the X Window System. View these files the same way as a regular man page.

- **/usr/doc/something...** – Files under `/usr/doc` can be in any number of different formats. Sometimes the end of the filename can provide a clue as to how it should be viewed:

   - **.html** – An HTML file. View with the web browser of your choice.
   - **.txt** – A text file. View with `cat` or `less`.
   - **.ps** – A Postscript file. You can print it to a Postscript printer, or you can view it with `gv`.
   - **.gz** – A file compressed with `gzip`. If you make a copy of the original file, you can use `gunzip` to decompress it (you'll probably want to keep the original file compressed to save space). You can then view the file as you would normally. The `zless` command combines `gunzip` and `less`, and makes it possible to read compressed text files without making interim copies. There are other, more elegant ways to work with compressed files, but this approach will work for those just starting to use Linux.

In general, most of the documentation files you'll find will be one of those listed above. If in doubt, it's a good bet that the file is text. You can always try the `file` command to see if the file's contents can be identified.

- **/usr/info...** – Files in `/usr/info` are meant to be viewed using the `info` (or Emacs' Info mode). If you use Emacs, press Ctrl-I, followed by I to view the main Info screen.

D.1 Amusements

This section lists the packages that provide fun and entertainment to Red Hat Linux system owners the world over.

D.1.1 Games

This section lists packages that contain a variety of games.

cxhextris – (Version 1.0, 39K)

CXHextris is a color version of the popular xhextris game, which is a Tetris-like game that uses hexagon shapes instead of square shapes. CXHextris runs within the X Window System.

Install cxhextris if you enjoy playing Tetris or Tetris-like games and you'd like to play one on your system. You'll need to have X installed in order to play CXHextris.

fortune-mod – (Version 1.0, 2,342K)

Fortune-mod contains the ever-popular fortune program. Want a little bit of random wisdom revealed to you when you log in? Fortune's your program. Fun-loving system administrators can add fortune to users' .login files, so that the users get their dose of wisdom each time they log in.

Install fortune if you want a program which will bestow these random bits o' wit.

gnome-games – (Version 1.0.2, 3,356K)   W

GNOME is the GNU Network Object Model Environment. That's a fancy name, but really GNOME is a nice GUI desktop environment. Its powerful, friendly and easy-to-configure interface makes using your computer easy.

This package installs some GNOME games on your system, such as gnothello, solitaire, tetris and others.

gnuchess – (Version 4.0.pl79, 1,428K)

The gnuchess package contains the GNU chess program. By default, GNUchess uses a curses text-based interface. Alternatively, GNUchess can be used in conjunction with the xboard user interface and the X Window System for a graphical chessboard.

You should install the gnuchess package if you would like to play chess on your computer. You'll also need to install the curses package. If you'd like to use a graphical interface with GNUchess, you'll also need to install the xboard package and the X Window System.

kdegames – (Version 1.1, 5,289K)

Games for the K Desktop Environment. Included with this package are: kabalone, kasteroids, kblackbox, kmahjongg, kmines, konquest, kpat, kpoker, kreversi, ksame, kshisen, ksokoban, ksmiletris, ksnake, ksirtet.

trojka – (Version 1.1, 16K)

The game of Trojka involves a set of falling blocks. The point is to move the blocks around as they fall, so that three of the same blocks end up next to each other, either horizontally or diagonally. Once the blocks fill up the entire game area, the game is over.

Install the trojka package if you want to play a non-X game of falling blocks.

xbill – (Version 2.0, 183K)

The xbill game tests your reflexes as you seek out and destroy all forms of Bill, establish new operating systems and boldly go where no geek has gone before. Xbill has become an increasingly attractive option as the Linux Age progresses, and it is very popular at Red Hat.

xboard – (Version 4.0.0, 601K)

Xboard is an X Window System based graphical chessboard which can be used with the GNUchess and Crafty chess programs, with Internet Chess Servers (ICSs), with chess via email, or with your own saved games.

Install the xboard package if you need a graphical chessboard.

xboing – (Version 2.4, 1,043K)

Xboing is an X Window System based game like the Breakout arcade game. The object of the game is to keep a ball bouncing on the bricks until you've broken through all of them.

xgammon – (Version 0.98, 3,282K)

Xgammon is an X Window System based backgammon game. Xgammon allows you to play against the computer, or you can play against another person. Xgammon also supports playing a game against another person on a remote X terminal, and will display a second board there for their use.

xjewel – (Version 1.6, 52K)

Xjewel is an X Window System game much like Domain/Jewelbox, Sega's Columns and/or Tetris. The point of the game is to move or rotate the blocks as they fall, to get jewels in patterns of three when they come to rest.

xpat2 – (Version 1.04, 456K)

Xpat2 is a generic patience or Solitaire game for the X Window System. Xpat2 can be used with different rules sets, so it can be used to play Spider, Klondike, and other card games.

xpilot – (Version 3.6.2, 1,617K)

Xpilot is an X Window System based multiplayer game of aerial combat. The object of the game is to shoot each other down, or you can use the race mode to just fly around. Xpilot resembles the Commodore 64 Thrust game, which is similar to Atari's Gravitar and Asteriods (note: this is not misspelled). Unless you already have an xpilot server on your network, you'll need to set up the server on one machine, and then set up xpilot clients on all of the players' machines.

xpuzzles – (Version 5.4.1, 469K)

A set of geometric puzzles and toys for the X Window System. Xpuzzles includes a version of Rubik's cube and various other geometric Rubik's cube style puzzles.

xtrojka – (Version 1.2.3, 216K)

The xtrojka game is an X Window System game of falling blocks, like Xjewel or Tetris.

D.1.2   Graphics

This section lists packages that provide graphics that are fun to look at.

mxp – (Version 1.0, 55K)

The mxp (Mandelbrot explorer) program is an X Window System application for computing and exploring Mandelbrot sets. Mxp supports zoom/un-zoom, dynamic resizing of drawing windows, setup save/load, asynchronous image generation, GIF outputs, animation, nine color schemes, color rotation, color change options, and detailed statistics.

Install the mxp package if you need a Mandelbrot set generator for the X Window System.

xbanner – (Version 1.31, 505K)   Ⓦ Ⓢ

The XBanner program allows the display of text, patterns and images in the root window, so users can customize the XDM style login screen and/or the normal X background.

Install XBanner if you'd like to change the look of your X login screen and/or X background.

xdaliclock – (Version 2.14, 80K)

The xdaliclock program displays a digital clock, with digits that merge into the new digits as the time changes. Xdaliclock can display the time in 12 or 24 hour modes and will display the date if you hold your mouse button down over it. Xdaliclock has two large fonts built in, but is capable of animating other fonts.

Install the xdaliclock package if you want a fairly large clock, with a melting special effect, for your system.

xearth – (Version 1.0, 192K)

Xearth is an X Window System based graphic that shows a globe of the Earth, including markers for major cities and Red Hat Software. The Earth is correctly shaded for the current position of the sun, and the displayed image is updated every five minutes.

xfishtank – (Version 2.0, 388K)

The xfishtank program displays an animated aquarium background on your screen. Xfishtank works with the X Window System.

xloadimage – (Version 4.1, 255K)

The xloadimage utility displays images in an X Window System window, loads images into the root window, or writes images into a file. Xloadimage supports many images types (GIF, TIFF, JPEG, XPM, XBM, etc.).

Install the xloadimage package if you need a utility for displaying images or loading images into the root window.

xlockmore – (Version 4.13, 759K)

The xlockmore utility is an enhanced version of the standard xlock program, which allows you to lock an X session so that other users can't access it. Xlockmore runs a provided screensaver until you type in your password.

Install the xlockmore package if you need a locking program to secure X sessions.

xmorph – (Version 1996.07.12, 127K) Ⓦ

Xmorph is a digital image warping (aka morphing) program. Xmorph provides the tools needed and comprehensible instructions for you to create morphs: changing one image into another. Xmorph runs under the X Window System.

Install the xmorph package if you need a program that will create morphed images.

xscreensaver – (Version 3.08, 3,172K) Ⓦ

The xscreensaver package contains a variety of screensavers for your mind-numbing, ambition-eroding, time-wasting, hypnotized viewing pleasure.

Install the xscreensaver package if you need screensavers for use with the X Window System.

xwpick – (Version 2.20, 50K)

The xwpick program allows you to choose an image or a rectangular piece of an image from an X Window System window and then write the image to a file in a variety of formats, incuding PostScript(TM), GIF, and PICT.

Install the xwpick program if you need to take screenshots from X Window System screens and write them to files.

D.2   Applications

This section contains packages that contain various applications for Red Hat Linux.

D.2.1   Archiving

This section contains packages that are associated with the efficient storing and/or copying of files.

cpio – (Version 2.4.2, 70K) Ⓑ

GNU cpio copies files into or out of a cpio or tar archive. Archives are files which contain a collection of other files plus information about them, such as their file name, owner, timestamps, and access permissions. The archive can be another file on the disk, a magnetic tape, or a pipe. GNU cpio supports the following archive formats: binary, old ASCII, new ASCII, crc, HPUX binary, HPUX old ASCII, old tar and POSIX.1 tar. By default, cpio creates binary format archives, so that they are compatible with older cpio programs. When it is extracting files from archives, cpio automatically recognizes which kind of archive it is reading and can read archives created on machines with a different byte-order.

Install cpio if you need a program to manage file archives.

dump – (Version 0.4b4, 153K)

The dump package contains both dump and restore. Dump examines files in a filesystem, determines which ones need to be backed up, and copies those files to a specified disk, tape or other storage medium. The restore command performs the inverse function of dump; it can restore a full backup of a filesystem. Subsequent incremental backups can then be layered on top of the full backup. Single files and directory subtrees may also be restored from full or partial backups.

Install dump if you need a system for both backing up filesystems and restoring filesystems after backups.

lha – (Version 1.00, 56K) Ⓦ

LHA is an archiving and compression utility for LHarc format archives. LHA is mostly used in the DOS world, but can be used under Linux to extract DOS files from LHA archives.

Install the lha package if you need to extract DOS files from LHA archives.

ncompress – (Version 4.2.4, 31K) Ⓑ

The ncompress package contains the compress and uncompress file compression and decompression utilities, which are compatible with the original UNIX compress utility (.Z file extensions). These utilities can't handle gzipped (.gz file extensions) files, but gzip can handle compressed files.

rmt – (Version 0.4b4, 12K) Ⓑ

The rmt utility provides remote access to tape devices for programs like dump (a filesystem backup program), restore (a program for restoring files from a backup) and tar (an archiving program).

sharutils – (Version 4.2, 221K) ⓌⓈ

The sharutils package contains the GNU shar utilities, a set of tools for encoding and decoding packages of files (in binary or text format) in a special plain text format called shell archives (shar). This format can be sent through email (which can be problematic for regular binary files). The shar utility supports a wide range of capabilities (compressing, uuencoding, splitting long files for multi-part mailings, providing checksums), which make it very flexible at creating shar files. After the files have been sent, the unshar tool scans mail messages looking for shar files. Unshar automatically strips off mail headers and introductory text and then unpacks the shar files.

Install sharutils if you send binary files through email very often.

taper – (Version 6.9, 847K)

Taper is a backup and restoration program with a user friendly interface. Files may be backed up to a tape drive or to a hard disk. The interface for selecting files to be backed up/restored is very similar to the Midnight Commander interface, and allows easy traversal of directories. Taper supports recursive selection of directories. Taper also supports backing up SCSI, ftape, zftape and removable drives. By default, taper is set for incremental backups and automatic most recent restore.

Install the taper package if you need a user friendly file backup and restoration program.

tar – (Version 1.12, 474K) Ⓑ

The GNU tar program saves many files together into one archive and can restore individual files (or all of the files) from the archive. Tar can also be used to add supplemental files to an archive and to update or list files in the archive.

Tar includes multivolume support, automatic archive compression/ decompression, the ability to perform remote archives and the ability to perform incremental and full backups.

If you want to use Tar for remote backups, you'll also need to install the rmt package.

You should install the tar package, because you'll find its compression and decompression utilities essential for working with files.

unarj – (Version 2.41a, 26K)

The UNARJ program is used to uncompress .arj format archives. The .arj format archive was mostly used on DOS machines.

Install the unarj package if you need to uncompress .arj format archives.

unzip – (Version 5.31, 370K) Ⓦ

The unzip utility is used to list, test, or extract files from a zip archive. Zip archives are commonly found on MS-DOS systems. The zip utility, included in the zip package, creates zip archives. Zip and unzip are both compatible with archives created by PKWARE(R)'s PKZIP for MS-DOS, but the programs' options and default behaviors do differ in some respects.

Install the unzip package if you need to list, test or extract files from a zip archive.

zip – (Version 2.1, 217K) Ⓦ

The zip program is a compression and file packaging utility. Zip is analogous to a combination of the UNIX tar and compress commands and is compatible with PKZIP (a compression and file packaging utility for MS-DOS systems).

Install the zip package if you need to compress files using the zip program.

D.2.2   Communications

This section contains packages that are associated with communications.

dip – (Version 3.3.7o, 88K) ⓌⓈ

Dip is a modem dialer. Dip handles the connections needed for dialup IP links like SLIP or PPP. Dip can handle both incoming and outgoing connections, using password security for incoming connections. Dip is useful for setting up PPP and SLIP connections, but isn't required for either. Netcfg uses dip for setting up SLIP connections.

Install dip if you need a utility which will handle dialup IP connections.

efax – (Version 0.8a, 205K)

Efax is a small ANSI C/POSIX program that sends and receives faxes using any Class 1, 2 or 2.0 fax modem.

You need to install efax if you want to send faxes and you have a Class 1, 2 or 2.0 fax modem.

getty_ps – (Version 2.0.7j, 127K) Ⓑ

The getty_ps package contains the getty and uugetty programs, basic programs for accomplishing the login process on a Red Hat Linux system. Getty and uugetty are used to accept logins on the console or a terminal. Getty is invoked by the init process to open tty lines and set their modes, to print the login prompt and get the user's name, and to initiate a login process for the user. Uugetty works just like getty, except that uugetty creates and uses lock files to prevent two or more processes from conflicting in their use of a tty line. Getty and uugetty can also handle answer a modem for dialup connections, but mgetty is recommended for that purpose.

kpilot – (Version 3.1b8, 876K)

KPilot allows you to synchronize your PalmPilot with your desktop. It allows you to backup and restore the various databases (Addressbook, ToDo List, Memos, etc.) as well as install applications to the pilot. Two "conduits" for the third party application KOrganizer are included which will let you sync your ToDo list and Calendar with that program.

lrzsz – (Version 0.12.20, 391K) Ⓦ Ⓢ

Lrzsz (consisting of lrz and lsz) is a cosmetically modified zmodem/ymodem/xmodem package built from the public-domain version of the rzsz package. Lrzsz was created to provide a working GNU copylefted Zmodem solution for Linux systems.

You should install lrzsz if you're also installing a Zmodem communications program that uses lrzsz. If you're installing minicom, you need to install lrzsz.

mgetty-sendfax – (Version 1.1.14, 272K)

Sendfax is a standalone backend program for sending fax files. The mgetty program (a getty replacement for handling logins over a serial line) plus sendfax will allow you to send faxes through a Class 2 modem.

If you'd like to send faxes over a Class 2 modem, you'll need to install the mgetty-sendfax and the mgetty packages.

mgetty-viewfax – (Version 1.1.14, 94K)

Viewfax displays the fax files received using mgetty in an X11 window. Viewfax is capable of zooming in and out on the displayed fax.

If you're installing the mgetty-viewfax package, you'll also need to install mgetty.

mgetty-voice – (Version 1.1.14, 651K)

The mgetty-voice package contains the vgetty system, which enables mgetty and your modem to support voice capabilities. In simple terms, vgetty lets your modem act as an answering machine. How well the system will work depends upon your modem, which may or may not be able to handle this kind of implementation.

Install mgetty-voice along with mgetty if you'd like to try having your modem act as an answering machine.

minicom – (Version 1.82, 302K) Ⓦ Ⓢ

Minicom is a simple text-based modem control and terminal emulation program somewhat similar to MSDOS Telix. Minicom includes a dialing directory, full ANSI and VT100 emulation, an (external) scripting language, and other features.

Minicom should be installed if you need a simple modem control program or terminal emulator.

pilot-link – (Version 0.9.0, 2,222K)

This suite of tools allows you to upload and download programs and data files between a *nix machine and the USR Pilot. It has a few extra utils that will allow for things like syncing the Pilot's calendar app with Ical. Note that you might still need to consult the sources for pilot-link if you would like the Python, Tcl, or Perl bindings.

sliplogin – (Version 2.1.1, 54K)

The sliplogin utility turns the terminal line on standard input into a SLIP (Serial Line Internet Protocol) link to a remote host. Sliplogin is usually used to allow dial-in SLIP connections.

Install the sliplogin package if you need to support dial-in SLIP connections.

uucp – (Version 1.06.1, 2,079K)   Ⓦ Ⓢ

The uucp command copies files between systems. Uucp is primarily used by remote machines downloading and uploading email and news files to local machines.

Install the uucp package if you need to use uucp to transfer files between machines.

D.2.3   Databases

This section contains packages that are associated with databases.

postgresql – (Version 6.4.2, 6,918K)   Ⓢ

Postgresql includes the programs needed to create and run a PostgreSQL server, which will in turn allow you to create and maintain PostgreSQL databases. PostgreSQL is an advanced Object-Relational database management system (DBMS) that supports almost all SQL constructs (including transactions, subselects and user-defined types and functions).

You should install postgresql if you want to create and maintain your own PostgreSQL databases and/or your own PostgreSQL server. If you are installing postgresql, you should also install postgresql-data, which will help you get started with PostgreSQL.

postgresql-clients – (Version 6.4.2, 917K)   Ⓢ

Postgresql-clients includes the client programs and client libraries that you'll need to access a PostgreSQL database management system server. This package contains the client libraries for C, C++ and PERL, as well as command-line utilities for managing PostgreSQL databases on a remote server. If you just want to connect to an existing remote PostgreSQL server, this package is all you need.

You should install postgresql-clients if you're installing postgresql. You should also install postgresql-clients if you're not installing postgresql, but you want to access PostgreSQL databases on a remote PostgreSQL server.

D.2.4   Editors

This section contains packages that are associated with editing text files.

GXedit – (Version 1.23, 570K)

Here is a fast, easy-to-use editor which is both network- oriented and very secure. GXedit is a graphical text editor which features a toolbar, network bar and tooltips, spell checking, inline help, the ability to send text as e-mail, macros and more. GXedit was designed to balance these and many other features without becoming too bloated.

You'll need GTK+ to use GXedit.

emacs – (Version 20.3, 17,340K)   ⓌⓈ

Emacs is a powerful, customizable, self-documenting, modeless text editor. Emacs contains special code editing features, a scripting language (elisp), and the capability to read mail, news and more without leaving the editor.

This package includes the libraries you need to run the Emacs editor, so you need to install this package if you intend to use Emacs. You also need to install the actual Emacs program package (emacs-nox or emacs-X11). Install emacs-nox if you are not going to use the X Window System; install emacs-X11 if you will be using X.

emacs-X11 – (Version 20.3, 5,782K)   Ⓦ

Emacs-X11 includes the Emacs text editor program for use with the X Window System (it provides support for the mouse and other GUI elements). Emacs-X11 will also run Emacs outside of X, but it has a larger memory footprint than the 'non-X' Emacs package (emacs-nox).

Install emacs-X11 if you're going to use Emacs with the X Window System. You should also install emacs-X11 if you're going to run Emacs both with and without X (it will work fine both ways). You'll also need to install the emacs package in order to run Emacs.

emacs-el – (Version 20.3, 21,631K)

Emacs-el contains the emacs-elisp sources for many of the elisp programs included with the main Emacs text editor package.

You need to install emacs-el only if you intend to modify any of the Emacs packages or see some elisp examples.

emacs-leim – (Version 20.3, 4,216K)

The Emacs Lisp code for input methods for various international character scripts.

emacs-nox – (Version 20.3, 2,434K)   ⓌⓈ

Emacs-nox is the Emacs text editor program without support for the X Window System.

You need to install this package only if you plan on exclusively using Emacs without the X Window System (emacs-X11 will work both in X and out of X, but emacs-nox will only work outside of X). You'll also need to install the emacs package in order to run Emacs.

gedit – (Version 0.5.1, 340K)   Ⓦ

gEdit is a small but powerful text editor designed expressly for GNOME.

It includes such features as split-screen mode, a plugin API, which allows gEdit to be extended to support many features while remaining small at its core, multiple document editing through the use of a 'tabbed' notebook and many more functions.

GNOME is required to use gEdit (Gnome-Libs and Gtk+).

gnotepad+ – (Version 1.1.3, 189K)   (W)

gnotepad+ is an easy-to-use, yet fairly feature-rich, simple text editor for systems running X11 and using GTK+. It is designed for as little bloat as possible, while still providing many of the common features found in a modern GUI-based text editor.

jed – (Version 0.98.7, 140K)

Jed is a fast, compact editor based on the slang screen library. Jed features include emulation of the Emacs, EDT, WordStar and Brief editors; support for extensive customization with slang macros, colors, keybindings, etc.; and a variety of programming modes with syntax highlighting.

You should install jed if you've used it before and you like it, or if you haven't used any text editors before and you're still deciding what you'd like to use. You'll also need to have slang installed.

jed-common – (Version 0.98.7, 1,502K)

The jed-common package contains files (such as .sl files) that are needed by any jed binary in order to run.

jed-xjed – (Version 0.98.7, 166K)

XJed is a version of the Jed text editor that will work with the X Window System.

You should install xjed if you like Jed and you'd like to use it with X. You'll also need to have the X Window System installed.

joe – (Version 2.8, 282K)

Joe is an easy to use, modeless text editor which would be very appropriate for novices. Joe uses the same WordStar keybindings used in Borland's development environment.

You should install joe if you've used it before and you liked it, or if you're still deciding what text editor you'd like to use, or if you have a fondness for WordStar. If you're just starting out, you should probably install joe because it is very easy to use.

vim-X11 – (Version 5.3, 1,395K)

VIM (VIsual editor iMproved) is an updated and improved version of the vi editor. Vi was the first real screen-based editor for UNIX, and is still very popular. VIM improves on vi by adding new features: multiple windows, multi-level undo, block highlighting and more. VIM-X11 is a version of the VIM editor which will run within the X Window System. If you install this package, you can run VIM as an X application with a full GUI interface and mouse support.

Install the vim-X11 package if you'd like to try out a version of vi with graphics and mouse capabilities. You'll also need to install the vim-common package.

vim-common – (Version 5.3, 4,355K)   (B)

VIM (VIsual editor iMproved) is an updated and improved version of the vi editor. Vi was the first real screen-based editor for UNIX, and is still very popular. VIM improves on vi by adding new features: multiple windows, multi-level undo, block highlighting and more. The vim-common package contains files which every VIM binary will need in order to run.

If you are installing any version of the VIM editor, you'll also need to the vim-common package installed.

vim-enhanced – (Version 5.3, 1,297K)

VIM (VIsual editor iMproved) is an updated and improved version of the vi editor. Vi was the first real screen-based editor for UNIX, and is still very popular. VIM improves on vi by adding new features: multiple windows, multi-level undo, block highlighting and more. The vim-enhanced package contains a version of VIM with extra, recently introduced features like Python and Perl interpreters.

Install the vim-enhanced package if you'd like to use a version of the VIM editor which includes recently added enhancements like interpreters for the Python and Perl scripting languages. You'll also need to install the vim-common package.

vim-minimal – (Version 5.3, 445K)   🅱

VIM (VIsual editor iMproved) is an updated and improved version of the vi editor. Vi was the first real screen-based editor for UNIX, and is still very popular. VIM improves on vi by adding new features: multiple windows, multi-level undo, block highlighting and more. The vim-minimal package includes a minimal version of VIM, which is installed into /bin/vi for use when only the root partition is present.

D.2.5   Emulators

This section contains packages associated with the emulation of other operating systems.

dosemu – (Version 0.99.10, 1,812K)   🅦

Dosemu is a DOS emulator. Once you've installed dosemu, start the DOS emulator by typing in the dos command.

You need to install dosemu if you use DOS programs and you want to be able to run them on your Red Hat Linux system. You may also need to install the dosemu-freedos package.

dosemu-freedos – (Version 0.99.10, 8,194K)

Generally, the dosemu DOS emulator requires either that your system have some version of DOS available or that your system's partitions were formatted and installed with DOS. If your system does not meet either of the previous requirements, you can instead use the dosemu- freedos package, which contains an hdimage file which will be installed in teh /var/lib/dosemu directory. The hdimage file is already bootable with FreeDOS.

You will need to edit your /etc/dosemu.conf file to add the image to the list of disk 'drives' used by dosemu.

Install dosemu-freedos if you are installing the dosemu package and you don't have a version of DOS available on your system, and your system's partitions were not formatted and installed with DOS.

xdosemu – (Version 0.99.10, 26K)   🅦

Xdosemu is a version of the dosemu DOS emulator that runs with the X]Window System. Xdosemu provides VGA graphics and mouse support.

Install xdosemu if you need to run DOS programs on your system, and you'd like to do so with the convenience of graphics support and mouse capabilities.

D.2.6   Engineering

This section contains packages that are associated with the engineering arts.

bc – (Version 1.05a, 128K) $\boxed{\mathcal{B}}$

The bc package includes bc and dc. Bc is an arbitrary precision numeric processing arithmetic language. Dc is an interactive arbitrary precision stack based calculator, which can be used as a text mode calculator.

Install the bc package if you need its number handling capabilities or if you would like to use its text mode calculator.

gnuplot – (Version 3.7, 918K)

Gnuplot is a command-line driven, interactive function plotting program especially suited for scientific data representation. Gnuplot can be used to plot functions and data points in both two and three dimensions and in many different formats.

Install gnuplot if you need a graphics package for scientific data representation.

units – (Version 1.0, 25K)

Units converts an amount from one unit to another, or tells you what mathematical operation you need to perform to convert from one unit to another. Units can only handle multiplicative scale changes (i.e., it can't tell you how to convert from Celsius to Fahrenheit, which requires an additive step in addition to the multiplicative conversion).

Units is a handy little program which contains a large number of conversions, from au's to parsecs and tablespoons to cups. You probably don't need to install it, but it comes in handy sometimes.

xlispstat – (Version 3.52.9, 2,871K)

The xlispstat package contains XLISP-PLUS, an implementation of the Lisp programming language for the X Window System. XLISP-PLUS also includes extensions for performing advanced statistical computations.

Install the xlispstat package if you need a version of the Lisp programming language for X with statistics extensions.

D.2.7   File

This section contains packages that are associated with file manipulation.

bzip2 – (Version 0.9.0b, 233K)

Bzip2 is a freely available, patent-free, high quality data compressor. Bzip2 compresses files to within 10 to 15 percent of the capabilities of the best techniques available. However, bzip2 has the added benefit of being approximately two times faster at compression and six times faster at decompression than those techniques. Bzip2 is not the fastest compression utility, but it does strike a balance between speed and compression capability.

Install bzip2 if you need a high quality compression utility.

file – (Version 3.26, 206K) 🅱

The file command is used to identify a particular file according to the type of data contained by the file. File can identify many different file types, including ELF binaries, system libraries, RPM packages, and different graphics formats.

You should install the file package, since the file command is such a useful utility.

fileutils – (Version 4.0, 1,283K) 🅱

The fileutils package includes a number of GNU versions of common and popular file management utilities. Fileutils includes the following tools: chgrp (changes a file's group ownership), chown (changes a file's ownership), chmod (changes a file's permissions), cp (copies files), dd (copies and converts files), df (shows a filesystem's disk usage), dir (gives a brief directory listing), dircolors (the setup program for the color version of the ls command), du (shows disk usage), install (copies files and sets permissions), ln (creates file links), ls (lists directory contents in color), mkdir (creates directories), mkfifo (creates FIFOs, which are named pipes), mknod (creates special files), mv (renames files), rm (removes/deletes files), rmdir (removes empty directories), sync (synchronizes memory and disk), touch (changes file timestamps), and vdir (provides long directory listings).

You should install the fileutils package, because it includes many file management utilities that you'll use frequently.

findutils – (Version 4.1, 118K) 🅱

The findutils package contains programs which will help you locate files on your system. The find utility searches through a hierarchy of directories looking for files which match a certain set of criteria (such as a filename pattern). The locate utility searches a database (create by updatedb) to quickly find a file matching a given pattern. The xargs utility builds and executes command lines from standard input arguments (usually lists of file names generated by the find command).

You should install findutils because it includes tools that are very useful for finding things on your system.

git – (Version 4.3.17, 715K) Ⓦ

GIT (GNU Interactive Tools) provides an extensible file system browser, an ASCII/hexadecimal file viewer, a process viewer/killer and other related utilities and shell scripts. GIT can be used to increase the speed and efficiency of copying and moving files and directories, invoking editors, compressing and uncompressing files, creating and expanding archives, compiling programs, sending mail and more. GIT uses standard ANSI color sequences, if they are available.

You should install the git package if you are interested in using its file management capabilities.

gzip – (Version 1.2.4, 242K) 🅱

The gzip package contains the popular GNU gzip data compression program. Gzipped files have a .gz extension.

Gzip should be installed on your Red Hat Linux system, because it is a very commonly used data compression program.

slocate – (Version 1.4, 19K) 🅱

slocate searches through a central database (updated nightly) for files which match a given glob pattern. This allows you to quickly find files anywhere on your system.

stat – (Version 1.5, 6K)   Ⓑ

The stat utility prints out filesystem level information about a specified file, including size, permissions, link count, inode, etc.

tree – (Version 1.2, 19K)

The tree utility recursively displays the contents of directories in a tree-like format. Tree is basically a UNIX port of the tree DOS utility.

Install tree if you think it would be useful to view the contents of specified directories in a tree-like format.

D.2.8   Internet

This section contains packages that are associated with the Internet.

elm – (Version 2.5.0, 616K)   ⓌⓈ

Elm is a popular terminal mode email user agent. Elm includes all standard mailhandling features, including MIME support via metamail.

Elm is still used by some people, but is no longer in development. If you've used Elm before and you're devoted to it, you should install the elm package. If you would like to use metamail's MIME support, you'll also need to install the metamail package.

exmh – (Version 2.0.2, 1,814K)   ⓌⓈ

Exmh provides an X interface for MH/nmh mail, a feature-rich email handling system. Exmh supports almost all (but not all) of MH's features: viewing the messages in a folder, reading/deleting/refiling messages, and sorting arriving mail into different folders before the messages are read. Exmh highlights which folders have new mail, and indicates which messages have not been read (so you don't lose the sorted, unread mail).

If you like MH/nmh mail, you should install exmh, because it makes the MH/nmh mail system much more user friendly. You may also want to use exmh if you prefer a graphical user interface for your mail client. Note that you will also have to install the nmh package.

faces – (Version 1.6.1, 144K)

Faces is a program for visually monitoring a list (typically a list of incoming mail messages, a list of jobs in a print queue or a list of system users). Faces operates in five different modes: monitoring for new mail, monitoring an entire mail file, monitoring a specified print queue, monitoring users on a machine and custom monitoring. Faces also includes a utility for including a face image (a compressed, scanned image) with mail messages. The image has to be compressed in a certain way, which can then be uncompressed and displayed on-the-fly in the mail program. This feature of faces is typically used with the exmh mail handling system.

Install faces if you'd like to use its list monitoring capability or its face image inclusion capability. If you would like to include face images in email, you'll also need to install the faces-xface package. If you would like to develop xface applications, you'll need to also install faces-devel.

faces-xface – (Version 1.6.1, 21K)

Faces-xface includes the utilities that mail user agent programs need to handle X-Face mail headers. When an email program reads the X-face header line in an email message, it calls these utilities to display the face image included in the message.

You'll need to install faces-xface if you want your mail program to display Faces' X-face images.

fetchmail – (Version 4.7.0, 538K) Ⓦ Ⓢ

Fetchmail is a remote mail retrieval and forwarding utility intended for use over on-demand TCP/IP links, like SLIP or PPP connections. Fetchmail supports every remote-mail protocol currently in use on the Internet (POP2, POP3, RPOP, APOP, KPOP, all IMAPs, ESMTP ETRN) for retrieval. Then Fetchmail forwards the mail through SMTP, so you can read it through your normal mail client.

Install fetchmail if you need to retrieve mail over SLIP or PPP connections.

fetchmailconf – (Version 4.7.0, 55K)

Fetchmailconf is a tcl/tk application for graphically configuring your .fetchmailrc preferences file. Fetchmail has many options which can be daunting to the new user. This utility takes some of the guesswork and hassle out of setting up fetchmail.

finger – (Version 0.10, 32K) Ⓦ Ⓢ

Finger is a utility which allows users to see information about system users (login name, home directory, name, how long they've been logged in to the system, etc.). The finger package includes a standard finger client and server. The server daemon (fingerd) runs from /etc/inetd.conf, which must be modified to disable finger requests.

You should install finger if your system is used by multiple users and you'd like finger information to be available.

ftp – (Version 0.10, 89K) Ⓦ Ⓢ

The ftp package provides the standard UNIX command-line FTP client. FTP is the file transfer protocol, which is a widely used Internet protocol for transferring files and for archiving files.

If your system is on a network, you should install ftp in order to do file transfers.

fwhois – (Version 1.00, 8K) Ⓦ Ⓢ

The fwhois program is a different style of the whois program. Both fwhois and whois query Internet whois databases to find information about system users. Fwhois is smaller and more compact than whois, and runs in a different manner.

Install fwhois if you or your system's users need a program for querying whois databases. You may also want to install whois, and then decide for yourself which program you prefer.

gftp – (Version 1.13, 553K) Ⓦ

gFTP is a multithreaded FTP client for X Windows written using Gtk. It allows to have simultaneous downloads, resuming of interrupted file transfers, file transfer queues, a very nice connection manager and many more features.

ircii – (Version 4.4, 997K)

IrcII is a popular Internet Relay Chat (IRC) client. IRC clients communicate with IRC servers, enabling users to "chat" via the Internet.

Install ircii if you want to participate in chat rooms.

kdenetwork – (Version 1.1, 7,317K)

Network applications for the K Desktop Environment.

Includes: karchie (ftp archive searcher); kbiff (mail delivery notification) kfinger ("finger" utility); kmail (mail client); knu (network utilities); korn (mailbox monitor tool); kppp (easy PPP connection configuration); krn (news reader); ktalkd (talk daemon); ksirc (irc client).

kpppload – (Version 1.04, 88K)

Monitors the load on your PPP connection. Looks a lot like xload.

lynx – (Version 2.8.1, 2,011K)   Ⓦ Ⓢ

Lynx is a text-based Web browser. Lynx does not display any images, but it does support frames, tables and most other HTML tags. Lynx's advantage over graphical browsers is its speed: Lynx starts and exits quickly and swiftly displays Web pages.

Install lynx if you would like to try this fast, non-graphical browser (you may come to appreciate its strengths).

mailx – (Version 8.1.1, 89K)   Ⓑ

The mailx package installs the /bin/mail program, which is used to send quick email messages (i.e., without opening up a full-featured mail user agent). Mail is often used in shell scripts.

You should install mailx because of its quick email sending ability, which is especially useful if you're planning on writing any shell scripts.

metamail – (Version 2.7, 341K)   Ⓦ Ⓢ

Metamail is a system for handling multimedia mail, using the mailcap file. Metamail reads the mailcap file, which tells Metamail what helper program to call in order to handle a particular type of non-text mail. Note that metamail can also add multimedia support to certain non-mail programs.

Metamail should be installed if you need to add multimedia support to mail programs and some other programs, using the mailcap file.

mutt – (Version 0.95.4us, 1,369K)   Ⓦ Ⓢ

Mutt is a text mode mail user agent. Mutt supports color, threading, arbitrary key remapping, and a lot of customization.

You should install mutt if you've used mutt in the past and you prefer it, or if you're new to mail programs and you haven't decided which one you're going to use.

nc – (Version 1.10, 105K)

The nc package contains Netcat (the program is actually nc), a simple utility for reading and writing data across network connections, using the TCP or UDP protocols. Netcat is intended to be a reliable back-end tool which can be used directly or easily driven by other programs and scripts. Netcat is also a feature-rich network debugging and exploration tool, since it can create many different connections and has many built-in capabilities.

You may want to install the netcat package if you are administering a network and you'd like to use its debugging and network exploration capabilities.

ncftp – (Version 3.0beta18, 725K)   Ⓦ Ⓢ

Ncftp is an improved FTP client. Ncftp's improvements include support for command line editing, command histories, recursive gets, automatic anonymous logins and more.

Install ncftp if you use FTP to transfer files and you'd like to try some of ncftp's additional features.

netscape-common – (Version 4.51, 7,128K)   Ⓦ Ⓢ

This package contains the files that are shared between the Netscape Navigator Web browser and the Netscape Communicator suite of tools (the Navigator Web browser, an e-mail client, a news reader and Web page editor).

Install the netscape-common package if you're installing the netscape-navigator and/or the netscape-communicator program.

netscape-communicator – (Version 4.51, 13,522K)   Ⓦ Ⓢ

Netscape Communicator is the industry-leading Web browser. It supports the latest HTML standards, Java, JavaScript and some style sheets. It also includes a full-featured Usenet news reader as well as a complete e-mail client.

Information on the Netscape Communicator license may be found in the file /usr/doc/netscape-common-4.51/-LICENSE.

netscape-navigator – (Version 4.51, 7,242K)

Netscape Navigator is the industry-leading Web browser. It supports the latest HTML standards, Java, JavaScript and some style sheets.

Information on the Netscape Navigator license may be found in the file /usr/doc/netscape-common-4.51/LICENSE.

This will install the basic Netscape Navigator Web browser. If you want additional features, such as the Usenet news reader and HTML editor, you should install the netscape-communicator package.

nmh – (Version 0.27, 4,646K)   Ⓦ Ⓢ

Nmh is an email system based on the MH email system and is intended to be a (mostly) compatible drop-in replacement for MH. Nmh isn't a single comprehensive program. Instead, it consists of a number of fairly simple single-purpose programs for sending, receiving, saving, retrieving and otherwise manipulating email messages. You can freely intersperse nmh commands with other shell commands or write custom scripts which utilize nmh commands. If you want to use nmh as a true email user agent, you'll want to also install exmh to provide a user interface for it–nmh only has a command line interface.

If you'd like to use nmh commands in shell scripts, or if you'd like to use nmh and exmh together as your email user agent, you should install nmh.

pine – (Version 4.10, 3,427K)   Ⓦ Ⓢ

Pine is a very popular, easy to use, full-featured email user agent which includes a simple text editor called pico. Pine supports MIME extensions and can also be used to read news. Pine also supports IMAP, mail and MH style folders.

Pine should be installed because Pine is a very commonly used email user agent and it is currently in development.

rsh – (Version 0.10, 127K)   Ⓦ Ⓢ

The rsh package contains a set of programs which allow users to run commmands on remote machines, login to other machines and copy files between machines (rsh, rlogin and rcp). All three of these commands use rhosts style authentication. This package contains the clients and servers needed for all of these services. It also contains a server for rexec, an alternate method of executing remote commands. All of these servers are run by inetd and configured using /etc/inetd.conf and PAM. The rexecd server is disabled by default, but the other servers are enabled.

The rsh package should be installed to enable remote access to other machines.

rsync – (Version 2.3.0, 223K)

Rsync uses a quick and reliable algorithm to very quickly bring remote and host files into sync. Rsync is fast because it just sends the differences in the files over the network (instead of sending the complete files). Rsync is often used as a very powerful mirroring process or just as a more capable replacement for the rcp command. A technical report which describes the rsync algorithm is included in this package.

Install rsync if you need a powerful mirroring program.

slrn – (Version 0.9.5.4, 425K)   Ⓦ Ⓢ

SLRN is a powerful, easy to use, threaded Internet news reader. SLRN is highly customizable and allows you to design complex filters to sort or kill news articles. SLRN works well over slow network connections, and includes a utility for reading news off-line.

Install slrn if you need a full-featured news reader, if you have a slow network connection, or if you'd like to save on-line time by reading your news off-line.

slrn-pull – (Version 0.9.5.4, 66K)

This package provides slrnpull, which allows set up of a small news spool for offline news reading.

talk – (Version 0.10, 33K)   Ⓦ Ⓢ

The ntalk package provides client and daemon programs for the Internet talk protocol, which allows you to chat with other users on different systems. Talk is a communication program which copies lines from one terminal to the terminal of another user.

Install ntalk if you'd like to use talk for chatting with users on different systems.

tcpdump – (Version 3.4, 214K)   Ⓦ Ⓢ

Tcpdump is a command-line tool for monitoring network traffic. Tcpdump can capture and display the packet headers on a particular network interface or on all interfaces. Tcpdump can display all of the packet headers, or just the ones that match particular criteria.

Install tcpdump if you need a program to monitor network traffic.

telnet – (Version 0.10, 180K)   Ⓦ Ⓢ

Telnet is a popular protocol for logging into remote systems over the Internet. The telnet package provides a command line telnet client as well as a telnet daemon, which will support remote logins into the host machine. The telnet daemon is enabled by default. You may disable the telnet daemon by editing /etc/inetd.conf.

Install the telnet package if you want to telnet to remote machines and/or support remote logins to your own machine.

tin – (Version 1.4_990216, 1,193K)   Ⓦ Ⓢ

Tin is a basic, easy to use Internet news reader. Tin can read news locally or remotely via an NNTP (Network News Transport Protocol) server.

Install tin if you need a basic news reader.

traceroute – (Version 1.4a5, 27K)   Ⓦ Ⓢ

The traceroute utility displays the route used by IP packets on their way to a specified network (or Internet) host. Traceroute displays the IP number and host name (if possible) of the machines along the route taken by the packets. Traceroute is used as a network debugging tool. If you're having network connectivity problems, traceroute will show you where the trouble is coming from along the route.

Install traceroute if you need a tool for diagnosing network connectivity problems.

trn – (Version 3.6, 446K)   Ⓦ Ⓢ

Trn is a basic news reader that supports threading. This version is configured to read news from an NNTP news server.

Install trn if you need a basic news reader that shows you newsgroup postings in threaded format.

urlview – (Version 0.7, 37K)

urlview extracts URLs from a given text file, and presents a menu of URLs to view using a user specified command.

wget – (Version 1.5.3, 335K)

GNU Wget is a file retrieval utility which can use either the HTTP or FTP protocols. Wget features include the ability to work in the background while you're logged out, recursive retrieval of directories, file name wildcard matching, remote file timestamp storage and comparison, use of Rest with FTP servers and Range with HTTP servers to retrieve files over slow or unstable connections, support for Proxy servers, and configurability.

Install wget if you need to retrieve large numbers of files with HTTP or FTP, or if you need a utility for mirroring web sites or FTP directories.

xchat – (Version 0.9.4, 205K)   Ⓦ

X-Chat is yet another IRC client for the X Window System, using the Gtk+ toolkit. It is pretty easy to use compared to the other Gtk+ IRC clients and the interface is quite nicely designed.

xmailbox – (Version 2.5, 33K)   Ⓦ Ⓢ

The xmailbox program is an X Window System program which notifies you when mail arrives. Xmailbox is similar to the xbiff program, but it offers more features and notification options.

Install the xmailbox package if you'd like a graphical program for X which will notify you when new mail arrives.

xrn – (Version 9.01, 253K)   Ⓦ Ⓢ

A simple Usenet News reader for the X Window System. Xrn allows you to point and click your way through reading, replying and posting news messages.

Install the xrn package if you need a simple news reader for X.

ytalk – (Version 3.1, 68K)

The YTalk program is essentially a chat program for multiple users. YTalk works just like the UNIX talk program and even communicates with the same talk daemon(s), but YTalk allows for multiple connections (unlike UNIX talk). YTalk also supports redirection of program output to other users as well as an easy-to-use menu of commands.

Install the ytalk package if you need a chat program for multiple users.

D.2.9   Multimedia

This section contains packages that are associated with multimedia.

ImageMagick – (Version 4.2.2, 3,150K)   Ⓦ Ⓢ

ImageMagick is a powerful image display, coversion and manipulation tool. It runs in an X session. With this tool, you can view, edit and display a variety of image formats.

This package installs the necessary files to run ImageMagick.

aktion – (Version 0.3.3, 314K)

Movie player for the K Desktop Environment. Requires 'xanim' to function.

aumix – (Version 1.18.2, 65K)   Ⓦ

Aumix is a tty based, interactive method of controlling a sound card mixer. It lets you adjust the input levels from the CD, microphone, and on board synthesizers, as well as the output volume. Aumix can adjust audio mixers from the command line, from a script, or interactively at the console or terminal with a full-screen ncurses-based interface.

Install aumix if you need to control an audio mixer. If you install aumix, you will also need to install ncurses (since aumix's interface is based on ncurses) and gpm (for mouse support).

awesfx – (Version 0.4.3a, 299K)   Ⓦ

The awesfx package contains necessary utilities for the AWE32 sound driver.

If you must use an AWE32 sound driver, you should install this package.

cdp – (Version 0.33, 39K)   Ⓦ

The cdp program plays audio CDs in your computer's CD-ROM drive. Cdp includes a full-screen interface version and a command line version.

Install cdp to play audio CDs on your system.

desktop-backgrounds – (Version 1.0.0, 5,451K)   Ⓦ

If you use a desktop environment like GNOME you can use these images to spruce up your background.

ee – (Version 0.3.8, 450K)   Ⓦ

The ee package contains the Electric Eyes image viewer for the GNOME desktop environment. Electric Eyes is primary an image viewer, but it also allows many types of image manipulations. Electric Eyes can handle almost any type of image.

Install the ee package if you need an image viewer.

giftrans – (Version 1.12.2, 22K)

Giftrans will convert an existing GIF87 file to GIF89 format. In other words, Giftrans can make one color in a .gif image (normally the background) transparent.

Install the giftrans package if you need a quick, small, one-purpose graphics program to make transparent .gifs out of existing .gifs.

gimp – (Version 1.0.4, 8,060K)   Ⓦ

The GIMP is an image manipulation program suitable for photo retouching, image composition and image authoring. Many people find it extremely useful in creating logos and other graphics for web pages. The GIMP has many of the tools and filters you would expect to find in similar commercial offerings, and some interesting extras as well.

The GIMP provides a large image manipulation toolbox, including channel operations and layers, effects, sub-pixel imaging and anti-aliasing, and conversions, all with multi-level undo.

This version of The GIMP includes a scripting facility, but many of the included scripts rely on fonts that we cannot distribute. The GIMP ftp site has a package of fonts that you can install by yourself, which includes all the fonts needed to run the included scripts. Some of the fonts have unusual licensing requirements; all the licenses are documented in the package. Get ftp://ftp.gimp.org/pub/gimp/fonts/freefonts-0.10.tar.gz and ftp://ftp.gimp.org/pub/gimp/fonts/sharefonts-0.10.tar.gz if you are so inclined. Alternatively, choose fonts which exist on your system before running the scripts.

gimp-data-extras – (Version 1.0.0, 7,825K)

Patterns, gradients etc. for gimp. This package isn't required, but contains lots of goodies for gimp.

gnome-audio – (Version 1.0.0, 828K)   ⓌⓈ

If you use the GNOME desktop environment, you may want to install this package of complementary sounds.

gnome-media – (Version 1.0.1, 291K) Ⓦ

GNOME (GNU Network Object Model Environment) is a user-friendly set of applications and desktop tools to be used in conjunction with a window manager for the X Window System. GNOME is similar in purpose and scope to CDE and KDE, but GNOME is based completely on Open Source software.

GNOME's powerful environment is pleasing on the eye, easy to configure and use.

This package will install such media features as the GNOME CD player.

kdegraphics – (Version 1.1, 2,685K)

Graphics applications for the K Desktop Environment.

Includes: kdvi (displays TeX .dvi files); kfax (displays fax files); kfract (a fractal generator); kghostview (displays postscript files); kiconedit (icon editor); kpaint (a simple drawing program); ksnapshot (screen capture utility); kview (image viewer for GIF, JPEG, TIFF, etc.).

kdemultimedia – (Version 1.1, 2,277K)

Multimedia applications for the K Desktop Environment. Included: kmedia (media player); kmid (midi/karaoke player); kmidi (midi-to-wav player/converter); kmix (mixer); kscd (CD audio player)

libgr-progs – (Version 2.0.13, 1,580K) Ⓦ Ⓢ

The libgr-progs package contains a group of scripts for manipulating the graphics files in formats which are supported by the libgr library. For example, libgr-progs includes the rasttopnm script, which will convert a Sun rasterfile into a portable anymap. Libgr-progs contains many other scripts for converting from one graphics file format to another.

If you need to use these conversion scripts, you should install libgr-progs. You'll also need to install the libgr package.

libungif-progs – (Version 4.1.0, 336K)

The libungif-progs package contains various programs for manipulating GIF format image files.

Install this package if you need to manipulate GIF format image files. You'll also need to install the libungif package.

mikmod – (Version 3.1.5, 784K) Ⓦ

MikMod is one of the best and most well known MOD music file players for UNIX-like systems. This particular distribution is intended to compile fairly painlessly in a Linux environment. MikMod uses the OSS /dev/dsp driver including all recent kernels for output, and will also write .wav files. Supported file formats include MOD, STM, S3M, MTM, XM, ULT, and IT. The player uses ncurses for console output and supports transparent loading from gzip/pkzip/zoo archives and the loading/saving of playlists.

Install the mikmod package if you need a MOD music file player.

mpg123 – (Version 0.59q, 207K) Ⓦ

Mpg123 is a fast, free and portable MPEG audio player for Unix. It supports MPEG 1.0/2.0 layers 1, 2 and 3 ("mp3" files). For full CD quality playback (44 kHz, 16 bit, stereo) a Pentium CPU is required. Mono and/or reduced quality playback (22 kHz or 11 kHz) is possible on 486 CPUs.

For information on the MP3 License, please visit: http://www.mpeg.org/

multimedia – (Version 2.1, 344K)   Ⓦ

The multimedia package contains several X Window System utilities for handling multimedia files: xplaycd, xmixer and xgetfile. Xplaycd is a CD player for playing audio CDs on your machine's CD-ROM drive. Xmixer controls the volume settings on your machine's sound card. Xgetfile is a versatile file browser, intended for use in shell scripts.

Install the multimedia package if you need an audio CD player, a sound card volume controller, or a file browser for use in shell scripts.

playmidi – (Version 2.4, 133K)   Ⓦ

Playmidi plays MIDI (Musicial Instrument Digital Interface) sound files through a sound card synthesizer. This package includes basic drum samples for use with simple FM synthesizers.

Install playmidi if you want to play MIDI files using your computer's sound card.

playmidi-X11 – (Version 2.4, 39K)   Ⓦ

Playmidi-X11 provides an X Window System interface for playing MIDI (Musical Instrument Digital Interface) sound files through a sound card synthesizer. This package includes basic drum samples for use with simple FM synthesizers.

Install playmidi-X11 if you want to use an X interface to play MIDI sound files using your computer's sound card.

rhsound – (Version 1.8, 11K)   Ⓦ

The rhsound package provides a script which can save and restore the mixer settings and volume level of the standard kernel sound drivers. These mixer settings are preserved through shutdowns and restarts.

Install the rhsound package if you need to preserve the kernel sound driver module's mixer settings through shutdowns and reboots.

sndconfig – (Version 0.31, 221K)   Ⓦ

Sndconfig is a text based tool which sets up the configuration files you'll need to use a sound card with a Red Hat Linux system. Sndconfig can be used to set the proper sound type for programs which use the /dev/dsp, /dev/audio and /dev/mixer devices. The sound settings are saved by the aumix and sysV runlevel scripts.

Install sndconfig if you need to configure your sound card.

sox – (Version 12.15, 233K)   Ⓦ

SoX (Sound eXchange) is a sound file format converter for Linux, UNIX and DOS PCs. The self-described 'Swiss Army knife of sound tools,' SoX can convert between many different digitized sound formats and perform simple sound manipulation functions, including sound effects.

Install the sox package if you'd like to convert sound file formats or manipulate some sounds.

transfig – (Version 3.2.1, 292K)

The transfig utility creates a makefile which translates FIG (created by xfig) or PIC figures into a specified LaTeX graphics language (for example, PostScript(TM)). Transfig is used to create TeX documents which are portable (i.e., they can be printed in a wide variety of environments).

x11amp – (Version 0.9_alpha3, 1,341K) (W)

X11amp is a X Windows based mp3 player with a nice interface borrowed from WinAMP.

For information on the MP3 License, please visit: http://www.mpeg.org/

xanim – (Version 27070, 847K) (W)

The XAnim program is an animation/video/audio viewer for the X Window System. XAnim can display a large variety of animation, audio and video formats.

Install the xanim package if you need a viewer for an animation, video or audio file.

xfig – (Version 3.2.2, 2,545K)

Xfig is an X Window System tool for creating basic vector graphics, including bezier curves, lines, rulers and more. The resulting graphics can be saved, printed on PostScript printers or converted to a variety of other formats (e.g., X11 bitmaps, Encapsulated PostScript, LaTeX).

You should install xfig if you need a simple program to create vector graphics.

xpaint – (Version 2.4.9, 448K) (W)

XPaint is an X Window System color image editing program which supports most standard paint program options. XPaint also supports advanced features like image processing algorithms. XPaint allows you to edit multiple images simultaneously and supports a variety of image formats, including PPM, XBM, TIFF, JPEG, etc.

Install the xpaint package if you need a paint program for X.

zgv – (Version 3.0, 175K)

Zgv is an image viewer which can display graphics in GIF, JPEG/JFIF, PNG, PBM/PGM/PPM, BMP, TGA, PCX and MRF formats on VGA and SVGA displays. Zgv can also display thumbnails of the images. Zgv is based on svgalib, which you will need to have on your system in order to use zgv.

Install zgv if you need an image viewer.

D.2.10   Productivity

This section contains packages that are associated with increasing productivity.

gnome-pim – (Version 1.0.3, 673K) (W)

The GNOME Personal Information Manager consists of applications to make keeping up with your busy life easier.

Currently these apps are present:

- gnomecal : personal calendar and todo list - gnomecard: contact list of friends and business associates

gnumeric – (Version 0.21, 5,008K) ⓦ

GNOME is the GNU Network Object Model Environment. This powerful environment is both easy to use and easy to configure.

This package will install Gnumeric the GNOME spreadsheet program. This program is intended to be a replacement for a commercial spreadsheet, so quite a bit of work has gone into the program.

Install this package if you want to use the GNOME spreadsheet Gnumeric.

ical – (Version 2.2, 790K) ⓦ Ⓢ

Ical is an X Window System based calendar program. Ical will easily create/edit/delete entries, create repeating entries, remind you about upcoming appointments, print and list item occurrences, and allow shared calendars between different users.

Install ical if you need a calendar program to track your schedule. You'll need to have the X Window System installed in order to use ical.

korganizer – (Version 1.1, 1,220K)

KOrganizer is a complete calendar and scheduling program for KDE. It allows interchange with other calendar applications through the industry standard vCalendar file format.

D.2.11   Publishing

This section contains packages that are associated with publishing.

enscript – (Version 1.6.1, 1,515K)

Enscript is a print filter. It can take ASCII input and format it into PostScript output. At the same time, it can also do nice transformations like putting two ASCII pages on one physical page (side by side) or changing fonts.

ghostscript – (Version 5.10, 3,330K) ⓦ Ⓢ

Ghostscript is a software set that provides a PostScript(TM) interpreter, a set of C procedures (the Ghostscript library, which implements the graphics capabilities in the PostScript language) and an interpreter for Portable Document Format (PDF) files. Ghostscript translates PostScript code into many common, bitmapped formats, like those understood by your printer or screen. Ghostscript is normally used to display PostScript files and to print PostScript files to non-PostScript printers.

If you need to display PostScript files or print them to non-PostScript printers, you should install ghostscript. If you install ghostscript, you also need to install the ghostscript-fonts package.

ghostscript-fonts – (Version 5.10, 1,490K) ⓦ Ⓢ

These fonts can be used by the GhostScript interpreter during text rendering. They are in addition to the shared fonts between GhostScript and X11.

groff – (Version 1.11a, 2,842K) Ⓑ

Groff is a document formatting system. Groff takes standard text and formatting commands as input and produces formatted output. The created documents can be shown on a display or printed on a printer. Groff's formatting commands allow you to specify font type and size, bold type, italic type, the number and size of columns on a page, and more.

You should install groff if you want to use it as a document formatting system. Groff can also be used to format man pages. If you are going to use groff with the X Window System, you'll also need to install the groff-gxditview package.

groff-gxditview – (Version 1.11a, 73K)

Gxditview displays the groff text processor's output on an X Window System display.

If you are going to use groff as a text processor, you should install gxditview so that you preview your processed text files in X. You'll also need to install the groff package and the X Window System.

gv – (Version 3.5.8, 424K)   Ⓦ Ⓢ

Gv provides a user interface for the ghostscript PostScript(TM) interpreter. Derived from the ghostview program, gv can display PostScript and PDF documents using the X Window System.

Install the gv package if you'd like to view PostScript and PDF documents on your system. You'll also need to have the ghostscript package installed, as well as the X Window System.

lout – (Version 3.08, 3,452K)

Lout is a high-level language for document formatting. Lout reads a high-level description of a document (similar in style to LaTeX) and can produce a PostScript(TM) file for printing or produce plain text. Lout supports the typesetting of documents which contain floating figures, table, diagrams, rotated and scaled text or graphics, footnotes, running headers, footers, an index, a table of contents and bibliography, cross-references, mathematical equations and statistical graphs. Lout can be extended with definitions that should be easier to write than other languages, since Lout is a high-level language. Lout supports (with hyphenation) a variety of languages: Czech, Danish, Dutch, English, Finnish, French, German, Norwegian, Russian, Slovenian, Spanish and Swedish.

Install the lout package if you'd like to try the Lout document formatting system. Unless you're already a Lout expert, you'll probably want to also install the lout-doc package, which contains the documentation for Lout.

lout-doc – (Version 3.08, 2,069K)

The lout-doc package includes all of the documentation for the Lout document formatting language. The documentation includes manuals for regular users and for experts, written in Lout and available as PostScript(TM) files. The documentation provides good examples for how to write large documents with Lout.

If you're installing the lout package, you should install the lout-doc package.

mpage – (Version 2.4, 90K)   Ⓦ Ⓢ

The mpage utility takes plain text files or PostScript(TM) documents as input, reduces the size of the text, and prints the files on a PostScript printer with several pages on each sheet of paper. Mpage is very useful for viewing large printouts without using up tons of paper. Mpage supports many different layout options for the printed pages.

Mpage should be installed if you need a useful utility for viewing long text documents without wasting paper.

printtool – (Version 3.40, 113K)   Ⓦ Ⓢ

The printtool is a printer configuration tool with a graphical user interface. Printtool can manage both local and remote printers, including Windows (SMB) and NetWare (NCP) printers.

Printtool should be installed so that you can manage local and remote printers.

rhs-printfilters – (Version 1.51, 101K)   Ⓦ Ⓢ

The rhs-printfilters package contains a set of print filters which are primarily meant to be used with the Red Hat printtool. These print filters provide an easy way for users to handle printing numerous file formats.

sgml-tools – (Version 1.0.9, 1,877K)

SGMLtools is a text formatting package based on SGML (Standard Generalized Markup Language). SGMLtools allows you to produce LaTeX, HTML, GNU info, LyX, RTF, plain text (via groff), and other format outputs from a single source. SGMLtools is intended for writing technical software documentation.

Install SGMLTools if you need a text formatting program that can produce a variety of different formats from a single source file. You should probably also install and try SGMLTtools if you're going to write technical software documentation.

tetex – (Version 0.9, 39,613K)   Ⓦ

TeTeX is an implementation of TeX for Linux or UNIX systems. TeX takes a text file and a set of formatting commands as input and creates a typesetter independent .dvi (DeVice Independent) file as output. Usually, TeX is used in conjunction with a higher level formatting package like LaTeX or PlainTeX, since TeX by itself is not very user-friendly.

Install tetex if you want to use the TeX text formatting system. If you are installing tetex, you will also need to install tetex-afm (a PostScript(TM) font converter for TeX), tetex-dvilj (for converting .dvi files to HP PCL format for printing on HP and HP compatible printers), tetex-dvips (for converting .dvi files to PostScript format for printing on PostScript printers), tetex-latex (a higher level formatting package which provides an easier-to-use interface for TeX) and tetex-xdvi (for previewing .dvi files in X). Unless you're an expert at using TeX, you'll also want to install the tetex-doc package, which includes the documentation for TeX.

tetex-afm – (Version 0.9, 3,030K)   Ⓦ

Tetex-afm provides afm2tfm, a converter for PostScript font metric files. PostScript fonts are accompanied by .afm font metric files which describe the characteristics of each font. To use PostScript fonts with TeX, TeX needs .tfm files that contain similar information. Afm2tfm will convert .afm files to .tfm files.

If you are installing tetex in order to use the TeX text formatting system, you will need to install tetex-afm. You will also need to install tetex-dvilj (for converting .dvi files to HP PCL format for printing on HP and HP compatible printers), tetex-dvips (for converting .dvi files to PostScript format for printing on PostScript printers), tetex-latex (a higher level formatting package which provides an easier-to-use interface for TeX) and tetex-xdvi (for previewing .dvi files in X). Unless you're an expert at using TeX, you'll probably also want to install the tetex-doc package, which includes documentation for TeX.

tetex-doc – (Version 0.9, 29,426K)

The tetex-doc package contains documentation for the TeX text formatting system.

If you want to use TeX and you're not an expert at it, you should install the tetex-doc package. You'll also need to install the tetex package, tetex-afm (a PostScript font converter for TeX), tetex-dvilj (for converting .dvi files to HP PCL format for printing on HP and HP compatible printers), tetex-dvips (for converting .dvi files to PostScript format for printing on PostScript printers), tetex-latex (a higher level formatting package which provides an easier-to-use interface for TeX) and tetex-xdvi (for previewing .dvi files).

tetex-dvilj – (Version 0.9, 351K)   ⟦W⟧

Dvilj and dvilj's siblings (included in this package) will convert TeX text formatting system output .dvi files to HP PCL (HP Printer Control Language) commands. Using dvilj, you can print TeX files to HP LaserJet+ and fully compatible printers. With dvilj2p, you can print to HP LaserJet IIP and fully compatible printers. And with dvilj4, you can print to HP LaserJet4 and fully compatible printers.

If you are installing tetex, so that you can use the TeX text formatting system, you will also need to install tetex-dvilj. In addition, you will need to install tetex-afm (for converting PostScript font description files), tetex-dvips (for converting .dvi files to PostScript format for printing on PostScript printers), tetex-latex (a higher level formatting package which provides an easier-to-use interface for TeX) and tetex-xdvi (for previewing .dvi files in X). If you're installing TeX and you're not a TeX expert, you'll also want to install the tetex-doc package, which contains documentation for TeX.

tetex-dvips – (Version 0.9, 856K)   ⟦W⟧

Dvips converts .dvi files produced by the TeX text formatting system (or by another processor like GFtoDVI) to PostScript(TM) format. Normally the PostScript file is sent directly to your printer.

If you are installing tetex, so that you can use the TeX text formatting system, you will also need to install tetex-dvips. In addition, you will need to install tetex-afm (for converting PostScript font description files), tetex-dvilj (for converting .dvi files to HP PCL format for printing on HP and HP compatible printers), tetex-latex (a higher level formatting package which provides an easier-to-use interface for TeX) and tetex-xdvi (for previewing .dvi files in X). If you're installing TeX and you're not an expert at it, you'll also want to install the tetex-doc package, which contains documentation for the TeX system.

tetex-latex – (Version 0.9, 7,898K)   ⟦W⟧

LaTeX is a front end for the TeX text formatting system. Easier to use than TeX, LaTeX is essentially a set of TeX macros which provide convenient, predefined document formats for users.

If you are installing tetex, so that you can use the TeX text formatting system, you will also need to install tetex-latex. In addition, you will need to install tetex-afm (for converting PostScript font description files), tetex-dvilj (for converting .dvi files to HP PCL format for printing on HP and HP compatible printers), tetex-dvips (for converting .dvi files to PostScript format for printing on PostScript printers) and tetex-xdvi (for previewing .dvi files in X). If you're not an expert at TeX, you'll probably also want to install the tetex-doc package, which contains documentation for TeX.

tetex-xdvi – (Version 0.9, 1,030K)   ⟦W⟧⟦S⟧

Xdvi allows you to preview the TeX text formatting system's output .dvi files on an X Window System.

If you are installing tetex, so that you can use the TeX text formatting system, you will also need to install tetex-xdvi. In addition, you will need to install tetex-afm (a PostScript font converter for TeX), tetex-dvilj (for converting .dvi files to HP PCL format for printing on HP and HP compatible printers), tetex-dvips (for converting .dvi files to PostScript format for printing on PostScript printers), and tetex-latex (a higher level formatting package which provides an easier-to-use interface for TeX). If you're not a TeX expert, you'll probably also want to install the tetex-doc package, which contains documentation for the TeX text formatting system.

texinfo – (Version 3.12f, 799K)   Ⓦ Ⓢ

Texinfo is a documentation system that can produce both online information and printed output from a single source file. Normally, you'd have to write two separate documents: one for online help or other online information and the other for a typeset manual or other printed work. Using Texinfo, you only need to write one source document. Then when the work needs revision, you only have to revise one source document. The GNU Project uses the Texinfo file format for most of its documentation.

Install texinfo if you want a documentation system for producing both online and print documentation from the same source file and/or if you are going to write documentation for the GNU Project.

xpdf – (Version 0.80, 1,351K)

Xpdf is an X Window System based viewer for Portable Document Format (PDF) files. PDF files are sometimes called Acrobat files, after Adobe Acrobat (Adobe's PDF viewer). Xpdf is a small and efficient program which uses standard X fonts.

Install the xpdf package if you need a viewer for PDF files.

D.2.12   System

This section contains packages that are associated with system-level operations.

SVGATextMode – (Version 1.8, 852K)

SVGATextMode is a utility for reprogramming (S)VGA hardware, which can improve the appearance of text consoles. You should install SVGATextMode if you want to alter the appearance of your text consoles. The utility uses a configuration file (Xconfig or XF86Config) to set up textmodes with higher resolution, larger fonts, higher display refresh rates, etc.

Although SVGATextMode can be used to program any text mode size, your results will depend on your VGA card.

arpwatch – (Version 2.1a4, 104K)

The arpwatch package contains arpwatch and arpsnmp. Arpwatch and arpsnmp are both network monitoring tools. Both utilities monitor Ethernet or FDDI network traffic and build databases of Ethernet/IP address pairs, and can report certain changes via email.

Install the arpwatch package if you need networking monitoring devices which will automatically keep traffic of the IP addresses on your network.

bind-utils – (Version 8.2, 1,320K)   Ⓦ Ⓢ

Bind-utils contains a collection of utilities for querying DNS (Domain Name Service) name servers to find out information about Internet hosts. These tools will provide you with the IP addresses for given host names, as well as other information about registered domains and network addresses.

You should install bind-utils if you need to get information from DNS name servers.

comanche – (Version 990330, 372K)

Comanche (COnfiguration MANager for apaCHE) is a front-end for the Apache Web server, the most popular Web server used on the Internet. Comanche aims to make it easier to manage and configure Apache.

Install the commanche package if you need a configuration manager for the Apache Web server. You'll also need to install the apache package.

console-tools – (Version 19990302, 1,393K)   Ⓑ

This package contains utilities to load console fonts and keyboard maps. It also includes a number of different fonts and keyboard maps.

control-panel – (Version 3.11, 186K)   ⓌⓈ

The Red Hat control panel is a configuration program launcher for the X Window System. Both convenient and pleasing, the Red Hat control panel allows you easy access to numerous X-based system administration tools included in your Red Hat Linux system.

Eventually, you'll want to work with many of your system administration tools; this package helps you locate and launch many of them.

dialog – (Version 0.6, 88K)   Ⓦ

Dialog is a utility that allows you to show dialog boxes (containing questions or messages) in TTY (text mode) interfaces. Dialog is called from within a shell script. The following dialog boxes are implemented: yes/no, menu, input, message, text, info, checklist, radiolist, and gauge.

Install dialog if you would like to create TTY dialog boxes.

ext2ed – (Version 0.1, 288K)

Ext2ed is a program which provides a text and window interface for examining and editing an ext2 filesystem. Ext2ed is supposed to be easier to use than debugfs, but debugfs is more powerful. Note that this program should only be used by someone who is very experienced at hacking filesystems.

Install ext2ed if you want to examine and/or edit your ext2 filesystem, and you know what you're doing.

fbset – (Version 2.0.19990118, 34K)

fbset is a utility for querying and changing video modes of fbcon consoles.

gnome-linuxconf – (Version 0.21, 320K)   ⓌⓈ

GNOME (GNU Network Object Model Environment) is a user-friendly set of applications and desktop tools to be used in conjunction with a window manager for the X Window System. The gnome-linuxconf package includes GNOME's front end for the Linuxconf system configuration utility.

gnome-utils – (Version 1.0.1, 774K)   Ⓦ

GNOME is the GNU Network Object Model Environment. This powerful environment is both easy to use and easy to configure.

This package will install some GNOME utilities, such as the calendar and calculator.

gnorpm – (Version 0.7, 374K)   ⓌⓈ

Gnome RPM is a graphical front end to RPM, similar to Glint, but written with the GTK widget set and the GNOME libraries. It is currently under development, so there are some features missing, but you can currently query packages in the filesystem and database, install upgrade, uninstall and verify packages.

gtop – (Version 1.0.1, 267K)   Ⓦ

GNOME is the GNU Network Object Model Environment. This powerful environment is both easy to use and easy to configure.

This package will install the GNOME system monitor gtop, which shows memory graphs and processes.

hdparm – (Version 3.3, 37K)   Ⓑ

Hdparm is a useful system utility for setting (E)IDE hard drive parameters. For example, hdparm can be used to tweak hard drive performance and to spin down hard drives for power conservation.

ipxutils – (Version 1.0, 53K)   Ⓢ

The ipxutils package includes utilities (ipx_configure, ipx_internal_net, ipx_interface, ipx_route) necessary for configuring and debugging IPX interfaces and networks under Linux. IPX is the low-level protocol used by Novell's NetWare file server system to transfer data.

Install ipxutils if you need to configure IPX networking on your network.

isicom – (Version 1.0, 38K)

Binary images and loader for Multitech IntelligentSerialInternal (ISI) data files.

kdeadmin – (Version 1.1, 1,378K)

System Administration tools for the K Desktop Environment.

Included with this package are: kdat (tape backup); ksysv (sysV init editor); kuser (user administration tool)

kdeutils – (Version 1.1, 2,977K)

Utilities for the K Desktop Environment. Includes: ark (tar/gzip archive manager); kab (address book); karm (personal time tracker); kcalc (scientific calculator); kedit (simple text editor); kfloppy (floppy formatting tool); khexedit (hex editor); kjots (note taker); klipper (clipboard tool); kljettool(HP printer configuration tool); klpq (print queue manager) knotes (post-it notes for the desktop); kpm (process manager similar to 'top', but more advanced);kwrite (improved text editor).

kernelcfg – (Version 0.5, 58K)   Ⓦ Ⓢ

The kernelcfg package contains an X Window System based graphical user interface tool for configuring the kernel daemon (kerneld). Kerneld automatically loads some hardware and software support into memory as needed and unloads the support when it is no longer being used. The kernel configurator tool can be used to tell kerneld what hardware support to load when it is presented with a generic hardware request.

Kernelcfg should be installed because it is a useful utility for managing the kernel daemon.

knfsd-clients – (Version 1.2, 10K)

The nfs-server-clients package contains the showmount program. Showmount queries the mount daemon on a remote host for information about the NFS (Network File System) server on the remote host. For example, showmount can display the clients which are mounted on that host. This package is not needed to mount NFS volumes.

Install nfs-server-clients if you'd like to use the showmount tool for querying NFS servers.

linuxconf – (Version 1.14r2, 11,322K) [B]

Linuxconf is an extremely capable system configuration tool. Linuxconf provides four different interfaces for you to choose from: command line, character-cell (like the installation program), an X Window System based GUI and a web-based interface. Linuxconf can manage a large proportion of your system's operations, including networking, user accounts, file systems, boot parameters, and more.

Linuxconf will simplify the process of configuring your system. Unless you are completely happy with configuring your system manually, you should install the Linuxconf package and use Linuxconf instead.

macutils – (Version 2.0b3, 218K)

The macutils package includes a set of utilities for manipulating files that are commonly used by Macintosh machines. Macutils includes utilities like binhex, hexbin, macunpack, etc.

Install macutils if you need to manipulate files that are commonly used by Macintosh machines.

mkdosfs-ygg – (Version 0.3b, 17K) [W]

The mkdosfs program is used to create an MS-DOS FAT file system on a Linux system device, usually a disk partition.

The mkdosfs package should be installed if your machine needs to support MS-DOS style file systems.

mkisofs – (Version 1.12b5, 153K)

The mkisofs program is used as a pre-mastering program; i.e., it generates the ISO9660 filesystem. Mkisofs takes a snapshot of a given directory tree and generates a binary image of the tree which will correspond to an ISO9660 filesystem when written to a block device. Mkisofs is used for writing CD-ROMs, and includes support for creating bootable El Torito CD-ROMs.

Install the mkisofs package if you need a program for writing CD-ROMs.

mkxauth – (Version 1.7, 15K) [W][S]

The mkxauth utility helps create and maintain X authentication databases (.Xauthority files). Mkxauth is used to create an .Xauthority file or to merge keys from another local or remote .Xauthority file. .Xauthority files are used by the xauth user-oriented access control program, which grants or denies access to X servers based on the contents of the .Xauthority file.

The mkxauth package should be installed if you're going to use user-oriented access control to provide security for your X Window System (a good idea).

modemtool – (Version 1.21, 15K) [W][S]

The modemtool is a simple graphical configuration tool for selecting the serial port to which your modem is connected.

Install modemtool if you use a modem.

mt-st – (Version 0.5b, 67K) Ⓑ

The mt-st package contains the mt and st tape drive management programs. Mt (for magnetic tape drives) and st (for SCSI tape devices) can control rewinding, ejecting, skipping files and blocks and more.

This package can help you manage tape drives.

mtools – (Version 3.9.1, 486K) Ⓦ

Mtools is a collection of utilities for accessing MS-DOS files. Mtools allow you to read, write and move around MS-DOS filesystem files (normally on MS-DOS floppy disks). Mtools supports Windows95 style long file names, OS/2 Xdf disks, and 2m disks.

Mtools should be installed if you need to use MS-DOS disks.

ncpfs – (Version 2.2.0.12, 553K) Ⓢ

Ncpfs is a filesystem which understands the Novell NetWare(TM) NCP protocol. Functionally, NCP is used for NetWare the way NFS is used in the TCP/IP world. For a Linux system to mount a NetWare filesystem, it needs a special mount program. The ncpfs package contains such a mount program plus other tools for configuring and using the ncpfs filesystem.

Install the ncpfs package if you need to use the ncpfs filesystem to use Novell NetWare files or services.

netcfg – (Version 2.20, 165K) Ⓦ Ⓢ

A Red Hat Linux tool which provides a graphical user interface for setting up and configuring networking for your machine.

open – (Version 1.4, 13K)

The open command starts a specified command with the first available virtual console, or on a virtual console that you specify.

Install the open package if you regularly use virtual consoles to run programs.

pciutils – (Version 1.99.4, 120K)

This package contains various utilities for inspecting and setting devices connected to the PCI bus.

It requires kernel version 2.1.82 or newer (supporting the /proc/bus/pci interface).

procinfo – (Version 16, 54K)

The procinfo command gets system data from the /proc directory (the kernel filesystem), formats it and displays it on standard output. You can use procinfo to acquire information about your system from the kernel as it is running.

Install procinfo if you'd like to use it to gather and display system data.

procps – (Version 2.0.2, 298K) Ⓑ

The procps package contains a set of system utilities which provide system information. Procps includes ps, free, skill, snice, tload, top, uptime, vmstat, w, and watch. The ps command displays a snapshot of running processes. The top command provides a repetitive update of the statuses of running processes. The free command displays the amounts of free and used memory on your system. The skill command sends a terminate command (or another specified signal) to a specified set of processes. The snice command is used to change the scheduling priority of specified processes. The tload command prints a graph of the current system load average to a specified tty. The uptime command displays the current time, how long the system has been running, how many users are logged on and system load averages for the past one, five and fifteen minutes. The w command displays a list of the users who are currently logged on and what they're running. The watch program watches a running program. The vmstat command displays virtual memory statistics about processes, memory, paging, block I/O, traps and CPU activity.

procps-X11 – (Version 2.0.2, 0K)

The procps-X11 package contains the XConsole shell script, a backwards compatibility wrapper for the xconsole program.

psacct – (Version 6.3, 87K)

The psacct package contains several utilities for monitoring process activities, including ac, lastcomm, accton and sa. The ac command displays statistics about how long users have been logged on. The lastcomm command displays information about previous executed commands. The accton command turns process accounting on or off. The sa command summarizes information about previously executed commmands.

Install the psacct package if you'd like to use its utilities for monitoring process activities on your system.

psmisc – (Version 18, 46K)   [B]

The psmisc package contains utilities for managing processes on your system: pstree, killall and fuser. The pstree command displays a tree structure of all of the running processes on your system. The killall command sends a specified signal (SIGTERM if nothing is specified) to processes identified by name. The fuser command identifies the PIDs of processes that are using specified files or filesystems.

rdate – (Version 0.960923, 5K)   [W][S]

The rdate utility retrieves the date and time from another machine on your network, using the protocol described in RFC 868. If you run rdate as root, it will set your machine's local time to the time of the machine that you queried. Note that rdate isn't scrupulously accurate. If you are worried about milliseconds, get the xntpd program instead.

rdist – (Version 6.1.5, 141K)   [W][S]

The rdist program maintains identical copies of files on multiple hosts. If possible, rdist will preserve the owner, group, mode and mtime of files and it can update programs that are executing.

rhmask – (Version 1.0, 8K)

The rhmask utility creates mask files from original and updated files. The mask files, which may be the latest new versions of software, can then be freely distributed on public Internet servers. The mask files are only useful for people who who already have a copy of the original package. The rhmask utility uses a simple XOR scheme for creating the file mask and uses file size and md5 sums to ensure the integrity of the result.

Install the rhmask package if you need a utility for creating file masks.

rhs-hwdiag – (Version 0.35, 75K)   [B]

The rhs-hwdiag package contains the Red Hat Hardware Discovery Tools. These tools probe the serial and parallel ports on your system, and are useful for finding and reporting hardware errors to Red Hat support if you're having problems. These tools could cause adverse side-effects in some situations, so you should use them carefully.

screen – (Version 3.7.6, 368K)

The screen utility allows you to have multiple logins on just one terminal. Screen is useful for users who telnet into a machine or are connected via a dumb terminal, but want to use more than just one login.

Install the screen package if you need a screen manager that can support multiple logins on one terminal.

setconsole – (Version 1.0, 3K)   [B]

Setconsole is a basic system utility for setting up the /etc/inittab, /dev/systty and /dev/console files to handle a new console. The console can be either the local terminal (i.e., directly attached to the system via a video card) or a serial console.

setserial – (Version 2.15, 37K)   [B]

Setserial is a basic system utility for displaying or setting serial port information. Setserial can reveal and allow you to alter the I/O port and IRQ that a particular serial device is using, and more.

You should install setserial because you may find it useful for detecting and/or altering device information.

setuptool – (Version 1.2, 17K)   [B]

Setuptool is a user-friendly text mode menu utility which allows you to access all of the text mode configuration programs included in the Red Hat Linx operating system.

You should install the setuptool package because you will find yourself using its features for essential system administration.

statserial – (Version 1.1, 289K)   [W] [S]

The statserial utility displays a table of the signals on a standard 9-pin or 25-pin serial port and indicates the status of the handshaking lines. Statserial is useful for debugging serial port and/or modem problems.

Install the statserial package if you need a tool to help debug serial port or modem problems.

swatch – (Version 2.2, 129K)

The Swatch utility monitors system log files, filters out unwanted data and takes specified actions (i.e., sending email, executing a script, etc.) based upon what it finds in the log files.

Install the swatch package if you need a program that will monitor log files and alert you in certain situations.

symlinks – (Version 1.2, 212K)

The symlinks utility performs maintenance on symbolic links. Symlinks checks for symlink problems, including dangling symlinks which point to nonexistent files. Symlinks can also automatically convert absolute symlinks to relative symlinks.

Install the symlinks package if you need a program for maintaining symlinks on your system.

time – (Version 1.7, 18K)   *B*

The GNU time utility runs another program, collects information about the resources used by that program while it is running and displays the results.

Time can help developers optimize their programs.

timeconfig – (Version 2.6, 107K)   *B*

The timeconfig package contains two utilities: timeconfig and setclock. Timeconfig provides a simple text mode tool for configuring the time parameters in /etc/sysconfig/clock and /etc/localtime. The setclock tool sets the hardware clock on the system to the current time stored in the system clock.

timetool – (Version 2.5, 22K)   *W* *S*

The timetool utility provides a graphical user interface for setting the current date and time on your system.

tksysv – (Version 1.0, 35K)   *W* *S*

Tksysv is an X Window System based graphical interface for editing the services provided by different runlevels. Tksysv is used to set which services are stopped and which services are started in the different runlevels on your system.

Install the tksysv package if you'd like to use a graphical tool for editing runlevel services.

tunelp – (Version 1.3, 9K)

The tunelp utility sets various parameters for lp devices (/dev/lp0, /dev/lp1, /dev/lp2). Tunelp can set parameters like the lp device's interrupt usage, polling rate, etc.

Install the tunelp package if you need a utility for setting lp device parameters.

ucd-snmp-utils – (Version 3.6.1, 253K)   *W* *S*

The ucd-snmp package contains various utilities for use with the UCD-SNMP network management project.

Install this package if you need utilities for managing your network using the SNMP protocol. You'll also need to install the ucd-snmp package.

usermode – (Version 1.6, 94K)   *W* *S*

The usermode package contains several graphical tools for users: userinfo, usermount and userpasswd. Userinfo allows users to change their finger information. Usermount lets users mount, unmount, and format filesystems. Userpasswd allows users to change their passwords.

Install the usermode package if you would like to provide users with graphical tools for certain account management tasks.

usernet – (Version 1.0.9, 24K)   *W* *S*

The usernet utility provides a graphical interface for manipulating network interfaces (bringing them up or down and viewing their status). Users can only manipulate interfaces that are user-controllable. The superuser can control all interfaces.

Install the usernet package if you'd like to provide a graphical utility for manipulating network interfaces.

vlock – (Version 1.3, 9K)

The vlock program locks one or more sessions on the console. Vlock can lock the current terminal (local or remote) or the entire virtual console system, which completely disables all console access. The vlock program unlocks when either the password of the user who started vlock or the root password is typed.

Install vlock if you need to disable access to one console or to all virtual consoles.

which – (Version 1.0, 7K)   [B]

The which command shows the full pathname of a specified program, if the specified program is in your PATH.

xcpustate – (Version 2.5, 33K)

The xcpustate utility is an X Window System based monitor which shows the amount of time that the CPU is spending in different states. On a Linux system, xcpustate displays a bar that indicates the amounts of idle, user, nice and system time (from left to right) used by the CPU.

Install the xcpustate package if you'd like to use a horizontal bar style CPU state monitor.

xosview – (Version 1.7.1, 109K)

The xosview utility displays a set of bar graphs which show the current system state, including memory usage, CPU usage, system load, etc. Xosview runs under the X Window System.

Install the xosview package if you need a graphical tool for monitoring your system's performance.

xsysinfo – (Version 1.6, 22K)

Xsysinfo is a graphic kernel monitoring tool for the X Window System. Xsysinfo displays vertical bars for certain kernel parameters: CPU load average, CPU load, memory and swap sizes.

Install the xsysinfo package if you'd like to use a graphical kernel monitoring tool.

xtoolwait – (Version 1.2, 10K)

Xtoolwait is a utility which starts an X client in the background, waits for a window to be mapped on the root window, and then exits. Xtoolwait can improve performance for users who start a bunch of X clients automatically (for example, xterm, xlock, xconsole, whatever) when the X session starts.

Install xtoolwait if you'd like to try to speed up the startup time for X sessions.

D.2.13   Text

This section contains packages that are associated with the manipulation of text.

diffutils – (Version 2.7, 152K)   [B]

Diffutils includes four utilities: diff, cmp, diff3 and sdiff. Diff compares two files and shows the differences, line by line. The cmp command shows the offset and line numbers where two files differ, or cmp can show the characters that differ between the two files. The diff3 command shows the differences between three files. Diff3 can be used when two people have made independent changes to a common original; diff3 can produce a merged file that contains both persons' changes and warnings about conflicts. The sdiff command can be used to merge two files interactively.

Install diffutils if you need to compare text files.

ed – (Version 0.2, 102K) $\boxed{B}$

Ed is a line-oriented text editor, used to create, display, and modify text files (both interactively and via shell scripts). For most purposes, ed has been replaced in normal usage by full-screen editors (emacs and vi, for example).

Ed was the original UNIX editor, and may be used by some programs. In general, however, you probably don't need to install it and you probably won't use it much.

gawk – (Version 3.0.3, 2,303K) $\boxed{B}$

The gawk packages contains the GNU version of awk, a text processing utility. Awk interprets a special-purpose programming language to do quick and easy text pattern matching and reformatting jobs. Gawk should be upwardly compatible with the Bell Labs research version of awk and is almost completely compliant with the 1993 POSIX 1003.2 standard for awk.

Install the gawk package if you need a text processing utility. Gawk is considered to be a standard Linux tool for processing text.

grep – (Version 2.3, 287K) $\boxed{B}$

The GNU versions of commonly used grep utilities. Grep searches one or more input files for lines which contain a match to a specified pattern and then prints the matching lines. GNU's grep utilities include grep, egrep and fgrep.

You should install grep on your system, because it is a very useful utility for searching through text files, for system administration tasks, etc.

indent – (Version 1.9.1, 81K)

Indent is a GNU program for beautifying C code, so that it is easier to read. Indent can also convert from one C writing style to a different one. Indent understands correct C syntax and tries to handle incorrect C syntax.

Install the indent package if you are developing applications in C and you'd like to format your code automatically.

ispell – (Version 3.1.20, 4,049K) $\boxed{W}$ $\boxed{S}$

Ispell is the GNU interactive spelling checker. Ispell will check a text file for spelling and typographical errors. When it finds a word that is not in the dictionary, it will suggest correctly spelled words for the misspelled word.

You should install ispell if you need a program for spell checking (and who doesn't...).

less – (Version 332, 142K) $\boxed{B}$

The less utility is a text file browser that resembles more, but has more capabilities. Less allows you to move backwards in the file as well as forwards. Since less doesn't have to read the entire input file before it starts, less starts up more quickly than text editors (for example, vi).

You should install less because it is a basic utility for viewing text files, and you'll use it frequently.

m4 – (Version 1.4, 120K)   Ⓦ Ⓢ

A GNU implementation of the traditional UNIX macro processor. M4 is useful for writing text files which can be logically parsed, and is used by many programs as part of their build process. M4 has built-in functions for including files, running shell commands, doing arithmetic, etc. The autoconf program needs m4 for generating configure scripts, but not for running configure scripts.

Install m4 if you need a macro processor.

mawk – (Version 1.2.2, 131K)

Mawk is a version of the awk programming language. Awk interprets a special-purpose programming language to do quick text pattern matching and reformatting. Mawk improves on awk in certain ways and can sometimes outperform gawk, the standard awk program for Linux. Mawk conforms to the POSIX 1003.2 (draft 11.3) definition of awk.

You should install mawk if you use awk.

rgrep – (Version 0.98.7, 17K)

The rgrep utility can recursively descend through directories as it greps for the specified pattern. Note that this ability does take a toll on rgrep's performance, which is somewhat slow. Rgrep will also highlight the matching expression.

Install the rgrep package if you need a recursive grep which can highlight the matching expression.

sed – (Version 3.02, 68K)   Ⓑ

The sed (Stream EDitor) editor is a stream or batch (non-interactive) editor. Sed takes text as input, performs an operation or set of operations on the text and outputs the modified text. The operations that sed performs (substitutions, deletions, insertions, etc.) can be specified in a script file or from the command line.

textutils – (Version 1.22, 694K)   Ⓑ

A set of GNU utilities for modifying the contents of files, including programs for splitting, joining, comparing and modifying files.

D.3   Base

This section contains packages that are associated with the part of Red Hat Linux that is common to all installations of the operating system.

redhat-logos – (Version 1.0.2, 239K)   Ⓑ

redhat-logos (the "Package") contains files of the Red Hat "Shadow Man" logo and the RPM logo (the "Logos").

Red Hat Software, Inc. grants you the right to use the Package during the normal operation of other software programs that call upon the Package. Red Hat Software, Inc. grants to you the right and license to copy and redistribute the Package, but only in conjunction with copying or redistributing additional software packages that call upon the Package during the normal course of operation. Such rights are granted to you without fee, provided that:

1. The above copyright notice and this license are included with each copy you make, and they remain intact and are not altered, deleted, or modified in any way; 2. You do not modify the Package, or the appearance of any or all of the Logos in any manner; and 3. You do not use any or all of the Logos as, or as part of, a trademark, trade name, or trade identifier; or in any other fashion except as set forth in this license.

NO WARRANTY. THIS PACKAGE IS PROVIDED "AS IS" AND ANY EXPRESS OR IMPLIED WARRANTIES, INCLUDING, BUT NOT LIMITED TO, THE IMPLIED WARRANTIES OF MERCHANTABILITY AND FITNESS FOR A PARTICULAR PURPOSE ARE DISCLAIMED. IN NO EVENT SHALL RED HAT SOFTWARE, INC. BE LIABLE FOR ANY DIRECT, INDIRECT, INCIDENTAL, SPECIAL, EXEMPLARY, OR CONSEQUENTIAL DAMAGES (INCLUDING, BUT NOT LIMITED TO, PROCUREMENT OF SUBSTITUTE GOODS OR SERVICES; LOSS OF USE, DATA OR PROFITS; OR BUSINESS INTERRUPTION) HOWEVER CAUSED AND ON ANY THEORY OF LIABILITY, WHETHER IN CONTRACT, STRICT LIABILITY, OR TORT (INCLUDING NEGLIGENCE OR OTHERWISE) ARISING IN ANY WAY OUT OF THE USE OF THIS PACKAGE, EVEN IF ADVISED OF THE POSSIBILITY OF SUCH DAMAGE.

redhat-release – (Version 5.9.5.2, 0K)   Ⓑ

Red Hat Linux release file

D.4   Development

This section contains packages that are associated with the development of software under Red Hat Linux.

D.4.1   Debuggers

This section contains packages that are associated with debugging programs under Red Hat Linux.

gdb – (Version 4.17.0.11, 1,171K)   Ⓦ Ⓢ

Gdb is a full featured, command driven debugger. Gdb allows you to trace the execution of programs and examine their internal state at any time. Gdb works for C and C++ compiled with the GNU C compiler gcc.

If you are going to develop C and/or C++ programs and use the GNU gcc compiler, you may want to install gdb to help you debug your programs.

lslk – (Version 1.19, 35K)

Lslk is a lock file lister. Lslk attempts to list all of the locks on the executing system's local files (i.e., on the active inodes).

Install lslk if you need a utility for listing file locks.

lsof – (Version 4.40, 547K)

Lsof's name stands for LiSt Open Files, and it does just that. It lists information about files that are open by the processes running on a UNIX system.

ltrace – (Version 0.3.6, 75K)

Ltrace is a debugging program which runs a specified command until the command exits. While the command is executing, ltrace intercepts and records both the dynamic library calls called by the executed process and the signals received by the executed process. Ltrace can also intercept and print system calls executed by the process.

You should install ltrace if you need a sysadmin tool for tracking the execution of processes.

strace – (Version 3.1, 123K)   Ⓦ Ⓢ

The strace program intercepts and records the system calls called and received by a running process. Strace can print a record of each system call, its arguments and its return value. Strace is useful for diagnosing problems and debugging, as well as for instructional purposes.

Install strace if you need a tool to track the system calls made and received by a process.

xxgdb – (Version 1.12, 103K)   Ⓦ

Xxgdb is an X Window System graphical interface to the GNU gdb debugger. Xxgdb provides visual feedback and supports a mouse interface for the user who wants to perform debugging tasks like the following: controlling program execution through breakpoints, examining and traversing the function call stack, displaying values of variables and data structures, and browsing source files and functions.

Install the xxgdb package if you'd like to use a graphical interface with the GNU gdb debugger. You'll also need to have the gdb package installed.

D.4.2   Languages

This section contains packages that are associated with the programming languages available under Red Hat Linux.

cpp – (Version 1.1.2, 135K)   Ⓦ Ⓢ

The C preprocessor is a 'macro processor' which is used automatically by the C compiler to transform your program before actual compilation. It is called a macro processor because it allows you to define 'macros,' which are abbreviations for longer constructs.

The C preprocessor provides four separate facilities that you can use as you see fit:

* Inclusion of header files. These are files of declarations that can be substituted into your program. * Macro expansion. You can define 'macros,' which are abbreviations for arbitrary fragments of C code, and then the C preprocessor will replace the macros with their definitions throughout the program. * Conditional compilation. Using special preprocessing directives, you can include or exclude parts of the program according to various conditions. * Line control. If you use a program to combine or rearrange source files into an intermediate file which is then compiled, you can use line control to inform the compiler about where each source line originated.

You should install this package if you are a programmer who is searching for such a macro processor.

egcs – (Version 1.1.2, 3,525K) Ⓦ Ⓢ

EGCS is a free software project that intends to further the development of GNU compilers using an open development environment. The egcs package contains the egcs compiler, a compiler aimed at integrating all the optimizations and features necessary for a high-performance and stable development environment.

Install egcs if you'd like to use an experimental GNU compiler.

egcs-c++ – (Version 1.1.2, 5,912K) Ⓦ

This package adds C++ support to the GNU C compiler. It includes support for most of the current C++ specification, including templates and exception handling. It does include the static standard C++ library and C++ header files; the library for dynamically linking programs is available separately.

egcs-g77 – (Version 1.1.2, 4,631K)

The egcs-g77 package provides support for compiling Fortran 77 programs with the GNU gcc compiler.

You should install egcs-g77 if you are going to do Fortran development and you would like to use the gcc compiler. You will also need to install the gcc package.

egcs-objc – (Version 1.1.2, 1,969K)

Egcs-objc provides Objective C support for the GNU C compiler (gcc). Mainly used on systems running NeXTSTEP, Objective C is an object-oriented derivative of the C language.

Install egcs-objc if you are going to do Objective C development and you would like to use the gcc compiler. You will also need to install the gcc package.

expect – (Version 5.28, 748K) Ⓦ Ⓢ

Expect is a tcl extension for automating interactive applications such as telnet, ftp, passwd, fsck, rlogin, tip, etc. Expect is also useful for testing the named applications. Expect makes it easy for a script to control another program and interact with it.

Install the expect package if you'd like to develop scripts which interact with interactive applications. You'll also need to install the tcl package.

gnome-objc – (Version 1.0.1, 497K)

This package installs basic libraries you must have to use GNOME programs that are built with Objective C.

GNOME is the GNU Network Object Model Environment. It's a powerful, pleasing, easy to use and configure environment for your computer.

guavac – (Version 1.2, 2,157K)

The guavac package includes guavac and guavad. Guavac is a stand-alone compiler for the Java programming language. Guavac was written entirely in C++ and it should be portable to any platform supporting GNU's C++ (gcc) or a similar compiler. Guavad is guavac's disassembler.

Install guavac if you need a Java compiler on your system.

guile – (Version 1.3, 1,029K) Ⓦ

GUILE (GNU's Ubiquitous Intelligent Language for Extension) is a library implementation of the Scheme programming language, written in C. GUILE provides a machine-independent execution platform that can be linked in as a library during the building of extensible programs.

Install the guile package if you'd like to add extensibility to programs that you are developing. You'll also need to install the guile-devel package.

itcl – (Version 3.0.1, 4,251K)

[incr Tcl] is an object-oriented extension of the Tcl language. It was created to support more structured programming in Tcl. Tcl scripts that grow beyond a few thousand lines become extremely difficult to maintain. This is because the building blocks of vanilla Tcl are procedures and global variables, and all of these building blocks must reside in a single global namespace. There is no support for protection or encapsulation.

[incr Tcl] introduces the notion of objects. Each object is a bag of data with a set of procedures or "methods" that are used to manipulate it. Objects are organized into "classes" with identical characteristics, and classes can inherit functionality from one another. This object-oriented paradigm adds another level of organization on top of the basic variable/procedure elements, and the resulting code is easier to understand and maintain.

kaffe – (Version 1.0.b3, 1,671K)

Kaffe is a free virtual machine designed to execute Java(TM) bytecode. Kaffe can be configured in two modes. In the first mode, it operates as a pure bytecode interpreter (not unlike Javasoft's machine). In the second mode, it performs "just-in-time" code conversion from the abstract code to the host machine's native code. The second mode will ultimately allow execution of Java code at the same speed as standard compiled code, while also maintaining the advantages and flexibility of code independence.

Install the kaffe package if you need a Java virtual machine.

p2c-devel – (Version 1.22, 26K)

The p2c-devel package contains the files necessary for development of the p2c Pascal to C translation system.

Install the p2c-devel package if you want to do p2c development.

perl – (Version 5.00502, 15,224K) Ⓑ

Perl is a high-level programming language with roots in C, sed, awk and shell scripting. Perl is good at handling processes and files, and is especially good at handling text. Perl's hallmarks are practicality and efficiency. While it is used to do a lot of different things, Perl's most common applications (and what it excels at) are probably system administration utilities and web programming. A large proportion of the CGI scripts on the web are written in Perl. You need the perl package installed on your system so that your system can handle Perl scripts.

perl-MD5 – (Version 1.7, 30K) Ⓢ

The perl-MD5 package provides the MD5 module for the Perl programming language. MD5 is a Perl interface to the RSA Data Security Inc. Message Digest Algorithm, which allows Perl programs to use the algorithm.

The perl-MD5 package should be installed if any Perl programs on your system are going to use RSA's Message Digest Algorithm.

pygnome – (Version 1.0.1, 1,650K)

PyGNOME is an extension module for python that gives you access to the base GNOME libraries. This means you have access to more widgets, simple configuration interface, metadata support and many other features.

pygtk – (Version 0.5.12, 2,259K)

PyGTK is an extension module for python that gives you access to the GTK+ widget set. Just about anything you can write in C with GTK+ you can write in python with PyGTK (within reason), but with all of python's benefits.

python – (Version 1.5.1, 5,829K)   Ⓦ Ⓢ

Python is an interpreted, interactive, object-oriented programming language often compared to Tcl, Perl, Scheme or Java. Python includes modules, classes, exceptions, very high level dynamic data types and dynamic typing. Python supports interfaces to many system calls and libraries, as well as to various windowing systems (X11, Motif, Tk, Mac and MFC).

Programmers can write new built-in modules for Python in C or C++. Python can be used as an extension language for applications that need a programmable interface. This package contains most of the standard Python modules, as well as modules for interfacing to the Tix widget set for Tk and RPM.

Note that documentation for Python is provided in the python-docs package.

tcl – (Version 8.0.4, 5,516K)   Ⓦ Ⓢ

Tcl is a simple scripting language designed to be embedded into other applications. Tcl is designed to be used with Tk, a widget set, which is provided in the tk package. This package also includes tclsh, a simple example of a Tcl application.

If you're installing the tcl package and you want to use Tcl for development, you should also install the tk and tclx packages.

tclx – (Version 8.0.4, 1,964K)   Ⓦ Ⓢ

TclX is a set of extensions which make it easier to use the Tcl scripting language for common UNIX/Linux programming tasks. TclX enhances Tcl support for files, network access, debugging, math, lists, and message catalogs. TclX can be used with both Tcl and Tcl/Tk applications.

Install TclX if you are developing applications with Tcl/Tk. You'll also need to install the tcl and tk packages.

tix – (Version 4.1.0.6, 2,732K)   Ⓦ Ⓢ

Tix (Tk Interface Extension), an add-on for the Tk widget set, is an extensive set of over 40 widgets. In general, Tix widgets are more complex and more capable than the widgets provided in Tk. Tix widgets include a ComboBox, a Motif-style FileSelectBox, an MS Windows-style FileSelectBox, a PanedWindow, a NoteBook, a hierarchical list, a directory tree and a file manager.

Install the tix package if you want to try out more complicated widgets for Tk. You'll also need to have the tcl and tk packages installed.

tk – (Version 8.0.4, 5,289K)   Ⓦ Ⓢ

Tk is a X Windows widget set designed to work closely with the tcl scripting language. It allows you to write simple programs with full featured GUI's in only a little more time then it takes to write a text based interface. Tcl/Tk applications can also be run on Windows and Macintosh platforms.

tkinter – (Version 1.5.1, 643K)   Ⓦ Ⓢ

The Tkinter (Tk interface) program is an graphical user interface for the Python scripting language.

You should install the tkinter package if you'd like to use a graphical user interface for Python programming.

umb-scheme – (Version 3.2, 1,211K)   Ⓦ

UMB Scheme is a public domain implementation of the Scheme programming language. Scheme is a statically scoped and properly tail-recursive dialect of the Lisp programming language, designed with clear and simple semantics and a minimal number of ways to form expressions.

Install the umb-scheme package if you need an implementation of the Scheme programming language.

D.4.3   Libraries

This section contains packages that are associated with the libraries used during the development of software under Red Hat Linux.

ImageMagick-devel – (Version 4.2.2, 1,594K)

If you want to create applications that will use ImageMagick code or APIs, you'll need to install these packages as well as ImageMagick. These additional packages aren't necessary if you simply want to use ImageMagick, however.

ImageMagick-devel is an addition to ImageMagick which includes static libraries and header files necessary to develop applications.

ORBit-devel – (Version 0.4.2, 1,471K)

ORBit is a high-performance CORBA ORB (object request broker) with support for the C language. It allows programs to send requests and receive replies from other programs, regardless of the locations of the two programs.

This package contains the header files, libraries and utilities necessary to write programs that use CORBA technology.

XFree86-devel – (Version 3.3.3.1, 7,875K)   Ⓦ

XFree86-devel includes the libraries, header files and documentation you'll need to develop programs which run in X clients. XFree86 includes the base Xlib library as well as the Xt and Xaw widget sets.

For guidance on programming with these libraries, O'Reilly & Associates produces a series on X programming which you might find useful.

Install XFree86-devel if you are going to develop programs which will run as X clients.

Xaw3d-devel – (Version 1.3, 657K)   Ⓦ

Xaw3d is an enhanced version of the MIT Athena widget set for the X Window System. Xaw3d adds a three-dimensional look to those applications with minimal or no source code changes. Xaw3d-devel includes the header files and static libraries for developing programs that take full advantage of Xaw3d's features.

You should install Xaw3d-devel if you are going to develop applications using the Xaw3d widget set. You'll also need to install the Xaw3d package.

apache-devel – (Version 1.3.6, 269K)

The apache-devel package contains the source code for the Apache 1.3.1 Web server and the APXS binary you'll need to build Dynamic Shared Objects (DSOs) for Apache.

If you are installing the Apache Web server version 1.3.1, and you want to be able to compile or develop additional modules for Apache, you'll need to install this package.

audiofile-devel – (Version 0.1.6, 100K)

Libraries, include files and other resources you can use to develop audiofile applications.

bind-devel – (Version 8.2, 1,294K)

The bind-devel package contains all the include files and the library required for DNS (Domain Name Service) development for bind versions 8.x.x.

You should install bind-devel if you want to develop bind DNS applications. If you install bind-devel, you'll need to install bind, as well.

control-center-devel – (Version 1.0.5, 38K)

If you're interested in developing panels for the GNOME control center, you'll want to install this package.

Control-center-devel helps you create the 'capplets' which are used in the control center.

e2fsprogs-devel – (Version 1.14, 260K)

E2fsprogs-devel contains the libraries and header files needed to develop second extended (ext2) filesystem-specific programs.

You should install e2fsprogs-devel if you want to develop ext2 filesystem-specific programs. If you install e2fsprogs-devel, you'll also want to install e2fsprogs.

esound-devel – (Version 0.2.9, 45K)

Libraries, include files and other resources you can use to develoop EsounD applications.

faces-devel – (Version 1.6.1, 22K) $\boxed{W}$

Faces-devel contains the faces program development environment, (i.e., the static libraries and header files).

If you want to develop Faces applications, you'll need to install faces-devel. You'll also need to install the faces package.

fnlib-devel – (Version 0.4, 34K)

Headers, static libraries and documentation for Fnlib.

freetype-devel – (Version 1.2, 511K)

This package is only needed if you intend to develop or compile applications which rely on the FreeType library.

If you simply want to run existing applications, you won't need this package.

gd-devel – (Version 1.3, 7K) Ⓦ

These are the development libraries and header files for gd, the .gif graphics library.

If you're installing the gd graphics library, you must install gd-devel.

gdbm-devel – (Version 1.7.3, 72K) Ⓦ

Gdbm-devel contains the development libraries and header files for gdbm, the GNU database system. These libraries and header files are necessary if you plan to do development using the gdbm database.

Install gdbm-devel if you are developing C programs which will use the gdbm database library. You'll also need to install the gdbm package.

gedit-devel – (Version 0.5.1, 8K)

gEdit is a small but powerful text editor for GTK+ and/or GNOME. This package allows you to develop plugins that work within gEdit. Plugins can create new documents and manipulate documents in arbitrary ways.

gimp-devel – (Version 1.0.4, 258K)

Static libraries and header files for writing GIMP plugins and extensions.

glib-devel – (Version 1.2.1, 309K) Ⓦ

Static libraries and header files for the support library for the GIMP's X libraries, which are available as public libraries. GLIB includes generally useful data structures.

glibc-devel – (Version 2.1.1, 32,857K) Ⓦ Ⓢ

To develop programs which use the standard C libraries (which nearly all programs do), the system needs to have these standard header files and object files available for creating the executables.

glibc-profile – (Version 2.1.1, 30,448K)

When programs are being profiled using gprof, they must use these libraries instead of the standard C libraries for gprof to be able to profile them correctly.

gmp-devel – (Version 2.0.2, 319K)

The static libraries, header files and documentation for using the GNU MP arbitrary precision library in applications.

If you want to develop applications which will use the GNU MP library, you'll need to install the gmp-devel package. You'll also need to install the gmp package.

gnome-core-devel – (Version 1.0.4, 122K)

Panel libraries and header files for creating GNOME panels.

gnome-games-devel – (Version 1.0.2, 42K)

This packages installs the libraries and files needed to develop some GNOME games.

gnome-libs-devel – (Version 1.0.5, 7,329K)

GNOME (GNU Network Object Model Environment) is a user-friendly set of applications and desktop tools to be used in conjunction with a window manager for the X Window System. GNOME is similar in purpose and scope to CDE and KDE, but GNOME is based completely on Open Source software. The gnome-libs-devel package includes the libraries and include files that you will need to develop GNOME applications.

You should install the gnome-libs-devel package if you would like to develop GNOME applications. You don't need to install gnome-libs-devel if you just want to use the GNOME desktop environment. If you are going to develop GNOME applications and/or you're going to use the GNOME desktop environment, you'll also need to install the gnome-core and gnome-libs packages. If you want to use Linuxconf with a GNOME front end, you'll also need to install the gnome-linuxconf package.

gnome-objc-devel – (Version 1.0.1, 694K)

Libraries, include files and other files you can use to develop Objective C GNOME applications.

If you're interested in developing GNOME applications, you should install this package.

gnome-pim-devel – (Version 1.0.3, 38K)

Files needed to develop apps which interact with gnome-pim applications via CORBA.

gpm-devel – (Version 1.17.5, 27K) Ⓦ

The gpm-devel program contains the libraries and header files needed for development of mouse driven programs. This package allows you to develop text-mode programs which use the mouse.

Install gpm-devel if you need to develop text-mode programs which will use the mouse. You'll also need to install the gpm package.

gtk+-devel – (Version 1.2.1, 2,461K) Ⓦ

The gtk+-devel package contains the static libraries and header files needed for developing GTK+ (GIMP ToolKit) applications. The gtk+-devel package contains glib (a collection of routines for simplifying the development of GTK+ applications), GDK (the General Drawing Kit, which simplifies the interface for writing GTK+ widgets and using GTK+ widgets in applications), and GTK+ (the widget set).

Install gtk+-devel if you need to develop GTK+ applications. You'll also need to install the gtk+ package.

guile-devel – (Version 1.3, 963K)

The guile-devel package includes the libraries, header files, etc., that you'll need to develop applications that are linked with the GUILE extensibility library.

You need to install the guile-devel package if you want to develop applications that will be linked to GUILE. You'll also need to install the guile package.

imlib-devel – (Version 1.9.4, 547K)

The header files, static libraries and documentation needed for developing Imlib applications. Imlib is an image loading and rendering library for X11R6.

Install the imlib-devel package if you want to develop Imlib applications. You'll also need to install the imlib and imlib_cfgeditor packages.

inn-devel – (Version 2.2, 1,737K)

The inn-devel package contains the INN (InterNetNews) library, which several programs that interface with INN need in order to work (for example, newsgate and tin).

If you are installing a program which must interface with the INN news system, you should install inn-devel.

libghttp-devel – (Version 1.0.2, 42K)

Libraries and includes files you can use for libghttp development

libgr-devel – (Version 2.0.13, 320K)   Ⓦ

The libgr-devel package contains the header files and static libraries, etc., for developing programs which can handle the various graphics file formats supported by the libgr library.

Install libgr-devel if you want to develop programs for handling the graphics file formats supported by the libgr library. You'll also need to have the libgr package installed.

libgtop-devel – (Version 1.0.1, 326K)

GNOME (GNU Network Object Model Environment) is a user-friendly set of applications and desktop tools to be used in conjunction with a window manager for the X Window System. GNOME is similar in purpose and scope to CDE and KDE, but GNOME is based completely on Open Source software. The gnome-libs-devel package includes the libraries and include files that you will need to develop GNOME applications.

You should install the gnome-libs-devel package if you would like to develop GNOME applications. You don't need to install gnome-libs-devel if you just want to use the GNOME desktop environment. If you are going to develop GNOME applications and/or you're going to use the GNOME desktop environment, you'll also need to install the gnome-core and gnome-libs packages. If you want to use Linuxconf with a GNOME front end, you'll also need to install the gnome-linuxconf package.

libjpeg-devel – (Version 6b, 233K)   Ⓦ

The libjpeg-devel package includes the header files and static libraries necessary for developing programs which will manipulate JPEG files using the libjpeg library.

If you are going to develop programs which will manipulate JPEG images, you should install libjpeg-devel. You'll also need to have the libjpeg package installed.

libpcap – (Version 0.4, 121K)

Libpcap provides a portable framework for low-level network monitoring. Libpcap can provide network statistics collection, security monitoring and network debugging. Since almost every system vendor provides a different interface for packet capture, the libpcap authors created this system-independent API to ease in porting and to alleviate the need for several system-dependent packet capture modules in each application.

Install libpcap if you need to do low-level network traffic monitoring on your network.

libpng-devel – (Version 1.0.3, 485K)   Ⓦ

The libpng-devel package contains the header files and static libraries necessary for developing programs using the PNG (Portable Network Graphics) library.

If you want to develop programs which will manipulate PNG image format files, you should install libpng-devel. You'll also need to install the libpng package.

libtermcap-devel – (Version 2.0.8, 12K) [W]

This package includes the libraries and header files necessary for developing programs which will access the termcap database.

If you need to develop programs which will access the termcap database, you'll need to install this package. You'll also need to install the libtermcap package.

libtiff-devel – (Version 3.4, 1,614K) [W]

This package contains the header files and static libraries for developing programs which will manipulate TIFF format image files using the libtiff library.

If you need to develop programs which will manipulate TIFF format image files, you should install this package. You'll also need to install the libtiff package.

libungif-devel – (Version 4.1.0, 271K)

This package contains the static libraries, header files and documentation necessary for development of programs that will use the libungif library to load and save GIF format image files.

You should install this package if you need to develop programs which will use the libungif library functions for loading and saving GIF format image files. You'll also need to install the libungif package.

libxml-devel – (Version 1.0.0, 127K)

This packages contains the libraries, include and other files you can use to develop libxml applications.

linuxconf-devel – (Version 1.14r2, 3,742K) [W]

Linuxconf is an extremely capable system configuration tool. It provides a variety of interfaces through which you can configure your Linux system and manage a large proportion of the system's operations.

This package provides the components necessary for developing Linuxconf modules outside of the Linuxconf source tree and/or developing stand-alone utilities using the Linuxconf interface toolkit.

Install linuxconf-devel if you want to develop Linuxconf modules. You must also have Linuxconf installed.

ncurses-devel – (Version 4.2, 7,149K) [W]

The header files and libraries for developing applications that use the ncurses CRT screen handling and optimization package.

Install the ncurses-devel package if you want to develop applications which will use ncurses.

newt-devel – (Version 0.40, 120K) [W]

The newt-devel package contains the header files and libraries necessary for developing applications which use newt. Newt is a development library for text mode user interfaces. Newt is based on the slang library.

Install newt-devel if you want to develop applications which will use newt.

pilot-link-devel – (Version 0.9.0, 1,635K)

This package contains the development headers that are used to build the pilot-link package. It also includes the static libraries necessary to build static pilot apps.

popt – (Version 1.2.3, 54K)

Popt is a C library for parsing command line parameters. Popt was heavily influenced by the getopt() and getopt_long() functions, but it improves on them by allowing more powerful argument expansion. Popt can parse arbitrary argv[] style arrays and automatically set variables based on command line arguments. Popt allows command line arguments to be aliased via configuration files and includes utility functions for parsing arbitrary strings into argv[] arrays using shell-like rules.

Install popt if you're a C programmer and you'd like to use its capabilities.

postgresql-devel – (Version 6.4.2, 662K)   Ⓢ

This package contains the header files and libraries needed to compile applications which will directly interact with a PostgreSQL server.

Install this package if you want to develop applications which will interact with a PostgreSQL server.

python-devel – (Version 1.5.1, 3,499K)

The Python programming language's interpreter can be extended with dynamically loaded extensions and can be embedded in other programs. This package contains the header files and libraries needed to do these types of tasks.

Install python-devel if you want to develop Python extensions. The python package will also need to be installed. You'll probably also want to install the python-docs package, which contains Python documentation.

qt-devel – (Version 1.44, 9,809K)

Contains the files necessary to develop applications using Qt: header files, the Qt meta object compiler, man pages, HTML documentation and example programs. See http://www.troll.no for more information about Qt, or file:/usr/lib/qt/html/index.html for Qt documentation in HTML.

readline-devel – (Version 2.2.1, 261K)   Ⓦ

The readline library will read a line from the terminal and return it. Use of the readline library allows programmers to provide an easy to use and more intuitive interface for users.

If you want to develop programs which will use the readline library, you'll need to have the readline-devel package installed. You'll also need to have the readline package installed.

rpm-devel – (Version 2.93, 338K)   Ⓦ

This package contains the RPM C library and header files. These development files will simplify the process of writing programs which manipulate RPM packages and databases and are intended to make it easier to create graphical package managers or any other tools that need an intimate knowledge of RPM packages in order to function.

This package should be installed if you want to develop programs that will manipulate RPM packages and databases.

slang-devel – (Version 1.2.2, 1,192K)   ⟨W⟩

This package contains the S-Lang extension language static libraries and header files which you'll need if you want to develop S-Lang based applications. Documentation which may help you write S-Lang based applications is also included.

Install the slang-devel package if you want to develop applications based on the S-Lang extension language.

sox-devel – (Version 12.15, 855K)

This package contains the library needed for compiling applications which will use the SoX sound file format converter.

Install sox-devel if you want to develop applications which will use SoX.

svgalib-devel – (Version 1.3.1, 505K)   ⟨W⟩

The svgalib-devel package contains the libraries and header files needed to build programs which will use the SVGAlib low-level graphics library.

Install the svgalib-devel package if you want to develop applications which will use the SVGAlib library.

ucd-snmp-devel – (Version 3.6.1, 275K)

The ucd-snmp-devel package contains the development libraries and header files for use with the UCD-SNMP project's network management tools.

Install the ucd-snmp-devel package if you would like to develop applications for use with the UCD-SNMP project's network management tools. You'll also need to have the ucd-snmp and ucd-snmp-utils packages installed.

w3c-libwww-devel – (Version 5.2.6, 1,512K)

Static libraries and header files for programs that use w3c-libwww.

x11amp-devel – (Version 0.9_alpha3, 13K)

Static libraries and header files for building x11amp plugins.

xpm-devel – (Version 3.4j, 221K)   ⟨W⟩

The xpm-devel package contains the development libraries and header files necessary for developing applications which will use the XPM library. The XPM library is used by many programs for displaying pixmaps in the X Window System.

Install the xpm-devel package if you want to develop applications using the XPM pixmap library. You'll also need to install the xpm package.

zlib-devel – (Version 1.1.3, 165K)   ⟨W⟩

The zlib-devel package contains the header files and libraries needed to develop programs that use the zlib compression and decompression library.

Install the zlib-devel package if you want to develop applications that will use the zlib library.

D.4.4 System

This section contains packages that are associated with building system-level software under Red Hat Linux.

kernel-headers – (Version 2.2.5, 2,692K) Ⓦ Ⓢ

Kernel-headers includes the C header files for the Linux kernel. The header files define structures and constants that are needed for building most standard programs. The header files are also needed for rebuilding the kernel.

kernel-source – (Version 2.2.5, 46,139K)

The kernel-source package contains the source code files for the Linux kernel. These source files are needed to build most C programs, since they depend on the constants defined in the source code. The source files can also be used to build a custom kernel that is better tuned to your particular hardware, if you are so inclined (and you know what you're doing).

D.4.5 Tools

This section contains packages that are associated with the various tools needed to develop software under Red Hat Linux.

ElectricFence – (Version 2.0.5, 44K) Ⓦ Ⓢ

If you know what malloc() violations are, you'll be interested in ElectricFence. ElectricFence is a tool which can be used for C programming and debugging. It uses the virtual memory hardware of your system to detect when software overruns malloc() buffer boundaries, and/or to detect any accesses of memory released by free(). ElectricFence will then stop the program on the first instruction that caused a bounds violation and you can use your favorite debugger to display the offending statement.

This package will install ElectricFence, which you can use if you're searching for a debugger to find malloc() violations.

autoconf – (Version 2.13, 580K) Ⓦ Ⓢ

GNU's Autoconf is a tool for configuring source code and Makefiles. Using Autoconf, programmers can create portable and configurable packages, since the person building the package is allowed to specify various configuration options.

You should install Autoconf if you are developing software and you'd like to use it to create shell scripts which will configure your source code packages. If you are installing Autoconf, you will also need to install the GNU m4 package.

Note that the Autoconf package is not required for the end user who may be configuring software with an Autoconf-generated script; Autoconf is only required for the generation of the scripts, not their use.

automake – (Version 1.4, 867K)   Ⓦ Ⓢ

Automake is an experimental Makefile generator. Automake was inspired by the 4.4BSD make and include files, but aims to be portable and to conform to the GNU standards for Makefile variables and targets.

You should install Automake if you are developing software and would like to use its capabilities of automatically generating GNU standard Makefiles. if you install Automake, you will also need to install GNU's Autoconf package.

bin86 – (Version 0.4, 73K)   Ⓦ Ⓢ

The bin86 package provides an assembler and linker for real mode 80x86 instructions. You'll need to have this package installed in order to build programs that run in real mode, including LILO and the kernel's bootstrapping code, from their sources.

You should install bin86 if you intend to build programs that run in real mode from their source code.

binutils – (Version 2.9.1.0.22b, 5,165K)   Ⓑ Ⓦ Ⓢ

Binutils is a collection of binary utilities, including ar (for creating, modifying and extracting from archives), nm (for listing symbols from object files), objcopy (for copying and translating object files), objdump (for displaying information from object files), ranlib (for generating an index for the contents of an archive), size (for listing the section sizes of an object or archive file), strings (for listing printable strings from files), strip (for discarding symbols), c++filt (a filter for demangling encoded C++ symbols), addr2line (for converting addresses to file and line), and nbnconv (for converting object code into an NLM).

Install binutils if you need to perform any of these types of actions on binary files. Most programmers will want to install binutils.

bison – (Version 1.27, 153K)   Ⓦ Ⓢ

Bison is a general purpose parser generator which converts a grammar description for an LALR context-free grammar into a C program to parse that grammar. Bison can be used to develop a wide range of language parsers, from ones used in simple desk calculators to complex programming languages. Bison is upwardly compatible with Yacc, so any correctly written Yacc grammar should work with Bison without any changes. If you know Yacc, you shouldn't have any trouble using Bison (but you do need to be very proficient in C programming to be able to use Bison). Many programs use Bison as part of their build process. Bison is only needed on systems that are used for development.

If your system will be used for C development, you should install Bison since it is used to build many C programs.

blt – (Version 2.4g, 4,007K)

BLT is an extension to the Tk toolkit. BLT's most useful feature is the provision of more widgets for Tk, but it also provides more geometry managers and miscellaneous other commands. Note that you won't need to do any patching of the Tcl or Tk source files to use BLT, but you will need to have Tcl/Tk installed in order to use BLT.

If you are programming with the Tk toolkit, you should install BLT. You will need to have Tcl/Tk installed.

byacc – (Version 1.9, 54K)   Ⓦ Ⓢ

Byacc (Berkeley Yacc) is a public domain LALR parser generator which is used by many programs during their build process.

If you are going to do development on your system, you will want to install this package.

cdecl – (Version 2.5, 80K) $\boxed{W}\boxed{S}$

The cdecl package includes the cdecl and c++decl utilities, which are used to translate English to C or C++ function declarations and vice versa.

You should install the cdecl package if you intend to do C and/or C++ programming.

cproto – (Version 4.6, 85K) $\boxed{W}\boxed{S}$

Cproto generates function prototypes and variable declarations from C source code. Cproto can also convert function definitions between the old style and the ANSI C style. This conversion will overwrite the original files, however, so be sure to make a backup copy of your original files in case something goes wrong. Since cproto uses a Yacc generated parser, it shouldn't be confused by complex function definitions (as much as other prototype generators) because it uses a Yacc generated parser.

Cproto will be useful for C programmers, so install cproto if you are going to do any C programming.

ctags – (Version 3.2, 146K) $\boxed{W}\boxed{S}$

Ctags generates an index (or tag) file of C language objects found in C source and header files. The index makes it easy for text editors or other utilities to locate the indexed items. Ctags can also generate a cross reference file which lists information about the various objects found in a set of C language files in human readable form. Exuberant Ctags improves on ctags because it can find all types of C language tags, including macro definitions, enumerated values (values inside enum...), function and method definitions, enum/struct/union tags, external function prototypes, typedef names and variable declarations. Exuberant Ctags is far less likely to be fooled by code containing #if preprocessor conditional constructs than ctags. Exuberant ctags supports output of emacs style TAGS files and can be used to print out a list of selected objects found in source files.

Install ctags if you are going to use your system for C programming.

cvs – (Version 1.10.5, 3,088K) $\boxed{W}\boxed{S}$

CVS means Concurrent Version System; it is a version control system which can record the history of your files (usually, but not always, source code). CVS only stores the differences between versions, instead of every version of every file you've ever created. CVS also keeps a log of who, when and why changes occurred, among other aspects.

CVS is very helpful for managing releases and controlling the concurrent editing of source files among multiple authors. Instead of providing version control for a collection of files in a single directory, CVS provides version control for a hierarchical collection of directories consisting of revision controlled files.

These directories and files can then be combined together to form a software release.

Install the cvs package if you need to use a version control system.

diffstat – (Version 1.25, 11K)

The diff command compares files line by line. Diffstat reads the output of the diff command and displays a histogram of the insertions, deletions and modifications in each file. Diffstat is commonly used to provide a summary of the changes in large, complex patch files.

Install diffstat if you need a program which provides a summary of the diff command's output. You'll need to also install diffutils.

flex – (Version 2.5.4a, 302K) Ⓦ Ⓢ

The flex program generates scanners. Scanners are programs which can recognize lexical patterns in text. Flex takes pairs of regular expressions and C code as input and generates a C source file as output. The output file is compiled and linked with a library to produce an executable. The executable searches through its input for occurrences of the regular expressions. When a match is found, it executes the corresponding C code. Flex was designed to work with both Yacc and Bison, and is used by many programs as part of their build process.

You should install flex if you are going to use your system for application development.

gettext – (Version 0.10.35, 889K) Ⓦ Ⓢ

The GNU gettext package provides a set of tools and documentation for producing multi-lingual messages in programs. Tools include a set of conventions about how programs should be written to support message catalogs, a directory and file naming organization for the message catalogs, a runtime library which supports the retrieval of translated messages, and stand-alone programs for handling the translatable and the already translated strings. Gettext provides an easy to use library and tools for creating, using, and modifying natural language catalogs and is a powerful and simple method for internationalizing programs.

If you would like to internationalize or incorporate multi-lingual messages into programs that you're developing, you should install gettext.

gperf – (Version 2.7, 122K)

Gperf is a perfect hash function generator written in C++. Simply stated, a perfect hash function is a hash function and a data structure that allows recognition of a key word in a set of words using exactly one probe into the data structure.

Install gperf if you need a program that generates perfect hash functions.

libtool – (Version 1.2f, 973K)

The libtool package contains the GNU libtool, a set of shell scripts which automatically configure UNIX and UNIX-like architectures to generically build shared libraries. Libtool provides a consistent, portable interface which simplifies the process of using shared libraries.

If you are developing programs which will use shared libraries, you should install libtool.

make – (Version 3.77, 265K) Ⓦ Ⓢ

A GNU tool for controlling the generation of executables and other non-source files of a program from the program's source files. Make allows users to build and install packages without any significant knowledge about the details of the build process. The details about how the program should be built are provided for make in the program's makefile.

The GNU make tool should be installed on your system because it is commonly used to simplify the process of installing programs.

patch – (Version 2.5, 99K) Ⓦ Ⓢ

The patch program applies diff files to originals. The diff command is used to compare an original to a changed file. Diff lists the changes made to the file. A person who has the original file can then use the patch command with the diff file to add the changes to their original file (patching the file).

Patch should be installed because it is a common way of upgrading applications.

pmake – (Version 2.1.33, 1,031K) $\boxed{W}\boxed{S}$

Make is a GNU tool which allows users to build and install programs without any significant knowledge of the build process. Details about how the program should be built are included in the program's Makefile. Pmake is a particular version (BSD 4.4) of make. Pmake supports some additional syntax which is not in the standard make program. Some Berkeley programs have Makefiles written for pmake.

Pmake should be installed on your system so that you will be able to build programs which require using pmake instead of make.

pmake-customs – (Version 2.1.33, 982K)

Customs is a remote execution facility for PMake. Customs is designed to run on a network of machines with a consistent, shared filesystem. Customs requires Sun RPC in order to use XDR (eXternal Data Representation) routines for logging functions.

A single server is designated as the master agent and is additionally responsible for noting when a machine goes down, from which machines any given machine will accept jobs and parcelling out available machines to requesting clients. The job of master is not given to any one machine but, rather, is decided among the active agents whenever the previous master dies.

Clients are provided to: - alter the availability criteria for the local machine (importquota) - find the status of all registered hosts on the net (reginfo). - abort, restart or ping any customs agent on the network (cctrl). - export a command from the shell (export). - accept log information from all hosts on the net (logd).

rcs – (Version 5.7, 536K) $\boxed{W}\boxed{S}$

The Revision Control System (RCS) is a system for managing multiple versions of files. RCS automates the storage, retrieval, logging, identification and merging of file revisions. RCS is useful for text files that are revised frequently (for example, programs, documentation, graphics, papers and form letters).

The rcs package should be installed if you need a system for managing different versions of files.

D.5   Documentation

This section contains packages that are associated with documentation for Linux in general and Red Hat Linux in particular.

bash2-doc – (Version 2.03, 2,275K)

This is a separate documentation package for the GNU Bourne Again shell.

faq – (Version 5.2, 891K)

The faq package includes the text of the Frequently Asked Questions (FAQ) about Linux from the SunSITE web-site (http://sunsite.unc.edu/pub/Linux/docs/faqs/linux-faq/Linux-FAQ). The Linux FAQ is a great source of information about Linux.

Install faq if you'd like to read the Linux FAQ off your own machine.

gimp-manual – (Version 1.0.0, 17,979K)

The gimp-manual package contains the GIMP (GNU Image Manipulation Program) User Manual (GUM) in HTML format. Please note that the HTML version of the GUM is not as good a quality as the other versions, which can be obtained from the GUM website at http://manual.gimp.org/pub/manual. On the GUM website, the manual is provided in HTML (for viewing the GUM online), in PostScript(TM) and PDF formats (for printing) as well as in FM (FrameMaker) source code. The FrameMaker source code is provided for people who would like to contribute to the Graphic Documentation Project. Submissions to the GUM are covered by the manual's license agreement and terms, included in the file COPYING.

The GUM is a complete guide for using the GIMP. This version of the GUM includes improvements over previous versions. Be sure to check out the new Gallery chapter, which provides a good overview of what the GIMP can do. The Gallery displays cool images and give you hints on how to create them with the GIMP.

For more information about the GUM, check the GUM website at http://manual.gimp.org/.

gnome-users-guide – (Version 1.0.5, 3,564K)   ⓦ

This package will install the users' guide for the GNOME Desktop Environment on your computer.

You should install this package if you are going to use GNOME and you want a quick, handy reference.

helptool – (Version 2.4, 23K)   ⓦⓢ

The helptool provides a unified graphical user interface for searching through many of the help sources available (including man pages and GNU texinfo documents).

Install helptool if you'd like to use it to search for help files. You'll need to have the X Window System installed to use the helptool.

howto – (Version 6.0, 11,103K)

Linux HOWTOs are detailed documents which describe a specific aspect of configuring or using Linux. Linux HOWTOs are a great source of practical information about your system. The latest versions of these documents are located at http://sunsite.unc.edu/linux.

Install the howto package if you'd like to be able to access the Linux HOWTO documentation from your own system.

howto-chinese – (Version 6.0, 13,445K)

The howto-chinese package contains the Linux HOWTO documents that have been translated into Chinese. Linux HOWTOs are detailed documents describing a specific aspect of configuring or using Linux.

Install the howto-chinese package if you'd like to use the Linux HOWTO documentation in Chinese. Please note that not all of the HOWTOs have been translated. If you need to have a complete set of HOWTOs, you'll need to install the English version (the howto package).

howto-croatian – (Version 6.0, 1,897K)

The howto-chinese package contains the Linux HOWTO documents that have been translated into Croatian. Linux HOWTOs are detailed documents which describe a specific aspect of configuring or using Linux.

Install the howto-croatian package if you'd like to use the Linux HOWTO documentation in Croatian. Please note that not all of the HOWTOs have been translated. If you need to have a complete set of HOWTOs, you'll need to install the English version (the howto package).

howto-french – (Version 6.0, 29,195K)

This package contains the Linux HOWTO documents that have been translated into French. Linux HOWTOs are detailed documents which describe a specific aspect of configuring or using Linux.

Install the howto-french package if you'd like to use the Linux HOWTOs in French. Please note that not all of the HOWTOs have been translated. If you need to have a complete set of HOWTOs, you'll need to install the English version (the howto package).

howto-german – (Version 6.0, 22,361K)

This package contains the Linux HOWTO documents that have been translated into German. Linux HOWTOs are detailed documents which describe a specific aspect of configuring or using Linux.

Install the howto-german package if you'd like to use the Linux HOWTOs in German. Please note that not all of the HOWTOs have been translated. If you need to have a complete set of HOWTOs, you'll need to install the English version (the howto package).

howto-greek – (Version 6.0, 7,712K)

This package contains the Linux HOWTO documents that have been translated into Greek. Linux HOWTOs are detailed documents which describe a specific aspect of configuring or using Linux.

Install the howto-greek package if you'd like to use the Linux HOWTOs in Greek. Please note that not all of the HOWTOs have been translated. If you need to have a complete set of HOWTOs, you'll need to install the English version (the howto package).

howto-html – (Version 6.0, 12,824K)

This package contains the Linux HOWTO documents in HTML format, so they can be viewed with a Web browser. Linux HOWTOs are detailed documents which describe a specific aspect of configuring or using Linux.

Install the howto-html package if you'd like to view the Linux HOWTOs with your Web browser off your own machine, or if you'd like to provide the HTML HOWTOs from your Web server.

howto-indonesian – (Version 6.0, 8,491K)

This package contains the Linux HOWTO documents that have been translated into Indonesian. Linux HOWTOs are detailed documents which describe a specific aspect of configuring or using Linux.

Install the howto-indonesian package if you'd like to use the Linux HOWTOs in Indonesian. Please note that not all of the HOWTOs have been translated. If you need to have a complete set of HOWTOs, you'll need to install the English version (the howto package).

howto-italian – (Version 6.0, 21,596K)

This package contains the Linux HOWTO documents that have been translated into Italian. Linux HOWTOs are detailed documents which describe a specific aspect of configuring or using Linux.

Install the howto-italian package if you'd like to use the Linux HOWTOs in Italian. Please note that not all of the

HOWTOs have been translated. If you need to have a complete set of HOWTOs, you'll need to install the English version (the howto package).

howto-japanese – (Version 6.0, 11,888K)

This package contains the Linux HOWTO documents that have been translated into Japanese. Linux HOWTOs are detailed documents which describe a specific aspect of configuring or using Linux.

Install the howto-japanese package if you'd like to use the Linux HOWTOs in Japanese. Please note that not all of the HOWTOs have been translated. If you need to have a complete set of HOWTOs, you'll need to install the English version (the howto package).

howto-korean – (Version 6.0, 19,242K)

This package contains the Linux HOWTO documents that have been translated into Korean. Linux HOWTOs are detailed documents which describe a specific aspect of configuring or using Linux.

Install the howto-korean package if you'd like to use the Linux HOWTOs in Korean. Please note that not all of the HOWTOs have been translated. If you need to have a complete set of HOWTOs, you'll need to install the English version (the howto package).

howto-polish – (Version 6.0, 9,474K)

This package contains the Linux HOWTO documents that have been translated into Polish. Linux HOWTOs are detailed documents which describe a specific aspect of configuring or using Linux.

Install the howto-polish package if you'd like to use the Linux HOWTOs in Polish. Please note that not all of the HOWTOs have been translated. If you need to have a complete set of HOWTOs, you'll need to install the English version (the howto package).

howto-serbian – (Version 6.0, 37K)

This package contains the Linux HOWTO documents that have been translated into Serbian. Linux HOWTOs are detailed documents which describe a specific aspect of configuring or using Linux.

Install the howto-serbian package if you'd like to use the Linux HOWTOs in Serbian. Please note that not all of the HOWTOs have been translated. If you need to have a complete set of HOWTOs, you'll need to install the English version (the howto package).

howto-sgml – (Version 6.0, 9,767K)

The howto-sgml package contains the Linux HOWTO documents in SGML format. The SGML format documents are the "source" files. Other file formats (text, PostScript(TM), DVI, HTML) are translated from the SGML documents. Linux HOWTOs are detailed documents which describe a specific aspect of configuring or using Linux.

Install the howto-sgml package if you'd like to use the Linux HOWTO documents in SGML format.

howto-slovenian – (Version 6.0, 3,791K)

This package contains the Linux HOWTO documents that have been translated into Slovenian. Linux HOWTOs are detailed documents which describe a specific aspect of configuring or using Linux.

Install the howto-slovenian package if you'd like to use the Linux HOWTOs in Slovenian. Please note that not all of the HOWTOs have been translated. If you need to have a complete set of HOWTOs, you'll need to install the

English version (the howto package).

howto-spanish – (Version 6.0, 7,739K)

This package contains the Linux HOWTO documents that have been translated into Spanish. Linux HOWTOs are detailed documents which describe a specific aspect of configuring or using Linux.

Install the howto-spanish package if you'd like to use the Linux HOWTOs in Spanish. Please note that not all of the HOWTOs have been translated. If you need to have a complete set of HOWTOs, you'll need to install the English version (the howto package).

howto-swedish – (Version 6.0, 4,009K)

This package contains the Linux HOWTO documents that have been translated into Swedish. Linux HOWTOs are detailed documents which describe a specific aspect of configuring or using Linux.

Install the howto-swedish package if you'd like to use the Linux HOWTOs in Swedish. Please note that not all of the HOWTOs have been translated. If you need to have a complete set of HOWTOs, you'll need to install the English version (the howto package).

howto-turkish – (Version 6.0, 816K)

This package contains the Linux HOWTO documents that have been translated into Turkish. Linux HOWTOs are detailed documents which describe a specific aspect of configuring or using Linux.

Install the howto-turkish package if you'd like to use the Linux HOWTOs in Turkish. Please note that not all of the HOWTOs have been translated. If you need to have a complete set of HOWTOs, you'll need to install the English version (the howto package).

indexhtml – (Version 5.8, 6K) Ⓦ Ⓢ

The indexhtml package contains the HTML page and graphics for a welcome page shown by your Web browser, which you'll see after you've successfully installed Red Hat Linux.

The Web page provided by indexhtml tells you how to register your Red Hat software and how to get any support that you might need.

install-guide – (Version 3.2, 1,373K)

The install-guide contains the Linux Documentation Project (LDP) Getting Started Guide in HTML format. The LDP Getting Started Guide is intended to be an installation manual and an entry-level guide to Linux. If you're installing the Red Hat Linux operating system, you should ignore the installation instructions included here and instead use Red Hat's Installation Guide.

You should install the install-guide package if you'd like to use the LDP's Getting Started Guide in HTML format using your Web browser off your own machine, or if you'd like to provide the LDP's Getting Started Guide on your Web server.

kernel-doc – (Version 2.2.5, 2,306K)

This package contains documentation files form the kernel source. Various bits of information about the Linux kernel and the device drivers shipped with it are documented in these files. You also might want install this package if you need a reference to the options that can be passed to Linux kernel modules at load time.

lpg – (Version 0.4, 1,739K)

The lpg package includes a generic guide for programming on Linux systems, in HTML format. You may want to check the Linux Documentation Project's website at http://sunsite.unc.edu/LDP/ for more information and possible updates to the programming guide.

If you'd like to view the Linux programming guide using your Web browser from files on your own machine, or if you'd like to provide it from your Web server, you should install the lpg package.

man-pages – (Version 1.23, 1,795K)   Ⓦ Ⓢ

A large collection of man pages (reference material) from the Linux Documentation Project (LDP). The man pages are organized into the following sections:

Section 1: User commands (intro only) Section 2: System calls Section 3: Libc calls Section 4: Devices (e.g., hd, sd) Section 5: File formats and protocols (e.g., wtmp, /etc/passwd, nfs) Section 6: Games (intro only) Section 7: Conventions, macro packages, etc. (e.g., nroff, ascii) Section 8: System administration (intro only)

nag – (Version 1.0, 1,217K)

The nag package contains the Linux Documentation Project's Network Administrators' Guide. The NAG covers the wide world of Linux networking, including TCP/IP, UUCP, SLIP, DNS, mail systems, NNTP and news systems, and NFS. Be sure to check the LDP's website at http://sunsite.unc.edu/linux/ldp.html for possible updates to the NAG.

Install the nag package if you'd like to use the LDP's Network Administrators' Guide off your own machine.

python-docs – (Version 1.5.1, 2,611K)

The python-docs package contains documentation on the Python programming language and interpreter. The documentation is provided in ASCII text files and in LaTeX source files.

Install the python-docs package if you'd like to use the documentation for the Python language.

rhl-alpha-install-addend-en – (Version 5.2, 200K)

The rhl-alpha-install-addend-en package contains the Red Hat Linux 5.2 Alpha Installation Addendum document in HTML format.

Install the rhl-alpha-install-addend-en package if you'd like to use an HTML version of the Alpha Installation Addendum loaded on your own machine.

rhl-install-guide-en – (Version 5.2, 2,245K)

The rhl-install-guide-en package contains the Red Hat Linux 5.2 Installation Guide in HTML format. An online copy of the Red Hat Linux 5.2 Installation Guide is available from the Red Hat Software Web page at http://www.redhat.com.

Install the rhl-install-guide-en package if you would like to use an HTML version of the Installation Guide from your own machine.

sag – (Version 0.6, 644K)

The Linux Documentation Project's System Administrators' Guide, provided in HTML format. This document provides a generic guide to Linux system administration. Check the Linux Documentation Project's website at http://sunsite.unc.edu/LDP/ldp.html for other formats of this document or for any updates.

Install the sag package if you'd like to use the HTML version of the LDP's System Administrators' Guide on your own machine.

sendmail-doc – (Version 8.9.3, 1,360K)

The sendmail-doc package contains documentation about the Sendmail Mail Transport Agent (MTA) program, including release notes, the Sendmail FAQ and a few papers written about Sendmail. The papers are provided in PostScript(TM) and troff formats.

Install the sendmail-doc package if you need documentation about Sendmail.

specspo – (Version 6.0, 850K)

The specspo package contains the portable object catalogues used to internationalize Red Hat packages.

D.6   System Environment

This section contains packages that are required to provide the Red Hat Linux system environment.

D.6.1   Base

This section contains packages that are required for the basic system environment.

MAKEDEV – (Version 2.4, 25K)   🅱

The /dev directory contains important files which correspond to the hardware on your system, such as sound cards, serial or printer ports, tape and CD-ROM drives and more. MAKEDEV is a script which helps you create and maintain the files in your /dev directory.

These are the files needed to install MAKEDEV.

SysVinit – (Version 2.74, 151K)   🅱

The SysVinit package contains a group of processes that control the very basic functions of your system. SysVinit is the first program started by the Linux kernel when the system boots, controlling the startup, running and shutdown of all other programs.

adjtimex – (Version 1.3, 23K)

Adjtimex is a kernel clock management program, which the superuser may use to correct any drift in the system's clock. Users can use adjtimex to view the time variables.

authconfig – (Version 1.7, 27K)   🅱

Authconfig is a terminal mode program for setting up Network Information Service (NIS) and shadow (more secure) passwords on your system. Authconfig also configures the system to automatically turn on NIS at system startup.

basesystem – (Version 6.0, 0K) Ⓑ

Basesystem defines the components of a basic Red Hat Linux system (for example, the package installation order to use during bootstrapping). Basesystem should be the first package installed on a system, and it should never be removed.

chkconfig – (Version 1.0.4, 69K) Ⓑ

Chkconfig is a basic system utility. It updates and queries runlevel information for system services. Chkconfig manipulates the numerous symbolic links in /etc/rc.d, so system administrators don't have to manually edit the symbolic links as often.

chkfontpath – (Version 1.3, 18K) ⓌⓈ

This is a simple terminal mode program for adding, removing and listing the directories contained in the X font server's path. It is mostly intended to be used 'internally' by RPM when packages with fonts are added or removed, but it may be useful as a stand-alone utility in some instances.

crontabs – (Version 1.7, 4K) Ⓑ

The crontabs package contains root crontab files. Crontab is the program used to install, uninstall or list the tables used to drive the cron daemon. The cron daemon checks the crontab files to see when particular commands are scheduled to be executed. If commands are scheduled, it executes them.

Crontabs handles a basic system function, so it should be installed on your system.

dev – (Version 2.7.3, 7K) Ⓑ

The Red Hat Linux operating system uses file system entries to represent devices (CD-ROMs, floppy drives, etc.) attached to the machine. All of these entries are in the /dev tree (although they don't have to be). This package contains the most commonly used /dev entries.

The dev package is a basic part of your Red Hat Linux system and it needs to be installed.

e2fsprogs – (Version 1.14, 1,134K) Ⓑ

The e2fsprogs package contains a number of utilities for creating, checking, modifying and correcting any inconsistencies in second extended (ext2) filesystems. E2fsprogs contains e2fsck (used to repair filesystem inconsistencies after an unclean shutdown), mke2fs (used to initialize a partition to contain an empty ext2 filesystem), debugfs (used to examine the internal structure of a filesystem, to manually repair a corrupted filesystem or to create test cases for e2fsck), tune2fs (used to modify filesystem parameters) and most of the other core ext2fs filesystem utilities.

You should install the e2fsprogs package if you need to manage the performance of an ext2 filesystem.

eject – (Version 2.0.2, 46K) Ⓑ

The eject program allows the user to eject removable media (typically CD-ROMs, floppy disks or Iomega Jaz or Zip disks) using software control. Eject can also control some multi- disk CD changers and even some devices' auto-eject features.

Install eject if you'd like to eject removable media using software control.

etcskel – (Version 1.6, 2K) Ⓑ

The etcskel package is part of the basic Red Hat system. Etcskel provides the /etc/skel directory's files. These files (.Xdefaults, .bash_logout, .bash_profile, .bashrc) are then placed in every new user's home directory when new accounts are created.

filesystem – (Version 1.3.4, 80K) Ⓑ

The filesystem package is one of the basic packages that is installed on a Red Hat Linux system. Filesystem contains the basic directory layout for a Linux operating system, including the correct permissions for the directories.

genromfs – (Version 0.3, 12K)

Genromfs is a tool for creating romfs filesystems, which are lightweight, read-only filesystems supported by the Linux kernel.

info – (Version 3.12f, 245K) Ⓑ

The GNU project uses the texinfo file format for much of its documentation. The info package provides a standalone TTY-based browser program for viewing texinfo files.

You should install info, because GNU's texinfo documentation is a valuable source of information about the software on your system.

initscripts – (Version 3.98, 148K) Ⓑ

The initscripts package contains the basic system scripts used to boot your Red Hat system, change run levels, and shut the system down cleanly. Initscripts also contains the scripts that activate and deactivate most network interfaces.

ipchains – (Version 1.3.8, 316K) ⓌⓈ

Linux IP Firewalling Chains is an update to (and hopefully an improvement upon) the normal Linux Firewalling code, for 2.0 and 2.1 kernels. It lets you do things like firewalls, IP masquerading, etc.

isapnptools – (Version 1.18, 237K) Ⓑ

The isapnptools package contains utilities for configuring ISA Plug-and-Play (PnP) cards/boards which are in compliance with the PnP ISA Specification Version 1.0a. ISA PnP cards use registers instead of jumpers for setting the board address and interrupt assignments. The cards also contain descriptions of the resources which need to be allocated. The BIOS on your system, or isapnptools, uses a protocol described in the specification to find all of the PnP boards and allocate the resources so that none of them conflict.

Note that the BIOS doesn't do a very good job of allocating resources. So isapnptools is suitable for all systems, whether or not they include a PnP BIOS. In fact, a PnP BIOS adds some complications. A PnP BIOS may already activate some cards so that the drivers can find them. Then these tools can unconfigure them or change their settings, causing all sorts of nasty effects. If you have PnP network cards that already work, you should read through the documentation files very carefully before you use isapnptools.

Install isapnptools if you need utilities for configuring ISA PnP cards.

kbdconfig – (Version 1.9, 40K) Ⓑ

The kbdconfig utility is a terminal mode program for setting the keyboard map for your system. Keyboard maps are necessary for using any keyboard besides the US default keyboard. Kbdconfig will load the selected keymap before exiting and configure your machine to use that keymap automatically after rebooting.

You should install kbdconfig if you need a utility for changing your keyboard map.

ld.so – (Version 1.9.5, 247K)   🅑

This package contains the shared library configuration tool, ldconfig, which is required by many packages. It also includes the shared library loader and dynamic loader for Linux libc 5.

ldconfig – (Version 1.9.5, 223K)   🅑

Ldconfig is a basic system program which determines run-time link bindings between ld.so and shared libraries. Ldconfig scans a running system and sets up the symbolic links that are used to load shared libraries properly. It also creates a cache (/etc/ld.so.cache) which speeds the loading of programs which use shared libraries.

lilo – (Version 0.21, 1,095K)   🅑

LILO (LInux LOader) is a basic system program which boots your Linux system. LILO loads the Linux kernel from a floppy or a hard drive, boots the kernel and passes control of the system to the kernel. LILO can also boot other operating systems.

logrotate – (Version 3.1, 52K)   🅑

The logrotate utility is designed to simplify the administration of log files on a system which generates a lot of log files. Logrotate allows for the automatic rotation compression, removal and mailing of log files. Logrotate can be set to handle a log file daily, weekly, monthly or when the log file gets to a certain size. Normally, logrotate runs as a daily cron job.

Install the logrotate package if you need a utility to deal with the log files on your system.

losetup – (Version 2.9, 8K)   🅑

Linux supports a special block device called the loop device, which maps a normal file onto a virtual block device. This allows for the file to be used as a "virtual file system" inside another file. Losetup is used to associate loop devices with regular files or block devices, to detach loop devices and to query the status of a loop device.

mailcap – (Version 2.0.1, 34K)   🅑

The mailcap file is used by the metamail program. Metamail reads the mailcap file to determine how it should display non-text or multimedia material. Basically, mailcap associates a particular type of file with a particular program that a mail agent or other program can call in order to handle the file.

Mailcap should be installed to allow certain programs to be able to handle non-text files.

man – (Version 1.5f, 217K)   🅑

The man package includes three tools for finding information and/or documentation about your Linux system: man, apropos and whatis. The man system formats and displays on-line manual pages about commands or functions on your system. Apropos searches the whatis database (containing short descriptions of system commands) for a string. Whatis searches its own database for a complete word.

The man package should be installed on your system because it is the primary way for finding documentation.

mgetty – (Version 1.1.14, 845K)

The mgetty package contains a "smart" getty which allows logins over a serial line (i.e., through a modem). If you're using a Class 2 or 2.0 modem, mgetty can receive faxes. If you also need to send faxes, you'll need to install the sendfax program.

If you'll be dialing in to your system using a modem, you should install the mgetty package. If you'd like to send faxes using mgetty and your modem, you'll need to install the mgetty-sendfax program. If you need a viewer for faxes, you'll also need to install the mgetty-viewfax package.

mingetty – (Version 0.9.4, 32K)   ⑬

The mingetty program is a lightweight, minimalist getty program for use only on virtual consoles. Mingetty is not suitable for serial lines (you should use the mgetty program instead for that purpose).

mkbootdisk – (Version 1.1, 5K)   ⑬

The mkbootdisk program creates a standalone boot floppy disk for booting the running system. The created boot disk will look for the root filesystem on the device mentioned in /etc/fstab and includes an initial ramdisk image which will load any necessary SCSI modules for the system.

mkinitrd – (Version 2.0, 7K)   ⑬

Mkinitrd creates filesystem images for use as initial ramdisk (initrd) images. These ramdisk images are often used to preload the block device modules (SCSI or RAID) needed to access the root filesystem.

In other words, generic kernels can be built without drivers for any SCSI adapters which load the SCSI driver as a module. Since the kernel needs to read those modules, but in this case it isn't able to address the SCSI adapter, an initial ramdisk is used. The initial ramdisk is loaded by the operating system loader (normally LILO) and is available to the kernel as soon as the ramdisk is loaded. The ramdisk image loads the proper SCSI adapter and allows the kernel to mount the root filesystem. The mkinitrd program creates such a ramdisk using information found in the /etc/conf.modules file.

mkkickstart – (Version 1.1, 4K)

The mkkickstart program writes a kickstart description from the host machine. The kickstart description can then be used, during a CD-ROM or NFS installation, to automatically build that machine's configuration of Red Hat Linux on one or more other machines.

Install mkkickstart if you want to use the kickstart method to automatically install Red Hat Linux.

mktemp – (Version 1.5, 8K)   ⑬

The mktemp utility takes a given file name template and overwrites a portion of it to create a unique file name. This allows shell scripts and other programs to safely create and use /tmp files.

Install the mktemp package if you need to use shell scripts or other programs which will create and use unique /tmp files.

mount – (Version 2.9, 115K)   ⑬

The mount package contains the mount, umount, swapon and swapoff programs. Accessible files on your system are arranged in one big tree or hierarchy. These files can be spread out over several devices. The mount command attaches a filesystem on some device to your system's file tree. The umount command detaches a filesystem from the tree. Swapon and swapoff, respectively, specify and disable devices and files for paging and swapping.

mouseconfig – (Version 3.7, 136K) 🅑

Mouseconfig is a text-based mouse configuration tool. Mouseconfig sets up the files and links needed for configuring and using a mouse on a Red Hat Linux system. The mouseconfig tool can be used to set the correct mouse type for programs like gpm, and can be used with Xconfigurator to set up the mouse for the X Window System.

net-tools – (Version 1.51, 395K) 🅑

The net-tools package contains the basic tools needed for setting up networking: arp, rarp, ifconfig, netstat, ethers and route.

ntsysv – (Version 1.0.4, 23K) 🅑

ntsysv updates and queries runlevel information for system services. ntsysv relieves system administrators of having to directly manipulate the numerous symbolic links in /etc/rc.d.

pam – (Version 0.66, 1,850K) 🅑

PAM (Pluggable Authentication Modules) is a system security tool which allows system administrators to set authentication policy without having to recompile programs which do authentication.

passwd – (Version 0.50, 28K) 🅑

The passwd package contains a system utility (passwd) which sets and/or changes passwords, using PAM (Pluggable Authentication Modules).

To use passwd, you should have PAM installed on your system.

pwdb – (Version 0.56, 417K) 🅑

The pwdb package contains libpwdb, the password database library. Libpwdb is a library which implements a generic user information database. Libpwdb was specifically designed to work with Linux's PAM (Pluggable Authentication Modules). Libpwdb allows configurable access to and management of security tools like /etc/passwd, /etc/shadow and network authentication systems including NIS and Radius.

quota – (Version 1.66, 79K) 🅑

The quota package contains system administration tools for monitoring and limiting users' and or groups' disk usage, per filesystem.

raidtools – (Version 0.90, 151K)

This package includes the tools you need to set up and maintain a software RAID device under Linux. It only works with Linux 2.2 kernels and later, or 2.0 kernel specifically patched with newer raid support.

rootfiles – (Version 5.2, 1K) 🅑

The rootfiles package contains basic required files that are placed in the root user's account. These files are basically the same as the files found in the etcskel package, which are placed in regular users' home directories.

rpm – (Version 2.93, 1,599K) 🅑

The Red Hat Package Manager (RPM) is a powerful command line driven package management system capable of installing, uninstalling, verifying, querying, and updating software packages. Each software package consists of an archive of files along with information about the package like its version, a description, etc.

setup – (Version 2.0.1, 15K) ⒝

The setup package contains a set of very important system configuration and setup files, such as passwd, group, profile and more.

You should install the setup package because you will find yourself using its many features for system administration.

shadow-utils – (Version 980403, 604K) ⒝

The shadow-utils package includes the necessary programs for converting UNIX password files to the shadow password format, plus programs for managing user and group accounts. The pwconv command converts passwords to the shadow password format. The pwunconv command unconverts shadow passwords and generates an npasswd file (a standard UNIX password file). The pwck command checks the integrity of password and shadow files. The lastlog command prints out the last login times for all users. The useradd, userdel and usermod commands are used for managing user accounts. The groupadd, groupdel and groupmod commands are used for managing group accounts.

shapecfg – (Version 2.0.36, 6K)

The Shapecfg program configures and adjusts traffic shaper bandwidth limiters. Traffic shaping means setting parameters to which traffic should conform - setting the standards for bandwidth consumption.

To use Shapecfg, you must have also installed the kernel which supports the shaper module (kernel versions 2.0.36 or later and late 2.1.x kernels).

Install the shapecfg package if you want to set traffic bandwidth parameters, and if you have the appropriate kernel.

termcap – (Version 9.12.6, 424K) ⒝

The termcap package provides the /etc/termcap file. /etc/termcap is a database which defines the capabilities of various terminals and terminal emulators. Certain programs use the /etc/termcap file to access various features of terminals (the bell, colors, and graphics, etc.).

tmpwatch – (Version 1.5.1, 9K) ⒝

The tmpwatch utility recursively searches through specified directories and removes files which have not been accessed in a specified period of time. Tmpwatch is normally used to clean up directories which are used for temporarily holding files (for example, /tmp). Tmpwatch ignores symlinks, won't switch filesystems and only removes empty directories and regular files.

utempter – (Version 0.3, 21K) ⒝

Utempter is a utility which allows programs to log information to a privledged file (/var/run/utmp), without compromising system security. It accomplishes this task by acting as a buffer between root and the programs.

util-linux – (Version 2.9o, 960K) ⒝

The util-linux package contains a large variety of low-level system utilities that are necessary for a Linux system to function. Among many features, Util-linux contains the fdisk configuration tool and login program.

You should install util-linux for its essential system tools.

vixie-cron – (Version 3.0.1, 57K)   Ⓑ

The vixie-cron package contains the Vixie version of cron. Cron is a standard UNIX daemon that runs specified programs at scheduled times. Vixie cron adds better security and more powerful configuration options to the standard version of cron.

yp-tools – (Version 2.1, 161K)   Ⓦ Ⓢ

The Network Information Service (NIS) is a system which provides network information (login names, passwords, home directories, group information) to all of the machines on a network. NIS can enable users to login on any machine on the network, as long as the machine has the NIS client programs running and the user's password is recorded in the NIS passwd database. NIS was formerly known as Sun Yellow Pages (YP).

This package's NIS implementation is based on FreeBSD's YP and is a special port for glibc 2.x and libc versions 5.4.21 and later. This package only provides the NIS client programs. In order to use the clients, you'll need to already have an NIS server running on your network. An NIS server is provided in the ypserv package.

Install the yp-tools package if you need NIS client programs for machines on your network. You will also need to install the ypbind package on every machine running NIS client programs. If you need an NIS server, you'll need to install the ypserv package on one machine on the network.

D.6.2   Daemons

This section contains packages associated with the daemon processes that run under Red Hat Linux.

ORBit – (Version 0.4.2, 1,273K)   Ⓦ Ⓢ

ORBit is a high-performance CORBA ORB (object request broker). It allows programs to send requests and receive replies from other programs, regardless of the locations of the two programs.

You will need to install this package and the related header files, libraries and utilities if you want to write programs that use CORBA technology.

XFree86-xfs – (Version 3.3.3.1, 505K)   Ⓦ Ⓢ

This is a font server for XFree86. You can serve fonts to other X servers remotely with this package, and the remote system will be able to use all fonts installed on the font server, even if they are not installed on the remote computer.

am-utils – (Version 6.0, 1,954K)

Am-utils includes an updated version of Amd, the popular BSD automounter. An automounter is a program which maintains a cache of mounted filesystems. Filesystems are mounted when they are first referenced by the user and unmounted after a certain period of inactivity. Amd supports a variety of filesystems, including NFS, UFS, CD-ROMS and local drives.

You should install am-utils if you need a program for automatically mounting and unmounting filesystems.

anonftp – (Version 2.8, 1,540K)   (S)

The anonftp package contains the files you need in order to allow anonymous FTP access to your machine. Anonymous FTP access allows anyone to download files from your machine without having a user account. Anonymous FTP is a popular way of making programs available via the Internet.

You should install anonftp if you would like to enable anonymous FTP downloads from your machine.

apache – (Version 1.3.6, 2,111K)   (S)

Apache is a powerful, full-featured, efficient and freely-available Web server. Apache is also the most popular Web server on the Internet.

This package will install the Apache Web server on your machine.

apmd – (Version 3.0beta5, 70K)

This is a Advanced Power Management daemon and utilities. It can watch your notebook's battery and warn all users when the battery is low.

Patches to Rik Faith's original version have been added for shutting down the PCMCIA sockets before a suspend.

at – (Version 3.1.7, 64K)   (B)

At and batch read commands from standard input or from a specified file. At allows you to specify that a command will be run at a particular time (now or a specified time in the future). Batch will execute commands when the system load levels drop to a particular level. Both commands use /bin/sh to run the commands.

You should install the at package if you need a utility that will do time-oriented job control. Note: you should use crontab instead, if it is a recurring job that will need to be repeated at the same time every day/week/etc.

autofs – (Version 3.1.3, 126K)

Autofs controls the operation of the automount daemons. The automount daemons automatically mount filesystems when you use them and unmount them after a period of inactivity. Filesystems can include network filesystems, CD-ROMs, floppies and others.

Install this package if you want a program for automatically mounting and unmounting filesystems. If your Red Hat Linux machine is on a network, you should install autofs.

bdflush – (Version 1.5, 10K)   (B)

The bdflush process starts the kernel daemon which flushes dirty buffers back to disk (i.e., writes all unwritten data to disk). This helps to prevent the buffers from growing too stale.

Bdflush is a basic system process that must run for your system to operate properly.

bind – (Version 8.2, 4,370K)   (S)

Bind includes the named name server, which resolves host names to IP addresses (and vice versa), and a resolver library (a set of routines in a system library that provide the interface for programs to use when accessing domain name services). A name server is a network service which enables clients to name resources or objects and share this information with other network machines. The named name server can be used on workstations as a caching name server, but is generally only needed on one machine for an entire network. Note that the configuration files for making bind act as a simple caching nameserver are included in the caching-nameserver package.

Install the bind package if you need a name server for your network. If you want bind to act a caching name server, you will also need to install the caching-nameserver package.

bootparamd – (Version 0.10, 18K)

The bootparamd process provides bootparamd, a server process which provides the information needed by disk-less clients in order for them to successfully boot. Bootparamd looks first in /etc/bootparams for an entry for that particular client; if a local bootparams file doesn't exist, it looks at the appropriate Network Information Service (NIS) map. Some network boot loaders (notably Sun's) rely on special boot server code on the server, in addition to the rarp and tftp servers. This bootparamd server process is compatible with SunOS bootparam clients and servers which need that boot server code.

You should install bootparamd if you need to provide boot information to diskless clients on your network.

caching-nameserver – (Version 6.0, 3K)   Ⓢ

The caching-nameserver package includes the configuration files which will make bind, the DNS name server, act as a simple caching nameserver. Many users on dialup connections use this package along with bind for such a purpose.

If you would like to set up a caching name server, you'll need to install the caching-nameserver package; you'll also need to install bind.

cleanfeed – (Version 0.95.7b, 107K)   Ⓢ

Cleanfeed is an automatic spam filter for Usenet news servers and routers (INN, Cyclone, Typhoon, Breeze and NNTPRelay). Cleanfeed is highly configurable, easily modified and very fast. It can be configured to block binary posts to non-binary newsgroups, to cancel already-rejected articles, and to reject some spamming from local users.

Install the cleanfeed package if you need a spam filter for a Usenet news server.

comsat – (Version 0.10, 17K)

The biff client and comsat server are an antiquated method of asynchronous mail notification. Although they are still supported, most users use their shell's MAIL variable (or csh shell's mail variable) to check for mail, or a dedicated application like xbiff or xmailbox. If the comsat service is not enabled, biff won't work and you'll need to use either the MAIL or mail variable.

You may want to install biff if you'd like to be notified when mail arrives. However, you should probably check out the more modern methodologies of mail notification (xbiff or xmailbox) instead.

dhcp – (Version 2.0b1pl6, 257K)

DHCP (Dynamic Host Configuration Protocol) is a protocol which allows individual devices on an IP network to get their own network configuration information (IP address, subnetmask, broadcast address, etc.) from a DHCP server. The overall purpose of DHCP is to make it easier to administer a large network. The dhcp package includes the DHCP server and a DHCP relay agent.

You should install dhcp if you want to set up a DHCP server on your network. You will also need to install the dhcpcd package, which provides the DHCP client daemon, on client machines.

esound – (Version 0.2.9, 178K)   Ⓦ Ⓢ

EsounD – the Enlightened Sound Daemon – is a server process that allows multiple applications to share a single sound card. For example, when you're listening to music from your CD and you receive a sound-related event from ICQ, your applications won't have to jockey for the attention of your sound card.

EsounD mixes several audio streams for playback by a single audio device.

Install esound if you'd like to allow for such event sharing by your audio device.

gated – (Version 3.5.10, 2,434K)

GateD is a modular software program consisting of core services, a routing database, and protocol modules which support multiple routing protocols (RIP versions 1 and 2, DCN HELLO, OSPF version 2, EGP version 2, BGP versions 2 through 4). GateD is designed to handle dynamic routing with a routing database built from the information exchanged by routing protocols.

Install gated if you need a routing daemon.

gpm – (Version 1.17.5, 258K) Ⓑ

Gpm provides mouse support to text-based Linux applications like the emacs editor, the Midnight Commander file management system, and other programs. Gpm also provides console cut-and-paste operations using the mouse and includes a program to allow pop-up menus to appear at the click of a mouse button.

Gpm should be installed if you intend to use a mouse with your Red Hat Linux system.

imap – (Version 4.5, 1,485K)

The imap package provides server daemons for both the IMAP (Internet Message Access Protocol) and POP (Post Office Protocol) mail access protocols. The POP protocol uses a "post office" machine to collect mail for users and allows users to download their mail to their local machine for reading. The IMAP protocol provides the functionality of POP, but allows a user to read mail on a remote machine without downloading it to their local machine.

Install the imap package if you need a server to support the IMAP or the POP mail access protocols.

inews – (Version 2.2, 74K)

The inews program is used by some news programs (for example, inn and trn) to post Usenet news articles to local news servers. Inews reads an article from a file or standard input, adds headers, performs some consistency checks and then sends the article to the local news server specified in the inn.conf file.

Install inews if you need a program for posting Usenet articles to local news servers.

inn – (Version 2.2, 6,246K) Ⓢ

INN (InterNetNews) is a complete system for serving Usenet news and/or private newsfeeds. INN includes innd, an NNTP (NetNews Transport Protocol) server, and nnrpd, a newsreader that is spawned for each client. Both innd and nnrpd vary slightly from the NNTP protocol, but not in ways that are easily noticed.

Install the inn package if you need a complete system for serving and reading Usenet news. You may also need to install inn-devel, if you are going to use a separate program which interfaces to INN, like newsgate or tin.

intimed – (Version 1.10, 210K)

The intimed package contains a server (in.timed), which keeps networked machines' clocks correctly synchronized to the server's time.

Install intimed if you need a network time server.

knfsd – (Version 1.2, 163K)   ⓦⓈ

This is the *new* kernel NFS server and related tools. It provides a much higher level of performance than the traditional Linux user-land NFS server.

lpr – (Version 0.35, 180K)   ⓦⓈ

The lpr package provides the basic system utility for managing printing services. Lpr manages print queues, sends print jobs to local and remote printers and accepts print jobs from remote clients.

If you will be printing from your system, you'll need to install the lpr package.

mars-nwe – (Version 0.99pl15, 657K)   Ⓢ

The mars_nwe (MARtin Stover's NetWare Emulator) package enables Linux to provide both file and print services for NetWare clients (i.e., providing the services of a Novell NetWare file server). Mars_nwe allows the sharing of files between Linux machines and Novell NetWare clients, using NetWare's native IPX protocol suite.

Install the mars_nwe package if you need a Novell NetWare file server on your Red Hat Linux system.

mcserv – (Version 4.5.29, 122K)

The Midnight Commander file management system will allow you to manipulate the files on a remote machine as if they were local. This is only possible if the remote machine is running the mcserv server program. Mcserv provides clients running Midnight Commander with access to the host's file systems.

Install mcserv on machines if you want to access their file systems remotely using the Midnight Commander file management system.

mod_perl – (Version 1.18, 1,261K)

Mod_perl incorporates a Perl interpreter into the Apache web server, so that the Apache web server can directly execute Perl code. Mod_perl links the Perl runtime library into the Apache web server and provides an object-oriented Perl interface for Apache's C language API. The end result is a quicker CGI script turnaround process, since no external Perl interpreter has to be started.

Install mod_perl if you're installing the Apache web server and you'd like for it to directly incorporate a Perl interpreter.

mod_php – (Version 2.0.1, 676K)

PHP is an HTML-embedded scripting language. PHP attempts to make it easy for developers to write dynamically generated web pages. PHP also offers built-in database integration for several commercial and non-commercial database management systems, so writing a database-enabled web page with PHP is fairly simple. The most common use of PHP coding is probably as a replacement for CGI scripts. The mod_php module enables the Apache web server to understand and process the embedded PHP language in web pages.

This package contains PHP/FI, or PHP version 2.01. Unless you use applications which specifically rely on PHP/FI, you should instead install the mod_php3 package, which contains PHP3. PHP3 is an improved and more capable update to PHP/FI.

mod_php3 – (Version 3.0.7, 3,892K)

PHP is an HTML-embedded scripting language. PHP attempts to make it easy for developers to write dynamically generated web pages. PHP also offers built-in database integration for several commercial and non-commercial database management systems, so writing a database-enabled web page with PHP is fairly simple. The most common use of PHP coding is probably as a replacement for CGI scripts. The mod_php module enables the Apache web server to understand and process the embedded PHP language in web pages.

This package contains PHP3, or PHP version 3.05. If you use applications which specifically rely on PHP/FI, you should instead install the PHP/FI module contained in the mod_php package. If you're just starting with PHP, you should install this package. You'll also need to install the Apache web server.

netkit-base – (Version 0.10, 61K) Ⓦ Ⓢ

The netkit-base package contains the basic networking tools ping and inetd. The ping command sends a series of ICMP protocol ECHO_REQUEST packets to a specified network host and can tell you if that machine is alive and receiving network traffic. Inetd listens on certain Internet sockets for connection requests, decides what program should receive each request, and starts up that program.

The netkit-base package should be installed on any machine that is on a network.

nscd – (Version 2.1.1, 33K)

nscd caches name service lookups; it can dramatically improve performance with NIS+, and may help with DNS as well.

You cannot use nscd with 2.0 kernels, due to bugs in the kernel-side thread support. nscd happens to hit these bugs particularly hard.

pidentd – (Version 2.8.5, 129K) Ⓦ Ⓢ

The pidentd package contains identd, which implements the RFC1413 identification server. Identd looks up specific TCP/IP connections and returns either the user name or other information about the process that owns the connection.

portmap – (Version 4.0, 49K) Ⓦ Ⓢ

The portmapper program is a security tool which prevents theft of NIS (YP), NFS and other sensitive information via the portmapper. A portmapper manages RPC connections, which are used by protocols like NFS and NIS.

The portmap package should be installed on any machine which acts as a server for protocols using RPC.

ppp – (Version 2.3.7, 301K) Ⓦ Ⓢ

The ppp package contains the PPP (Point-to-Point Protocol) daemon and documentation for PPP support. The PPP protocol provides a method for transmitting datagrams over serial point-to-point links.

The ppp package should be installed if your machine need to support the PPP protocol.

procmail – (Version 3.13, 207K) Ⓑ

The procmail program is used by Red Hat Linux for all local mail delivery. In addition to just delivering mail, procmail can be used for automatic filtering, presorting and other mail handling jobs. Procmail is also the basis for the SmartList mailing list processor.

pump – (Version 0.4, 30K) Ⓑ

DHCP (Dynamic Host Configuration Protocol) and BOOTP (Boot Protocol) are protocols which allow individual devices on an IP network to get their own network configuration information (IP address, subnetmask, broadcast address, etc.) from network servers. The overall purpose of DHCP and BOOTP is to make it easier to administer a large network.

Pump is a combined BOOTP and DHCP client daemon, which allows your machine to retrieve configuration information from a server. You should install this package if you are on a network which uses BOOTP or DHCP.

routed – (Version 0.10, 39K) ⓌⓈ

The routed routing daemon handles incoming RIP traffic and broadcasts outgoing RIP traffic about network traffic routes, in order to maintain current routing tables. These routing tables are essential for a networked computer, so that it knows where packets need to be sent.

The routed package should be installed on any networked machine.

rusers – (Version 0.10, 36K) ⓌⓈ

The rusers program allows users to find out who is logged into various machines on the local network. The rusers command produces output similar to who, but for the specified list of hosts or for all machines on the local network.

Install rusers if you need to keep track of who is logged into your local network.

rwall – (Version 0.10, 18K)

The rwall command sends a message to all of the users logged into a specified host. Actually, your machine's rwall client sends the message to the rwall daemon running on the specified host, and the rwall daemon relays the message to all of the users logged in to that host. The rwall daemon is run from /etc/inetd.conf and is disabled by default on Red Hat Linux systems (it can be very annoying to keep getting all those messages when you're trying to play Quake–I mean trying to get some work done).

Install rwall if you'd like the ability to send messages to users logged in to a specified host machine.

rwho – (Version 0.10, 25K) ⓌⓈ

The rwho command displays output similar to the output of the who command (it shows who is logged in) for all machines on the local network running the rwho daemon.

Install the rwho command if you need to keep track of the users who are logged in to your local network.

samba – (Version 2.0.3, 6,498K) Ⓢ

Samba provides an SMB server which can be used to provide network services to SMB (sometimes called "Lan Manager") clients, including various versions of MS Windows, OS/2, and other Linux machines. Samba also provides some SMB clients, which complement the built-in SMB filesystem in Linux. Samba uses NetBIOS over TCP/IP (NetBT) protocols and does NOT need NetBEUI (Microsoft Raw NetBIOS frame) protocol.

Samba-2 features an almost working NT Domain Control capability and includes the new SWAT (Samba Web

Administration Tool) that allows samba's smb.conf file to be remotely managed using your favourite web browser. For the time being this is being enabled on TCP port 901 via inetd.

Please refer to the WHATSNEW.txt document for fixup information. This binary release includes encrypted password support. Please read the smb.conf file and ENCRYPTION.txt in the docs directory for implementation details.

NOTE: Red Hat Linux 5.X Uses PAM which has integrated support for Shadow passwords. Do NOT recompile with the SHADOW_PWD option enabled. Red Hat Linux has built in support for quotas in PAM.

sendmail – (Version 8.9.3, 526K)   Ⓑ

The Sendmail program is a very widely used Mail Transport Agent (MTA). MTAs send mail from one machine to another. Sendmail is not a client program, which you use to read your email. Sendmail is a behind-the-scenes program which actually moves your email over networks or the Internet to where you want it to go.

If you ever need to reconfigure Sendmail, you'll also need to have the sendmail.cf package installed. If you need documentation on Sendmail, you can install the sendmail-doc package.

sendmail-cf – (Version 8.9.3, 503K)

This package includes the configuration files which you'd need to generate the sendmail.cf file distributed with the sendmail package. You'll need the sendmail-cf package if you ever need to reconfigure and rebuild your sendmail.cf file. For example, the default sendmail.cf file is not configured for UUCP. If someday you needed to send and receive mail over UUCP, you'd need to install the sendmail-cf package to help you reconfigure Sendmail.

Install the sendmail-cf package if you need to reconfigure your sendmail.cf file.

squid – (Version 2.2.DEVEL3, 1,861K)

Squid is a high-performance proxy caching server for web clients, supporting FTP, gopher, and HTTP data objects. Unlike traditional caching software, Squid handles all requests in a single, non-blocking, I/O-driven process.

Squid keeps meta data and especially hot objects cached in RAM, caches DNS lookups, supports non-blocking DNS lookups, and implements negative caching of failed requests.

Squid supports SSL, extensive access controls, and full request logging. By using the lightweight Internet Cache Protocol, Squid caches can be arranged in a hierarchy or mesh for additional bandwidth savings.

Squid consists of a main server program squid, a Domain Name System lookup program dnsserver, a program for retrieving FTP data ftpget, and some management and client tools. When squid starts up, it spawns a configurable number of dnsserver processes, each of which can perform a single, blocking Domain Name System (DNS) lookup. This reduces the amount of time the cache waits for DNS lookups.

Squid is derived from the ARPA-funded Harvest project.

syslogd – (Version 1.3.31, 112K)   Ⓑ

The syslogd package contains two system utilities (syslogd and klogd) which provide support for system logging. Syslogd and klogd run as daemons (background processes) and log system messages to different places, like sendmail logs, security logs, error logs, etc.

tcp_wrappers – (Version 7.6, 270K)   Ⓦ Ⓢ

The tcp_wrappers package provides small daemon programs which can monitor and filter incoming requests for systat, finger, ftp, telnet, rlogin, rsh, exec, tftp, talk and other network services.

Install the tcp_wrappers program if you need a security tool for filtering incoming network services requests.

tftp – (Version 0.10, 34K)   Ⓦ Ⓢ

The Trivial File Transfer Protocol (TFTP) is normally used only for booting diskless workstations. The tftp package provides the user interface for TFTP, which allows users to transfer files to and from a remote machine. This program, and TFTP, provide very little security, and should not be enabled unless it is expressly needed. The TFTP server is run from /etc/inetd.conf, and is disabled by default on Red Hat Linux systems.

timed – (Version 0.10, 74K)   Ⓦ Ⓢ

The timed package contains the timed daemon and the timedc program for controlling the timed program. Timed synchronizes its host machine's time with the time on other local network machines. The timedc program is used to control and configure the operation of timed.

Install the timed package if you need a system for keeping networked machines' times in synchronization.

ucd-snmp – (Version 3.6.1, 1,504K)   Ⓦ Ⓢ

SNMP (Simple Network Management Protocol) is a protocol used for network management (hence the name). The UCD-SNMP project includes various SNMP tools: an extensible agent, an SNMP library, tools for requesting or setting information from SNMP agents, tools for generating and handling SNMP traps, a version of the netstat command which uses SNMP, and a Tk/Perl mib browser. This package contains the snmpd and snmptrapd daemons, documentation, etc.

Install the ucd-snmp package if you need network management tools. You will probably also want to install the ucd-snmp-utils package, which contains UCD-SNMP utilities.

wu-ftpd – (Version 2.4.2b18, 398K)   Ⓢ

The wu-ftpd package contains the wu-ftpd FTP (File Transfer Protocol) server daemon. The FTP protocol is a method of transferring files between machines on a network and/or over the Internet. Wu-ftpd's features include logging of transfers, logging of commands, on the fly compression and archiving, classification of users' type and location, per class limits, per directory upload permissions, restricted guest accounts, system wide and per directory messages, directory alias, cdpath, filename filter and virtual host support.

Install the wu-ftpd package if you need to provide FTP service to remote users.

xntp3 – (Version 5.93, 968K)

The Network Time Protocol (NTP) is used to synchronize a computer's time with another reference time source. The xntp3 package contains utilities and daemons which will synchronize your computer's time to Coordinated Universal Time (UTC) via the NTP protocol and NTP servers. Xntp3 includes ntpdate (a program for retrieving the date and time from remote machines via a network) and xntpd (a daemon which continuously adjusts system time).

Install the xntp3 package if you need tools for keeping your system's time synchronized via the NTP protocol.

ypbind – (Version 3.3, 48K)   Ⓦ Ⓢ

The Network Information Service (NIS) is a system which provides network information (login names, passwords, home directories, group information) to all of the machines on a network. NIS can enable users to login on any machine on the network, as long as the machine has the NIS client programs running and the user's password is recorded in the NIS passwd database. NIS was formerly known as Sun Yellow Pages (YP).

This package provides the ypbind daemon. The ypbind daemon binds NIS clients to an NIS domain. Ypbind must be running on any machines which are running NIS client programs.

Install the ypbind package on any machines which are running NIS client programs (included in the yp-tools package). If you need an NIS server, you'll also need to install the ypserv package to a machine on your network.

ypserv – (Version 1.3.6.91, 289K)

The Network Information Service (NIS) is a system which provides network information (login names, passwords, home directories, group information) to all of the machines on a network. NIS can enable users to login on any machine on the network, as long as the machine has the NIS client programs running and the user's password is recorded in the NIS passwd database. NIS was formerly known as Sun Yellow Pages (YP).

This package provides the NIS server, which will need to be running on your network. NIS clients do not need to be running the server.

Install ypserv if you need an NIS server for your network. You'll also need to install the yp-tools and ypbind packages onto any NIS client machines.

D.6.3   Kernel

This section contains packages that are related to the Linux kernel on which Red Hat Linux is based.

kernel – (Version 2.2.5, 9,812K)   [B]

The kernel package contains the Linux kernel (vmlinuz), the core of your Red Hat Linux operating system. The kernel handles the basic functions of the operating system: memory allocation, process allocation, device input and output, etc.

kernel-BOOT – (Version 2.2.5, 5,881K)

This package includes a trimmed down version of the Linux 2.2.5 kernel. This kernel is used on the installation boot disks only and should not be used for an installed system, as many features in this kernel are turned off because of the size constraints.

kernel-pcmcia-cs – (Version 2.2.5, 561K)   [B]

Many laptop machines (and some non-laptops) support PCMCIA cards for expansion. Also known as "credit card adapters," PCMCIA cards are small cards for everything from SCSI support to modems. PCMCIA cards are hot swappable (i.e., they can be exchanged without rebooting the system) and quite convenient to use. The kernel-pcmcia-cs package contains a set of loadable kernel modules that implement an applications program interface, a set of client drivers for specific cards and a card manager daemon that can respond to card insertion and removal events by loading and unloading drivers on demand. The daemon also supports hot swapping, so that the cards can be safely inserted and ejected at any time.

Install the kernel-pcmcia-cs package if your system uses PCMCIA cards.

kernel-smp – (Version 2.2.5, 9,494K)

This package includes a SMP version of the Linux 2.2.5 kernel. It is required only on machines with two or more CPUs, although it should work fine on single-CPU boxes.

modutils – (Version 2.1.121, 841K) [B]

The modutils packages includes the kerneld program for automatic loading of modules under 2.0 kernels and unloading of modules under 2.0 and 2.2 kernels, as well as other module management programs.

Loaded and unloaded modules are device drivers and filesystems, as well as other things.

D.6.4   Libraries

This section contains the packages associated with the libraries that are required to run programs under Red Hat Linux.

XFree86-libs – (Version 3.3.3.1, 2,060K) [W][S]

XFree86-libs contains the shared libraries that most X programs need to run properly. These shared libraries are in a separate package in order to reduce the disk space needed to run X applications on a machine without an X server (i.e, over a network).

If you are installing the X Window System on your machine, you will need to install XFree86-libs. You will also need to install the XFree86 package, the XFree86-75dpi-fonts package or the XFree86-100dpi-fonts package (depending upon your monitor's resolution), the Xconfigurator package and the X11R6-contrib package. And, finally, if you are going to be developing applications that run as X clients, you will also need to install XFree86-devel.

Xaw3d – (Version 1.3, 292K) [W][S]

Xaw3d is an enhanced version of the MIT Athena Widget set for the X Window System. Xaw3d adds a three-dimensional look to applications with minimal or no source code changes.

You should install Xaw3d if you are using applications which incorporate the MIT Athena widget set and you'd like to incorporate a 3D look into those applications.

audiofile – (Version 0.1.6, 183K) [W][S]

Library to handle various audio file formats. Used by the esound daemon.

cracklib – (Version 2.7, 75K) [B]

CrackLib tests passwords to determine whether they match certain security-oriented characteristics. You can use CrackLib to stop users from choosing passwords which would be easy to guess. CrackLib performs certain tests:

* It tries to generate words from a username and gecos entry and checks those words against the password; * It checks for simplistic patterns in passwords; * It checks for the password in a dictionary.

CrackLib is actually a library containing a particular C function which is used to check the password, as well as other C functions. CrackLib is not a replacement for a passwd program; it must be used in conjunction with an existing passwd program.

Install the cracklib package if you need a program to check users' passwords to see if they are at least minimally secure. If you install CrackLib, you'll also want to install the cracklib-dicts package.

cracklib-dicts – (Version 2.7, 235K)   Ⓑ

The cracklib-dicts package includes the CrackLib dictionaries. CrackLib will need to use the dictionary appropriate to your system, which is normally put in /usr/dict/words. Cracklib-dicts also contains the utilities necessary for the creation of new dictionaries.

If you are installing CrackLib, you should also install cracklib-dicts.

fnlib – (Version 0.4, 352K)   Ⓦ

Fnlib is a library that provides full, scalable 24-bit color font rendering abilities for X.

freetype – (Version 1.2, 937K)   ⓌⓈ

The FreeType engine is a free and portable TrueType font rendering engine. It has been developed to provide TT support to a great variety of platforms and environments. Note that FreeType is a library, not a stand-alone application, though some utility applications are included.

gd – (Version 1.3, 314K)   Ⓑ

Gd is a graphics library for drawing .gif files. Gd allows your code to quickly draw images (lines, arcs, text, multiple colors, cutting and pasting from other images, flood fills) and write out the result as a .gif file. Gd is particularly useful in web applications, where .gifs are commonly used as inline images. Note, however, that gd is not a paint program.

Install gd if you are developing applications which need to draw .gif files. If you install gd, you'll also need to install the gd-devel package.

gdbm – (Version 1.7.3, 28K)   Ⓑ

Gdbm is a GNU database indexing library, including routines which use extensible hashing. Gdbm works in a similar way to standard UNIX dbm routines. Gdbm is useful for developers who write C applications and need access to a simple and efficient database or who are building C applications which will use such a database.

If you're a C developer and your programs need access to simple database routines, you should install gdbm. You'll also need to install gdbm-devel.

gimp-libgimp – (Version 1.0.4, 173K)   Ⓦ

Libraries used to communicate between The GIMP and other programs which may function as "GIMP plugins".

glib – (Version 1.2.1, 317K)   ⒷⓌ

Glib is a handy library of utility functions. This C library is designed to solve some portability problems and provide other useful functionality which most programs require.

Glib is used by GDK, GTK+ and many applications. You should install Glib because many of your applications will depend on this library.

glib10 – (Version 1.0.6, 54K)   ⓌⓈ

The glib package contains a useful library of utility functions, which are necessary for the successful operation of many different programs on your Red Hat Linux system.

glibc – (Version 2.1.1, 25,792K) Ⓑ

Contains the standard libraries that are used by multiple programs on the system. In order to save disk space and memory, as well as to ease upgrades, common system code is kept in one place and shared between programs. This package contains the most important sets of shared libraries, the standard C library and the standard math library. Without these, a Linux system will not function. It also contains national language (locale) support and timezone databases.

gmp – (Version 2.0.2, 117K) Ⓑ

The gmp package contains GNU MP, a library for arbitrary precision arithmetic, signed integers operations, rational numbers and floating point numbers. GNU MP is designed for speed, for both small and very large operands. GNU MP is fast for several reasons: It uses fullwords as the basic arithmetic type, it uses fast algorithms, it carefully optimizes assembly code for many CPUs' most common inner loops and it generally emphasizes speed over simplicity/elegance in its operations.

Install the gmp package if you need a fast arbitrary precision library.

gnome-audio-extra – (Version 1.0.0, 2,659K) Ⓦ

This package contains extra sound files useful for customizing the sounds that the GNOME desktop environment makes.

gnome-libs – (Version 1.0.5, 2,210K) ⓌⓈ

GNOME (GNU Network Object Model Environment) is a user-friendly set of applications and desktop tools to be used in conjunction with a window manager for the X Window System. GNOME is similar in purpose and scope to CDE and KDE, but GNOME is based completely on Open Source software. The gnome-libs package includes libraries that are needed by GNOME.

You should install the gnome-libs package if you would like to use the GNOME desktop environment. You'll also need to install the gnome-core package. If you would like to develop GNOME applications, you'll also need to install gnome-libs-devel. If you want to use Linuxconf with a GNOME front end, you'll also need to install the gnome-linuxconf package.

gsl – (Version 0.3f, 868K)

The gsl package includes the GNU Scientific Library (GSL). The GSL is a collection of routines for numerical analysis, written in C. The GSL is in alpha development. It now includes a random number suite, an FFT package, simulated annealing and root finding. In the future, it will include numerical and Monte Carlo integration and special functions. Linking against the GSL allows programs to access functions which can handle many of the problems encountered in scientific computing.

Install the gsl package if you need a library for high-level scientific numerical analysis.

gtk+ – (Version 1.2.1, 1,981K) ⓌⓈ

The gtk+ package contains the GIMP ToolKit (GTK+), a library for creating graphical user interfaces for the X Window System. GTK+ was originally written for the GIMP (GNU Image Manipulation Program) image processing program, but is now used by several other programs as well.

If you are planning on using the GIMP or another program that uses GTK+, you'll need to have the gtk+ package installed.

gtk+10 – (Version 1.0.6, 1,139K) Ⓦ Ⓢ

The X libraries originally written for the GIMP, which are now used by several other programs as well.

This RPM is a set of compatibility libraries needed to run applications linked against the 1.0 series of gtk+ and glib.

gtk-engines – (Version 0.5, 2,387K) Ⓦ

These are the graphical engines for the various GTK+ toolkit themes. Included themes are:

- Notif - Redmond95 - Pixmap - Metal (swing-like)

imlib – (Version 1.9.4, 423K) Ⓦ Ⓢ

Imlib is a display depth independent image loading and rendering library. Imlib is designed to simplify and speed up the process of loading images and obtaining X Window System drawables. Imlib provides many simple manipulation routines which can be used for common operations.

Install imlib if you need an image loading and rendering library for X11R6. You may also want to install the imlib-cfgeditor package, which will help you configure Imlib.

imlib-cfgeditor – (Version 1.9.4, 333K) Ⓦ

The imlib-cfgeditor package contains the imlib_config program, which you can use to configure the Imlib image loading and rendering library. Imlib_config can be used to control how Imlib uses color and handles gamma corrections, etc.

If you're installing the imlib package, you should also install imlib_cfgeditor.

kdelibs – (Version 1.1, 5,771K)

Libraries for the K Desktop Environment: KDE Libraries included: kdecore (KDE core library), kdeui (user interface), kfm (file manager), khtmlw (HTML widget), kfile (file access), kspell (spelling checker), jscript (javascript), kab (addressbook), kimgio (image manipulation), mediatool (sound, mixing and animation).

kdesupport – (Version 1.1, 2,138K)

Support Libraries for the K Desktop Environment, but not part of it.

Libraries included: QwSpriteField, js (javascript), uulib, mimelib, rdb; depending on the Red Hat release, libraries gdbm jpeg and gif are either also included, or the versions supplied by Red Hat are required.

This package also provides extra KDE support for Red Hat Linux: a script "usekde" that users can run to set up KDE as their default desktop (which is also done automatically when a new user is created), and scripts for activating the KDE X Display Manager "kdm" to replace "xdm".

libPropList – (Version 0.8.3, 111K)

The purpose of PL is to closely mimic the behavior of the property lists used in the GNUstep/OPENSTEP (they're formed with the NSString, NSData, NSArray and NSDictionary classes) and to be duly compatible.

PL enables programs that use configuration or preference3 files to make these compatible with GNUstep/-OPENSTEP's user defaults handling mechanism, without needing to use Objective-C or GNUstep/ OPENSTEP themselves.

libc – (Version 5.3.12, 5,259K)   *B*

Older Linux systems (including all Red Hat Linux releases between 2.0 and 4.2, inclusive) were based on libc version 5. The libc package includes the libc5 libraries and other libraries based on libc5. With these libraries installed, old applications which need them will be able to run on your glibc (libc version 6) based system.

The libc package should be installed so that you can run older applications which need libc version 5.

libelf – (Version 0.6.4, 76K)

The libelf package contains a library for accessing ELF object files. Libelf allows you to access the internals of the ELF object file format, so you can see the different sections of an ELF file.

Libelf should be installed if you need access to ELF object file internals.

libghttp – (Version 1.0.2, 85K)   *W* *S*

Library for making HTTP 1.1 requests.

libgr – (Version 2.0.13, 235K)   *W* *S*

The libgr package contains a library of functions which support programs for handling various graphics file formats, including .pbm (portable pitmaps), .pgm (portable graymaps), .pnm (portable anymaps), .ppm (portable pixmaps) and others.

libgtop – (Version 1.0.1, 431K)   *W*

A library that fetches information about the running system such as CPU and memory useage, active processes and more.

On Linux systems, this information is taken directly from the /proc filesystem while on other systems a server is used to read that information from other /dev/kmem, among others.

libgtop-examples – (Version 1.0.1, 937K)

These are examples for LibGTop, a library which retrieves information about your system, such as CPU and memory usage.

libjpeg – (Version 6b, 239K)   *W* *S*

The libjpeg package contains a library of functions for manipulating JPEG images, as well as simple client programs for accessing the libjpeg functions. Libjpeg client programs include cjpeg, djpeg, jpegtran, rdjpgcom and wrjpgcom. Cjpeg compresses an image file into JPEG format. Djpeg decompresses a JPEG file into a regular image file. Jpegtran can perform various useful transformations on JPEG files. Rdjpgcom displays any text comments included in a JPEG file. Wrjpgcom inserts text comments into a JPEG file.

libjpeg6a – (Version 6a, 137K)

This package is a library of functions that manipulate jpeg images, along with simple clients for manipulating jpeg images.

This version of the package includes only a library that is needed for preserving the backwards compatibility with previous releases of Red Hat Linux.

libpng – (Version 1.0.3, 270K) Ⓦ Ⓢ

The libpng package contains a library of functions for creating and manipulating PNG (Portable Network Graphics) image format files. PNG is a bit-mapped graphics format similar to the GIF format. PNG was created to replace the GIF format, since GIF uses a patented data compression algorithm.

Libpng should be installed if you need to manipulate PNG format image files.

libstdc++ – (Version 2.9.0, 3,421K) Ⓑ

EGCS is a free software project that intends to further the development of GNU compilers using an open development environment. The egcs package contains the egcs compiler, a compiler aimed at integrating all the optimizations and features necessary for a high-performance and stable development environment. EGCS includes the shared libraries necessary for running C++ appplications, along with additional GNU tools.

Install egcs if you'd like to use an experimental GNU compiler.

libtermcap – (Version 2.0.8, 58K) Ⓑ

The libtermcap package contains a basic system library needed to access the termcap database. The termcap library supports easy access to the termcap database, so that programs can output character-based displays in a terminal-independent manner.

libtiff – (Version 3.4, 568K) Ⓦ Ⓢ

The libtiff package contains a library of functions for manipulating TIFF (Tagged Image File Format) image format files. TIFF is a widely used file format for bitmapped images. TIFF files usually end in the .tif extension and they are often quite large.

The libtiff package should be installed if you need to manipulate TIFF format image files.

libungif – (Version 4.1.0, 80K) Ⓦ Ⓢ

The libungif package contains a shared library of functions for loading and saving GIF format image files. The libungif library can load any GIF file, but it will save GIFs only in uncompressed format (i.e., it won't use the patented LZW compression used to save "normal" compressed GIF files).

Install the libungif package if you need to manipulate GIF files. You should also install the libungif-progs package.

libxml – (Version 1.0.0, 154K) Ⓦ Ⓢ

This library allows you to manipulate XML files.

ncurses – (Version 4.2, 2,627K) Ⓑ

The curses library routines are a terminal-independent method of updating character screens with reasonable optimization. The ncurses (new curses) library is a freely distributable replacement for the discontinued 4.4BSD classic curses library.

ncurses3 – (Version 1.9.9e, 330K)

The curses library routines are a terminal-independent method of updating character screens with reasonable optimization. The ncurses (new curses) library is a freely distributable replacement for the discontinued 4.4BSD classic curses library.

newt – (Version 0.40, 128K)   ⒝

Newt is a programming library for color text mode, widget based user interfaces. Newt can be used to add stacked windows, entry widgets, checkboxes, radio buttons, labels, plain text fields, scrollbars, etc., to text mode user interfaces. This package also contains the shared library needed by programs built with newt, as well as a /usr/bin/dialog replacement called whiptail. Newt is based on the slang library.

p2c – (Version 1.22, 723K)

P2c is a system for translating Pascal programs into the C language. P2c accepts input source files in certain Pascal dialects: HP Pascal, Turbo/UCSD Pascal, DEC VAX Pascal, Oregon Software Pascal/2, Macintosh Programmer's Workshop Pascal and Sun/Berkeley Pascal. P2c outputs a set of .c and .h files which make up a C program equivalent to the original Pascal program. The C program can then be compiled using a standard C compiler, such as gcc.

Install the p2c package if you need a program for translating Pascal code into C code.

pythonlib – (Version 1.22, 236K)   ⓦⓢ

The pythonlib package contains Python code used by a variety of Red Hat Linux programs. Pythonlib includes code needed for multifield listboxes and entry widgets with non-standard keybindings, among other things.

qt – (Version 1.44, 2,093K)

Qt is a GUI software toolkit. Qt simplifies the task of writing and maintaining GUI (graphical user interface) applications for X Windows.

Qt is written in C++ and is fully object-oriented. It has everything you need to create professional GUI applications. And it enables you to create them quickly.

Qt is a multi-platform toolkit. When developing software with Qt, you can run it on the X Window System (Unix/X11) or Microsoft Windows NT and Windows 95/98. Simply recompile your source code on the platform you want.

This package contains the shared library needed to run Qt applications, as well as the README files for Qt.

readline – (Version 2.2.1, 262K)   ⒝

The readline library reads a line from the terminal and returns it, allowing the user to edit the line with standard emacs editing keys. The readline library allows programmers to provide an easy to use and more intuitive interface for users.

If you want to develop programs that will use the readline library, you'll also need to install the readline-devel package.

slang – (Version 1.2.2, 250K)   ⒝

S-Lang is an interpreted language and a programming library. The S-Lang language was designed so that it can be easily embedded into a program to provide the program with a powerful extension language. The S-Lang library, provided in this package, provides the S-Lang extension language. S-Lang's syntax resembles C, which makes it easy to recode S-Lang procedures in C if you need to.

svgalib – (Version 1.3.1, 489K) Ⓦ

The svgalib package provides the SVGAlib low-level graphics library for Linux. SVGAlib is a library which allows applications to use full screen graphics on a variety of hardware platforms. Many games and utilities use SVGAlib for their graphics.

You'll need to have the svgalib package installed if you use any of the programs which rely on SVGAlib for their graphics support.

w3c-libwww – (Version 5.2.6, 2,097K)

Libwww is a general-purpose Web API written in C for Unix and Windows (Win32). With a highly extensible and layered API, it can accommodate many different types of applications including clients, robots, etc. The purpose of libwww is to provide a highly optimized HTTP sample implementation as well as other Internet protocols and to serve as a testbed for protocol experiments.

words – (Version 2, 411K) Ⓑ

The words file is a dictionary of English words for the /usr/dict directory. Programs like ispell use this database of words to check spelling.

xpm – (Version 3.4j, 60K) ⓌⓈ

The xpm package contains the XPM pixmap library for the X Window System. The XPM library allows applications to display color, pixmapped images, and is used by many popular X programs.

zlib – (Version 1.1.3, 61K) Ⓑ

The zlib compression library provides in-memory compression and decompression functions, including integrity checks of the uncompressed data. This version of the library supports only one compression method (deflation), but other algorithms may be added later, which will have the same stream interface. The zlib library is used by many different system programs.

D.6.5   Shells

This section contains packages that are associated with the shells that provide the command-line user interface on Red Hat Linux.

ash – (Version 0.2, 361K) Ⓑ

The ash shell is a clone of Berkeley's Bourne shell. Ash supports all of the standard sh shell commands, but is considerably smaller than bash. The ash shell lacks some features (for example, command-line histories), but needs a lot less memory.

You should install ash if you need a lightweight shell with many of the same capabilities as the bash shell.

bash – (Version 1.14.7, 1,218K) Ⓑ

Bash is a GNU project sh-compatible shell or command language interpreter. Bash (Bourne Again shell) incorporates useful features from the Korn shell (ksh) and the C shell (csh). Most sh scripts can be run by bash without modification.

Bash offers several improvements over sh, including command line editing, unlimited size command history, job control, shell functions and aliases, indexed arrays of unlimited size and integer arithmetic in any base from two to 64. Bash is ultimately intended to conform to the IEEE POSIX P1003.2/ISO 9945.2 Shell and Tools standard.

Bash is the default shell for Red Hat Linux. You should install bash because of its popularity and power. You'll probably end up using it.

bash2 – (Version 2.03, 1,168K)

Bash is a GNU project sh-compatible shell or command language interpreter. Bash (Bourne Again shell) incorporates useful features from the Korn shell (ksh) and the C shell (csh). Most sh scripts can be run by bash without modification.

Bash offers several improvements over sh, including command line editing, unlimited size command history, job control, shell functions and aliases, indexed arrays of unlimited size and integer arithmetic in any base from two to 64. Bash is ultimately intended to conform to the IEEE POSIX P1003.2/ISO 9945.2 Shell and Tools standard.

mc – (Version 4.5.29, 2,449K)   Ⓦ

Midnight Commander is a visual shell much like a file manager, only with way more features. It is text mode, but also includes mouse support if you are running GPM. Its coolest feature is the ability to ftp, view tar, zip files, and poke into RPMs for specific files. :-)

pdksh – (Version 5.2.13, 402K)

The pdksh package contains PD-ksh, a clone of the Korn shell (ksh). The ksh shell is a command interpreter intended for both interactive and shell script use. Ksh's command language is a superset of the sh shell language.

Install the pdksh package if you want to use a version of the ksh shell.

sash – (Version 2.1, 402K)   Ⓑ

Sash is a simple, standalone, statically linked shell which includes simplified versions of built-in commands like ls, dd and gzip. Sash is statically linked so that it can work without shared libraries, so it is particularly useful for recovering from certain types of system failures. Sash can also be used to safely upgrade to new versions of shared libraries.

sh-utils – (Version 1.16, 355K)   Ⓑ

The GNU shell utilities are a set of useful system utilities which are often used in shell scripts. The sh-utils package includes basename (to remove the path prefix from a specified pathname), chroot (to change the root directory), date (to print/set the system time and date), dirname (to remove the last level or the filename from a given path), echo (to print a line of text), env (to display/modify the environment), expr (to evaluate expressions), factor (to print prime factors), false (to return an unsuccessful exit status), groups (to print the groups a specified user is a member of), id (to print the real/effective uid/gid), logname (to print the current login name), nice (to modify a scheduling priority), nohup (to allow a command to continue running after logging out), pathchk (to check a file name's portability), printenv (to print environment variables), printf (to format and print data), pwd (to print the current directory), seq (to print numeric sequences), sleep (to suspend execution for a specified time), stty (to print/change terminal settings), su (to become another user or the superuser), tee (to send output to multiple files), test (to evaluate an expression), true (to return a successful exit status), tty (to print the terminal name), uname (to print system information), users (to print current users' names), who (to print a list of the users who are currently logged in), whoami (to print the effective user id), and yes (to print a string indefinitely).

tcsh – (Version 6.08.00, 488K)   Ⓑ

Tcsh is an enhanced but completely compatible version of csh, the C shell. Tcsh is a command language interpreter which can be used both as an interactive login shell and as a shell script command processor. Tcsh includes a command line editor, programmable word completion, spelling correction, a history mechanism, job control and a C language like syntax.

zsh – (Version 3.0.5, 956K)

The zsh shell is a command interpreter usable as an interactive login shell and as a shell script command processor. Zsh resembles the ksh shell (the Korn shell), but includes many enhancements. Zsh supports command line editing, built-in spelling correction, programmable command completion, shell functions (with autoloading), a history mechanism and more.

Install the zsh package if you'd like to try out a different shell.

D.7   User Interface

This section contains packages that are associated with providing a user interface on Red Hat Linux.

D.7.1   Desktops

This section contains packages that are associated with the desktop environments available on Red Hat Linux.

AfterStep – (Version 1.7.75, 3,870K)   ⓌⓈ

AfterStep is a continuation of the BowMan window manager which was originally put together by Bo Yang. BowMan was based on the fvwm window manager, written by Robert Nation. Fvwm was based on code from twm. And so on... It was originally designed to emulate some of the look and feel of the NEXTSTEP user interface, but has since taken steps towards adding more useful, requested, and neat features especially in 1.4 version ! The changes which comprise AfterStep's personality were originally part of bowman development, but due to a desire to move past simple emulation and into a niche as its own valuable window manager, AfterStep designers decided to change the project name and move on.

Important features of AfterStep include:

1. Wharf: a free-floating application loader which can "Swallow" running programs and also can contain "Folders" of more applications. 2. Gradient filled TitleBars with 5 button : help/zap, action/tasks, iconize/maximise, shade/stick & close/destroy buttons 3. Gradient filled root window PopUp menus which can be configured to accomodate different tastes and styles of management 4. NEXTSTEP style icons which give a consistent look to the entire desktop 5. Pixmapped Pager with desktop pixmmaping 6. Easy to use look files, to share you desktop appearance with your friends 7. Start menu entries in a hierarchy of directories 8. WinList : a tasklist which can be horizontal or vertical 9. Many modules & asapps to give a good look to your X window station

AfterStep-APPS – (Version 990329, 1,119K)   ⓌⓈ

What's a cool window manager without some cool applets? Well... it's still cool, but these applets which can be used in the Wharf module for AfterStep or Window Maker can add both spice and productivity to your preferred window manager, such as a handy clock and information about system resources.

If you've installed the AfterStep packages, you should also install these packages. Enjoy!

AnotherLevel – (Version 0.8, 302K) Ⓦ Ⓢ

AnotherLevel is a custom configuration of the popular fvwm2 window manager. Fvwm stands for (?) virtual window manager. You can fill in the blank for the 'f': fast, flexible, friendly and fabulous all could apply. This window manager is based on TheNextLevel desktop configuration, created by Greg J. Badros, which won the 1996 Red Hat Desktop Contest.

AnotherLevel is designed to be easily configured by the user.

WindowMaker – (Version 0.51.2, 3,933K)

Window Maker is an X11 window manager which emulates the look and feel of the NeXTSTEP (TM) graphical user interface. It is relatively fast, feature rich and easy to configure and use. Window Maker is part of the official GNU project, which means that Window Maker can interoperate with other GNU projects, such as GNOME.

Window Maker allows users to switch themes 'on the fly,' to place favorite applications on either an application dock, similar to AfterStep's Wharf or on a workspace dock, a 'clip' which extends the application dock's usefulness.

You should install the WindowMaker package if you use Window Maker as your window manager or if you'd like to try using it. If you do install the WindowMaker package, you may also want to install the AfterStep-APPS package, which includes applets that will work with both AfterStep and Window Maker window managers.

control-center – (Version 1.0.5, 981K) Ⓦ

Control-center is a configuration tool for easily setting up your GNOME environment.

GNOME is the GNU Network Object Model Environment. That's a fancy name, but really GNOME is a nice GUI desktop environment.

It's a powerful, easy to configure environment which helps to make your computer easy to use.

enlightenment – (Version 0.15.5, 3,703K) Ⓦ

Enlightenment is a window manager for the X Window System that is designed to be powerful, extensible, configurable and pretty darned good looking! It is one of the more graphically intense window managers.

Enlightenment goes beyond managing windows by providing a useful and appealing graphical shell from which to work. It is open in design and instead of dictating a policy, allows the user to define their own policy, down to every last detail.

This package will install the Enlightenment window manager.

enlightenment-conf – (Version 0.15, 386K) Ⓦ

A Configuration tool for easily setting up Enlightenment

fvwm – (Version 1.24r, 573K) Ⓦ Ⓢ

FVWM (the F stands for whatever you want, but the VWM stands for Virtual Window Manager) is a window manager for the X Window System. FVWM was derived from the twm window manager. FVWM is designed to minimize memory consumption, to provide window frames with a 3D look, and to provide a simple virtual desktop. FVWM can be configured to look like Motif.

Install the fvwm package if you'd like to use the FVWM window manager. If you install fvwm, you'll also need to install fvwm2-icons.

fvwm2 – (Version 2.2, 1,730K)   Ⓦ Ⓢ

FVWM2 (the F stands for whatever you want, but the VWM stands for Virtual Window Manager) is an improved version of the FVWM window manager for the X Window System and shares the same characteristics as FVWM.

Install the fvwm2 package if you'd like to use the FVWM2 window manager. If you install fvwm2, you'll also need to install fvwm2-icons.

fvwm2-icons – (Version 2.2, 408K)   Ⓦ Ⓢ

The fvwm2-icons package contains icons, bitmaps and pixmaps used by the FVWM and FVWM2 X Window System window managers.

You'll need to install fvwm2-icons if you are installing fvwm and/or fvwm2.

gmc – (Version 4.5.29, 7,078K)   Ⓦ

Midnight Commander is a visual shell much like a file manager, only with way more features. This is the GNOME version. It's coolest feature is the ability to ftp, view tar, zip files and poke into RPMs for specific files. The GNOME version of Midnight Commander is not yet finished though. :-(

gnome-core – (Version 1.0.4, 3,253K)   Ⓦ

GNOME (GNU Network Object Model Environment) is a user-friendly set of applications and desktop tools to be used in conjunction with a window manager for the X Window System. GNOME is similar in purpose and scope to CDE and KDE, but GNOME is based completely on Open Source software. The gnome-core package includes the basic programs and libraries that are needed to install GNOME.

You should install the gnome-core package if you would like to use the GNOME desktop environment. You'll also need to install the gnome-libs package. If you want to use Linuxconf with a GNOME front end, you'll also need to install the gnome-linuxconf package.

kdebase – (Version 1.1, 11,806K)

Core applications for the K Desktop Environment. Included are: kdm (replacement for xdm), kwm (window manager), kfm (filemanager, web browser, ftp client, ...), konsole (xterm replacement), kpanel (application starter and desktop pager), kaudio (audio server), kdehelp (viewer for kde help files, info and man pages), plus other KDE components (kcheckpass, kikbd, kvt, kscreensaver, kcontrol, kfind, kfontmanager, kmenuedit, kappfinder).

PAM password authentication is supported via PAM service: kde.

switchdesk – (Version 1.5, 90K)   Ⓦ

The Desktop Switcher is a tool which enables users to easily switch between various desktop environments that they have installed. The tool includes support for GNOME, KDE, and AnotherLevel. Support for different environments on different computers is available, as well as setting a "global default."

switchdesk-gnome – (Version 1.5, 10K) [W]

Provides the desktop switching tool with a GNOME look and feel.

switchdesk-kde – (Version 1.5, 22K)

Provides the desktop switching Tool with a KDE look and feel.

wmakerconf – (Version 1.7, 569K)

Wmakerconf is a GTK+ based graphical user interface configuration tool for the Window Maker window manager. Wmakerconf supports all Window Maker attributes. Wmakerconf provides a font selection browser, a pixmap preview browser, a color selection dialog, a shortcut dialog, and a file selection dialog. Wmakerconf also provides tooltips in multiple languages.

If you use the Window Maker window manager, you should probably install the wmakerconf package, because it will make configuration a little easier.

wmconfig – (Version 0.9.3, 53K) [W] [S]

The wmconfig program is a helper program which provides output for use in configuring window managers. Wmconfig will produce a list of menu definitions for a specified X window manager (currently, FVWM2, FVWM95, AfterStep, MWM, IceWM and KDE are supported). Wmconfig's output can be placed into your .rc file or you can use the output for other configuration purposes.

xfm – (Version 1.3.2, 706K) [W]

Xfm is a file manager for the X Window System. Xfm supports moving around the directory tree, multiple windows, moving/copying/deleting files, and launching programs.

Install xfm if you would like to use a graphical file manager program.

D.7.2   X Hardware Support

This section contains packages that are associated with providing hardware support for specific video cards under Red Hat Linux.

XFree86-3DLabs – (Version 3.3.3.1, 2,211K)

X server for cards built around 3D Labs GLINT and Permedia chipsets, including GLINT 500TX with IBM RGB526 RAMDAC, GLINT MX with IBM RGB526 and IBM RGB640 RAMDAC, Permedia with IBM RGB526 RAMDAC and the Permedia 2 (classic, 2a, 2v).

XFree86-8514 – (Version 3.3.3.1, 1,743K)

If you are installing the X Window System and the video card in your system is an older IBM 8514 or a compatible from a company such as ATI, you should install XFree86-8514.

To install the X Window System, you will need to install the XFree86 package, one or more of the XFree86 fonts packages, the X11R6-contrib package, the Xconfigurator package and the XFree86-libs package.

If you are going to develop applications that run as X clients, you will also need to install the XFree86-devel package.

XFree86-AGX – (Version 3.3.3.1, 1,925K)

This is the X server for AGX-based cards, such as the Boca Vortex, Orchid Celsius, Spider Black Widow and Hercules Graphite.

If you are installing the X Window System and the video card in your system is an AGX, you'll need to install XFree86-AGX. To install the X Window System, you will need to install the XFree86 package, one or more of the XFree86 fonts packages, the X11R6-contrib package, the Xconfigurator package and the XFree86-libs package.

Finally, if you are going to develop applications that run as X clients, you will also need to install the XFree86-devel package.

XFree86-FBDev – (Version 3.3.3.1, 2,001K)

This is the X server for the generic frame buffer device used on Amiga, Atari and Macintosh/m68k machines.

Support for Intel and Alpha architectures is included in the Linux 2.2 kernel, as well.

XFree86-I128 – (Version 3.3.3.1, 2,182K)

This is the X server for the #9 Imagine 128 and similar video boards.

XFree86-Mach32 – (Version 3.3.3.1, 1,886K)

XFree86-Mach32 is the X server package for video cards built around ATI's Mach32 chip, including the ATI Graphics Ultra Pro and Ultra Plus.

If you are installing the X Window System and the video card in your system is based on the Mach32 chip, you need to install XFree86-Mach32. You will also need to install the XFree86 package, one or more of the XFree86 fonts packages, the X11R6-contrib package, the Xconfigurator package and the XFree86-libs package. And, finally, if you are going to develop applications that run as X clients, you will also need to install XFree86-devel.

XFree86-Mach64 – (Version 3.3.3.1, 2,008K)

XFree86-Mach64 is the server package for cards based on ATI's Mach64 chip, such as the Graphics Xpression, GUP Turbo, and WinTurbo cards. Note that this server is known to have problems with some Mach64 cards. Check http://www.xfree86.org for current information on updating this server.

If you are installing the X Window System and the video card in your system is based on the Mach64 chip, you need to install XFree86-Mach64. You will also need to install the XFree86 package, one or more of the XFree86 fonts packages, the X11R6-contrib package, the Xconfigurator package and the XFree86-libs package. And, finally, if you are going to be developing applications that run as X clients, you will also need to install XFree86-devel.

XFree86-Mach8 – (Version 3.3.3.1, 1,755K)

XFree86-Mach 8 is the X server for video cards built around ATI's Mach8 chip, including the ATI 8514 Ultra and Graphics Ultra.

If you are installing the X Window System and the video card in your system is based on the Mach8 chip, you need to install XFree86-Mach8. You will also need to install the XFree86 package, one or more of the XFree86 fonts packages, the X11R6-contrib package, the Xconfigurator package and the XFree86-libs package. And, finally, if you are going to be developing applications that run as X clients, you will also need to install XFree86-devel.

XFree86-Mono – (Version 3.3.3.1, 2,052K)

XFree86-Mono is a generic monochrome (2 color) server for VGA cards. XFree86-Mono will work for nearly all VGA compatible cards, but will only support a monochrome display.

If you are installing the X Window System and your VGA card is not currently supported, you should install and try either XFree86-Mono or XFree86-VGA16, depending upon the capabilities of your display. You will also need to install the XFree86 package, one or more of the XFree86 fonts packages, the X11R6-contrib package, the Xconfigurator package and the XFree86-libs package. And, finally, if you are going to develop applications that run as X clients, you will also need to install XFree86-devel.

XFree86-P9000 – (Version 3.3.3.1, 1,945K)

XFree86-P9000 is the X server for video cards built around the Weitek P9000 chip, such as most Diamond Viper cards and the Orchid P9000 card.

If you are installing the X Window System and you have a Weitek P9000 based video card, you should install XFree86-P9000. You will also need to install the XFree86 package, one or more of the XFree86 fonts packages, the X11R6-contrib package, the Xconfigurator package and the XFree86-libs package. And, finally, if you are going to develop applications that run as X clients, you will also need to install XFree86-devel.

XFree86-S3 – (Version 3.3.3.1, 2,431K)

XFree86-S3 is the X server for video cards based on S3 chips, including most #9 cards, many Diamond Stealth cards, Orchid Farenheits, Mirco Crystal 8S, most STB cards, and some motherboards with built-in graphics accelerators (such as the IBM ValuePoint line). Note that if you have an S3 ViRGE based video card, you'll need XFree86-S3V instead of XFree86-S3.

If you are installing the X Window System and you have a video card based on an S3 chip, you should install XFree86-S3. You will also need to install the XFree86 package, one or more XFree86 fonts packages, the X11R6-contrib package, the Xconfigurator package and the XFree86-libs package. And, finally, if you are going to develop applications that run as X clients, you will also need to install XFree86-devel.

XFree86-S3V – (Version 3.3.3.1, 2,160K)

XFree86-S3V is the X server for video cards based on the S3 ViRGE chipset.

If you are installing the X Window System and you have a video card based on an S3 ViRGE chip, you should install XFree86-S3V. You will also need to install the XFree86 package, one or more of the XFree86 fonts packages, the X11R6-contrib package, the Xconfigurator package and the XFree86-libs package. And, finally, if you are going to develop applications that run as X clients, you will also need to install XFree86-devel.

XFree86-SVGA – (Version 3.3.3.1, 3,097K)

X server for most simple framebuffer SVGA devices, including cards built from ET4000 chips, Cirrus Logic chips, Chips and Technologies laptop chips, Trident 8900 and 9000 chips, and Matrox chips. It works for Diamond Speedstar, Orchid Kelvins, STB Nitros and Horizons, Genoa 8500VL, most Actix boards, the Spider VLB Plus, etc. It also works for many other chips and cards, so try this server if you are having problems.

XFree86-VGA16 – (Version 3.3.3.1, 1,944K)

XFree86-VGA16 is a generic 16 color server for VGA boards. XFree86-VGA16 will work on nearly all VGA style graphics boards, but will only support a low resolution, 16 color display.

If you are installing the X Window System and your VGA video card is not specifically supported by another X server package, you should install either XFree86-Mono or XFree86-VGA16, depending upon the capabilities of your display. You will also need to install the XFree86 package, one or more of the XFree86 fonts packages, the X11R6-contrib package, the Xconfigurator package and the XFree86-libs package. And, finally, if you are going to be develop applications that run as X clients, you will also need to install XFree86-devel.

XFree86-W32 – (Version 3.3.3.1, 1,793K)

XFree86-W32 is the X server for cards built around ET4000/W32 chips, including the Genoa 8900 Phantom 32i, the Hercules Dynamite, the LeadTek WinFast S200, the Sigma Concorde, the STB LightSpeed, the TechWorks Thunderbolt, and the ViewTop PCI.

If you are installing the X Window System and your VGA video card is based on the ET4000/W32 chipset, you should install XFree86-W32. You will also need to install the XFree86 package, one or more of the XFree86 fonts packages, the X11R6-contrib package, the Xconfigurator package and the XFree86-libs package. And, finally, if you are going to develop applications that run as X clients, you will also need to install XFree86-devel.

XFree86-XF86Setup – (Version 3.3.3.1, 596K)

XF86Setup is a graphical user interface configuration tool for setting up and configuring XFree86 servers. XF86Setup can configure video settings, keyboard layouts, mouse types, etc. XF86Setup can't be used with non-VGA compatible video cards, with fixed-frequency monitors, or with OS/2.

Install XF86Setup if you have used it before and prefer to keep using it to configure your X server. If you do not have a preference for XF86Setup, you should instead install and use Xconfigurator, Red Hat's graphical user interface configuration tool for the X Window System.

XFree86-Xnest – (Version 3.3.3.1, 2,242K)

Xnest is an X Window System server which runs in an X window. Xnest is a 'nested' window server, actually a client of the real X server, which manages windows and graphics requests for Xnest, while Xnest manages the windows and graphics requests for its own clients.

You will need to install Xnest if you require an X server which will run as a client of your real X server (perhaps for testing purposes).

XFree86-Xvfb – (Version 3.3.3.1, 2,707K)

Xvfb (X Virtual Frame Buffer) is an X Windows System server that is capable of running on machines with no display hardware and no physical input devices. Xvfb emulates a dumb framebuffer using virtual memory. Xvfb doesn't open any devices, but behaves otherwise as an X display. Xvfb is normally used for testing servers. Using Xvfb, the mfb or cfb code for any depth can be exercised without using real hardware that supports the desired depths. Xvfb has also been used to test X clients against unusual depths and screen configurations, to do batch processing with Xvfb as a background rendering engine, to do load testing, to help with porting an X server to a new platform, and to provide an unobtrusive way of running applications which really don't need an X server but insist on having one.

If you need to test your X server or your X clients, you may want to install Xvfb for that purpose.

Xconfigurator – (Version 4.1.3, 433K)   Ⓦ Ⓢ

Xconfigurator is a full-screen, menu-driven program which walks you through setting up your X server. Xconfigurator is based on the sources for xf86config, a utility from XFree86.

You should install Xconfigurator if you are installing the X Window System.

D.7.3   X

This section contains packages associated with the X Window System graphical user interface.

X11R6-contrib – (Version 3.3.2, 474K)   Ⓦ Ⓢ

If you want to use the X Window System, you should install X11R6-contrib. This package holds many useful programs from the X Window System, version 11, release 6 contrib tape. The programs, contributed by various users, include listres, xbiff, xedit, xeyes, xcalc, xload and xman, among others.

You will also need to install the XFree86 package, the XFree86 package which corresponds to your video card, one or more of the XFree86 fonts packages, the Xconfigurator package and the XFree86-libs package.

Finally, if you are going to develop applications that run as X clients, you will also need to install XFree86-devel.

XFree86-100dpi-fonts – (Version 3.3.3.1, 1,228K)

If you're going to use the X Window System and you have a high resolution monitor capable of 100 dpi, you should install XFree86-100dpi-fonts. This package contains a set of 100 dpi fonts used on most Linux systems.

If you are installing the X Window System, you will also need to install the XFree86 package, the XFree86 package corresponding to your video card, the X11R6- contrib package, the Xconfigurator package and the XFree86-libs package. If you need to display certain fonts, you may also need to install other XFree86 fonts packages.

And finally, if you are going to develop applications that run as X clients, you will also need to install the XFree86-devel package.

XFree86 – (Version 3.3.3.1, 14,458K)   Ⓦ Ⓢ

If you want to install the X Window System (TM) on your machine, you'll need to install XFree86.

The X Window System provides the base technology for developing graphical user interfaces. Simply stated, X draws the elements of the GUI on the user's screen and builds methods for sending user interactions back to the application. X also supports remote application deployment–running an application on another computer while viewing the input/output on your machine. X is a powerful environment which supports many different applications, such as games, programming tools, graphics programs, text editors, etc. XFree86 is the version of X which runs on Linux, as well as other platforms.

This package contains the basic fonts, programs and documentation for an X workstation. However, this package doesn't provide the program which you will need to drive your video hardware. To control your video card, you'll need the particular X server package which corresponds to your computer's video card.

In addition to installing this package, you will need to install the XFree86 package which corresponds to your video card, the X11R6-contrib package, the Xconfigurator package and the XFree86-libs package. You may also need to install one of the XFree86 fonts packages.

And finally, if you are going to develop applications that run as X clients, you will also need to install XFree86-devel.

XFree86-75dpi-fonts – (Version 3.3.3.1, 1,060K)   Ⓦ Ⓢ

XFree86-75dpi-fonts contains the 75 dpi fonts used on most X Window Systems. If you're going to use the X Window System, you should install this package, unless you have a monitor which can support 100 dpi resolution. In that case, you may prefer the 100dpi fonts available in the XFree86-100dpi-fonts package.

You may also need to install other XFree86 font packages.

To install the X Window System, you will need to install the XFree86 package, the XFree86 package corresponding to your video card, the X11R6-contrib package, the Xconfigurator package and the XFree86-libs package.

Finally, if you are going to develop applications that run as X clients, you will also need to install the XFree86-devel package.

XFree86-ISO8859-2 – (Version 1.0, 77K)

If you use the X Window System and you want to display Central European fonts, you should install the XFree86-ISO8859-2 package.

This package contains a full set of Central European fonts, in compliance with the ISO 8859-2 standard. The fonts included in this package are distributed free of charge and can be used freely, subject to the accompanying copyright:

Copyright (c) 1996, 1997 BIZNET Poland, Inc. All Rights Reserved. BIZNET is a registered trademark of BIZNET Poland, Inc.

You may also need to install one or more other XFree86 fonts packages.

To install the X Window System, you will need to install the XFree86 package, the XFree86 package which corresponds to your video card, the X11R6-contrib package, the Xconfigurator package and the XFree86-libs package.

Finally, if you are going to develop applications that run as X clients, you will also need to install XFree86-devel.

XFree86-ISO8859-2-100dpi-fonts – (Version 1.0, 1,003K)

The XFree86-ISO8859-2-100dpi-fonts package includes Central European (ISO 8859-2) fonts, in 100 dpi resolution, for the X Window System.

If you need to display the special characters used by Central European languages on your X Window System, and your monitor can support 100 dpi resolution, you should install the XFree86-ISO8859-2-100dpi-fonts package. You may need to install one or more of the other XFree86 fonts packages, as well. To install the X Window System, you will need to install the XFree86 package, the XFree86 video card package which corresponds to your video card, the X11R6-contrib package, the Xconfigurator package and the XFree86-libs package. If you're going to develop applications which run as X clients, you'll also need to install XFree86-devel.

XFree86-ISO8859-2-75dpi-fonts – (Version 1.0, 877K)

The XFree86-ISO8859-2-75dpi-fonts package contains a set of Central European language fonts in 75 dpi resolution for the X Window System. If you have a high resolution monitor capable of supporting 100 dpi, you should install the 100 dpi version of this package instead.

If you are installing the X Window System and you need to display Central European language characters in 75 dpi resolution, you should install this package. You may also need to install one or more of the other XFree86 fonts packages as well. To install the X Window System, you will need to install the XFree86 package, the XFree86 video card package that corresponds to your video card, the X11R6-contrib package, the Xconfigurator package and the XFree86-libs package. If you are going to develop applications that will run as X clients, you will also need to install XFree86-devel.

XFree86-ISO8859-2-Type1-fonts – (Version 1.0, 1,905K)

The XFree86-ISO8859-2-Type1-fonts package contains Central European Type 1 fonts for the X Window System. This set of fonts is known as the ulT1mo (or ultimo) collection. All of the included fonts are copyrighted to their authors and freeware. Original fonts were taken from the Internet or CDs.

If you need to display Central European language fonts on your X Window System, you should install the XFree86-ISO8859-2-Type1-fonts package. You may need to also install one or more of the other XFree86 fonts packages. To install the X Window System, you will need to install the XFree86 package, the XFree86 video card package which corresponds to your video card, the X11R6-contrib package, the Xconfigurator package and the XFree86-libs package. Finally, if you are going to develop applications that will run as X clients, you'll need to install XFree86-devel.

XFree86-ISO8859-9-100dpi-fonts – (Version 2.1.2, 1,142K)

The XFree86-ISO8859-9-100dpi-fonts package contains a set of Turkish language fonts in 100 dpi resolution and in accordance with the ISO8859-9 standard for the X Window System.

If you need to display Turkish language fonts for the X Window System, and your monitor is capable of supporting 100 dpi resolution, you should install this package. You may also need to install one or more of the other XFree86 fonts packages. To install the X Window System, you will need to install the XFree86 package, the XFree86 video card package which corresponds to your video card, the X11R6-contrib package, the Xconfigurator package and the XFree86-libs package.

If you are going to develop applications that will run as X clients, you will also need to install XFree86-devel.

XFree86-ISO8859-9 – (Version 2.1.2, 85K)

The XFree86-ISO8859-9 package contains Turkish language (ISO8859-9) terminal fonts, modmaps for the Q and F style of Turkish keyboard mappings and a simple utility for changing the modmap.

If you need to display Turkish language fonts on your X Window System, or if you need a to use the Q and F style keyboard mappings, you should install the XFree86-ISO8859-9 package. You may also need to install other XFree86 font packages. If you're installing the X Window System, you'll need to install the XFree86 package, the XFree86 video card package which corresponds to your video card, the X11R6-contrib package, the Xconfigurator package and the XFree86-libs package. If you're going to develop applications that run as X clients, you will also need to install XFree86-devel.

XFree86-ISO8859-9-75dpi-fonts – (Version 2.1.2, 1,032K)

The XFree86-ISO8859-9-75dpi-fonts package contains a set of Turkish language (ISO8859-9) fonts in 75 dpi resolution for the X Window System.

If you need to display Turkish language fonts on your X Window System, you should install this package. If your monitor is capable of supporting 100 dpi resolution, you should instead install the 100 dpi font package. You may also need to install one or more of the other XFree86 fonts packages. If you're installing the X Window System, you need to install the XFree86 package, the XFree86 video card package which corresponds to your video card, the X11R6-contrib package, the Xconfigurator package and the XFree86-libs package. Finally, if you are going to develop applications that will run as X clients, you will also need to install XFree86-devel.

XFree86-cyrillic-fonts – (Version 3.3.3.1, 301K)

The Cyrillic fonts included with XFree86 3.3.2 and higher. Those who use a language requiring the Cyrillic character set should install this package.

gdm – (Version 1.0.0, 246K) W

GNOME Display Manager allows you to log into your system with the X Window System running. It is highly configurable, allowing you to run several different X sessions at once on your local machine, and can manage login connections from remote machines as well.

gqview – (Version 0.6.0, 186K) W

GQview is a browser for graphics files. Offering single click viewing of your graphics files. Includes thumbnail view, zoom and filtering features. And external editor support.

kterm – (Version 6.2.0, 154K)

The kterm package provides a terminal emulator for the Kanji Japanese character set.

Install kterm if you need a Kanji character set terminal emulator. You'll also need to have the X Window System installed.

rxvt – (Version 2.6.PRE2, 490K) W S

Rxvt is a color VT102 terminal emulator for the X Window System. Rxvt is intended to be an xterm replacement for users who don't need the more esoteric features of xterm, like Tektronix 4014 emulation, session logging and toolkit style configurability. Since it doesn't support those features, rxvt uses much less swap space than xterm uses. This is a significant advantage on a machine which is serving a large number of X sessions.

The rxvt package should be installed on any machine which serves a large number of X sessions, if you'd like to improve that machine's performance.

urw-fonts – (Version 1.1, 2,160K) W S

Free versions of the 35 standard PostScript fonts. With newer releases of ghostscript quality versions of the standard 35 Type 1 PostScript fonts are shipped. They were donated and licenced under the GPL by URW. The fonts.dir was specially made to match the original Adobe names of the fonts, e.g. Times, Helvetica etc. With X, LaTeX, or Ghostscript, these fonts are a must to have!

x3270 – (Version 3.1.1.6, 561K)

The x3270 program opens a window in the X Window System which emulates the actual look of an IBM 3278/3279 terminal, commonly used with mainframe applications. x3270 also allows you to telnet to an IBM host from the x3270 window.

Install the x3270 package if you need to access IBM hosts using an IBM 3278/3279 terminal emulator.

xinitrc – (Version 2.1, 8K) W S

The xinitrc package contains the xinitrc file, a script which is used to configure your X Window System session or to start a window manager.

The xinitrc package should be installed if you use the X Window System.

General Parameters and Modules

This appendix is provided to illustrate *some* of the possible parameters that may be needed by certain drivers. It should be noted that, in most cases, these additional parameters are unnecessary. Also included is a list of network hardware and the associated modules required by that hardware.

Please keep in mind that if a device you are attempting to use requires one of these parameters, and support for that device is *not* compiled into the kernel, the traditional method of adding the parameter to the LILO boot command will not work. Drivers loaded as modules require that these parameters are specified when the module is loaded. The Red Hat Linux installation program gives you the option to specify module parameters when a driver is loaded.

For more information concerning the device support compiled into the kernel used by the Red Hat Linux installation program, please refer to Section 2.9 on page 32.

Please Note: Not all of the cards that are listed are supported. Please check the hardware compatibility list on Red Hat Software's World Wide Web site at
`http://www.redhat.com/support/docs/hardware.html` to make sure your card is supported.

One of the more commonly used parameters, the `hdX=cdrom` parameter, *can* be entered at the boot prompt, as it deals with support for IDE/ATAPI CD-ROMs, which is part of the kernel.

In the tables below, most modules without any parameters listed are either able to auto-probe to find the hardware, or require you to manually change settings in the module source code, and recompile.

E.1 CD-ROM parameters

Hardware	Module	Parameters
ATAPI/IDE CD-ROM Drives		hdX=cdrom
Aztech CD268-01A, Orchid CD-3110, Okano/Wearnes CDD110, Conrad TXC, CyCDROM CR520 CyCDROM CR540 (non-IDE)	aztcd.o	aztcd=io_port
Sony CDU 31A or 33A CD-ROM	cdu31a.o	cdu31a=io_port,IRQ[,PAS] cdu31a_port=base_addr cdu31a_irq=irq
Philips/LMS CDROM drive 206 with cm260 host adapter card	cm206.o	cm206=io_port,IRQ
Goldstar R420 CD-ROM	gscd.o	gscd=io_port
ISP16, MAD16, or Mozart sound card CD-ROM interface (OPTi 82C928 and OPTi 82C929) with Sanyo/Panasonic, Sony, or Mitsumi drives	isp16.o	isp16=io_port,IRQ,dma,drive_type isp16_cdrom_base=io_port isp16_cdrom_irq=IRQ isp16_cdrom_dma=dma isp16_cdrom_type=drive_type
Mitsumi CD-ROM, Standard	mcd.o	mcd=io_port,IRQ
Mitsumi CD-ROM, Experimental	mcdx.o	mcdx=io_port_1,IRQ_1,io_port_n,IRQ_n
Optics storage 8000 AT CD-ROM "Dolphin" drive; Lasermate CR328A	optcd.o	optcd =io_port
SB Pro 16 compatible	sbpcd.o	sbpcd=io_port,sb_pro_Setting
Sanyo CDR-H94A	sjcd.o	sjcd=io_port sjcd_base=io_port
Sony CDU-535 & 531 (some Procomm drives)	sonycd535.o	sonycd535=io_port

Here are some examples of these modules in use:

Configuration	Example
ATAPI CD-ROM, jumpered as master on 2nd IDE channel	hdc=cdrom
non-IDE Mitsumi CD-ROM on port 340, IRQ 11	mcd=0x340,11
Three non-IDE Mitsumi CD-ROM drives using the experimental driver, io ports 300, 304, and 320 with IRQs 5, 10 and 11	mcdx=0x300,5,0x304,10,0x320,11
Sony CDU 31 or 33 at port 340, no IRQ	cdu31=0x340,0

Configuration (module arguments for above)	Example
	cdu31_port=0x340 cdu31a.irq=0
Aztech CD-ROM at port 220	aztcd=0x220
Panasonic-type CD-ROM on a SoundBlaster interface at port 220	sbpcd=0x230,1
Phillips/LMS cm206 and cm260 at IO 340 and IRQ 11	cm206=0x340,11
Goldstar R420 at IO 300	gscd=0x300
Mitsumi drive on a MAD16 soundcard at IO Addr 330 and IRQ 1, probing DMA	isp16=0x330,11,0,Mitsumi
Sony CDU 531 at IO address 320	sonycd535=0x320

Please Note: Most newer Sound Blaster cards come with IDE interfaces. For these cards, you do not need to use sbpcd parameters, only use hdx parameters.

E.2 SCSI parameters

Hardware	Module	Parameters
NCR53c810/820/720, NCR53c700/710/700-66	53c7,8xx.o	
AM53/79C974 PC-SCSI Driver Qlogic PCI-Basic	AM53C974.o	AM53C974=host-scsi-id, target-scsi-id,max-rate, max-offset
Most Buslogic (now Mylex) cards with "BT" part number	BusLogic.o	BusLogic_Options=option,option,... (See /usr/src/linux/drivers/scsi/README.BusLogic)
	NCR53c406a.o	ncr53c406a=io-port[,IRQ[,FASTPIO]] ncr53c406a io=io-port irq=IRQ fastpio=FASTPIO
Advansys SCSI Cards	advansys.o	
Adaptec AHA 152x	aha152x.o	aha152x=io_base,IRQ,scsiid,reconnect,parity
Adaptec AHA 1542	aha1542.o	aha1542=io_base,buson,busoff,dmaspeed
Adaptec AHA 1740	aha1740.o	
Adaptec AHA-274x, AHA-284x, AHA-29xx, AHA-394x, AHA-398x, AHA-274x, AHA-274xT, AHA-2842, AHA-2910B, AHA-2920C, AHA-2930/U/U2, AHA-2940/W/U/UW/AU/U2W/U2/U2B/, U2BOEM, AHA-2944D/WD/UD/UWD,	aic7xxx.o	aic7xxx=string

Hardware	Module	Parameters
AHA-2950U2/W/B, AHA-3940/U/W/UW/, AUW/U2W/U2B, AHA-3950U2D, AHA-3985/U/W/UW, AIC-777x, AIC-785x, AIC-786x, AIC-787x, AIC-788x, AIC-789x, AIC-3860		
Data Technology Corp DTC3180/3280	dtc.o	
DTP SCSI host adapters (EATA/DMA) PM2011B/9X ISA, PM2021A/9X ISA, PM2012A, PM2012B, PM2022A/9X EISA, PM2122A/9X, PM2322A/9X, SmartRAID PM3021, PM3222, PM3224	eata.o	eata=port0,port1,port2,...options eata io_port=port0,port1,port2,...option=value
DTP SCSI Adapters PM2011, PM2021, PM2041, PM3021, PM2012B, PM2022, PM2122, PM2322, PM2042, PM3122, PM3222, PM3332, PM2024, PM2124, PM2044, PM2144, PM3224, PM3334	eata_dma.o	
DTP EATA-PIO boards	eata-pio.o	
Future Domain TMC-16x0- based cards TMC-1800, TMC-18C50, TMC-18C30, TMC-36C70, Future Domain TMC-1650, TMC-1660, TMC-1670, TMC-1680, TMC-1610M/MER/MEX, TMC-3260 (PCI), Quantum ISA-200S, ISA-250MG Adaptec AHA-2920A (PCI) (NOT AHA-2920C)	fdomain.o	fdomain=io_base,IRQ[,ADAPTER_ID]
NCR5380 and NCR53c400 cards	g_NCR5380.o	ncr5380=io_port,IRQ,dma ncr53c400=io_port,IRQ ncr5380 io=io_port irq=IRQ dma=dma ncr53c400 io=io_port irq=IRQ
GDT ISA/EISA/PCI Disk Array Controller	gdth.o	gdth=IRQ0,IRQ1,IRQ2,...options:values
IOMEGA MatchMaker parallel port SCSI adapter	imm.o	
Always IN2000 ISA SCSI card	in2000.o	in2000=setup_string:value in2000 setup_string=value
Initio INI-9X00U/UW SCSI host adapters	initio.o	
AMI MegaRAID 418, 428, 438, 466, 762	megaraid.o	
NCR SCSI controllers with 810/810A/815/ 825/825A/860/875/876/895 chipsets	ncr53c8xx.o	ncr53c8xx=option1:value1,option2:value2,... ncr53c8xx="option1:value1 option2:value2..."
Pro Audio Spectrum/Studio 16	pas16.o	pas16=port,irq
IOMEGA PPA3 parallel port SCSI host adapter	ppa.o	

Hardware	Module	Parameters
Perceptive Solutions PSI-2401 EIDE	psi240i.o	
QLogic Fast SCSI FASXXX ISA/VLB/PCMCIA	qlogicfas.o	
QLogic ISP2100 SCSI-FCP	qlogicfc.o	
QLogic ISP1020 Intelligent SCSI cards IQ-PCI, IQ-PCI-10, IQ-PCI-D	qlogicisp.o	
Seagate ST01/ST02	seagate.o	controller_type=1 base_address=base_addr irq=irq
Future Domain TMC-885, TMC-950	seagate.o	controller_type=2 base_address=base_addr irq=irq
Cards with the sym53c416 chipset	sym53c416.o	sym53c416=PORTBASE[,IRQ] sym53c416 io=PORTBASE irq=IRQ
Trantor T128/T128F/T228 SCSI Host Adapter	t128.o	
Tekram DC390 and other AMD53C974A based PCI SCSI adapters	tmscsim.o	tmscsim=ID,SPEED
UltraStor 14F/34F SCSI host adapters (14F, 24F, 34F)	u14-34f.o	u14-34f=io_port1,io_port2,...io_port10 u14-34f io=io_port1,io_port2,...io_port10
UltraStor 14F, 24F, and 34F	ultrastor.o	
WD7000-FASST2,WD7000-ASC, WD7000-AX/MX/EX	wd7000.o	wd7000=IRQ,dma,io_port wd7000 io=io_port irq=IRQ dma=dma

Here are some examples of these modules in use:

Configuration	Example
Adaptec AHA1522 at port 330, IRQ 11, SCSI ID 7	aha152x=0x330,11,7
Adaptec AHA1542 at port 330	bases=0x330
Future Domain TMC-800 at CA000, IRQ 10	controller_type=2 base_address=0xca000 irq=10

When a parameter has commas, make sure you do *not* put a space after a comma.

E.3 Ethernet parameters

Hardware	Module	Parameters
3Com 3c501	3c501.o	3c501=io_port,IRQ
3Com 3c503 and 3c503/16	3c503.o	3c503=io_port,IRQ

Hardware	Module	Parameters
3Com EtherLink Plus (3c505)	3c505.o	3c503 io=io_port_1,io_port_n irq=IRQ_1,IRQ_n 3c505=io_port,IRQ,DMA 3c505 io=io_port_1,io_port_n irq=IRQ_1,IRQ_2 dma=dma_1,dma_n
3Com EtherLink 16	3c507.o	3c507=io_port,IRQ 3c507 io=io_port irq=IRQ
3Com EtherLink III	3c509.o	3c509=IRQ
3Com ISA EtherLink XL "Corkscrew"	3c515.o	
3Com EtherLink PCI III/XL Vortex (3c590, 3c592, 3c595, 3c597) Boomerang (3c900, 3c905, 3c595)	3c59x.o	
Apricot 680x0 VME, 82596 chipset	82596.c	82596=IRQ 82596 irq=IRQ
Ansel Communications AC3200 EISA	ac3200.o	ac3200=io_port,IRQ ac3200 io=io_port_1,io_port_n irq=IRQ_1,IRQ_n
Alteon AceNIC Gigabit Ethernet driver	acenic.o	acenic=trace,link acenic trace=trace link=val
Allied Telesis AT1700	at1700.o	at1700=io_port,IRQ at1700 io=io_port irq=IRQ
Tangent ATB-II, Novel NL-10000, Daystar Digital LT-200, Dayna DL2000, DaynaTalk PC (HL), COPS LT-95, Farallon PhoneNET PC II, III	cops.o	cops=io_port,IRQ cops io=io_port irq=IRQ
Modular driver for the COSA or SRP synchronous serial card	cosa.c	cosa=io_port,IRQ,dma
Crystal LAN CS8900/CS8920	cs89x0.o	cs89x0=io_port,IRQ,MEDIA_TYPE cs89x0 io=io_port irq=IRQ media=TYPE
EtherWORKS DE425 TP/COAX EISA, DE434 TP PCI, DE435/450 TP/COAX/AUI PCI DE500 10/100 PCI Kingston, LinkSys, SMC8432, SMC9332, Znyx31[45], and Znyx346 10/100 cards with DC21040 (no SROM), DC21041[A], DC21140[A], DC21142, DC21143 chipsets	de4x5.o	de4x5=io_port de4x5 io=io_port de4x5 args='ethX[fdx] autosense=MEDIA_STRING'
D-Link DE-600 Ethernet Pocket Adapter	de600.o	

Hardware	Module	Parameters
D-Link DE-620 Ethernet Pocket Adapter	de620.o	de620 io=io_port irq=IRQ bnc=1 utp=1
DIGITAL DEPCA & EtherWORKS DEPCA, DE100, DE101, DE200 Turbo, DE201Turbo DE202 Turbo TP/BNC, DE210, DE422 EISA	depca.o	depca=io_port,IRQ depca io=io_port irq=IRQ
Digi Intl. RightSwitch SE-X EISA and PCI	dgrs.o	
Cabletron E2100 series ethercards	e2100.o	e2100=io_port,IRQ e2100 io=io_port irq=IRQ
Intel i82595 ISA EtherExpressPro10/10+ driver	eepro.o	eepro=io_port,IRQ,mem eepro io=io_port irq=IRQ mem=mem
Intel i82557/i82558 PCI EtherExpressPro driver	eepro100.o	
Intel EtherExpress 16 (i82586)	eexpress.o	eexpress=io_port,IRQ eexpress io=io_port irq=IRQ
SMC EtherPower II 9432 PCI (83c170/175 EPIC series)	epic100.o	
Racal-Interlan ES3210 EISA Network Adapter	es3210.o	es3210=io_port,IRQ,mem es3210 io=io_port irq=IRQ mem=mem
ICL EtherTeam 16i/32	eth16i.o	eth16i=io_port,mediatype eth16i ioaddr=io_port mediatype=type
EtherWORKS 3 (DE203, DE204 and DE205)	ewrk3.o	ewrk=io_port,IRQ ewrk io=io_port irq=IRQ
Fujitsu FMV-181/182/183/184	fmv18x.o	fmv18x=io_port,IRQ fmv18x io=io_port irq=IRQ
Modular driver for the Comtrol Hostess SV11	hostess_sv11.o	hostess_sv11=io_port,IRQ,DMABIT hostess_sv11 io=io_port irq=IRQ dma=DMABIT
HP PCLAN/plus	hp-plus.o	hp-plus=io_port,IRQ hp-plus io=io_port irq=IRQ
HP LAN Ethernet	hp.o	hp=io_port,IRQ hp io=io_port irq=IRQ
100VG-AnyLan Network Adapters HP J2585B, J2585A, J2970, J2973, J2573 Compex ReadyLink ENET100-VG4, FreedomLine 100/VG	hp100.o	hp100=io_port,name hp100 hp100_port=io_port hp100_name=name
IBM Token Ring 16/4	ibmtr.o	ibmtr=io_port,IRQ,mem ibmtr io=io_port irq=IRQ mem=mem

Hardware	Module	Parameters
AMD LANCE/PCnet Allied Telesis AT1500, HP J2405A, NE2100, NE2500	lance.o	lance=io-port,IRQ,dma lance io=io-port.1,io-port.n irq=IRQ.1,IRQ.2 dma=dma.1,dma.n
Mylex LNE390 EISA cards (LNE390A, LNE390B)	lne390.o	lne390=io-port,IRQ,mem lne390 io=io-port irq=IRQ mem=mem
	ltpc.o	ltpc=io-port,IRQ ltpc io=io-port irq=IRQ
NE1000 / NE2000 (non-pci)	ne.o	ne=io-port,IRQ ne io=io-port irq=IRQ
PCI NE2000 cards RealTek RTL-8029, Winbond 89C940, Compex RL2000, KTI ET32P2, NetVin, NV5000SC, Via 82C926, SureCom NE34,	ne2k-pci.o	
Novell NE3210 EISA Network Adapter	ne3210.o	ne3210=io-port,IRQ,mem ne3210 io=io-port irq=IRQ mem=mem
MiCom-Interlan NI5010 ethercard	ni5010.o	ni5010=io-port,IRQ ni5010 io=io-port irq=IRQ
NI5210 card (i82586 Ethernet chip)	ni52.o	ni52=io-port,IRQ ni52 io=io-port irq=IRQ
NI6510, ni6510 EtherBlaster	ni65.o	ni65=io-port,IRQ,dma ni65 io=io-port irq=IRQ dma=dma
AMD PCnet32 and AMD PCnetPCI	pcnet32.o	
RedCreek Communications PCI	rcpci.o	
RealTek cards using RTL8129 or RTL8139 Fast Ethernet chipsets	rtl8139.o	
Sangoma S502/S508 multi-protocol FR	sdla.o	
Sangoma S502A, ES502A, S502E, S503, S507, S508, S509	sdladrv.o	
SysKonnect Token Ring ISA/PCI Adapter, TR4/16(+) ISA or PCI, TR4/16 PCI, and older SK NET TR4/16 ISA cards	sktr.o	sktr=io-port,IRQ,mem sktr io=io-port irq=IRQ mem=mem
SMC Ultra and SMC EtherEZ ISA ethercard (8K, 83c790)	smc-ultra.o	smc-ultra=io-port,IRQ smc-ultra io=io-port irq=IRQ
SMC Ultra32 EISA Ethernet card (32K)	smc-ultra32.o	
SMC 9000 series of Ethernet cards	smc9194.o	smc9194=io-port,IRQ smc9194 io=io-port irq=IRQ ifport=[0,1,2]

Hardware	Module	Parameters

Compaq Netelligent 10/100 TX PCI UTP
Compaq Netelligent 10 T PCI UTP
Compaq Integrated NetFlex 3/P
Compaq Netelligent Dual 10/100 TX PCI UTP
Compaq Netelligent Integrated 10/100 TX UTP
Compaq Netelligent 10/100 TX Embedded UTP
Compaq Netelligent 10 T/2 PCI UTP/Coax
Compaq Netelligent 10/100 TX UTP
Compaq NetFlex 3/P
Olicom OC-2325, OC-2183, OC-2326
	`tlan.o`	`tlan=io_port,IRQ,aui,debug`
		`tlan io=io_port irq=IRQ`
		Other Module Options:
		`speed=10Mbs,100Mbs`
		`debug=0x0[1,2,4,8]`
		`aui=1`
		`duplex=[1,2]`

Digital 21x4x Tulip PCI Ethernet cards SMC EtherPower 10 PCI(8432T/8432BT) SMC EtherPower 10/100 PCI(9332DST) DEC EtherWorks 100/10 PCI(DE500-XA) DEC EtherWorks 10 PCI(DE450) DEC QSILVER's, Znyx 312 etherarray Allied Telesis LA100PCI-T Danpex EN-9400, Cogent EM110	`tulip.o`	
VIA Rhine PCI Fast Ethernet cards with either the VIA VT86c100A Rhine-II PCI or 3043 Rhine-I D-Link DFE-930-TX PCI 10/100	`via-rhine.o`	
AT&T GIS (nee NCR) WaveLan ISA Card	`wavelan.o`	`wavelan=[IRQ,0],io_port,NWID`
WD8003 and WD8013 "compatible" ethercards	`wd.o`	`wd=io_port,IRQ,mem,mem_end` `wd io=io_port irq=IRQ mem=mem mem_end=end`
Packet Engines Yellowfin	`yellowfin.o`	
G-NIC PCI Gigabit Ethernet adapter Z8530 based HDLC cards for AX.25	`z85230.o`	

Here are some examples of these modules in use:

Configuration	Example
NE2000 ISA card at IO address 300 and IRQ 11	`ne=0x300,11` `ether=0x300,11,eth0`
Wavelan card at IO 390, autoprobe for IRQ, and use the NWID to 0x4321	`wavelan=0,0x390,0x4321` `ether=0,0x390,0x4321,eth0`

E.3.1   Using Multiple Ethernet Cards

You can use multiple Ethernet cards in one machine. If each card uses a different driver (e.g., a 3c509 and a DE425), you simply need to add `alias` (and possibly `options`) lines for each card to `/etc/conf.modules`. See Section 8.2.2 on page 165 for more information.

If any two Ethernet cards use the same driver (e.g., two 3c509's or a 3c595 and a 3c905), you will need to either give the two card addresses on the driver's `options` line (in the case of ISA cards), or (for PCI cards) simply add one `alias` line for each card.

For more information about using more than one Ethernet card, see the *Linux Ethernet-HOWTO*. If you installed the `howto` package when you installed Red Hat Linux, you can find it in the file `/usr/doc/HOWTO/Ethernet-HOWTO`.

Information Specific to Red Hat Linux/SPARC

This appendix describes the differences between Red Hat Linux/SPARC and Red Hat Linux/Intel installations. While it provides a good overview of these differences, you will find it easier to read chapters 2, 3, 4, 5 and 6 in order. These chapters will refer you to the appropriate parts of this appendix at the appropriate time.

In addition, there is a Linux/SPARC homepage at
`http://www.geog.ubc.ca/s_linux.html`. It has a wealth of information for people considering Red Hat Linux/SPARC, and is a great resource.

F.1 Supported Hardware

Red Hat Linux/SPARC supports a variety of hardware based on the SPARC architecture. The most recent list of hardware supported by Red Hat Linux/SPARC can be found at Red Hat Software's World Wide Web site at
`http://www.redhat.com/hardware`.

The following list is current as of the time this manual was produced:

- sun4c architecture machines (IPC, SS1, etc)

- sun4m architecture machines (Classic, SS5, SS10, etc)
- sun4u (UltraSparc1, UltraSparc2, EnterPrise UltraSparc servers)
- bwtwo, cg3, cg6, TCX framebuffers (24 bit on the TCX)
- cg14 framebuffer (in cg3 mode)
- SCSI and Ethernet on all of the above
- type 4 and type 5 keyboards and mice
- external SCSI drives
- CD-ROM drives (external and internal)
- SCSI/Ether SBUS expansion cards
- Any original equipment Sun monitor for the above framebuffers

Unsupported Hardware – The following list contains hardware that is currently unsupported:

- VME based sun4m machines, such as the 4/690
- SPARC 5 Model 170 machines
- sun4d (SS1000, SS2000)
- sun4 architecture
- Eurocard sun4c machines, called the "sun4e" under Solaris2.4 and others, are not supported. These are VME-bus sun4c machines, to which the kernel has not been ported yet.
- The following types of CD-ROMs are unsupported (for more information on CD-ROM compatibility issues, please visit
  `http://saturn.tlug.org/suncdfaq`):
  - All NEC models
  - Some Toshiba XM-4101B revisions
  - Toshiba XM-3201B
  - AppleCD 300 Plus on older SPARC PROM
  - Apple CD600i

F.2   Installation Overview

Installing Red Hat Linux on a SPARC system is slightly more complex than installing Red Hat Linux/Intel, mostly due to differences in machine architecture. In general, the main steps to a successful installation are:

1. Determine which console commands your SPARC systems supports.
2. Determine whether you have sufficient memory to use a ramdisk-based installation.
3. Determine how you will boot the installation program.
4. Determine what installation method you will use.
5. Determine whether you will install Red Hat Linux/SPARC from a serial terminal.
6. Load and run the Red Hat Linux installation program.

Let's look at each of these steps in more detail.

F.3   Console Commands

SPARC systems have two different types of boot commands available, depending on the version of the system's console PROM. Systems with a PROM version less than 2.0 use what is known as the "old" style boot command, while systems whose PROM is at version 2.0 or greater can use either the old or the new style boot commands. If your SPARC system's console prompt is "ok," then your system is in new command mode, and can use the new style boot command.

In general, it's preferable to use the new style boot command if your system supports it. Of course, it's possible to use the old style boot command, but you'll need to know a bit more about your hardware configuration. An excellent reference on older Sun hardware in general (and the old-style boot commands in particular) can be found in *The Sun Hardware Reference*, by James W. Birdsall. It can be found at `ftp://ftp.picarefy.com/pub/Sun-Hardware-Ref/parts/`. The file `part2` contains an in-depth description of the various "ROM monitors" present in older Sun Systems.

In general, the new style boot command is `boot`, followed by a descriptive device name (such as `floppy`, `cdrom`, or `net`).

The old style boot command is `b`, followed by a device specifier in the form:

```
xx(a,b,c)
```

Where `xx` is used to specify the device type (such as `sd` for SCSI disks), `a` is the controller number, `b`, is the device's unit number, and `c` is the partition number. Please refer to *The Sun Hardware Reference* if you have an older SPARC system, and require additional information on its boot command syntax.

F.4   Ramdisk-based Installation Criteria

When the Red Hat Linux/SPARC installation starts, normally a ramdisk is loaded into memory. This ramdisk contains data and programs required to perform the installation, and is approximately 4 MB in size. Since the ramdisk takes memory away from the Red Hat Linux/SPARC installation program, your SPARC system must have at least 12 MB of memory in order to sucessfully use a ramdisk-based installation.

For SPARC systems with less than 12 MB of RAM, another approach is available. It is known as an *NFS-mounted root*. As the name implies, instead of using a ramdisk to hold parts of the Red Hat Linux/SPARC installation program, an NFS server is used to export the necessary files to the SPARC system. While this approach uses less memory, it is somewhat more complex to set up.

Please Note: Red Hat Linux/SPARC may also be installed by booting from the Red Hat Linux/-SPARC CD-ROM. This method uses neither a ramdisk or an NFS-mounted root, as the necessary files are already present on the
Red Hat Linux/SPARC CD-ROM. We will discuss booting from CD-ROM in Section F.5.2 on page 363.

F.4.1   Preparing to Use an NFS-Mounted Root

If you will be using an NFS-mounted root for the installation program, you'll need a network connection for your SPARC system, an NFS server capable of exporting the Red Hat Linux/SPARC CD-ROM (or equivalent files), and the ability to respond to `rarp` requests, so that your SPARC system can obtain its IP address. The necessary commands for `rarp` would be:

```
rarp -s ip.address.of.sparc hw:address:of:sparc
arp -s ip.address.of.sparc hw:address:of:sparc
```

As you might surmise, replace `ip.address.of.sparc` with the IP address of your SPARC system, and replace `hw:address:of:sparc` with the MAC address of your SPARC system's network adapter. The IP address is assigned by your network administrator, and the MAC address is displayed on your SPARC system's console at power-up.

To use an NFS-mounted root during the installation, add the following argument to your boot command:

```
linux nfsroot=nfs.server.ip.address:/path/to/RH/image
```

The word `linux` should always be included in a boot command that includes one or more arguments, and must precede the first argument. Replace
`nfs.server.ip.address` with the NFS server's IP address, and
`/path/to/RH/image` with the path to the exported directory containing the appropriate Red Hat Linux/SPARC files.

F.5   Choosing a Boot Method

This section describes how to start (or *boot*) the installation program. Once the installation program is running, you will be able to choose from several installation methods. You can choose from the following installation methods: CD-ROM, hard disk, NFS, FTP and HTTP. (Note that if the installation program is booted directly from CD-ROM, the installation will automatically proceed from that CD-ROM.)

There are three different ways a Red Hat Linux/SPARC installation can be started:

Boot From Diskette – The installation program is read from a diskette.

Boot From CD-ROM – The installation program is read directly from the Red Hat Linux/SPARC CD-ROM.

Boot From the Network – The installation program is read from a TFTP server.

F.5.1 Booting From Diskette

If your SPARC system has a diskette drive, you can boot the Red Hat Linux/SPARC installation program from a diskette. The boot diskette image (known as `boot32.img` for Sun4c and Sun4m; and `bootimg64.img` for UltraSparc) is located in the `images/` directory on your Red Hat Linux/-SPARC CD-ROM. A ramdisk diskette image (known as `ramdisk.img`) is also available. Please refer to Appendix B on page 237 for instructions on writing the image file to a diskette. Make sure you label the boot and ramdisk diskettes appropriately.

Diskette Boot Commands

For SPARC systems with a PROM version of 2.0 or greater, the proper boot command (when in new command mode) is:

```
boot floppy
```

On the other hand, SPARC systems with PROM versions less than 2.0 should use the following command at the > prompt:

```
b fd()
```

Please Note: There have been reports that some systems with pre-2.0 PROMs cannot boot the Red Hat Linux/SPARC installation program from diskette. If you find this to be the case with your SPARC system, you will need to use another boot method.

F.5.2 Booting From CD-ROM

If your SPARC system has a fully Sun-supported CD-ROM drive, you can boot directly from the Red Hat Linux/SPARC CD-ROM. For SPARC systems with a PROM version of 2.0 or better, use the following command when in new command mode:

```
boot cdrom
```

SPARC systems with PROM versions less than 2.0 may not be able to boot from a CD-ROM at all, although we've received reports that at least some PROM 1.3 systems have been able to boot from CD-ROM. If your SPARC system has a CD-ROM at SCSI id 6, the following command should boot the Red Hat Linux/SPARC installation program:

```
b sd(0,6,0)
```

Note that using an NFS-mounted root after booting from CD-ROM is not supported, as the filesystem on the Red Hat Linux/SPARC CD-ROM performs the same function as an NFS-mounted root. Therefore, no additional boot command arguments should be given for CD-ROM boots.

F.5.3   Booting From the Network

There are two types of network boots supported by the Red Hat Linux/SPARC installation program:

1. Network boot with NFS-mounted root. This method is required for SPARC systems with less than 16 MB of RAM.
2. Network boot with network-loaded ramdisk. This method can be used by systems with at least 16 MB of RAM.

While booting your SPARC system from the network is fairly straightforward, there are several requirements:

- Your SPARC system must have a network connection.

- Your network must be able to give your SPARC system its IP address via a `rarp`.

- You must have a TFTP server that can download the Red Hat Linux/SPARC kernel and installation program to your SPARC system.

- If you are going to use an NFS-mounted root, an NFS server capable of exporting the Red Hat Linux/SPARC CD-ROM (or equivalent files).

Setting up RARP   If you are going to use `rarp`, please refer to Section F.4.1 on page 362.

TFTP Server Setup   If you are going to set up a TFTP server on a Red Hat Linux system, simply install the latest `tftp` package using RPM, and make sure the line in `inetd.conf` that will run `tftp` is uncommented. Don't forget to `kill -HUP` inetd if you needed to make any changes to `inetd.conf`.

Next, you'll need to make a symlink describing the SPARC system to be booted, and pointing to the file from which it should boot. The name of the symlink contains two items:

1. The IP address of the system to be booted, in hexadecimal.
2. A string describing the architecture of the system to be booted.

To convert the more common "dotted decimal" IP address into its hex equivalent, convert each of the address' four groups of numbers into hex. If the resulting hex number is only one digit, add a leading zero to it. Then append all four hex numbers together. For example, take the IP address 10.0.2.254. Convert each set of four numbers into hex, and add a leading zero where necessary:

```
 10 = A  or 0A
  0 = 0  or 00
  2 = 2  or 02
254 = FE or FE
```

Therefore, the IP address 10.0.2.254 in hex is: 0A0002FE.

If you have perl available on a system, you can use the following command (modified to include your system's IP address, of course) to have your IP address converted for you:

```
# perl -e 'printf "%02x"x4 ."\n",10,0,2,254;'
0a0002fe
#
```

Here we've had perl convert 10.0.2.254 for us.

The second part of the symlink name is the SPARC system's architecture. For our example, we'll use SUN4M. The IP address and architecture are separated by a dot, resulting in this symlink name:

```
0A0002FE.SUN4M
```

The last step is figuring out what this symlink should point to. There are two choices. If you want to use an NFS-mounted root, use the file:

```
/kernels/vmlinux32 -- for Sun4c and Sun4m
/kernels/vmlinux64 -- for UltraSparc
```

If you would rather use a ramdisk, use the file

```
/images/tftp32.img -- for Sun4c and Sun4m
/images/tftp64.img -- for UltraSparc
```

Place the appropriate file in the TFTP server's directory, and create the symlink. In this example, we're using the image that includes a ramdisk:

```
ln -s tftp32.img 0A0002FE.SUN4M or
ln -s tftp64.img 0A0002FE.SUN4U
```

Network Boot Commands

You're now ready to boot. If you're going to boot tftp32.img or tftp64.img, simply use the following command (in new command mode):

```
boot net
```

On the other hand, if you're going boot from vmlinux32 or vmlinux64 and use an NFS-mounted root, use this command:

```
boot net linux nfsroot=nfs.server.IP.address:/path/to/RH/image
```

Replace `nfs.server.ip.address` with the NFS server's IP address, and
`/path/to/RH/image` with the path to the exported directory containing the appropriate Red Hat
Linux/SPARC files.

SPARC systems with PROM versions less than 2.0 should use this boot command, appending the
usual NFS root argument if required:

```
b le()
```

F.6   Choosing an Installation Method

Once your SPARC systems has booted, and the installation program is running, you'll be asked to
choose an installation method (unless you've booted directly from CD-ROM, in which case a CD-
ROM installation method is assumed). Red Hat Linux/SPARC can be installed by any of the following methods:

- Installing packages from CD-ROM.
- Installing packages from an FTP site.
- Installing packages from an NFS server.
- Installing packages from a locally-attached hard disk.
- Installing packages from an HTTP site.

F.6.1   CD-ROM Installation

This is the most straightforward method. It requires a Red Hat Linux/SPARC CD-ROM, and a Sun-
supported CD-ROM connected to your SPARC system.

F.6.2   FTP Installation

This installation method requires a local area network connection and access to an FTP site with the
Red Hat Linux/SPARC CD-ROM (or equivalent files).

F.6.3   NFS Installation

Installing via NFS requires a local area network connection and access to an NFS server that can
export the contents of the Red Hat Linux/SPARC CD-ROM (or equivalent files).

F.6.4   Hard Disk Installation

This installation method requires that the contents of the Red Hat Linux/SPARC CD-ROM (or equivalent files) have been copied to a hard disk directly attached to your SPARC system. It is important to note that the partition holding these files cannot be used for any other purpose during the installation (ie, it cannot be given a mount point during the installation). In addition, the partition must be in ext2 format.

F.6.5   HTTP Installation

This installation method requires a local area network connection and access to an HTTP site with the Red Hat Linux/SPARC CD-ROM (or equivalent files).

F.7   Installation Using a Serial Terminal

You can also install Red Hat Linux/SPARC using a serial terminal attached to your SPARC system. Any terminal which can emulate a VT100 (or a computer with terminal emulation software) will work fine. Boot as you would normally, and at the SILO prompt enter:

```
linux serial
```

The installation program runs on the first serial port at 9600 baud, 8 bits, no parity, 1 stop bit (often called 9600,8,N,1). The installation program can run in color, if your serial terminal supports color. Note that a computer running kermit and connected to your SPARC system will display in color.

At any prompt dialog during a serial installation (any dialog with an **Ok** button), you can press [Ctrl]-[Z] to start a subshell. To return to the installation program, enter exit at the shell prompt.

When the installation is complete, simply boot normally, and Red Hat Linux should come up on your serial terminal.

Please Note: If you want to have a "headless" installation, you must use a serial terminal to perform the installation, and make sure you disable GPM.

F.8   SILO Configuration

SILO configuration is nearly identical to LILO configuration. See Section 6.9 on page 105 for more details.

Please Note: Unlike LILO, SILO cannot be configured to boot other operating systems during the installation. However, information on configuring SILO to boot other operating systems is available. Please read the file README in

`/usr/doc/silo*/docs` after installation.

F.9   Partitioning

Please Note: If you decide to use Disk Druid to partition your system's hard drive, be aware that, at this time, Disk Druid cannot initialize disk labels on the SPARC. Therefore, the drive must have a valid disk label on it prior to attempting to use Disk Druid. A disk label can be written using `fdisk` – after that, Disk Druid should work normally.

There is one additional step required when partitioning a hard drive for Red Hat Linux/SPARC. You must create the third partition of every disk as type `Whole Disk` spanning from cylinder 0 to the end of the disk. It shouldn't be used in any way, but it must exist. You can still create other partitions as you normally would.

Note that this partition will already exist on any disk that has been used under SunOS or Solaris. If you are partitioning a new disk, you can use `fdisk`'s "s" command to create a standard disk label (which includes the whole-disk partition). If you don't care for the size of the other partitions created by "s", you can delete those partitions and recreate them with the sizes you want.

G

Glossary

Alpha A RISC (*Reduced Instruction Set Computer*) architecture developed by Digital Equipment Corporation.

ATAPI An abbreviation for *AT Attachement Packet Interface*. ATAPI is the protocol by which CD-ROM drives communicate with a computer system over an IDE interface.

Binary Although the base two-numbering system used by computers is known as binary, the word often refers to the executable form of a program. Contrast with "source code."

BIOS An abbreviation for *Basic Input/Output System*. On PC-compatible systems, the BIOS is used to perform all necessary functions to properly initialize the system's hardware when power is first applied. The BIOS also controls the boot process, provides low-level input/output routines (hence its name) and (usually) allows the user to modify details of the system's hardware configuration.

Boot Short for "bootstrap." The process by which a computer starts running an operating system when power is applied.

Boot Diskette A diskette used to start many Red Hat Linux installations.

Bootstrap See "Boot."

CISC An abbreviation for *Complex Instruction Set Computer*. A design philosophy for computers whereby the processor is designed to execute a relatively large number of different instructions, each taking a different amount of time to execute (depending on the complexity of the instruction). Contrast with RISC.

CMOS Originally an abbreviation for *Complementary Metal Oxide Semiconductor* – a semiconductor technology used in many integrated circuits. Now often used to describe the low-level hardware that contains a personal computer's BIOS setting, and the computer's hardware clock.

Cylinder When referring to disk drives, the number of different positions the disk drive's read/write heads can take over the unit's disk platters. When viewed from above the platters, each head position describes an imaginary circle of different diameters on the platter's surface, but when viewed from the side, these circles can be thought of as a series of cylinders nested within each other, hence the term. See also Geometry.

Daemon A daemon is a program that runs, without human intervention, to accomplish a given task. For example, lpd is a daemon that controls the flow of print jobs to a printer.

Dependencies When referring to packages, dependencies are requirements that exist between packages. For example, package foo may require files that are installed by package bar. In this example, bar must be installed, or else foo will have unresolved dependencies. RPM will not normally allow packages with unresolved dependencies to be installed.

Device Driver Software that controls a device that is connected to, or part of, a computer.

Disk Drive See Hard Disk.

Disk Druid Disk Druid is a component of the Red Hat Linux installation program that is used to partition disk drives during the installation process.

Diskette A small mass storage device in a removable cartridge, meant to be read/written to, in a compatible drive.

Distribution An operating system (usually Linux) that has been packaged so as to be easily installed.

Domain Name A domain name is used to identify computers as belonging to a particular organization. Domain names are hierarchical in nature, with each level in the hierarchy being separated from other levels with a period (pronounced "dot"). For example, Foo Incorporated's Finance department might use the domain name "finance.foo.com."

Driver See Device Driver.

Dual Boot   The act of configuring a computer system to boot more than one operating system. The name is something of a misnomer, as it is possible to boot more than the two operating systems the word "dual" implies.

EIDE   An abbreviation for *Enhanced Integrated Drive Electronics*, which is a newer version of the IDE interface standard and another term for a particular implementation for IDE interfaces. EIDE makes larger and faster disk drives possible; most systems sold today use EIDE.

Errata   Errata is Latin for "Ooops."[1] When software is found to have bugs, quite often the software is fixed, and released as errata. Red Hat Linux is no exception to the rule; we have an Errata web page at http://www.redhat.com/errata.

Extended Partition   A segment of a disk drive that contains other partitions. See Partition.

FAQ   An abbreviation for Frequently Asked Questions. Linux information is often presented in the form of lists of questions and answers called FAQs.

fdisk   fdisk is a utility program that is used to create, delete or modify partitions on a disk drive.

Filesystem   A filesystem is the method by which information is stored on disk drives. Different operating systems normally use different filesystems, making it difficult to share the contents of a disk drive between two operating systems. However, Linux supports multiple filesystems, making it possible, for example, to read/write a partition dedicated to Windows.

Floppy   A somewhat historical term for a small mass storage device in a removable cartridge, meant to be read/written to in a compatible drive. See "diskette."

Formatting   The act of writing a filesystem on a disk drive.

FQDN   An abbreviation for *Fully Qualified Domain Name*. An FQDN is the human-readable name that includes a computer's hostname and associated domain name. For example, given a hostname of "foo," and a domain name of "bar.com," the FQDN would be "foo.bar.com."

FTP   An abbreviation for *File Transfer Protocol*. Also the name of a program that, as the name implies, permits the copying of files from one system on a network to another.

Gateway   In networking terms, refers to a device that connects one or more computers on a network to other networks. The device may be specialized hardware (such as a router), or may be a general-purpose computer system configured to act as a gateway.

---

[1]Well, it should be. . .

Geometry   When referring to disk drives, the physical characteristics of the disk drive's internal organization. Note that a disk drive may report a "logical geometry" that is different from its "physical geometry," normally to get around BIOS-related limitations. See also Cylinder, Head and Sector.

GID   Short for Group *ID*. The means by which a user's membership in a group is identified to various parts of Red Hat Linux. GIDs are numeric, although human-readable names are stored in the `/etc/group` file.

Group   Groups are a way of assigning specific access rights to certain classes of users. For example, all users working on Project X could be added to group `xproj`. System resources (such as disk space) devoted to Project X could then be configured to permit only members of `xproj` full access.

Hard Disk   A hard disk contains rotating magnetic media (in the shape of disks) that spin rapidly. Small heads float over the surface of each disk, and are used to write to and read from the disk as it rotates.

Head   When referring to disk drives, the number of read/write heads within a disk drive. For each platter in a disk drive, there are normally two heads for each platter – one for each surface – although one surface may go unused. See also Geometry.

Hostname   A hostname is a human-readable string of characters used to identify a particular computer system.

I18n   See Internationalization.

IDE   An abbreviation for *Integrated Drive Electronics*, which is the name of a standard interface used to connect primarily disk and CD-ROM drives to a computer system. See also "EIDE" and "ATAPI."

Intel   Company responsible for producing the microprocessors that most commonly appear in PC-compatible personal computers. These processors include the 80386, 80486, Pentium, Pentium Pro, and Pentium II.

Internationalization   The practice of designing and writing programs that can be easily configured to interact with the user in more than one language. Often referred to as "i18n," due to the number of letters between the starting "i" and the ending "n."

IP Address   IP addresses are the method by which individual computer systems (or from a more strictly accurate interpretation, the network interfaces on those computer systems) are identified on a TCP/IP network. All IP addresses consist of four number blocks, each ranging from 0 to 255, and separated by periods.

Kernel   The central part of an operating system upon which the rest of the operating system is based.

Library   When speaking of computers, refers to a collection of routines that perform operations which are commonly required by programs. Libraries may be shared, meaning that the library routines reside in a file separate from the programs that use them. Library routines may also be "statically linked" to a program, meaning that copies of the library routines required by that program are physically added to the program. Such statically linked binaries do not require the existence of any library files in order to execute. Programs linked against shared libraries will not execute unless the required libraries have been installed.

LILO   A commonly-used bootstrap loader for Linux systems based on an Intel-compatible processor.

Linus Torvalds   Created Linux in 1991 while a university student.

Linuxconf   A versatile system configuration program written by Jacques Gelinas. Linuxconf provides a menu-based approach to system configuration via several different user interfaces.

Linux   A full-featured, robust, freely-available operating system originally developed by Linus Torvalds.

Logical Partition   A partition that exists within an extended partition. See also "partition" and "extended partition."

Master Boot Record   The master boot record (or MBR) is a section of a disk drive's storage space that is set aside for the purpose of saving information necessary to begin the bootstrap process on a personal computer.

MBR   See "Master Boot Record."

Memory   When referring to computers, memory (in general) is any hardware that can store data for later retrieval. In this context, memory usually specifically refers to RAM.

MILO   A commonly-used bootstrap loader for Linux systems based on the Alpha processor.

Module   In Linux, a module is a collection of routines that perform a system-level function, and may be dynamically loaded and unloaded from the running kernel as required. Often containing device drivers, modules are tightly bound to the version of the kernel; most modules built from one version of a kernel will not load properly on a system running another kernel version.

Mount Point   The directory under which a filesystem is accessible after being mounted.

Mount   The act of making a filesystem accessible to a system's users.

Nameserver   In TCP/IP networking terms, a nameserver is a computer that can translate a human-readable name (such as "foo.bar.com") into a numeric address (such as "10.0.2.14").

Netmask   A netmask is a set of four number blocks separated by periods. Each number is normally represented as the decimal equivalent of an eight-bit binary number, which means that each number may take any value between 0 (all eight bits cleared) and 255 (all eight bits set). Every IP address consist of two parts (the network address and the host number). The netmask is used to determine the size of these two parts. The positions of the bits that are set in the netmask are considered to represent the space reserved for the network address, while the bits that are cleared are considered to represent the space set aside for the host number.

NFS   An abbreviation for Network File System, NFS is a method of making the filesystem on a remote system accessible on the local system. From a user's perspective, an NFS-mounted filesystem is indistinguishable from a filesystem on a directly-attached disk drive.

Operating System   A collection of software that controls various resources of a computer.

Packages   Files that contain software, and written in a particular format that enables the software to be easily installed and removed.

PAM   An acronym for *Pluggable Authentication Modules*. PAM is an authentication system that controls access to Red Hat Linux.

Partition   A segment of a disk drive's storage space that can be accessed as if it was a complete disk drive.

Partition Table   The partition table is a section of a disk drive's storage space set aside to define the partitions that exist on that disk drive.

Partition Type   Partitions contain a field that is used to define the type of filesystem the partition is expected to contain. The partition type is actually a number, although many times the partition type is referred to by name. For example, the "Linux Native" partition type is 82. Note that this number is hexadecimal.

PC Card   See PCMCIA.

PCMCIA   Acronym for *Personal Computer Memory Card International Association*. This organization produced a series of standards that define the physical, electrical and software characteristics of small, credit card-sized devices that can contain memory, modems, network adapters and more. Also known as PC Cards, these devices are mainly used in laptop computers (although some desktop systems can use PCMCIA cards, too).

PCMCIA Support Diskette   A diskette required for Red Hat Linux installations that require the use of a PCMCIA device during the install.

Permissions   The set of identifiers that control access to files. Permissions consist of three fields: user, group, and world. The user field controls access by the user owning the file, while the group field controls access by anyone matching the file's group specification. As the name implies, the world field controls access by everyone else. Each field contains the same set of bits that specify operations that may or may not be performed, such as reading, writing and executing.

PLIP   An abbreviation for *Parallel Line Internet Protocol*. PLIP is a protocol that permits TCP/IP communication over a computer's parallel port using a specially-designed cable.

POSIX   A somewhat mangled abbreviation for *Portable Operating System Interface*. A set of standards that grew out of the UNIX operating system.

Process   A process (in somewhat simplistic terms) is one instance of a running program on a Linux system.

PS/2 Mouse   A PS/2 mouse gets its name from the original computer in which this type of mouse was first used – the IBM PS/2. A PS/2 mouse can be easily identified by the small, round connector at the end of its cable.

RAM   An acronym for *Random Access Memory*. RAM is used to hold programs while they are being executed, and data while it is being processed. RAM is also volatile, meaning that information written to RAM will disappear when the computer's power is turned off.

Reboot   To restart the boot process. See also "Boot."

Red Hat Software   A North Carolina software company. Produces and markets sofware for the Linux operating system, including Red Hat Linux.

Rescue Diskette   A diskette containing a rudimentary system environment. As the name implies, a rescue diskette is normally used in an attempt to "rescue" an ailing system from the necessity of re-installing the entire operating system.

RISC   An abbreviation for *Reduced Instruction Set Computer*. A design philosophy for computers whereby the processor is optimized to execute a relatively small number of different instructions in a predictably small amount of time. Contrast with CISC.

ROM   An abbreviation for *Read Only Memory*. ROM is used to hold programs and data that must survive when the computer is turned off. Because ROM is non-volatile; data in ROM will remain unchanged the next time the computer is turned back on. As the name implies, data cannot be easily written to ROM; depending on the technology used in the ROM, writing may require special hardware, or may be impossible. A computer's BIOS may be stored in ROM.

Root   The name of the login account given full and complete access to all system resources. Also used to describe the directory named "/"as in, "the root directory."

RPM   An abbreviation that stands for *Red Hat Package Manager*. RPM is also the name of a program that enables the installation, upgrading and removal of packages.

SCSI   An abbreviation for *Small Computer System Interface*, SCSI is a standard interface for connecting a wide variety of devices to a computer. Although the most popular SCSI devices are disk drives, SCSI tape drives and scanners are also common.

Sector   When referring to disk drives, the number of fixed-size (normally 512 byte) areas that can be accessed by one of the disk drive's read/write heads, in one rotation of the disk, without that head changing position. See Also Geometry.

Serial Mouse   A serial mouse is a mouse that is designed to be connected to a computer's serial port. A serial mouse can be easily identified by the rectangular-shaped connector at the end of its cable.

setgid   A system call that can be used to set the GID of a process. Programs can be written using setgid such that they can assume the group ID of any group on the system.

setuid   A system call that can be used to set the UID of a process. Programs can be written using setuid such that they can assume the user ID of any process on the system. This is considered a possible security problem if a program is "setuid root."

Shadow Password   Normally, each user's password is stored, encrypted, in the file /etc/passwd. This file must be readable by all users so that certain system functions will operate correctly. However, this means that copies of user's encrypted passwords are easily obtained, making it possible to run an automated password-guessing program against them. Shadow passwords, on the other hand, store the encrypted passwords in a separate highly-protected file, making it much more difficult to crack passwords.

SILO   A commonly-used bootstrap loader for Linux systems based on the SPARC processor.

SLIP   An acronym for *Serial Line Internet Protocol*. SLIP is a protocol that permits TCP/IP communication over serial line (typically over a dial-up modem connection).

source code The human-readable form of instructions that comprise a program. Also known as "sources." Without a program's source code, it is very difficult to modify the program.

SPARC A RISC (*Reduced Instruction Set Computer*) architecture developed by Sun Microsystems.

Swap Also known as "swap space." When a program requires more memory than is physically available in the computer, currently-unused information can be written to a temporary buffer on the hard disk, called swap, thereby freeing memory. Some operating systems support swapping to a specific file, but Linux normally swaps to a dedicated swap partition. A misnomer, the term swap in Linux is used to define damand paging.

System Call A system call is a routine that accomplishes a system-level function on behalf of a process.

TCP/IP An abbreviation for *Transmission Control Protocol/Internet Protocol*, TCP/IP is the name given to the networking standard commonly used on the Internet today.

Torvalds, Linus See Linus Torvalds.

UID Short for *User ID*. The means by which a user is identified to various parts of Red Hat Linux. UIDs are numeric, although human-readable names are stored in the /etc/passwd file.

UNIX A set of Linux-like operating systems that grew out of an original version written by some guys at a phone company.[2]

Unmount The act of revoking access to a filesystem. (Note that the program that unmounts filesystems is called umount.)

Virtual Console Virtual consoles provides multiple "screens" on which a user may log in and run programs. One screen is displayed on the computer's monitor at any given time; a key sequence is used to switch between virtual consoles.

Widget A standardized on-screen representation of a control that may be manipulated by the user. Scroll bars, buttons, and text boxes are all examples of widgets.

X Window System Also known as "X," this graphical user interface provides the well-known "windows on a desktop" metaphor common to most computer systems today. Under X, application programs act as clients, accessing the X server, which manages all screen activity. In addition, client applications may be on a different system than the X server, permitting the remote display of the applications graphical user interface.

---

[2]Just kidding – thank you Ken Thompson and Dennis Ritchie of Bell Telephone Laboratories for your inspired operating system design!

XFree86   A free implementation of the X Window System.

Kickstart Installations

Due to the need for automated installation, Red Hat Software has created the *kickstart* installation method. With this method, a system administrator can create a single file containing the answers to all the questions that would normally be asked during a typical Red Hat Linux installation. The kickstart installation method is powerful enough that often a single kickstart file can be used to install Red Hat Linux on multiple machines.

Please Note: Kickstart installations can only be performed using the CD-ROM and NFS installation methods. FTP, HTTP, SMB, or local hard disk installations cannot be automated using kickstart mode.

H.1   Where to Put A Kickstart File

To use kickstart mode, you must first create a kickstart file, and make it available to the Red Hat Linux installation program. Normally this is done by copying the kickstart file to the boot diskette, or making it available on the network. The network-based approach is most commonly used, as most kickstart installations tend to be performed on networked computers. This also makes it easier to install Red Hat Linux on many computers, as the kickstart files can be kept on single server system, and read by the individual computers during the installation.

Let's take a more in-depth look at the locations where the kickstart file may be placed.

H.1.1   On Diskette

To perform a diskette-based kickstart installation, the kickstart file must be named `ks.cfg`, and reside in the boot diskette's top-level directory. Note that the Red Hat Linux boot diskettes are in MS-DOS format, making it easy to copy the kickstart file under Linux using the `mcopy` command (or, if you insist, you can also use Windows). Although there's no technological requirement for it, most diskette-based kickstart installations install Red Hat Linux from CD-ROM.

H.1.2   On the Network

Network installations using kickstart are quite common, because system administrators can easily automate the installation of many networked computers quickly and painlessly. In general, the approach most commonly used is for the administrator to have both a BOOTP/DHCP server and an NFS server on the local network. The BOOTP/DHCP server is used to give the client system its networking information, while the NFS server serves the actual files used during the installation. Often these two servers run on the same physical machine, but there is no requirement for this.

To do a network-based kickstart installation, you must have a BOOTP/DHCP server on your network, and it must include configuration information for the machine you are attempting to install. The BOOTP/DHCP server will be used to give the client its networking information as well as the location of the kickstart file.

If a kickstart file is specified by the BOOTP/DHCP server, the client system will attempt an NFS mount of the file's path, and will copy the specified file to the client, using it as the kickstart file. The exact settings required vary depending on the BOOTP/DHCP server you use.

Here's an example for the DHCP server shipped with Red Hat Linux:

```
filename "/usr/new-machine/kickstart/";
next-server blarg.redhat.com;
```

Note that you should use `filename` for the kickstart file's name (or the directory in which the kicstart file resides) and `next-server` to set the NFS server name.

If the filename returned by the BOOTP/DHCP server ends with a slash ("/"), then it is interpreted as a path only. In this case, the client system mounts that path using NFS, and searches for a specially-named file. The filename the client searches for is:

```
<ip-addr>-kickstart
```

The `<ip-addr>` section of the filename should be replaced with the client's IP address in dotted decimal notation. For example, the filename for a computer with an IP address of 10.10.0.1 would be `10.10.0.1-kickstart`.

Note that if you don't specify a server name, then the client system will attempt to use the server that answered the BOOTP/DHCP request as its NFS server. If you don't specify a path or filename, the client system will try to mount `/kickstart` from the BOOTP/DHCP server, and will try to find the kickstart file using the same `<ip-addr>-kickstart` filename as described above.

H.2   Starting a Kickstart Installation

To begin a kickstart installation, you must boot the system from a Red Hat Linux boot diskette, and enter a special boot command at the boot prompt. If the kickstart file resides on the boot diskette, the proper boot command would be:

```
boot: linux ks=floppy
```

If, on the other hand, the kickstart file resides on a server, the appropriate boot command would be:

```
boot: linux ks
```

H.3   The Kickstart File

Now that you have some background information on kickstart installations, let's take a look at the kickstart file itself. The kickstart file is a simple text file, containing a list of items, each identified by a keyword. You can create it by editing a copy of the README.ks file found in the docs/ directory of a Red Hat Linux CD-ROM, or you can create it from scratch. You should be able to edit it with any text editor or word processor that can save files as ASCII text.

First, some ground rules to keep in mind while creating your kickstart file:

- Items must be specified *in order*. It is not a good idea to try to change the order of the required items.
- Items that aren't required can be omitted.
- For kickstart *upgrades*, the following items are required:

    - language
    - installation method
    - device specification
    - keyboard setup
    - the upgrade keyword
    - LILO configuration

    If any other items are specified for an upgrade, those items will be ignored (note that this includes package selection).

- Omitting any required item will result in the installation process prompting the user for an answer to that question, just as during a normal installation. If this happens, once the answer is given the installation will continue unattended (unless it comes across another missing item).
- Lines starting with a pound sign ("#") are treated as comments, and are ignored.

Let's take a look at each item in order.

H.3.1 `lang` – Language Setting

The first item that must appear is the language setting. The language you specify will be used during the installation as well as to configure any language-specific aspect of the installed system. The language specification must be a two letter ISO language code, such as en for English, de for German, fr for French, and so on. For example, to set the language to English, the kickstart file should contain the following line:

```
lang en
```

H.3.2 `network` – Networking Configuration

The next item is the network configuration information. This line is used to tell the system how it should configure networking for itself. It is optional, and if omitted, the system will be configured for stand-alone operation.

There are three different methods of network configuration:

- DHCP
- BOOTP
- static

The DHCP method uses a DHCP server system to obtain its networking configuration. As you might guess, the BOOTP method is similar, requiring a BOOTP server to supply the networking configuration.

The static method requires that you enter all the required networking information in the kickstart file. As the name implies, this information is static, and will be used during the installation, and after the installation as well.

To direct a system to use DHCP to obtain its networking configuration, use the following line:

```
network --bootproto dhcp
```

To direct a machine to use BOOTP to obtain its networking configuration, use the following line in the kickstart file:

```
network --bootproto bootp
```

The line for static networking is more complex, as you must include all network configuration information on one line. You'll need to specify:

- IP address
- netmask
- gateway IP address

- nameserver IP address

Here's an example static line:

```
network --bootproto static ↩
--ip 10.0.2.15 ↩
--netmask 255.255.255.0 ↩
--gateway 10.0.2.254 ↩
--nameserver 10.0.2.1
```

Please Note: The entire `network` configuration *must* appear on one line! We've wrapped it here to make it easier to read.

There are two restrictions you must keep in mind should you use the static method:

- All static networking configuration information must be specified on *one* line; you cannot wrap lines using a backslash, for example.
- You can only specify one nameserver here. However, you can use the kickstart file's `%post` section (described in Section H.3.22 on page 392) to add more nameservers, if needed.

H.3.3   Installation Methods

The next required item is the installation method. This item directs the installation program for the rest of the files required to install Red Hat Linux. There are two choices: NFS or CD-ROM. Let's look at both, starting with NFS.

H.3.4   `nfs` – The NFS Installation Method

For the NFS installation method, you must include the NFS server's name and the directory to be mounted. Here's an example:

```
nfs --server hostname.of.server --dir /path/to/RH/CD/image
```

H.3.5   `cdrom` – The CD-ROM Installation Method

For a CD-ROM-based kickstart installation, simply use the following line:

```
cdrom
```

H.3.6 `device` – **Optional Hardware Information**

The next set of items in the kickstart file is used to specify optional hardware information. For most PCI-based hardware you can omit this step, as this information can be obtained directly from the hardware. Note that IDE hard disks and common PCI cards fall into this category. Any other hardware may need to be specified here.

To specify a device, start with the `device` keyword, followed by the type of device:

- `ethernet` (for Ethernet cards)
- `scsi` (for SCSI cards)
- `cdrom` (for non-SCSI, non-IDE CD-ROM drives; usually sound cards with proprietary CD-ROM interfaces)

If a kernel module is required to support the device, the module name follows the device type.

Finally, if there are any parameters that are required by a device, they can be specified by using the `--opts` option. Enclose the parameters in quotes after `--opts`. We'll show you some examples below.

Note that you can specify more than one type of device in a given kickstart file. For example, if you know the machines you'll be kickstart-installing have either an Adaptec 1542 or a Buslogic SCSI card, you can enter both in the kickstart file. But be aware that the installation program uses only the first card found, so order the device entries appropriately.

An example for an ISA 3com Ethernet card would be:

```
device ethernet 3c509 --opts "io=0x330, irq=7"
```

Here's an example line for an Adaptec 1542 SCSI card:

```
device scsi aha154x
```

An example of a SoundBlaster CD-ROM might look like this:

```
device cdrom --opts "io=0x240"
```

H.3.7 `keyboard` – **Keyboard Type**

The next item you'll need to specify is the correct code for your keyboard type. For US keyboards, the type is `us`. For the others, please run the `/usr/sbin/kbdconfig` program on an already-installed Red Hat Linux system. (An alternative approach would be to set the keyboard type to `us` and run `kbdconfig` on the installed system to set it properly after the installation completes.)

An example of this would be:

```
keyboard us
```

H.3.8 `noprobe`

If you do not want your system device controllers to be automatically probed then you can issue the command:

```
noprobe
```

By configuring this command, your system will not probe for any device controllers, SCSI or otherwise. This is to be used only if you wish to manually specify the devices that are on your system.

Please Note: You will not be prompted to enter devices at any point. You will have to manually enter them into the kickstart configuration file or else you will not be able to continue with the installation.

H.3.9 **device** `--continue`

Your system is normally set up to take or find one device of a type. Without changes, the kickstart configuration will load the modules for one type of device, such as loading the module for one SCSI adapter type. Beyond that, the program will not load further modules for that type of device.

In order to load modules for more than 1 adapter type, (for example, two different SCSI adapters) you will need to add the command

```
device --continue
```

So, if you need to have modules for a Adaptec and a BusLogic adapter, then you will need to have both of these specified in the configuration file and you will need to have `--continue` after the first one in the configuration file:

```
device scsi aic7xxx --continue
device scsi BusLogic
```

However, if you have multiple adapters of the same type, then you will not need to be concerned with this line, as the single module insertion is enough to control all adapters of that type. For example, if you have three Adaptec adapters, then the single line

```
device scsi aic7xxx
```

will load and allow all three adapters to function.

H.3.10 **Partitioning**

The hard drive in the machine must be partitioned before Red Hat Linux can be installed. In this section, we will describe how to specify disk partitioning in the kickstart file.

H.3.11   `zerombr` – Partition table initialization

First, if you are installing Red Hat Linux on a new machine, you should use the `zerombr` keyword to clear the current partition information. This is a good idea, because the partition table on new hard drives is usually bogus. Here's an example of `zerombr` on a new system:

```
zerombr yes
```

On the other hand, if you are installing machines that have a valid partition table, even if you want to change part (or all) of it, you should use `zerombr` this way:

```
zerombr no
```

H.3.12   `clearpart` – Removing partitions based on partition type

The next command is optional, but can come in handy. If you'd like to remove all partitions, or just any Linux-related partitions, you can use `clearpart`. For example, to clear all partitions of type "Linux native" and "Linux swap," you could add this line:

```
clearpart --linux
```

To clear *all* partitions from a disk, this line would do the trick:

```
clearpart --all
```

The only options `clearpart` supports are `--linux` and `--all`.

H.3.13   `part` – Partition definition

The next step is to specify the partitions you want to create. These will only be created using the system's unpartitioned free space. (In other words, if the machine had Windows-related partitions, and you had done `clearpart --linux` those Windows partitions would remain untouched.) You must enter one partition per line using the following format:

```
part <mntpt> --size <size in megs> [--grow] ↩
[--maxsize <size in megs>]
```

(This `part` line was broken to make it more readable.)

<mntpt> is the location you are going to mount that partition in your installed system (for example, the root partition would have a mount point of `/`, while you may decide that another partition should have a mount point of `/home`).

<size in megs> is the size of the partition in megabytes. You can optionally specify that the partition is *growable* by adding the `--grow` option. Note that making a partition growable does *not* mean that you can later increase its size. Instead, a growable partition will be automatically resized to use all available unpartitioned free space (after all fixed-size partitions have been created).

Since the amount of unpartitioned free space can vary, and you probably want to use it all, by tagging partitions as growable you can easily make sure no space is wasted. If you have multiple partitions tagged as growable, the free space is split evenly among them.

Note that you can also limit the size of growable partitions with the optional `--maxsize` argument.

Here's an example of kickstart partitioning in action. Let's say you know the smallest disk out of a set of machines you plan to kickstart-install is 1GB. You'd like to use the same kickstart file. You could use the following partitioning scheme:

```
zerombr no
clearpart --all
part / --size 250
part swap --size 50
part /usr --size 500 --grow --maxsize 800
part /tmp --size 100 --grow
```

When defined this way, the installation program will first clear all partitions. It will then set up a 250MB root filesystem, followed by a 50MB swap partition. Next the installation program will create a `/usr` partition of at least 500MB (remember, it's growable), but it cannot grow beyond 800MB. Finally, the last line will create a `/tmp` partition of at least 100MB (again, it's growable).

So for that 1GB system, you would end up with a 250MB root, a 50MB swap, a 550MB `/usr`, and a 150MB `/tmp` partition. If another system has a 2GB drive, you would get a 250MB root, a 50MB swap, a 800MB `/usr`, and a 900MB `/tmp`.

H.3.14 `install` and `upgrade` – Install/Upgrade Selection

The next item to specify is whether you are doing a fresh install, or an upgrade of an already-installed system. For a fresh install, use:

```
install
```

For an upgrade of an existing system, use:

```
upgrade
```

Keep in mind that for upgrades, the only items that matter are:

- installation media (CD-ROM or NFS)
- device specification (if necessary)

- keyboard setup
- install/upgrade specification (which should be `upgrade`, of course!)
- LILO configuration

H.3.15 `mouse` – Mouse Configuration

To define the type of mouse your system has, you must use the `mouse` keyword. Run `mouseconfig --help` on an already-installed Red Hat Linux for a list of mouse types.

Depending on the type of mouse, you may also need to specify the device to which the mouse is attached. The default device is correctly set for bus mice. For serial mice, the default device is `/dev/cua0`, but can be overridden with the `--device` option followed by the device name, such as `cua1`.

For example, for a three-button PS/2 mouse, you would use:

```
mouse --kickstart generic3ps/2
```

For a two-button PS/2 mouse, use:

```
mouse --kickstart genericps/2
```

For a two-button Microsoft mouse on your second serial port, use:

```
mouse --kickstart microsoft --device cua1
```

H.3.16 `timezone` – Timezone Definition

Red Hat Linux is timezone-aware, so you'll need to specify the timezone in which the machine will operate. This is done using the `timezone` keyword. There are *many* different timezones; the best way to find yours is to run `/usr/sbin/timeconfig` on an already-installed Red Hat Linux system.

If you would like to have your system's hardware clock set to use GMT/UTC, add the `--utc` option to your timezone line. Here's an example that defines the timezone as US Eastern with the system clock set to GMT:

```
timezone --utc US/Eastern
```

H.3.17 `xconfig` – X Window Setup

The next item is the X Window setup line. The installation program will normally find common PCI video hardware and will know which X server to install. The keyword for X configuration is `xconfig`.

If your video card isn't autoprobed properly, you can use the `--card` option to explicitly specify the card. You can use `Xconfigurator --help` on a running Red Hat Linux system to get a list of supported cards to choose from.

If your card isn't in the list but *is* supported by one of the existing servers, you can simply install the proper server by using the `--server` option. Again, use `Xconfigurator --help` to get the list of server names.

You also need to specify a monitor type. If you don't, the installation will assume a generic monitor capable of 640x480@60hz. Use the `--monitor` option to specify something other than the default. Again, `Xconfigurator --help` will list all valid monitor types.

If your monitor isn't listed, you can enter the actual monitor specifications by using the `--hsync` and `--vsync` options for horizontal and vertical sync rates, respectively. The rates may be single numbers (representing kilohertz and megahertz, as appropriate), groups of numbers separated by commas, or two numbers separated by a dash (signifying a range). For example:

```
xconfig --hsync "31.5,35.5,50-65" --vsync "50-70"
```

An example for a machine where the video card can be autoprobed properly would be:

```
xconfig --monitor "tatung cm14uhe"
```

An example for a machine where nothing is probed and the monitor isn't in the list might be:

```
xconfig --server "Mach64" --hsync "31.5,35.5,50-65" --vsync "50-70"
```

H.3.18 `rootpw` – Setting the Root Password

You can put the root passwd in a kickstart file in the clear (in which case it would go over the network in the clear on an NFS install) or you can specify that an encrypted password is to be used. To specify an unencrypted password in the kickstart file, use the `rootpw` keyword, followed by the cleartext password:

```
rootpw mypasswd
```

If you would rather use an encrypted password, grab it out of `/etc/passwd` (or wherever you have the encrypted version stored), and add the `--iscrypted` option:

```
rootpw --iscrypted encryptedpasswdstring
```

H.3.19 `authconfig` – Setting up Authentication Configuration

After you have set the root password, you have the ability to set up different network password authentications:

- **Enable NIS** – allows you to run a group of computers in the same Network Information Service domain with a common password and group file. There are two options here to choose from:
  - **NIS Domain** – this option allows you to specify which domain or group of computers your system will belong to.
  - **NIS Server** – this option causes your computer to use a specific NIS server, rather than "broadcasting" a message to the local area network asking for any available server to host your system.
- **Enable Shadow Passwords** – provides a very secure method of retaining passwords for you.
- **MD5 Password** allows a long password to be used up to 256 characters, instead of the standard eight letters or less.

The `authconfig` format for kickstart looks similiar to:

```
auth --enablenis --nisdomain foo.redhat.com --nisserver
server.foo.redhat.com [--useshadow] [--enablemd5]
```

Please Note: The commands in the square brackets are optional. If you choose to set them up, you do not need to use the brackets.

You are able to change `authconfig` using these commands to set up the different password options:

```
--enablenis            enable nis by default
--nisdomain <domain>   default NIS domain
--nisserver <server>   default NIS server
--useshadow            use shadow passwords
--enablemd5            enable MD5 passwords
```

H.3.20 `lilo` – LILO Configuration

For machines that use LILO (Intel-based systems), you can specify the LILO configuration using the `lilo` keyword. The default line can be as simple as this:

```
lilo
```

This will install LILO in the hard drive's master boot record (MBR), and automatically configure boot entries for your Linux installation as well as a DOS or Windows installation (if one is present).

If you don't want LILO installed in the MBR, you can do so with by using the `--location` option. There are three possible places where LILO can be installed:

- `mbr` - put LILO on the master boot record (default)
- `partition` - put LILO on the beginning of the root partition

- `none` - don't install LILO at all (in which case you'll need your own method of booting the installed system)

You can also use the `--append` option to add an `append=` line to the Linux boot entry. This is handy if you need to do things like set memory sizes, etc. For example, to install LILO on the MBR on a machine with 128MB of RAM, you would add the following `lilo` line:

```
lilo --append "mem=128M" --location mbr
```

(Due to the new kernel in Red Hat Linux 6.0, the `mem` boot-time option shouldn't be necessary, but we needed an example.)

H.3.21 `%packages` – Package Selection

You can use the `%packages` keyword to start the beginning of a kickstart file section that lists the packages you'd like to install (note that this is for installs only, as package selection during upgrades is not supported).

Packages can be specified by component or by individual package name. The installation program defines several components that group together related packages. See the `RedHat/base/comps` file on any Red Hat Linux CD-ROM for a list of components. The components are defined by the lines that begin with a number followed by a space, and then the component name. Each of the packages in that component are then listed, line-by-line, until the `end` keyword. Individual packages lack the leading number found in front of component lines.

In most cases, it's only necessary to list the desired components and not individual packages. Note that the `Base` component is always selected by default, so it's not necessary to specify it in the `%packages` section.

Here's an example `%packages` section:

```
%packages
@ Networked Workstation
@ C Development
@ Web Server
@ X Window System
bsd-games
```

As you can see, components are specified, one to a line, starting with an "@" symbol, a space, and then the full component name as given in the `comps` file. Specify individual packages with no additional characters (the `bsd-games` line in the example above is an individual package).

Please Note: You can also direct the kickstart install to use the workstation- and server-class installation methods. To do this, simply add *one* of the following lines to the `%packages` section:

```
@ Workstation
@ Server
```

H.3.22 %post — Post-Installation Configuration Section

You have the option of adding commands to be run on the installed system after the installation is complete. This section must be at the end of the kickstart file and must start with the %post keyword. Note that you can access the network in the %post section; however, nameservice has not yet been configured at this point, so only IP addresses will work. Here's an example %post section:

```
%post

# add comment to /etc/motd
echo "Kickstart-installed Red Hat Linux '/bin/date'" > /etc/motd

# add another nameserver
echo "nameserver 10.10.0.2" >> /etc/resolv.conf
```

This section creates a message-of-the-day file containing the date the kickstart installation took place, and gets around the network keyword's one-nameserver-only limitation by adding another name-server to /etc/resolv.conf.

Index

Symbols

/dev directory 196
/etc directory 196
/etc/hosts file, managing 168
/etc/sysconfig, files in 217
/lib directory 196
/proc directory 196
/sbin directory 196
/usr directory 196
/usr/local directory 197, 199
/var directory 198
/etc/pam.conf 207
/etc/pam.d 207

A

account management 123, 124
account modification 126, 127
acknowledgments xii
addendum, Alpha 7
administration, system 195
Alpha addendum 7
Alpha computer x
Alpha-specific information6–9, 11, 14, 15, 20, 30, 37,
        49, 75
AMD 211
anonymous FTP 215
ATAPI CD-ROM
        unrecognized, problems with 44
authentication configuration 103
        kickstart 389
        MD5 Password 103
        NIS 103
        Shadow Password 103
autoboot 38
autostart, selecting services for 95

B

BIOS, issues related to LILO 31

boot diskette 104
boot method selection for SPARC 362
boot process 217
bootable CD-ROM 38
booting
        rescue mode 228
                a trick 228
                using diskettes 228
                using LILO 228
        single user 225
booting from diskette for SPARC 363
booting installation program 37

C

CD-ROM
        ATAPI 43
        ATAPI, unrecognized, problems with 44
        bootable 38
        IDE 43
        IDE, unrecognized, problems with 44
        other 44
        SCSI 43
CD-ROM boot commands, SPARC 363
CD-ROM Installation 15
        for SPARC 366
CD-ROM installation 43
CD-ROM module parameters 350
changing passwords 128, 129
changing root password 130
changing time/date 172
chkconfig utility 227
class
        installation 19, 46, 72
clock 95
clone network devices 169
comp.os.linux 117
Compact Discs
        Linux Applications Pack 8
Compact Discs, Red Hat Linux 7

components
   missing 9
   selecting 61, 86
configuration
   system .... *see* Linuxconf
   anonymous FTP 215
   clock 95
   ethernet 171
   GnoRPM 188
   hosts 168
   kerneld 165
      adding modules 166
      changing modules 165
      module options 165
      restarting 166
   LAN manager printer 163
   local printer 162
   NCP printer 163
   NetWare printer 163
   network 92, 167
   network device, adding 169
   network dialogs 93
   network routes 171
   NFS 216
   PLIP 171
   pocket network adapters 171
   PPP 169
   printer 96, 160
   printer test page 164
   remote printer 163
   selecting nameservers 168
   SILO 367
   SLIP 169
   SMB printer 163
   system 119
   time 95
   time zone 95
   token ring 171
   X Window System 108
   XFree86 109
configuration, hardware 10
   finding with Windows 11
configuration, video 13
configuring console access 203
console access
   configuring 203
   defining 204
   disabling 203
   disabling all 203
   enabling 205
   making files accessible 204

console commands for SPARC 361
consoles, virtual 35
control panel .... *see* controlpanel
controlpanel 158
Copyright ii
Costales, Bryan 214
CSLIP 32
Cyrix 211

D

daemon, kernel 165
date
   setting 172
dd, creating installation diskette with ... 238
deleting accounts 132, 133
deleting groups 135, 136
dependencies, packages 62, 89
destructive partitioning 24
devices
   network, clone 169
directories
   /dev 196
   /etc 196
   /lib 196
   /proc 196
   /sbin 196
   /usr 196
   /usr/local 197, 199
   /var 198
disabling accounts 131
Disk Druid 48, 74
   aborting 54, 80
   adding NFS with 54, 80
   adding partitions with 52, 78
   buttons 51, 77
   current partitions screen 49, 75
   deleting partitions with 53, 79
   drive summary screen 50, 76
   editing partitions with 54, 79
   function keys 51, 77
   problems adding partitions 53, 79
   starting over 54, 80
   using 49, 75
   when finished with 54, 81
disk partitioning, SPARC 368
disk, partitioning 21
disk-based installation for SPARC 367
diskette
   boot 104
   boot, creating 237

network boot, creating 237
    PCMCIA support, creating 237
diskette boot commands, SPARC 363
diskette, making under Linux-like O/S 238
diskette, making with MS-DOS 238
diskettes 8, 18
    boot 8
    images, updated 10
    network boot 18
    support 8, 18
documentation 111
    FAQs 115
    finding 114
    HOWTOs 115
    HTML 115
    info pages 116
    locate command 115
    makewhatis, searching with 113
    man pages 112
        printing 112
        searching 113
        section 112
    on-line 111
    package documentation 114
    PAM 209
    READMEs 114
documentation, how to improve xiii
documentation, obtaining additional 6
drivers, kernel 32

E

editor's acknowledgements xiv
editor's notes xiii
emacs 116
enabling accounts 132
errata 10
ethernet 171
Ethernet module parameters 353
Ethernet, supporting multiple cards 358
expert installation mode 37
exporting NFS filesystems 216
extended partitions 244

F

FAQ
    ATAPI CD-ROM
        unrecognized, problems with 44
    IDE CD-ROM
        unrecognized, problems with 44

technical support 234
FAQs 115
FAT32 filesystems, accessing 143
fdisk 48, 74
    overview of 56, 81
    using 54, 81
features, new to 6.0 1
feedback, how to give xiii
filesystem
    how to review 141, 142
    overview of 140
    standard 196
    structure 195
filesystem configuration 57, 83
    other partitions 57, 83
    root partition 57, 83
filesystem formats, overview of 240
filesystems
    NFS, exporting of 216
    NFS, mounting of 216
finishing installation 91
fips partitioning utility 27
floppy group, use of 205
formatting partitions 60, 85
Frequently Asked Questions . . . . *see* FAQs
friends, impressing with RPM 180
FSSTND 196
FTP
    anonymous 215
    ftpaccess 215
    ftphosts 215
    ftpusers 215
FTP Installation 16, 65, 69
    for SPARC 366

G

getting started xii
Getting Started Guide 7
GLINT . . . . *see* GnoRPM
glossary 369
GnoRPM 183
    configuration 188
    installing packages 187
    package display 185
    package manipulation 191
    querying packages 191
    removing packages with 192
    selecting packages 186
    starting 184
    uninstalling packages with 192

upgrading packages with 194
verifying packages 192
group creation 135
group management 134
group modification 137–139
groups 199
floppy, use of 205
standard 200
user-private 199, 200
rationale 202

H

halt 196, 227
hard disk
basic concepts 239
extended partitions 244
filesystem formats 240
partition introduction 242
partition types 244
partitioning of 239
hard disk installation
for SPARC 367
hard drive installation 18, 45
hardware configuration 10
finding with Windows 11
hardware supported by SPARC 359
hostname 168
hosts, managing 168
hosts.allow 215
example 215
hosts.deny 215
HOWTOs 115
HTTP Installation 17, 65, 69
for SPARC 367
HTTP installation, method 2

I

IDE CD-ROM
unrecognized, problems with 44
info pages 116
information
Alpha-specific 6–9, 11, 14, 15, 20, 30, 37, 49, 75
Intel-specific 7–9, 15–18, 20, 27, 29, 30, 38
license 8
registration 8
SPARC-specific ... 8, 9, 11, 14, 15, 31, 37, 49, 74
information, network 14
information, pre-installation 10
init, SysV-style 224

initrd 213
initscript utilities 227
install
CD-ROM 15, 41, 43
component selection 61, 86
finishing 91, 109
FTP 16, 41
getting Red Hat Linux 6
Hard Drive 18, 41
hard drive 45
HTTP 17, 41
NFS 17, 68
NFS Image 41
NFS server information 68
package information 62, 87
package selection 60, 61, 86
PCMCIA support 15, 40
preparing for 5
selecting network drivers 65
TCP/IP networking 66
upgrade 45, 70
installation
class 19
kickstart .... see kickstart installations
language, selecting 39
printer 96
installation class 46, 72
installation guide 7
installation method
CD-ROM 41, 43
FTP 41
hard drive 41, 45
HTTP 41
NFS Image 41
selecting 41, 43, 65
installation method, choosing for SPARC 366
installation methods 14
installation mode, expert 37
installation overview for SPARC 360
installation problems
IDE CD-ROM related 44
installation program
booting 37
booting without diskette 38
keyboard navigation 34
starting 36
user interface 33
virtual consoles 35
installation, starting 33, 39
installing packages 60, 86
Intel 211

Intel-specific information . 7–9, 15–18, 20, 27, 29, 30, 38

K

kernel 32
    building 210, 213
    custom 210, 213
    initrd image for 213
    modular 210
    monolithic 213
kernel daemon 165
kernel drivers 32
kernel options 38
kerneld 165
    adding modules 166
    changing modules 165
    module options 165
    restarting 166
keyboard navigation, installation program 34
keyboard type, selecting 40
keymap . . . . *see* keyboard type, selecting
kickstart file
    authconfig 389
    cdrom keyword 383
    clearpart keyword 386
    device keyword 384
    diskette-based 380
    format of 381
    install keyword 387
    keyboard keyword 384
    lang keyword 382
    lilo keyword 390
    MD5 389
    mouse keyword 388
    network keyword 382
    network-based 380
    nfs keyword 383
    NIS 389
    package selection specification 391
    part keyword 386
    post-installation configuration 392
    rootpw keyword 389
    Shadow Password 389
    timezone keyword 388
    upgrade keyword 387
    xconfig keyword 388
    zerombr keyword 386
kickstart installations 379
    --continue 385
    noprobe 385

disk partitions 385
diskette-based 380
    file format 381
    file locations 379
    network-based 380
    partitions 385
    starting 381

L

language
    selecting 39
LDP 111, 115
license information 8
LILO 105, 196
    /etc/lilo.conf 212
    Adding options to 107
    alternatives to 108
        commercial products 108
        LOADLIN 108
        SYSLINUX 108
    installing 105
    MBR, installing on 105
    root partition, installing on 106
    SMP Motherboards 106
LILO, BIOS-related issues 31
LILO, partition-related issues 30
Linux
    defined ix
Linux Applications CD Pack 8
Linux Documentation Project . . . . *see* LDP, 115
Linux-like O/S
    creating installation diskette with 238
Linuxconf 120
    with Linuxconf 157
    account management with 123, 124
    account modification with 126, 127
    changing password with 128, 129
    changing root password with 130
    deleting account with 132, 133
    deleting group with 135, 136
    disabling account with 131
    enabling account with 132
    filesystem review with 141, 142
    group creation with 135
    group management with 134
    group modification with 137–139
    modem configuration with 146
    nameserver specification with 155
    network configuration with 145, 152
    NFS mount addition with 144

overview of 120
PPP configuration modification 149, 150
PPP configuration with 146
running 121
SLIP configuration modification 149, 150
SLIP configuration with 146
time setting with 157
tree menu 122
users, adding with 123, 124
web access 123
LOADLIN 108
local media installations 43
CD-ROM 43
hard drive 45
local printer, configuring 96, 97
locate command, finding documentation with .. 115
lpd printer, configuring 96, 97

M

mailing lists
apollo-list 117
applixware-list 117
axp-list 117
blinux-list 117
cde-list 117
gnome-announce 117
gtk-list 117
hurricane-list 117
linux-alert 117
linux-security 117
m68k-list 117
pam-list 117
redhat-announce-list 117
redhat-devel-list 117
redhat-install-list 117
redhat-list 117
redhat-ppp-list 117
rpm-list 117
sound-list 117
sparc-list 117
support from 117
makewhatis 113
man pages 112
how to read 113
printing 112
searching 113
sections 112
master boot record .... see MBR
Maximum RPM 182
MBR, installing LILO on 105

methods, installation 14
missing components 9
mkswap 196
modem configuration 146
module parameters 349
modules
PAM 206
mount points and partitions 29
mounting NFS filesystems 216
mouse, configuring 91
MS-DOS
creating installation diskette with 238
mtools and the floppy group 205

N

nameserver
selecting 168
nameservers, specifying 155
netnews, support from 117
NetWare printer, configuration 99
Netware printer, configuration 96
network
interface
aliasing 168
network adapters, pocket 171
network boot commands, SPARC 364
network boot commands, SPARC install 365
network boot diskette 18
network configuration 92, 145, 152, 167
adding device 169
network configuration dialogs 93
network devices, clone 169
network information 14
network installations 65
FTP 69
HTTP 69
NFS 68
network routes, managing 171
networking 169
new features 1
2.2 kernel 4
APM enabled kernel 2
Authentication Configuration 2
Enlightenment 3
font support 4
GNOME 3
Initscripts 4
installation method 2
installation-related 1
KDE 3

miscellaneous 4
new boot disks 2
Optimized kernels 2
package selection 2
pcmcia support disk 2
SMP Motherboard support 2
switchdesk 4
TrueType font support 4
Xconfigurator 3
NFS
configuration 216
exporting 216
mounting 216
NFS Installation 17, 65, 68
for SPARC 366
NFS mount, adding 57, 83
NFS mounts, adding 144
NFS-mounted root, SPARC install using 362
non-destructive partitioning 25
notes, editor's xiii
ntsysv utility 227

O

O'Reilly & Associates 214, 217
on-line documentation 111
options, kernel 38
OS/2 . . . . 29, 105
overview xi

P

package
installation screen 64, 89
package list index 403
package manipulation with GnoRPM 191
packages
dependencies 62, 89, 176
determining file ownership 180
documentation 114
finding deleted files from 180
freshening with RPM 177
handy hints 180
installing 60, 86, 175
keys for viewing packages 61, 87
list of 247
locating documentation for 181
obtaining information on 62, 87
obtaining list of files 181
preserving config files 177
querying 178

querying uninstalled 181
removing 176
removing with glint 192
selecting 60, 86
selecting individual 61, 86
uninstalling with GnoRPM 192
upgrading 177
upgrading with GnoRPM 194
verifying 179
verifying with GnoRPM 191, 192
packages, GnoRPM 187
PAM 206
additional information 209
configuration files 207
modules 206
rexec, access to 208
services 206
parameters, CD-ROM modules 350
parameters, Ethernet modules 353
parameters, module 349
partition
/boot 30
MILO 30
root 30
swap 30
partitioning 21
basic concepts 239
destructive 24
introduction to 242
LILO issues related to 30
non-destructive 25
other operating systems 29
using free space 22
using in-use partition 24
using unused partition 22
partitions
basic concepts 239
changing table of 57, 82
creating 48, 74
extended 244
formatting 60, 85
how many 29
introduction to 242
making room for 22
mount points relation with 29
naming of 28
numbering of 28
types of 244
password
root, setting 102
passwords

shadow 208
PCMCIA support 40
PCMCIA, support during installation 15
PLIP 32, 171
plip .... see PLIP
pluggable authentication modules .... see PAM
pocket network adapters 171
PPP 32, 169
ppp .... see PPP
PPP configuration 146
    modification of 149, 150
pre-installation information 10
printer configuration 96, 160
    finalizing 99
    LAN manager 163
    local 96, 97, 162
    NCP 163
    NetWare 99, 163
    netware 96
    remote 163
    remote lpd 96, 97
    SMB 163
    SMB, Windows 95/NT 96, 99
    test page 164
    verifying 102
processor
    AMD 211
    Cyrix 211
    Intel 211
programs, running at boot time 227

Q

querying packages with GnoRPM 191
quick start xii

R

ramdisk, criteria for use on SPARC 361
RARP commands, SPARC install 364
rawrite, creating installation diskette with 238
rc.local, modifying 227
reading man pages 113
README files 114
recursion .... see recursion
Red Hat Linux
    what it is x
Red Hat Linux boxed set, contents of 6
Red Hat Linux CDs 7
Red Hat Linux, methods of installing 14
Red Hat newsgroups 118

Red Hat Package Manager .... see RPM
Red Hat Software
    mailing lists 117
        apollo-list 117
        applixware-list 117
        axp-list 117
        blinux-list 117
        cde-list 117
        gnome-announce 117
        gtk-list 117
        hurricane-list 117
        linux-alert 117
        linux-security 117
        m68k-list 117
        pam-list 117
        redhat-announce-list 117
        redhat-devel-list 117
        redhat-install-list 117
        redhat-list 117
        redhat-ppp-list 117
        rpm-list 117
        sound-list 117
        sparc-list 117
        WWW 117
Red Hat-specific file locations 199
registration information 8
remote lpd printer, configuring 96, 97
removing packages with GnoRPM 192
rescue mode 228
    using a trick 228
    using diskettes 228
    using LILO 228
restarting kerneld 166
rexec, access to 208
root password 102
root password, changing 130
routes, managing 171
RPM .... see rpm
rpm 173
    book written about 182
    dependencies 176
    design goals 174
    determining file ownership with 180
    file conflicts, resolving 175
    finding deleted files with 180
    freshen 177
    freshening 177
    handy hints 180
    installing 175
    locating documentation with 181
    mailing list devoted to 182

other resources...........................182
preserving config files...................177
querying.................................178
querying for file list.....................181
querying uninstalled packages...........181
uninstalling.............................176
upgrading...............................177
using...................................174
verifying................................179
web site devoted to.....................182

S

SCSI..32
SCSI support...............................47, 74
selecting components.......................61, 86
selecting packages.........................60, 86
selecting packages with GnoRPM.............186
sendmail...................................214
    aliases.................................214
    masquerading..........................214
    with UUCP.............................214
serial terminal installation for SPARC.........367
services
    PAM..................................206
services, controlling access to................215
services, selecting for autostart...............95
shadow passwords..........................208
shadow utilities............................209
shutdown.............................196, 227
SILO configuration.........................367
SLIP..................................32, 169
slip...............................see SLIP
SLIP configuration.........................146
    modification of....................149, 150
SMB, Windows 95/NT printer, configuring..96, 99
SMP Motherboards
    LILO.................................106
SPARC
    boot method, choosing.................362
    booting
        from diskette......................363
    CD-ROM boot commands................363
    CD-ROM installation...................366
    choosing installation method............366
    console commands......................361
    disk partitioning.......................368
    diskette boot commands.................363
    FTP installation........................366
    hard disk installation...................367
    HTTP installation......................367

installation overview.....................360
installation with serial terminal..........367
network boot commands..................364
NFS installation..........................366
NFS-mounted root, installation using....362
overview of information specific to.......359
ramdisk criteria.........................361
SILO configuration......................367
supported hardware.....................359
unsupported CD-ROMs..................360
unsupported hardware..................360
using network boot commands..........365
using RARP during install..............364
using TFTP during install..............364
SPARC computer...........................x
SPARC-specific information..8, 9, 11, 14, 15, 31, 37,
    49, 74, 359
standard groups............................200
standard users.............................199
starting installation........................39
starting installation program................36
structure, filesystem.......................195
support from mailing lists..................117
support from Usenet.......................117
support, technical..........................229
swap space, initializing..................58, 85
swapoff..............................113, 196
swapon..............................113, 196
sysconfig information.......................217
SYSLINUX................................108
system administration......................195
System Commander.........................108
system configuration...........119, see Linuxconf
system shutdown..........................227
SysV init..................................224
    directories used by......................225
    runlevels used by.......................226

T

TCP wrapper...............................215
tcpd......................................215
technical support...........................229
    FAQ...................................234
    how to send questions for...............233
    how to state problem for................233
    obtaining.............................231
    overview..............................229
    registering............................231
        via email...........................232
        via fax.............................232

        via snail mail 232
        via WWW 232
        where to send support request 234
test page, printer 164
TFTP setup, SPARC install 364
time
        setting 172
time zone, setting 95
time, setting 157
token ring 171
Torvalds, Linus . . . . ix, xii

U

uninstalling packages with GnoRPM 192
upgrade x
upgrade, description of 46, 72
upgrade, performing 45, 70
upgrading packages with GnoRPM 194
upgrading, how to xii
Usenet 117
        Red Hat-specific groups 118
user interface, installation program 33
user-private groups 199, 200
user-private groups, rationale behind 202
users 199
        standard 199
users, adding 123, 124
utilities
        shadow 209

V

verifying packages with GnoRPM 192
video configuration 13
virtual consoles 35

W

Windows
        finding hardware configuration with 11
with Linuxconf 157

X

X Windows, configuring 108
Xconfigurator 109
XFree86
        configuration 109

Index of Packages

A

adjtimex 311
AfterStep 337
AfterStep-APPS 337
aktion 268
am-utils 318
anonftp 319
AnotherLevel 338
apache 319
apache-devel 294
apmd 319
arpwatch 277
ash 335
at 319
audiofile 328
audiofile-devel 294
aumix 268
authconfig 311
autoconf 301
autofs 319
automake 302
awesfx 268

B

basesystem 312
bash 335
bash2 336
bash2-doc 305
bc 260
bdflush 319
bin86 302
bind 319
bind-devel 294
bind-utils 277
binutils 302
bison 302
blt 302
bootparamd 320

byacc 302
bzip2 260

C

caching-nameserver 320
cdecl 303
cdp 269
chkconfig 312
chkfontpath 312
cleanfeed 320
comanche 277
comsat 320
console-tools 278
control-center 338
control-center-devel 294
control-panel 278
cpio 252
cpp 289
cproto 303
cracklib 328
cracklib-dicts 329
crontabs 312
ctags 303
cvs 303
cxhextris 249

D

desktop-backgrounds 269
dev 312
dhcp 320
dialog 278
diffstat 303
diffutils 285
dip 254
dosemu 259
dosemu-freedos 259
dump 253

E

e2fsprogs 312
e2fsprogs-devel 294
ed 286
ee 269
efax 254
egcs 290
egcs-c++ 290
egcs-g77 290
egcs-objc 290
eject 312
ElectricFence 301
elm 262
emacs 257
emacs-el 257
emacs-leim 257
emacs-nox 257
emacs-X11 257
enlightenment 338
enlightenment-conf 338
enscript 273
esound 320
esound-devel 294
etcskel 313
exmh 262
expect 290
ext2ed 278

F

faces 262
faces-devel 294
faces-xface 263
faq 305
fbset 278
fetchmail 263
fetchmailconf 263
file 261
filesystem 313
fileutils 261
findutils 261
finger 263
flex 304
fnlib 329
fnlib-devel 294
fortune-mod 249
freetype 329
freetype-devel 294
ftp 263
fvwm 338
fvwm2 339
fvwm2-icons 339
fwhois 263

G

gated 321
gawk 286
gd 329
gd-devel 295
gdb 288
gdbm 329
gdbm-devel 295
gdm 347
gedit 257
gedit-devel 295
genromfs 313
gettext 304
getty_ps 255
gftp 263
ghostscript 273
ghostscript-fonts 273
giftrans 269
gimp 269
gimp-data-extras 269
gimp-devel 295
gimp-libgimp 329
gimp-manual 306
git 261
glib 329
glib-devel 295
glib10 329
glibc 330
glibc-devel 295
glibc-profile 295
gmc 339
gmp 330
gmp-devel 295
gnome-audio 269
gnome-audio-extra 330
gnome-core 339
gnome-core-devel 295
gnome-games 249
gnome-games-devel 295
gnome-libs 330
gnome-libs-devel 296
gnome-linuxconf 278
gnome-media 270
gnome-objc 290
gnome-objc-devel 296
gnome-pim 272
gnome-pim-devel 296

gnome-users-guide 306
gnome-utils 278
gnorpm 278
gnotepad+ 258
gnuchess 249
gnumeric 273
gnuplot 260
gperf 304
gpm 321
gpm-devel 296
gqview 347
grep 286
groff 273
groff-gxditview 274
gsl 330
gtk+ 330
gtk+-devel 296
gtk+10 331
gtk-engines 331
gtop 279
guavac 290
guile 291
guile-devel 296
gv 274
GXedit 257
gzip 261

H

hdparm 279
helptool 306
howto 306
howto-chinese 306
howto-croatian 306
howto-french 307
howto-german 307
howto-greek 307
howto-html 307
howto-indonesian 307
howto-italian 307
howto-japanese 308
howto-korean 308
howto-polish 308
howto-serbian 308
howto-sgml 308
howto-slovenian 308
howto-spanish 309
howto-swedish 309
howto-turkish 309

I

ical 273
ImageMagick 268
ImageMagick-devel 293
imap 321
imlib 331
imlib-cfgeditor 331
imlib-devel 296
indent 286
indexhtml 309
inews 321
info 313
initscripts 313
inn 321
inn-devel 297
install-guide 309
intimed 321
ipchains 313
ipxutils 279
ircii 263
isapnptools 313
isicom 279
ispell 286
itcl 291

J

jed 258
jed-common 258
jed-xjed 258
joe 258

K

kaffe 291
kbdconfig 313
kdeadmin 279
kdebase 339
kdegames 250
kdegraphics 270
kdelibs 331
kdemultimedia 270
kdenetwork 264
kdesupport 331
kdeutils 279
kernel 327
kernel-BOOT 327
kernel-doc 309
kernel-headers 301
kernel-pcmcia-cs 327
kernel-smp 328

kernel-source 301
kernelcfg 279
knfsd 322
knfsd-clients 279
korganizer 273
kpilot 255
kpppload 264
kterm 347

L

ld.so 314
ldconfig 314
less 286
lha 253
libc 332
libelf 332
libghttp 332
libghttp-devel 297
libgr 332
libgr-devel 297
libgr-progs 270
libgtop 332
libgtop-devel 297
libgtop-examples 332
libjpeg 332
libjpeg-devel 297
libjpeg6a 332
libpcap 297
libpng 333
libpng-devel 297
libPropList 331
libstdc++ 333
libtermcap 333
libtermcap-devel 298
libtiff 333
libtiff-devel 298
libtool 304
libungif 333
libungif-devel 298
libungif-progs 270
libxml 333
libxml-devel 298
lilo 314
linuxconf 280
linuxconf-devel 298
logrotate 314
losetup 314
lout 274
lout-doc 274
lpg 310

lpr 322
lrzsz 255
lslk 288
lsof 289
ltrace 289
lynx 264

M

m4 287
macutils 280
mailcap 314
mailx 264
make 304
MAKEDEV 311
man 314
man-pages 310
mars-nwe 322
mawk 287
mc 336
mcserv 322
metamail 264
mgetty 315
mgetty-sendfax 255
mgetty-viewfax 255
mgetty-voice 255
mikmod 270
mingetty 315
minicom 255
mkbootdisk 315
mkdosfs-ygg 280
mkinitrd 315
mkisofs 280
mkkickstart 315
mktemp 315
mkxauth 280
mod_perl 322
mod_php 322
mod_php3 323
modemtool 280
modutils 328
mount 315
mouseconfig 316
mpage 274
mpg123 270
mt-st 281
mtools 281
multimedia 271
mutt 264
mxp 251

N

nag...310
nc..264
ncftp......................................265
ncompress..............................253
ncpfs.....................................281
ncurses...................................333
ncurses-devel.........................298
ncurses3.................................333
net-tools................................316
netcfg....................................281
netkit-base.............................323
netscape-common...................265
netscape-communicator...........265
netscape-navigator..................265
newt.......................................334
newt-devel..............................298
nmh.......................................265
nscd......................................323
ntsysv...................................316

O

open.......................................281
ORBit.....................................318
ORBit-devel............................293

P

p2c..334
p2c-devel...............................291
pam.......................................316
passwd...................................316
patch.....................................304
pciutils..................................281
pdksh....................................336
perl..291
perl-MD5...............................291
pidentd..................................323
pilot-link...............................256
pilot-link-devel......................299
pine.......................................265
playmidi.................................271
playmidi-X11..........................271
pmake...................................305
pmake-customs......................305
popt......................................299
portmap................................323
postgresql.............................256
postgresql-clients..................256
postgresql-devel....................299

ppp..323
printtool.................................275
procinfo.................................281
procmail.................................323
procps...................................281
procps-X11.............................282
psacct...................................282
psmisc...................................282
pump.....................................324
pwdb.....................................316
pygnome...............................291
pygtk.....................................292
python...................................292
python-devel..........................299
python-docs...........................310
pythonlib...............................334

Q

qt..334
qt-devel.................................299
quota....................................316

R

raidtools.................................316
rcs...305
rdate.....................................282
rdist......................................282
readline.................................334
readline-devel........................299
redhat-logos..........................287
redhat-release.......................288
rgrep.....................................287
rhl-alpha-install-addend-en.....310
rhl-install-guide-en.................310
rhmask..................................282
rhs-hwdiag............................283
rhs-printfilters.......................275
rhsound.................................271
rmt..253
rootfiles.................................316
routed...................................324
rpm.......................................316
rpm-devel..............................299
rsh..266
rsync....................................266
rusers...................................324
rwall.....................................324
rwho.....................................324
rxvt......................................347

S

sag 310
samba 324
sash 336
screen 283
sed 287
sendmail 325
sendmail-cf 325
sendmail-doc 311
setconsole 283
setserial 283
setup 317
setuptool 283
sgml-tools 275
sh-utils 336
shadow-utils 317
shapecfg 317
sharutils 253
slang 334
slang-devel 300
sliplogin 256
slocate 261
slrn 266
slrn-pull 266
sndconfig 271
sox 271
sox-devel 300
specspo 311
squid 325
stat 262
statserial 283
strace 289
svgalib 335
svgalib-devel 300
SVGATextMode 277
swatch 283
switchdesk 339
switchdesk-gnome 340
switchdesk-kde 340
symlinks 283
sysklogd 325
SysVinit 311

T

talk 266
taper 253
tar 253
tcl 292
tclx 292

tcp_wrappers 325
tcpdump 266
tcsh 337
telnet 267
termcap 317
tetex 275
tetex-afm 275
tetex-doc 275
tetex-dvilj 276
tetex-dvips 276
tetex-latex 276
tetex-xdvi 276
texinfo 277
textutils 287
tftp 326
time 284
timeconfig 284
timed 326
timetool 284
tin 267
tix 292
tk 292
tkinter 293
tksysv 284
tmpwatch 317
traceroute 267
transfig 271
tree 262
trn 267
trojka 250
tunelp 284

U

ucd-snmp 326
ucd-snmp-devel 300
ucd-snmp-utils 284
umb-scheme 293
unarj 254
units 260
unzip 254
urlview 267
urw-fonts 347
usermode 284
usernet 284
utempter 317
util-linux 317
uucp 256

V

vim-common 258

vim-enhanced 259
vim-minimal 259
vim-X11 258
vixie-cron 318
vlock 285

W

w3c-libwww 335
w3c-libwww-devel 300
wget 267
which 285
WindowMaker 338
wmakerconf 340
wmconfig 340
words 335
wu-ftpd 326

X

x11amp 272
x11amp-devel 300
X11R6-contrib 344
x3270 347
xanim 272
Xaw3d 328
Xaw3d-devel 293
xbanner 251
xbill 250
xboard 250
xboing 250
xchat 267
Xconfigurator 343
xcpustate 285
xdaliclock 251
xdosemu 259
xearth 251
xfig 272
xfishtank 251
xfm 340
XFree86 344
XFree86-100dpi-fonts 344
XFree86-3DLabs 340
XFree86-75dpi-fonts 344
XFree86-8514 340
XFree86-AGX 341
XFree86-cyrillic-fonts 346
XFree86-devel 293
XFree86-FBDev 341
XFree86-I128 341
XFree86-ISO8859-2 345

XFree86-ISO8859-2-100dpi-fonts 345
XFree86-ISO8859-2-75dpi-fonts 345
XFree86-ISO8859-2-Type1-fonts 346
XFree86-ISO8859-9 346
XFree86-ISO8859-9-100dpi-fonts 346
XFree86-ISO8859-9-75dpi-fonts 346
XFree86-libs 328
XFree86-Mach32 341
XFree86-Mach64 341
XFree86-Mach8 341
XFree86-Mono 342
XFree86-P9000 342
XFree86-S3 342
XFree86-S3V 342
XFree86-SVGA 342
XFree86-VGA16 342
XFree86-W32 343
XFree86-XF86Setup 343
XFree86-xfs 318
XFree86-Xnest 343
XFree86-Xvfb 343
xgammon 250
xinitrc 347
xjewel 250
xlispstat 260
xloadimage 251
xlockmore 252
xmailbox 268
xmorph 252
xntp3 326
xosview 285
xpaint 272
xpat2 250
xpdf 277
xpilot 250
xpm 335
xpm-devel 300
xpuzzles 251
xrn 268
xscreensaver 252
xsysinfo 285
xtoolwait 285
xtrojka 251
xwpick 252
xxgdb 289

Y

yp-tools 318
ypbind 326
ypserv 327

ytalk..268

Z

zgv...272
zip 254
zlib..335
zlib-devel.....................................300
zsh..337